# Struggle and Survival
# in the Modern Middle East

# Struggle and Survival in the Modern Middle East

EDITED BY

## Edmund Burke, III

**UNIVERSITY OF CALIFORNIA PRESS**

Berkeley   Los Angeles

University of California Press
Berkeley and Los Angeles, California

© 1993 by
The Regents of the University of California

Library of Congress Cataloging-in-Publication Data

Struggle and survival in the modern Middle East / edited by Edmund
Burke III.
    p.   cm.
    Includes bibliographical references.
    ISBN 0-520-07988-4 (pbk. : alk. paper)
    1. Middle East—Biography.  I. Burke, Edmund, 1940– .
CT1866.S77   1993
920.056—dc20
   [B]                               91-45869
                                                CIP

Printed in the United States of America

10   09   08   07   06   05   04   03
12   11   10   9   8   7   6   5

A version of the essay by Ashraf Ghani was previously published under the title
"Afghanistan's Sorrow and Pity" in *Natural History* 89 (July 1980): 64–77.

The paper used in this publication meets the minimum requirements of
ANSI/NISO Z39.48-1992 (R 1997) (*Permanence of Paper*). ∞

*For Carolyn*

# CONTENTS

CONTENTS

# PREFACE

The present book draws its inspiration from David G. Sweet and Gary B. Nash's collection of biographies of ordinary men and women from colonial Latin America and the United States, *Struggle and Survival in the Colonial-Americas.** In an era of increasing specialization, Sweet and Nash provide a human dimension to the colonial history of the Americas, offering vivid glimpses into the lived lives of real people, rather than the sterile abstractions of strict historical analysis. Their book illuminates how nonelite people managed their lives, often in the face of extreme hardship and oppression.

I believe that a similar approach has great potential for opening up the history of the modern Middle East. This book is a collaborative effort of twenty-seven individuals, for the most part unknown to one another. Through the lives of ordinary Middle Eastern men and women, it presents Middle Eastern history as it might appear when viewed from the bottom up. In the process, it exposes the discrepancy between the abstractions that are used to characterize Middle Eastern history as it is taught and written—modernization, imperialism, and nationalism—and how events were actually experienced by most people.

When I sat down to write the introduction, I was quite unprepared for the power with which this message emerged from a reading of the stories included in the volume. Official sources and the dominance of political and institutional history have masked the range of variation in views. Together, the biographies suggest some ways that Middle Eastern

*David G. Sweet and Gary B. Nash, eds., *Struggle and Survival in the Colonial Americas* (Berkeley: University of California Press, 1981). See also William H. Beezley and Judith Ewell, eds., *The Human Tradition in Latin America: The Twentieth Century* (Wilmington: Scholarly Resources, Inc., 1989).

history may be rewritten to take full account of the perspectives of most Middle Easterners.

That the book exists at all is a minor miracle. This diverse collection of biographies was drawn together with no financial backing (save small grants from the University of California, Santa Cruz, Faculty Research Committee and Division of Humanities) and no commitment from anyone but the authors. In seeking to discover and enlist the participation of authors for what must have seemed to many a somewhat dubious enterprise, I distributed at conferences and by mail over one hundred copies of a prospectus. Not all invited to contribute were able to accept. Our disciplines are after larger, more prestigious quarry than the biographies of ordinary people. Every contribution is therefore precious.

The gestation period of a book of this size is regrettably somewhat longer than that of an elephant. I am therefore grateful for the patience and understanding of the contributors, some of whom no doubt grew to wonder what they had enrolled themselves in. I hope they find in the finished book some recompense for their labor and forbearance. Many others have contributed to the successful completion of this work. My friend and colleague David Sweet provided the original impetus and encouragement for this book. (Had I listened more carefully to him about the work involved, I might have decided against undertaking it!) I am especially grateful to the Faculty Research Committee and the former Dean of Humanities Michael Cowan of the University of California, Santa Cruz, for providing funds for typing the manuscript. The John D. and Catherine T. MacArthur Foundation provided a fellowship at the Institute for Advanced Study, Princeton, which enabled me to complete the editing of the manuscript. My thanks to the fellowship program and to Clifford Geertz, Director of the School of Social Sciences. Parts of the manuscript have been read and commented upon by Dilip Basu, Lois Beck, Steven Caton, Nicholas Dirks, Takashi Fujitani, Clifford Geertz, Michael Gilsenan, Albert Hourani, Akram Khater, Sherry Ortner, Richard Randolph, Lawrence Rosen, and Joan Scott. May they all here receive my thanks for their interest and support. Helen Wheatley, Amanda Wilbur, and Patricia Sanders assisted in typing and editing various incarnations of this manuscript with much good humor and efficiency. Their high standards and critical judgment helped make it a better work. My gratitude to them is immense. Finally, the editorial support of Lynne Withey of the University of California Press and Albert Hourani and Anna Enayat of I. B. Tauris Press was invaluable to me at a crucial juncture.

Transliteration is always a problem when one is dealing with Middle Eastern languages. Because this book is addressed to a wide audience, a simplified system of transliteration from Arabic, Persian, and Turkish has been adopted. Diacritical marks and the Arabic letters hamza and ayn have usually been omitted. Standard Arabic terms used in variant versions in different countries have generally been spelled in their modified Arabic forms (e.g., Sharia, ulama). Geographical and proper names and terms peculiar to particular regions have been included in the form to which people reading the regional literatures are accustomed. A glossary at the back of the book provides complete transliterations and definitions of key terms.

Each chapter is preceded by a brief editorial introduction. Its purpose is to contextualize the story and to suggest some connections between it and other selections. Readers are encouraged to develop their own connections between the selections as well.

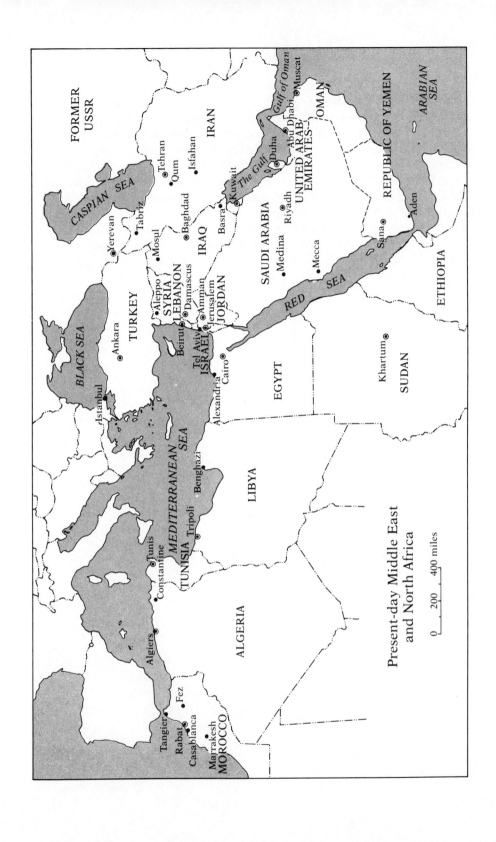

Present-day Middle East
and North Africa

0    200    400 miles

ONE

# Middle Eastern Societies and Ordinary People's Lives

*Edmund Burke, III*

### RETHINKING MIDDLE EASTERN HISTORY

Despite a great deal of useful research on the histories of modern Middle Eastern societies we know little of the lives of ordinary Middle Eastern men and women. Instead we see the Middle East over the shoulders of diplomats, military officers, entrepreneurs, and bureaucrats. This essentially elite perspective has focused on the "big story": the coming to modernity of Middle Eastern states and societies, and the operation of large-scale historical forces. In the process, the perspectives of those who were on the receiving end of these changes have generally been neglected.

As a result, we tend to see the fate of the Middle East, or of Islamic societies, as determined by one or another impersonal historical force whose operation was decisive. For some authors this force is religion, for others capitalism, imperialism, oriental despotism, or economic dependency. These views, despite their often contradictory explanations of the mainsprings of change, have portrayed Middle Easterners as marionettes in a historical drama not of their devising, rather than as flesh-and-blood individuals with some capacity to affect their own life chances. Deprived of agency, they have become what Eric Wolf calls "peoples without history."[1]

Often unexamined, these determinisms still govern the way most of us think about the Middle East. However, they fail to take account of the complex historical processes, structural forms, and cultural patterns that have shaped the context within which individuals have lived. Instead they provide us with a kind of just-so story (or rather a series of often conflicting just-so stories). By privileging particular groups' understanding of the past, such views have skewed our sense of how that

*1*

past actually came about, and have simultaneously delegitimized the self-understanding of other groups.

Politics, however, was not always or invariably the determining factor in most people's lives, and the ups and downs of the economic roller coaster affected different people in different ways. No one schema can make sense of the quite varied historical experiences covered in this book: those of Middle Easterners from Morocco to Afghanistan and from the middle of the nineteenth century to the present.

Instead of starting from broad generalizations about Islam or the Ottoman state, or from stereotypes about the Arab mind or Islam, a rereading of the history of the Middle East should put the experiences of ordinary men and women at its center. This new kind of history would begin with the notion that different ecologies, ways of life, and ethnic, class, and gender situations shaped individual possibilities of action. The biographies of ordinary Middle Eastern men and women in this book provide a series of vantage points from which to undertake such a rereading. (Below I reflect on the nature of such a rereading, based on the contributions in this book.)

This book focuses on the biographies of ordinary people, rather than on the lives of officials, military officers, and intellectuals. By "ordinary people" I mean the "peoples without history"—which includes nonelite men and most women (for example, tribal elite women)—namely, those whose experiences have generally been left out of the history books. This is not to say that the individuals whose lives are chronicled here are ordinary. The very fact that enough information exists about them to make possible a brief biography makes them by definition extraordinary. As we will soon see, some of those whose lives are chronicled here were of humble origins and later moved up in the social pecking order or became well known locally for one or another reason. Others started and remained artisans, peasants, and tribespeople and might have remained unknown but for a chance event—the opening of an official file, an encounter with an anthropologist, the desire of a descendant to explore the family tree.

A question that may arise concerns the extent to which the biographies included in this volume can be seen as typical of Middle Easterners. Despite an energetic effort to cast the net as widely as possible, not all groups are represented within these pages. Given the ethnic, linguistic, and religious diversity of the region, a comprehensive inclusiveness—a kind of Noah's Ark principle of coverage—is quite impossible. Rather, the not entirely random selection of biographies provides a set of core samples aimed at helping us understand the transformations that Middle Eastern societies have undergone since the beginning of the nineteenth century. They spotlight the dynamism of Middle Eastern men and women, as well as their attachment to old ways of doing things. At a time when the Middle East is often harshly caricatured in Western society, these portraits of ordinary men and women and their struggles and attempts to survive in a context of great uncertainty and risk serve to assert our common humanity. The sheer variety of so broad a historical and geographical sample also suggests the need to rethink much of the conventional wisdom about Middle Eastern society. In this sense, it is hoped that the present volume is not an end but a beginning.

To provide a framework for readers lacking a knowledge of the histories of particular Middle Eastern societies, this book is organized chronologically. Other arrangements (geographical or regional or by gender, class, or way of life) can, however, be imagined, and the reader is encouraged to develop his or her own alternative thematic or regional focus. (For example, one might wish to group the biographies of peasants, North Africans, women, or minorities.) To promote alternative foci, each chapter is preceded by a brief introduction by the editor. The chapter introductions have two purposes: to provide a historical, political, and methodological context for the essay in question and to suggest connections with some of the other selections.

Given the uneven impact of change between and within modern Middle Eastern societies from Morocco to Afghanistan, the chronological structure of the book should be taken as a set of floating benchmarks, not a fixed Procrustean scheme. Its purpose is to draw attention to what is similar in the historical experiences of the different societies of the area, not to argue for a particular unilinear sequence of causality. The specific pace of change varied from place to place and mattered crucially both for ordinary people and for the particular outcomes in particular places. The arrangement of the chapters in this volume has been shaped by these considerations.

Middle Eastern men and women responded to often difficult circumstances in different ways. Struggle was one dimension of their individual stories: defiance of the guild master, the cruel government official, the "system" in all its manifestations. Such efforts were by their very nature uncommon, for those in power possessed not only superior force but also (even under colonialism) a measure of cultural hegemony, what Eugene Genovese in another context has referred to as "invisible shackles of the mind."[2] Some of the individuals we will encounter in these pages were nonetheless heroes of a sort. But (as we will see) even anticolonial resistance was not an unalloyed impulse. Rather it could, and did, often mask the settling of old scores, the chance for quick gain. (To study the roots of nationalism through the lives of ordinary people is to encounter the density and confusion of micropolitics, where moral choices were not always clear and options not unlimited.) Moreover, seen in one way a strategy of resistance might seem heroic, when from another optic it could seem quixotic. When we look at the successive strategies of an individual's entire life, coherence is hard to find.

More common was the tenacious and often courageous effort of common folk to hang in there, to survive against all odds. Rascals and scoundrels might prove better survivors for a time, but the operation of the wheel of fortune did not permit many to escape from misfortune for long. The possibilities for individual action derived in part from the social cards an individual was dealt at birth (gender, class, and ethnicity foremost among them). But they were also determined by personal character and chance. Struggle and survival, then, are not exclusive, mutually contradictory categories, but dimensions within a field of power in which the terms are constantly shifting over time.

Part 1, entitled "Precolonial Lives," contains biographies of individuals whose lives were largely untouched by the shadow of the West. Most, but not all, of them lived in the period from 1850 to World War I. Their existence was shaped by the structures of the old society: artisan guilds, kinship groups, ethnic communities. Although already in the throes of change when the nineteenth century began, as several examples show, these structures proved remarkably resilient. They also provided considerable resources for resistance and accommodation to change.

Part 2, "Colonial Lives," contains essays about persons whose lives were primarily shaped by the experience of nationalism and colonialism.[3] Because the chronology of European rule differed from country to country within the region as a whole,[4] this section includes individuals who lived in the nineteenth as well as the twentieth century. The colonial encounter was complex and affected people differently depending upon their specific situations. Some were able to trade upon their skills and connections to advance their personal and family fortunes. Others, less favorably situated, found the going rough. Navigating in the constantly shifting political and economic tides presented tricky problems to all.

In Part 3, "Contemporary Lives," we encounter Middle Easterners who came to maturity after World War II. Shaped by the harsher realities of nationalist and Islamic movements, the boom-and-bust cycles of the world oil market, wars, civil strife, and foreign occupation, individuals who came to maturity in this period had substantially different experiences than their parents and grandparents. Taken together, they give us a portrait, incomplete it is true, of some of the ways people have tried to cope with a dizzying transformations of the postwar era.

### Social Biography and Social Theory

In a sense, this volume brings the field of Middle Eastern history full circle. Biography gave an early impetus to the writing of Islamic history,

largely because of the central place in Islamic piety and scholarship occupied by the figure of Muhammad. The need for information about his
life, seen by Muslims as a model of correct behavior, spawned a host of
biographies. The most famous, Ibn Ishaq's *Sirat rasul Allah* (c. 809
A.C.E.), quickly acquired canonical status. For information about Muhammad, Muslims looked not only to the Quran but also to the living
memory of the community. Eventually these traditions, called *hadith* reports, were collected and written down. Over time, the Quran and *hadith*
reports came to form the basis of Islamic law, the Sharia.[5]

The need to distinguish reliable *hadith* reports from pious legend provided a second impulse to the writing of biography. This took the form
of a new genre of Islamic scholarship known as *tabaqat,* which contained
biographies of the first generations of Muslims that focused on their ethical character and hence reliability as transmitters of *hadith* reports.[6]
Later, *tabaqat* came to include not just the lives of the early companions
of the Prophet but also of Islamic scholars (ulama), Sufi mystics, and notables (*ayan*) of particular cities. The *tabaqat* literature is voluminous, and
more continues to be produced to this day. While *tabaqat* writings lack
much that we would recognize as biography (including a sense of individual psychology), their focus on the person provides a valuable source
for social history, especially for prosopography (group biography).[7] Of
course, biography provided only one of the sources for Islamic history
writing. Other sources included pre-Islamic Arabian tribal sagas and imperial chronicles (the best-known example of which is the monumental
*History* of Tabari).[8]

In the West, biography is a well-established genre, though until recently a disfavored one in historical writing. Because it is a primary site
for exploring the connections of social and cultural processes, biography
has grown in importance if anything in recent times. Some exemplary
histories that utilize biography in this way include Natalie Davis's *Return
of Martin Guerre,* Carlo Ginzburg's *Cheese and the Worms,* and Jonathan
Spence's *Death of Woman Wang.*[9]

There has been a resurgence of interest in biography in the social sciences as well, notably in anthropology and sociology. In anthropology,
where the relationship of the anthropologist to his or her indigenous
collaborator has been a constant incitement to "read" the culture
through the life of the informant, the genre has been well established
since Franz Boas.[10] Recently, anthropologists have begun to acknowledge the role of their informants in their work and to recognize that
anthropological knowledge by its nature is a joint product reflecting
the field situation.[11] In sociology, too, biography may now once again
be coming to the fore, against the background of the statistical mod-
eling that has become increasingly typical in that discipline. This move

represents a renewal of an earlier tradition embodied in such classics as Eliott Liebow's *Tally's Corner.*[12]

Because social theories tend to be partial rather than totalizing (focusing, for example, on political or economic behavior), while real lives sprawl in their sheer exuberance across conventional categories, the patterns of individual lives elude even the best theories. The biographical approach holds out the promise of reinvigorating the relation between social theory and empirical research. The credibility of biographies comes from the concrete details they convey about a particular life and how it was lived. The more accounts of lives we have, the better we will be able to assess their typicality and to understand individual survival strategies. It is because biography can provide fundamental insights into social and cultural processes that it was privileged by Wilhelm Dilthey and his followers.[13]

I use the term *social biography* to refer to the use of biography to explore the complex ways in which individuals navigate amidst social structures, processes, and cultural interactions. Social biography can be distinguished from literary biography, which tends to center upon the inner world or psychology of the subject and its relationship to the dynamics of the life of the individual.[14] Social biographies, especially when deployed as part of a broader research strategy, can test and refine social theories, as well as provide an alternative vantage point from which to think about the historical processes by which societies have been continually transformed.

Since World War II growing epistemological self-consciousness has made us aware of the ways in which language structures the ways that we think about the world. Much of the heightened awareness focuses on the act of writing in the production of social scientific knowledge.[15] Literary and scientific activities are not as distinct as previously thought. Both are primarily interpretive and focus on the analysis and the production of texts (whether literary or social). Cultural interpretation and social scientific knowledge in general are inextricably connected to the specific rhetorical envelope in which they are conveyed.[16] Put more directly, there is no easily discoverable distinction between literature and social science. The facts are not separable from their literary embodiment. Rather their very "factness" derives from the way in which they are related.

What are the implications of these reflections for the biographies in this volume? First we must recognize that the essays in this volume are *stories.* They seek to make sense of the life of a single individual or related individuals. As stories (some more self-conscious than others) they *represent* to us the experience of people whose culture differs from our own. This they do on the basis of information gathered from historical documents or from the fading memories of family members and anthropological informants or from both together. Like all good stories, their narratives are designed to lead the reader to have a degree of sympathy and understanding for the main characters. Their manner of doing so, however, varies considerably.

To recognize that biographies are manifestly literary products as well as products of the historical/sociological imagination is not to discount their truth value, but only to qualify it. Like all other exercises in the human sciences, social biographies are constrained by the ways language struggles to mediate between that which is observed and that which is said, knowing that the gap is not fully bridgeable because the "factness" of what is seen is always potentially debatable, contingent, and partial. The point is not that anything goes, but that history has only the sense we give to it, and that sense necessarily changes along with the world we live in.[17]

While we have acquired a vast amount of knowledge about the Middle East and its diverse peoples, that knowledge tends not to be reflected in the stereotypical images of the region current in the West. Each major political development in the Middle East is confidently analyzed by self-proclaimed experts as demonstrating the existence of a supposedly perennial "Muslim fanaticism," or the unchanging nature of the "Arab mind." The contrast between the knowledge that has been accumulated and the persistent racist nonsense about Middle Eastern people is striking.

Since the appearance of Edward Said's *Orientalism*,[18] we have become aware of the ways in which Western representations of Middle Eastern culture have been intertwined with the fact of European dominance of the area. Orientalism was a discipline that studied Asian civilizations through an examination of their allegedly characteristic cultural products (the Quran or other texts). By privileging certain texts as the sole authoritative sources of religious and cultural norms and neglecting others that qualify or contradict them, orientalists claimed to provide an explanation for Muslim behavior valid for all times and places.

The intersecting series of more or less connected cultural stereotypes about Islam and Middle Easterners can be called the colonial vulgate. In it, Middle Easterners are represented as congenitally fatalistic, fanatical, cowardly, treacherous, despotic, sexually repressed, and patriarchal (among other things).[19] The colonial vulgate constitutes an ever-present reservoir of stereotypes of the Middle Eastern "other" that purports to explain why "they" differ from "us."[20]

Biographies of Middle Easterners have helped to disseminate these popular images. They play an important role in shaping Daniel Lerner's *Passing of Traditional Societies*, a classic of 1950s modernization theory in which the stereotypical biographies of the Grocer and the Chief serve as a central organizing motif.[21] Another example is Richard Critchfield's widely read *Shahhat: An Egyptian*,[22] which through the portrait of an allegedly typical peasant seeks to represent all Egyptian peasants. Shahhat, the subject of this study, is a quarrelsome, superstitious youth whose personality traits nicely conform to standard Western cultural stereotypes about shiftless Egyptian peasants. A recent critical review has suggested that there are particular reasons to distrust this work.[23] Whatever the circumstances of its preparation, what interests me about Critchfield's account in the present context is the way in which it recycles the colonial vulgate image of Egyptians.

Because the complexities of the area are so daunting, it is tempting to read Middle Eastern society through the lives of a few individuals. A homogenized and essentialist Middle East enables us to avoid engaging the historical and cultural specificities of the various groups and peoples who live there. Cultural stereotypes, by contrast, enable us to attain a misleading mastery. When those stereotypes also reinforce our sense of cultural superiority they may well appear irresistible. There is, therefore, reason for reflection—reading the society through the lives of a few supposedly typical individuals is ultimately a quixotic venture.

How then to avoid falling into this trap? It is important to be wary of explanations that invoke allegedly innate psychological traits, such as "the Arab mind," "the fatalism of the Egyptian peasant," and the like, in place of a more historically grounded examination. While for some it may seem satisfying to view the turbulent politics of the 1980s as deriving from "tribes with flags,"[24] it is well to question such essentialist metaphors closely if we would seek a deeper understanding. More successful works, such as Roy Mottahedeh's portrait of an Iranian *mullah* in *The Mantle of the Prophet* or Erika Friedl's *Women of Deh Koh*,[25] locate their subjects in particular sociological and cultural, as well as historical, contexts and do not invoke broad psychological or cultural traits in explanation. They are social biographies in their commitment to change and complexity, as well as to the individuality of their subjects.[26]

By their sheer variety, the twenty-four lives presented in this book constitute a potent antidote to the homogenizing and essentialist impulse. While different themes can be traced in these biographies, no one of them applies to all cases. The absolute diversity of the lives works to undermine the "verities" of the colonial vulgate. The very number of lives is an incitement to thought, for one is compelled to consider the particular factors that appear to have been significant in shaping the individual lives recounted here and to locate them in a complex and historical context. Different sources, authorial viewpoints, and connections to the subject also work to undermine efforts to extract a particular theme or lesson about Arabs, Muslims, or Middle Easterners that can apply to all experiences.

So many different cases offer one the opportunity to ask some interesting questions about the impact of change, and how particular groups and individuals responded. How much did women or tribespeople or villagers (to select a few examples) appear to have been influenced by the particular social structures in which they existed? How important were family and patron/client connections in providing access to crucial resources? How did the modernization of society affect the life chances of particular individuals? How important was individual personality or historical conjuncture?

The biographies included here allow us to refine our understanding of how particular groups were affected by large-scale historical processes like Ottoman modernization, European colonialism, and nationalism. In this way we can begin to develop a new understanding of the history of the region keyed to gender, ethnicity, religion, class, ecology, and way of life. In the remainder of this chapter, I explore how the history of the Middle East might be rethought from the vantage point of the ordinary people whose lives are described in this book.

## MIDDLE EASTERN HISTORY AND THE EXPERIENCE OF ORDINARY PEOPLE

### Precolonial Lives

The lives of the men and women we encounter in part 1 were shaped by the urban and agrarian structures of the Ottoman Empire and the Iranian and Moroccan monarchies. Their identities derived from their family, occupation, and religion (for some, tribal affiliation was also important) rather than from their nationality or class position. Most nineteenth-century Middle Easterners expected to contend with adversity and cyclical change. But few could have imagined the extent to which their world would be altered by far-reaching forces of social change persisting over time.

Essentially, the changes they confronted were of three sorts: (1) the Ottoman *tanzimat* reforms, (2) the incorporation of the Middle East into the world economy, and (3) the growing power of the West. Each type of change had consequences that affected not just the state but also the society and individuals, opening options for some and closing them off for others. In the process, old social groups and old ways of doing things were supplemented and eventually supplanted by new classes and new ways of behaving.

Since we sometimes tend to forget that many of the chief features of the contemporary Middle East are of recent origin, it is important to add that these changes affected different groups at different rates, and some regions more than others. Until 1880 neither nationalism nor Western power, both of which were significantly to mark the region in the twentieth century, was as yet a dominant factor outside of the Balkan provinces of the Ottoman Empire. This is not to suggest that premodern Middle Eastern society was static and unchanging, as has sometimes been proposed. Nor were the old structures so oppressive as to exclude even relatively poor and powerless individuals from the possibility of some modest social mobility.

The main sources of disruption of people's lives during the nineteenth century were the *tanzimat* reforms and the incorporation of the Middle East into the world economy. Everyday life was gradually remade in response to the outcomes of the struggles around the expanding role of the state, which was the most visible source of change to contemporaries. The encroachment of the *tanzimat* reforms upon the traditional liberties of urban quarters and villages provoked opposition, migration, and accommodation. While some sought to ride the waves of change, others tried to ride them out in the interstices of the society.

By following the differential impact of the *tanzimat* reforms on different groups in Ottoman society, it is possible to gain a different perspective on them. On the level of the elite, the attempt by nineteenth-century Ottoman reformers to build a modern army, a modern bureaucracy, and a modern system of education was opposed by powerful vested interests. Most important were the janissaries, court officials, and ulama of the old regime. For the janissaries, the *tanzimat* reforms were a calamity. They were brutally eliminated in a series of purges. Court officials and ulama who opposed the reforms were marginalized, but supporters prospered.[27]

The impact of the *tanzimat* reforms on local and provincial elites similarly cut both ways. On the one hand, the creation of local and provincial administrative councils, mixed courts, and other new organizations provided unprecedented access to power and patronage resources. On the other hand, by abolishing some of the special privileges and exemptions that had benefited the elite, the reforms brought ruin to some.[28]

We have few accounts of the impact of the *tanzimat* on nonelites. But what we know about the experience of ordinary people indicates that it was similarly mixed. Military conscription, forced labor, and a more efficient fiscal administration encroached upon the traditional liberties of populations whose survival in the best of times was precarious, while the trickle down of new jobs in the bureaucracy was inadequate and the jobs mostly menial. Some peasants and villagers, threatened with ruin, sought refuge in flight or became bandits.[29] What the reforms meant in practice to a poor Lebanese peasant can be seen in the life of Assaf Khater, recounted in this section.

The transformation from subject to citizen experienced by Middle Easterners is another theme of the *tanzimat* era. For the non-Muslim populations it was a transition fraught with peril. Since the minorities benefited from the semiautonomous status accorded them as "peoples of the Book," or *dhimma* under Islamic law, by which they were accorded religious toleration and protection in return for their cooperation, they had a considerable stake in the existing system. Under the *millet* system, by which the Ottomans regulated the affairs of their non-Muslim subjects, local religious communities enjoyed freedom of worship and control over their local affairs, subject to certain conditions. By abolishing these privileges, the *tanzimat* reforms thus posed a significant challenge to the non-Muslim elites.[30]

The situation of non-Muslim elites was complicated by the fact that in the course of the period many of them acquired special privileges and exemptions as a result of their employment by European businesses or governments. These extraterritorial privileges, called *barat,* had originally been granted by the Ottoman government to official representatives of European states as part of capitulatory agreements. They carried exemption from local taxes, justice, military service, and civic obligations. Similar arrangements existed in independent states like Afghanistan, Iran, and Morocco.

In the nineteenth century, such privileges were often extended to the local employees (and their families) of European officials and businessmen in the Ottoman Empire. Many elite Moroccan Jews held analogous extraterritorial privileges granted by the Moroccan government. Similar arrangements existed in Iran. From the point of view of the state, the system resulted in a significant loss to the state treasury and threatened the success of the reform program. Because it unfairly loaded the dice against Muslim merchants and businessmen, the capitulation system constituted a flash point of popular Muslim indignation as well.[31]

Another theme of Ottoman modernization was reform of the educational system. The development of an efficient and modern cadre of administrative agents, as well as a modern officer corps for the army, required modern schools, books, and ideas to succeed. Secular ideas began to spread throughout the society, aided by the development of the press and of a modern education system. In the process, the authority of the local clergy (Muslim, Christian, and Jewish alike) was undermined.[32] We are relatively well informed on how this process played itself out in the Ottoman Empire at the level of the elite, but know far less about how it worked for ordinary people.

The incorporation of the Middle East into the emerging world economy is a second major source of change in the period. The increasingly closer mesh between the economies of the area and the international economy caused the erosion of many of the basic structures of the old regime—guilds, Sufi orders and other religious groupings, quarter- and village-based communities. These, however, continued to exist and to provide a semblance of order and meaning in the lives of the people. At the same time, new opportunities stimulated the development of new activities. By the end of the period increased rural security and better communication stimulated commercial agriculture throughout the region. In the cities the old artisan guild structures, once a mainstay of the urban economy, were significantly affected.

Three contrasting studies focus on individuals whose lives were profoundly shaped by the structures of the guild system. Deli Mehmet, a member of the Cairo slave dealers' guild, exposed the guild to public ridicule by his flagrant abuse of the regulations of the organization. Shemsigul, the Circassian slave woman whom he raped and made pregnant, brought suit in the Sharia court. Her story, told by Ehud Toledano, throws an interesting light on a neglected corner of Egyptian history: the Ottoman elite household and the slave trade that helped to sustain it. The abolition of slavery in the Ottoman Empire at the end of the nineteenth century brought an end to the Ottoman elite household. Sherry Vatter's contribution, a collective biography of the journeyman weavers of Damascus, focuses on the response of journeymen weavers to the nineteenth-century changes that buffeted the Syrian textile handicraft industry. She argues that while the importation of cheap British cottons had an important effect on local textile producers in Damascus, the expansion of the market in the nineteenth century enabled some sectors to ride out the mid-century crisis.

Another image of the perdurance of guild structures is provided by Nels Johnson's portrait of Ahmad, a pearl diver in the now defunct Persian Gulf pearling industry. (Although Ahmad's life falls mostly in the present century, given the different rhythms of Kuwaiti history it is more usefully studied in part 1 than alongside the lives of those who are his literal contemporaries.) Ahmad's experience suggests that the guild system continued to structure people's existence in the Persian Gulf fisheries after it had lost most of its relevance in economically more dynamic areas. It also serves to remind us of how recent is the impact of the oil boom on the area. The fragile ecology of the Gulf has now been drastically affected by the development of the Gulf region and by the 1991 war.

Nineteenth-century Ottomans, even fairly far-sighted ones, had little doubt that the empire would survive for some time, despite its manifest weaknesses. European rule (which was to pose a fundamental cultural challenge to all Middle Easterners) lay on the horizon, not yet fully actualized. (Of course exception must be made here for the Maghrib, most of which slipped under French rule in the nineteenth century.) Over time, European political domination gradually altered the context within which culture and society existed, and with it the way most people led their lives.

Similarly, despite our present-day sense that Middle Eastern nationalisms are basic to the area, until the defeat and breakup of the Ottoman Empire in World War I, nationalism was not a major force among the Muslim populations outside of the Balkans. Only after the defeat of the Ottoman Empire in World War I did nationalism become a major political force among Turks and Arabs. By 1880, the nationalist "traditions" that were later to reshape the cultural and political landscape of the region were still being "invented."[33]

Since North Africa was the first portion of the Middle East to be subjected to European conquest, it is there that we must look for the first stirrings of anticolonial resistance. In this prenationalist age, resistance inevitably drew upon deeply rooted cultural and political forms, especially that of *jihad*. Yet despite the received pieties of official nationalist discourse, according to which opposition was general, the realities of the European threat were differently assessed by different people at different times. Given the overwhelming superiority of European arms, the decision to take up weapons was neither simple nor automatic. The portraits of Mohand N'Hamoucha, a Moroccan Berber tribesman, and Ramadan al-Suwayhli, a Libyan notable from Tripoli, underscore the complex process by which some individuals were led to become involved in resistance.

To understand how Mohand N'Hamoucha became a local leader of opposition to French imperialism one must consider first the ambiguous situation of his tribe, the Aith Ndhir, between the government-dominated central plain and the Middle Atlas Mountains, home to large pastoralist tribal groups. While some of his kinsmen were drawn into urban networks at Fez and Meknes and were subsequently exposed to French intimidation and blandishments, Mohand and his friends took the road to resistance. How and why he did so is the subject of my contribution. Together with Lisa Anderson's essay on Ramadan al-Suwayhli, Mohand's story helps distance us from the pieties of the official history, according to which there was widespread popular support for anticolonial resistance. As perceptions of the European threat and possible options changed, both essays suggest, individuals were led to reassess their situations constantly.

The final essay in this section is Julie Oehler's account of the dramatic role played by Bibi Maryam, an elite woman of the Bakhtiyari tribal confederacy in southwestern Iran during World War I. In some ways the situation of the Bakhtiyari resembles that of the Aith Ndhir, trapped between a would-be modernizing state and European power. But the dynamics of history in early twentieth-century Iran diverge from those in Morocco in important ways and shaped a different context for action. Most crucially, the hierarchical structures of the Bakhtiyari, and thus of elite women's scope for political action, were quite different from the much more diffuse and egalitarian organization of the Aith Ndhir. Oehler's contribution also illuminates the public role of women in the Middle East and is usefully placed alongside Julia Clancy-Smith's chapter in the following section.

## The Colonial Experience

World War I and its aftermath constituted a watershed of unprecedented significance that led to far-reaching political changes throughout the area. According to the conventional narrative, the politics of the Middle East from 1918 until 1967 revolved around the struggle of nationalism and imperialism. For the most part the history of this period has been viewed primarily from the perspective of the elite. Part 2 of this volume brings together biographies of individuals who lived through this era. As a group, they provide the basis for an alternative reading of the history of the period.

Changes in the world of politics are the most obvious. With the collapse of the Ottoman Empire and the abolition of the caliphate (1924) and sultanate (1925), basic cultural assumptions about identity and the nature of the state were transformed. The old elites and social groups, already weakened by the nineteenth-century changes, declined rapidly, while new ones, tied to new economic and political forces, emerged. Simultaneously, personal identity became increasingly based upon linguistically defined nationality, instead of upon membership in a religious community under the Ottoman sultan/padishah. The resultant rise of nationalisms constituted an unparalleled mental revolution for many.

While one world was vanishing, another was establishing itself. After 1918 European colonial empires, which had already embraced all of Arab Africa, were extended to Arab Asia as well. Even the weak Iranian and Afghan states were made to accept sharp limitations on their sovereignty. Only Turkey managed to elude this particular fate, and then only after Ataturk had defeated the Greeks, British, and French. European rule not only changed the nature of the emerging political struggle within each country, it affected to varying degrees the lives of all.

The men and women whose biographies are included in part 2 of this book are a varied group. One of the things they have in common is the fact that they were all profoundly marked by the experience of colonialism—that complex of racist attitudes, policies, and politics predicated upon notions of European superiority and virtue—which shaped the societies of the region for two generations. Thus their experiences and expectations were significantly different from those of their parents and grandparents. As European dominance pervaded society, life was irrevocably transformed, even for peasants and tribespeople. The degree to which particular groups were affected varied, of course.

In the conventional account, colonialism is portrayed as a victimless crime that brought far more benefits than disadvantages to the area. As a consequence, we know a great deal more about colonial policymakers and the policies they implemented than we do about the ways in which colonial rule was experienced by Middle Eastern men and women.[34]

After the establishment of European rule, the folly of *jihad* and other traditional forms of armed resistance gradually became evident. European occupation drastically reduced the available options for individuals. The case of Algeria helped set the mold for what was to follow. While some elite families emigrated to other parts of the Ottoman Empire following the French takeover in 1830, most remained behind. Tacit cooperation with the French colonial authorities alternated with petty acts of resistance (such as feigning laziness, or minor acts of theft and sabotage).[35]

The experience of colonialism as it emerges in the biographies included here ran the gamut from heroism to opportunism. Julia Clancy-Smith provides a portrait of an Algerian popular Islamic saintly lineage in the mid-nineteenth century. Her essay focuses on the stratagems employed by Zaynab, the eldest daughter of a popular Sufi leader, or marabout, who succeeded her father as head of the Sufi *zawiya,* and her struggles against the French authorities on the one hand and family rivals on the other.

David Seddon's brief biography of Muhammad El Merid introduces us to a cunning opportunist who was able to reap a sizable fortune by exploiting his privileged connections to the Spanish and French colonial rulers. El Merid's life may be usefully contrasted with that of Muhammad Ameur. Ameur, a Tunisian peasant and café philosopher whose story is related by Kenneth Brown, tried a variety of ways of coping with French colonial rule in Tunisia, including collaboration and membership in the Tunisian Communist party. A master of many disguises, he remains a quixotic figure.

For non-Muslims, the period was one of narrowing options. Some were able to survive and even thrive. Others found themselves gradually marginalized in the new circumstances of the post-Ottoman Middle East. Hagob Hagobian, whose portrait is written by David Yaghoubian, is one of the first sort. Hagobian was an Armenian Christian born in eastern Anatolia whose life began with the tragic death of his parents in the massacres of Armenians during World War I. Raised in an orphanage in northwestern Iran, he became a long-distance truck driver on the route from Tehran to the Gulf. Later in his life he migrated to California.

The narrowing personal options of the post-1918 Middle East can also be seen in Sami Zubaida's account of the life of Dr. Naji, an Iraqi Jewish provincial physician. Like many other Iraqi middle-class Jews, he was a nationalist opponent of the corrupt monarchy that ruled Iraq for Britain in the interwar period. During his career as an employee of the Iraqi Ministry of Health he moved from one provincial post to another. His devotion to his profession eventually collided with decreasing possibilities for professional advancement and the sterner politics of the post-1948 period. As a result, he too took the path of exile.

No subject in the modern history of the Middle East has received greater attention from scholars than nationalism. The conventional account stresses the ways in which in response to heroic leaders the masses mobilized to overthrow Western rule. The obvious contradiction between the reality of ethnic diversity and the nationalist assumption of ethnic unity in Middle Eastern states is simply elided in most accounts. While we know quite a bit about nationalism as an ideology and a political movement, we are much less well informed about how it became the language of politics.[36] The role of nationalism as an ideology in serving the interests of indigenous elites in maintaining their dominance is generally not examined. It is here that the study of ordinary people's lives can contribute a great deal.

As presented in the literature, the triumph of nationalism seems foreordained and in no way problematic. Yet the terrible simplifications of the nationalist ideologues ran against the grain of the old social forms, personal attachments, and ways of thinking. By asking us to reimagine the specific context in which nationalisms emerged, the biographies provide us with the materials of a more complex and culturally sensitive understanding of this elusive phenomenon. The rise of nationalism, these biographies suggest, needs to be situated not only in the context of Arab nationalist ideology but also in that of local politics and the specific options available to individuals.

This theme clearly emerges in Abdullah Schleifer's biography of Izz al-Din al-Qassam. Schleifer shows that Palestinian popular resistance to British and Zionist domination of mandatory Palestine arose from multiple roots. These included Islamic reformism, Sufism, and late Ottoman pan-Islam, as well as urban-based secular nationalism. Philip Khoury's portrait of Abu Ali al-Kilawi shows us an old-style neighborhood enforcer, or *qabaday*, rooted in quarter-based youth gangs, whose ideology derived from Islamic notions of chivalry and the cult of masculine physical prowess. With the changes in Damascene society, the old patronage networks grew less important, and new political forms gradually emerged. Eventually Abu Ali and those like him were replaced by a new style of resolutely modern nationalist organizers. M'hamed Ali, a Tunisian labor leader and early nationalist, is a third figure whose biography is especially revealing of the way nationalism came to the area. In his case, involvement in labor organizing followed service in the Ottoman army during World War I and exile in Berlin in the last years of World War I. Through him we get a sense of the complex relations between the chief nationalist party, the Néo-Destour, the chief Tunisian labor union, the CGTT, and the various groups on the colonial left. It is a theme that can be found elsewhere in the region.

While the major story of the period is one of the transformation of the political world, the social and cultural worlds were no less affected. Artisan shops were gradually supplemented by factories and industrial enterprises. Smokestacks increasingly rivaled minarets along the new urban skyline, and new forms of communication such as the telegraph and telephone, railroads, trucks, and airplanes displaced human and animal transport. (The old forms did not so much disappear as coexist with the new.)

As part of a trend already established by the nineteenth-century Ottoman *tanzimat* reformers, governments, whether colonial or indigenous, became insulated from the people by bureaucracies modeled on modern lines. The cityscape was transformed by masses of rural migrants, who erected shantytowns around the old *qasba* and invaded the core of the old city. Simultaneously the elite gradually relocated to expensive villas constructed in the suburbs. The social gulf between elites and the masses widened and was bridged only by nationalism.

Despite these dramatic changes, important continuities remained. Kinship and family patterns proved remarkably resilient, even as large numbers of rural folk migrated to the cities. The extended family survived because it provided alternative possibilities for coping with new situations: finding schools and jobs, arranging marriages, sharing scarce resources.[37] Similarly, ethnic and religious communities developed unforeseen staying power in the face of the rising tide of nationalism. In part this was due to the deliberate policies of European colonial rulers, who played divide-and-rule games the better to establish their dominance. Thus Berbers, Kurds, Alawis, Druze, and other rural (often tribal) minorities were accorded varying degrees of privilege. So too non-Muslim groups were often the beneficiaries of favorable treatment. But ethnic communities prospered also because they continued to meet the spiritual, cultural, and material needs of large numbers of people. Nor, for all of that, did colonial efforts to foster discord necessarily succeed. Part of the success of secular nationalism derived from its ability to invent a national community in which cultural difference was authorized or at least tolerated.

Many social continuities between old and new remained as well. Artisan guild structures not only survived but were extended into new trades. (Consider, for example, the case of Hagob Hagobian, who proudly wore the badge of the long-distance truck drivers' guild.) Long-established forms of male and female sociability based in homes, *hammams,* and cafés helped to maintain sexual segregation and to provide many women and men with emotional support and networks for coping. (Note the importance of cafés in the lives of many of the men whose biographies appear in this volume.)[38]

A final theme that might be noted here is the impact of World War II. This is most evident in the case of the North Africans, since the Maghrib was the site of some of the war's major battles. For Muhammad Ameur, the Tunisian protagonist in Kenneth Brown's essay, the war brought tragedy; his village suffered a racist pogrom by the occupying Italian Fascist troops. Because of the wartime role of the Middle East in Allied strategic planning, Iranians were mobilized by the Allies in support of the Russian front, while the Middle East Supply Center was located in Cairo. Both Hagob Hagobian and Amir Agha were affected (though differently) by the war. The changes wrought by the war so undermined the world of Dr. Naji, the Iraqi Jewish physician whose life is presented by Sami Zubaida, that he eventually had to leave Iraq for Britain, where he lives today. World War II was a major defining period in the life of the group of the Egyptian bedouin woman Migdim, profiled by Lila Abu-Lughod in the next section. Migdim remembers how things used to be before the bedouin were sedentarized by the government. Her reminiscences afford us a privileged glimpse of some of the stratagems for survival employed by a proud and independent woman. They also give us a sense of her ironic and earthy sense of humor.

*Contemporary Lives*

For contemporary Middle Easterners, the period since 1945 has been one of extraordinary change. Hopes have been raised periodically, only to be dashed by some new turn of the historical wheel. The biographies that comprise this section are a sobering reminder of the human costs of much of this change—as well as the ability of people to survive even under the most appalling conditions.

The most dramatic transformation in the contemporary period lay in the political arena: namely, the final act of the colonial drama—the triumph of nationalist movements and the emergence of independent states. Yet independence did not bring solutions to the many problems of the societies of the region. Instead, the blighted dream of nationalism has increasingly provided the focus of political debate. As regimes lost legitimacy due to their inability to resolve the problems of independence, opposition movements sprang up first on the secular left (inspired by the Algerian FLN and the Palestinian commandos) and later on the Islamist right (where the Islamic revolution in Iran was the major catalyst).

Global superpower rivalries deriving from the cold war, Western support for Israel, and Western dependence on Middle Eastern oil all combined to skew internal debate, foreclose options, and dampen dissent even as they weakened the legitimacy of states in the area. By the late 1970s the splintering of the coalitions that had sustained the nationalist movements led to a loss of confidence in the capacity of the providential state to deliver the goods of modernity. Also in the 1970s, the boom-and-bust cycles of the oil economy led to the erosion of the living standard of the many and to the scandalous enrichment of the few. Civil conflict in Afghanistan, Lebanon, and the Sudan and the bloody Iran-Iraq war established the limits of the political stalemate throughout the region. The attractiveness of Islamic alternative solutions to many people must be understood in this context.

The rupture of the nationalist consensus and the differential impact of economic change make it difficult to find a common thread among the biographies in this section. Some individuals became political militants; others remained quiescent. Some experienced real gains in their living standard after independence, while for others (notably tribal peoples) the ambitious plans of modernizing regimes meant the destruction of a traditional way of life. Finally, although the increased integration of the region into the world economy facilitated large-scale labor migration (a benefit to some), the globalization of politics has led to a rash of civil wars and an upsurge in violence (especially of regimes toward domestic opponents).

The effort to find continuities founders for other reasons as well. In the transformation of the Middle East since 1800, two global historical trends, prior to and analytically distinguishable from the phenomenon of European imperialism, loom large: the expansion of the role of the state and the integration of the Middle East into the world economy. Under colonialism, the third major force for change, centralization and economic change appeared as consequences of imperialism. The specifically Western cultural auspices under which the transformation to modernity occurred thus masked its global character. Nationalists denounced colonial abuses. Yet their ambitions to modernize and develop their societies differed little from those pursued by the imperialists. Because the nationalists assumed that states were independent actors, instead of inextricably bound into the world economy and international political systems, they were bound not only to provoke dissent but also to fail.

The contemporary era was affected by two additional conjunctural factors. The first was the cold war. Fear of Soviet expansionism led the United States and its allies to seek to establish alliance schemes like the Baghdad Pact (1955). It also led Western policymakers to view nationalist leaders such as Nasser, Ben Bella, and Qasim as potential Communist agents. This fundamental misreading had serious consequences. Because Western leaders never understood the indigenous roots of nationalism, they were propelled into a series of military adventures (Suez, Algeria, Iran, Lebanon) that by the 1980s had drastically eroded whatever moral capital they retained. European and American interests in Middle Eastern oil and the Suez Canal in the postwar era further intensified the tendency toward interventionism.

To this must be added the Arab sense of injury stemming from the establishment of Israel. For Jews, Israel represented a haven from oppression, the fulfillment of age-old dreams, and the possibility of forging a new Jewish people outside the heritage of European racism and the Hitlerian genocide. For the Palestinian people, however, it meant the loss of their homeland. Middle Eastern peoples did not share in European anti-Semitism, and they perceived the Zionist project as a form of colonialism. In Israel the contradictions of European history encountered those of Middle Eastern history. The roots of current Middle Eastern bitterness and distrust of the West are to be sought in this tangled history.

For most people World War II marked the point of rupture with the colonial period. The war not only inflicted suffering and death upon Middle Easterners (especially North Africans, many of whom found themselves caught in the crossfire), it also raised questions about the continued viability of the colonial empires. Whereas World War I was followed by the dismantling of the Ottoman Empire and the establishment of the colonial mandates in the Arab East, the aftermath of World War II led to the emergence of independent states throughout the region.

The rise of national states led by charismatic nationalist leaders like Gamal Abdel Nasser, Ahmed Ben Bella, and Habib Bourguiba (respectively, the heads of Egypt, Algeria, and Tunisia in the 1960s) was the most important source of change in the period. Ambitious programs of national development and more prosaic efforts on the part of newly independent governments to reward their followers led to a vast expansion of state bureaucracies. They also led to a steady extension of the involvement of the state in people's lives, with both positive and negative consequences.

What the increased role of the state meant for most people depended upon their access to government bureaucrats who might intervene on their behalf, and on their vulnerability to government policies. Both Gulab, the Afghan schoolteacher whose story is presented by Ashraf Ghani, and Haddou, the Moroccan migrant worker whose life is limned by David McMurray, benefited from the favorable decisions of government bureaucrats. Gulab became a schoolteacher, while Haddou obtained a coveted government authorization to work in Europe.

In contrast, government reforms confronted tribal peoples like Migdim or Rostam, the Iranian Qashqa'i rebel whom Lois Beck discusses in her contribution, with impossible choices. To go along with government plans and assimilate would cut them off irrevocably from their tribal roots, while opposition would be pitilessly crushed. Migdim and her bedouin group decided to submit. Rostam, on the other hand, found himself drawn into radical opposition to the shah's forced modernization efforts. The differences between Rostam's and Migdim's responses to modernization define the options of tribal peoples throughout the region. Thus the bedouin of Arabia, Syria, Iraq, and Jordan and the pastoralist Berbers of North Africa have tended to follow the route of sedentarization, while groups like the Kurds and the Baluch have been more divided in their responses. (In part as well, these variations can be glossed as reflections of the different relative power positions of tribes and states in the different societies.)[39]

The differential responses of ordinary people to the political appeals of governments and oppositions in the contemporary period are a revealing sign of the limits of charisma. Attempts at political mobilization served chiefly to raise popular expectations and frustration. The lives of activists like Gulab, the Afghan teacher, were transformed by their political choices. Others, like the Iranian Amir Agha, whose portrait is presented by Fakhreddin Azimi, remained resolutely apolitical. Amir Agha's life revolved around his family and friends in the local café. This, given the politicization of modern Iran, must be rated no mean achievement. Reading about his life, we have a sense of the limits of political enthusiasm. The skepticism of people like Amir Agha sets real limits on both the shah's power and that of the Islamic Republic.

The contrast between Amir Agha's life and that of Gulab could not be greater. Gulab's biography is the story of the political education of a provincial youth. Plunged into the seething cauldron of student politics in Kabul, Gulab was hard-pressed to choose between different groups, each of which proclaimed it had the solution to what they saw as a backward country's problems. The sharp social divisions in prerevolutionary Afghanistan—between wealth and poverty, urban and rural, and between Persian-speakers and speakers of Pashtu—only made the political footing more slippery. Eventually Gulab found himself trapped between left and right, Marxists and Islamic fundamentalists. Through his dilemma we come to understand the social choices Afghans were forced to make following the overthrow of Taraki in 1978.

Since 1973, when the population of the Middle East was 85 to 90 percent rural and agricultural and mostly nonliterate, the pace of social change has quickened dramatically throughout the region. By 1990, the majority of the population of the region was urban, nonagricultural, and literate (although the percentages vary with each country). Despite sharp rises in oil revenues, population increases have swamped the ability of the states outside the Persian Gulf to provide even rudimentary services. The unprecedented movement from the countryside to the cities and the simultaneous huge increase in the percentage of the population under the age of twenty-five (more than 60 percent in some countries) have blighted dreams of development. The difficulties of negotiating the transition from a predominantly rural and agricultural society to a predominantly urbanized one were bound to have political consequences. The wonder is that (till now at least) they have not been greater.

These contradictions are largely responsible for the increased violence of the last decade, including the Lebanese and Afghan civil wars, the Iranian revolution, and the Iran-Iraq war. As confidence in secular nationalism has waned, political interest in Islam has grown rapidly.[40] Given this context, the survival of most of the regimes in the area must be rated one of the biggest surprises of all. With the exception of Afghanistan, Lebanon, and Iran, the same regimes (and often the same leaders) that were in power in 1973 are still in place in 1992.

The Lebanese and Afghan civil wars both resulted from failed leftist efforts to transform their respective societies into modern secular states. Nominally a democracy, Lebanon was stalemated by class and ethnic divisions. The presence of three hundred thousand Palestinian refugees and the existence of a PLO quasi government constituted another flash point of tension. When a left-wing coalition (including the PLO) sought to introduce major reforms in 1975, right-wing Maronites, supported first by Syria and subsequently by Israel, intervened, setting off a conflict unprecedented in its complexity and savagery. The struggle took on an international dimension when the different Lebanese factions acquired foreign backers.[41]

Leila Fawaz's biography of Sumaya, a Lebanese housemaid, implicitly challenges the grim determinisms that shape our image of the Lebanese conflict. Partially crippled, illiterate, and poor, Sumaya seemed destined for a life of drudgery when she left her village to take up employment as a domestic servant in a bourgeois household in Beirut. The outlook for her future remained bleak until the outbreak of civil war in 1975. While the war was a calamity for Lebanese society and led to the emigration of her employers, it paradoxically seemed to provide Sumaya with new reserves of energy and self-confidence. As the war intensified, her role in the household became increasingly assertive. Fawaz has provided us with a fascinating and deeply problematic portrait.

In 1973 the monarchy of Afghanistan was displaced by a coup that brought to power the government of Muhammad Daud. When the left-leaning Daud was in turn ousted by a faction of the Afghan Communist party under Muhammad Taraki in 1978, the society exploded. While Communist party factions battled for power, tribal and Islamic religious leaders sought to organize resistance. As in Lebanon, the conflict swiftly became an international one, although in this case along orthodox cold war lines. The Soviet Union backed the government, while the United States, Pakistan, Saudi Arabia, and Iran supported different factions among the *mujahidin*.

Ashraf Ghani's biography of Gulab sheds light on the hopes and expectations of the Afghan intelligentsia in the period of rising tension and conflict that immediately preceded the outbreak of the civil war. Through it we come to appreciate the ways in which families found themselves torn and lifelong friends became bitterly estranged. The stakes for both sides were high: the chance for a modern secular state on the one hand, the preservation of deeply rooted customs and religious values on the other.

Of the political earthquakes that have reshaped the political landscape of the contemporary Middle East, the most important is assuredly the Iranian revolution. Media stereotypes about the Islamic revolution, while providing the smug with a sense of superiority, have been more notable for their vulgar otherizing than their ability to provide a coherent explanation of events. A more complex understanding of the stakes for ordinary Iranians is provided by the biographies included in this volume.

The quasi-autobiographical portrait of Mehdi Abedi (cowritten with Michael Fischer) describes what it was like to grow up in an Iranian village in the shah's Iran. From it we acquire a sense of the firmly entrenched popular traditions of Shiite Islam, and their capacity to instill a love of religious learning in young men like Abedi. Abedi's personal odyssey was to lead him deep into the political factions of provincial Iran and then to the struggles between the Islamists and Marxists in Tehran and on college campuses in the United States. In a very different fashion from Amir Agha, he managed to avoid being drawn into the violence of politics, and although, like Gulab, he debated activists, he managed to retain an independent spirit.[42]

Mehdi Abedi's biography contrasts with those of Rostam, the Qashqa'i tribal rebel, and Amir Agha, the ne'er-do-well truck driver and shop-keeper, the other Iranians whose portraits are drawn here. The three portraits permit us to see the quite different individual strategies pursued by Iranians in the conditions of rapid change and political repression that pertained in the 1970s.

The final two chapters underscore the costs of the changes that the region has undergone in the contemporary period. Joost Hiltermann's biography of Abu Jamal, a Palestinian urban villager, provides a sharply etched study of life under the *intifada* in Arab Jerusalem, while David McMurray's evocative portrait of Haddou, a Moroccan migrant worker in Germany, gives us a sense of the dreams, as well as the harsh realities, that govern the lives of North Africans who work in Europe.

## NOTES

1. Eric Wolf, *Europe and the People without History* (Berkeley: University of California Press, 1982).

2. Eugene Genovese, *Roll, Jordan, Roll* (New York: Vintage Books, 1976).

3. Strictly speaking, the term *colonialism* implies settlers, and applies only to the Maghrib and Palestine. In this book, I use the term to refer to incorporation into a European colonial empire. What mattered to individuals were the ways Western rule altered how their societies were run.

4. European rule came gradually to the area. Some countries (Afghanistan, Iran, Saudi Arabia, and Yemen are some examples) were never officially incorporated into a colonial empire, though all came under Western hegemony in varying degrees. Prior to World War I the order of acquisition was as follows: Algeria (France, 1830), Aden (Britain, 1839), South Arabia (Britain, 1879), Tunisia (France, 1881), Egypt (Britain, 1882), Libya (Italy, 1911), and Morocco (France and Spain, 1912). As part of the World War I peace settlement, the British and French acquired mandates from the League of Nations over Iraq, Jordan, Lebanon, Palestine, and Syria. Kuwait became a formal British dependency at this time as well.

5. See P. M. Holt and Bernard Lewis, eds., *Historians of the Middle East* (Oxford: Oxford University Press, 1964).

6. On the genre of *tabaqat*, see R. Stephen Humphrys, *Islamic History: A Framework for Inquiry* (Minneapolis: Bibliotheca Islamica, 1988).

7. For an example, see Richard Bulliet, *The Patricians of Nishapur* (Cambridge, Mass.: Harvard University Press, 1972).

8. *The History of al-Tabari* (*Tarikh al-rusul wa'l-muluk*), translated from the Arabic in 37 vols. (New York: State University of New York Press, 1981–).

9. Natalie Davis, *The Return of Martin Guerre* (Cambridge, Mass.: Harvard University Press, 1983); Carlo Ginzburg, *The Cheese and the Worms: The Cosmos of a Sixteenth-Century Miller* (Baltimore: Johns Hopkins University Press, 1980); Jonathan Spence, *The Death of Woman Wang* (New York: Viking, 1978).

10. For a recent survey, see L. L. Langness and Gelya Frank, *Lives: An Anthropological Approach to Biography* (Novato, Calif.: Chandler and Sharp, 1987).

11. Several recent works treat this theme. See George E. Marcus and Michael M. J. Fischer, eds., *Anthropology as Cultural Critique* (Chicago: University of Chicago Press, 1986); James Clifford and George E. Marcus, eds., *Writing Culture: The Poetics and Politics and Ethnography* (Berkeley: University of California Press, 1986); and James Clifford, *The Predicament of Culture* (Cambridge, Mass.: Harvard University Press, 1988). In this volume the joint article of Michael Fischer and Mehdi Abedi is an example of this new genre.

12. Eliott Liebow, *Tally's Corner* (Boston: Little, Brown, 1967). For an example of the new tendency see the work of the French sociologist Daniel Bertaux, *Destins personnels et structures de classe: Pour une critique de l'anthropométrie politique* (Paris: P.U.F., 1977). Also D. Bertaux, ed., *Biography and Society: The Life History Approach in the Social Sciences* (Beverly Hills: Sage, 1981); and the journal *Life Stories/Récits de vie*.

13. Wilhelm Dilthey, *Pattern and Meaning in History* (New York: Harper, 1961).

14. See also Dale Eickelman, *Knowledge and Power in Morocco: The Education of a Twentieth-Century Notable* (Princeton: Princeton University Press, 1985), who refers to "biography as social document."

15. On this subject see Clifford Geertz, *Local Knowledge* (New York: Basic Books, 1983), and *Le mal de voir*, Cahiers Jussieu, no. 2 (Paris: Collection 10/18, 1976). See also the works mentioned in n. 10 above.

16. For an overview, see Peter Schottler, "Historians and Discourse Analysis," *History Workshop Journal* 27 (1989): 37–65. For more on "deconstruction" see Jacques Derrida, *Of Grammatology* (Baltimore: Johns Hopkins University Press, 1976); Sande Cohen, *Historical Culture: On the Recoding of an Academic Discipline* (Berkeley: University of California Press, 1986); Christopher Norris, *Deconstruction: Theory and Practice* (London: Methuen, 1982).

17. For an introduction to these issues, see Peter Novick, *That Noble Dream: The "Objectivity Question" and the American Historical Profession* (Cambridge: Cambridge University Press, 1988). Also Joan Scott, "History in Crisis? The Others' Side of the Story," *American Historical Review* 94 (1989): 680–92; and more generally Michel Foucault, *The Archeology of Knowledge* (New York: Harper, 1972).

18. Edward Said, *Orientalism* (New York: Vintage Books, 1978).

19. For an analysis of media stereotypes, see Edward Said, *Covering Islam* (New York: Pantheon, 1981).

20. How this works out in the case of French orientalism is discussed in my "The French Tradition of the Sociology of Islam," in *Islamic Studies: A Tradition and Its Problems*, ed. Malcolm Kerr (Santa Monica: Undena University Press, 1980), 73–88. See also my *Orientalism Observed: France, Islam and the Colonial Encounter* (Princeton: Princeton University Press, in preparation).

21. Daniel Lerner, *The Passing of Traditional Societies: Modernizing the Middle East* (Glencoe, Ill.: Free Press, 1958).

22. Richard Critchfield, *Shahhat: An Egyptian* (Syracuse: Syracuse University Press, 1978).

23. Tim Mitchell, "The Invention and Reinvention of the Egyptian Peasant," *IJMES* 22 (1990): 129–50.

24. The title of a book by Charles Glass, *Tribes with Flags: A Dangerous Passage through the Chaos of the Middle East* (New York: Atlantic Monthly Press, 1990).

25. Roy Mottahedeh, *The Mantle of the Prophet: Religion and Politics in Iran* (New York: Pantheon, 1985); and Erika Friedl, *The Women of Deh Koh: Lives in an Iranian Village* (Washington, D.C.: Smithsonian Institution Press, 1989).

26. For some others, see Nayra Atiya, *Khul Khaal: Five Egyptian Women Tell Their Stories* (Syracuse: Syracuse University Press, 1982); Vincent Crappanzano, *Tuhami, Portrait of a Moroccan* (Chicago: University of Chicago Press, 1980); Eickelman, *Knowledge and Power in Morocco;* Martin Lings, *A Sufi Saint in the Modern World* (London: Allen and Unwin, 1971); John Waterbury, *North for the Trade* (Berkeley: University of California Press, 1972).

27. On the officials, see Carter Findlay, *Ottoman Civil Officialdom: A Social History* (Princeton: Princeton University Press, 1989). On the ulama, see the chapters by Richard Chambers and Richard Repp in *Scholars, Saints and Sufis,* ed. Nikki Keddie (Berkeley: University of California Press, 1973).

28. Albert Hourani, "Ottoman Reform and the Politics of Notables," in *The Beginnings of Modernization in the Middle East,* ed. William Polk and Richard Chambers (Chicago: University of Chicago Press, 1968), 41–68, and the other articles in this volume.

29. Yashar Kemal's *Memed My Hawk* (New York: Pantheon, 1961) chronicles one such personal itinerary.

30. Benjamin Braude and Bernard Lewis, eds., *Christians and Jews in the Ottoman Empire,* 2 vols. (New York: Holmes and Meier, 1982).

31. On the system of extraterritoriality, see Stanford J. Shaw and Ezel K. Shaw, *History of the Ottoman Empire and Modern Turkey,* vol. 2 (Cambridge: Cambridge University Press, 1977). Also M. E. Yapp, *The Making of the Modern Near East, 1792–1923* (London and New York: Longman, 1987).

32. Niyazi Berkes, *The Rise of Secularism in Turkey* (Montreal: McGill University Press, 1966); and Bernard Lewis, *The Emergence of Modern Turkey* (Oxford: Oxford University Press, 1964). For the non-Muslim groups see the relevant chapters in Braude and Lewis, *Christians and Jews in the Ottoman Empire.*

33. E. J. Hobsbawm and Terence Ranger, eds., *The Invention of Tradition* (Cambridge: Cambridge University Press, 1983).

34. For representative studies, see Robert Fernea, *Shaykh and Effendi: Changing Patterns of Authority among the El Shabana of Southern Iraq* (Cambridge, Mass.: Harvard University Press, 1970); Lerner, *Passing of Traditional Societies;* S. H. Longrigg, *Syria and Lebanon under French Mandate* (Oxford: Oxford University Press, 1956); Daniel Rivet, *Lyautey et l'institution du protectorat français au Maroc, 1912–1925,* 3 vols. (Paris: Harmattan, 1988); Robert Tignor, *Modernization and British Colonial Rule in Egypt, 1882–1914* (Princeton: Princeton University Press, 1966). On the experience of colonialism see among others Jacques Berque, *French North Africa: The Maghrib between Two Wars* (New York: Praeger, 1962); and Timothy Mitchell, *Colonizing Egypt* (Cambridge: Cambridge University Press, 1988).

35. Pierre Bourdieu, *The Algerians* (Boston: Beacon Press, 1962). On peasant behavior more generally, see James Scott, *Weapons of the Weak: Everyday Forms of Peasant Resistance* (New Haven: Yale University Press, 1985).

36. See Albert Hourani, *Arabic Thought in the Liberal Age* (Oxford: Oxford University Press, 1962).

37. Samih Farsoun, "Family Structure and Society in Modern Lebanon," in *Peoples and Cultures of the Middle East,* ed. Louise Sweet (New York: Natural History Press, 1970).

38. Ralph Hattox, *Coffee and Coffee Houses: The Origins of a Social Beverage in the Medieval Near East* (Seattle: University of Washington Press, 1985).

39. Philip Khoury and Joseph Kostiner, eds., *Tribes and State Formation in the Middle East* (Berkeley: University of California Press, 1990).

40. See the preface to the second edition of Fatima Mernissi's *Beyond the Veil* (Bloomington, Ind.: Indiana University Press, 1987) for this suggestion.

41. On the Lebanese civil war, see Kamal Salibi, *Crossroads to Civil War: Lebanon, 1958–1976* (Delmar, N.Y.: Caravan Books, 1976). Also Jonathan Randal, *Going All the Way* (New York: Viking Press, 1983).

42. For the full tale, see Mehdi Abedi and Michael Fischer, *Debating Muslims: Cultural Dialogues in Tradition and Postmodernity* (Madison: University of Wisconsin Press, 1990).

# PART ONE

# Precolonial Lives

# TWO

# Assaf: A Peasant of Mount Lebanon

*Akram F. Khater and Antoine F. Khater*

Lebanon in the nineteenth century was part of the Ottoman Empire. It was administratively divided into several districts, the core of which was Mount Lebanon, the historic homeland of the Christian Maronite population. (It was not until the establishment of the French Mandate after World War I that Lebanon acquired its present borders.) Other important religious and linguistic ethnic groups existed: chiefly Druze (a heterodox Muslim sect), Sunni Muslims, Orthodox Christians, and in the south and east, Shii Muslims as well. Lesser numbers of Catholic Christians, Armenian Christians, and others could also be found.

The incorporation of the Middle East into the world economy had rather dramatic consequences for Lebanon. For centuries, Lebanese silk had been prized in Europe; starting in the 1840s, demand for silk thread by French manufacturers rose rapidly. Silk production increased sharply, then collapsed in 1877 and 1888 as the result of mechanization, silkworm disease, and problems with quality control. The booms and collapses seriously weakened the Maronite grip of the quasi-feudal elite on the rural populations. It also permitted the Ottoman government and foreign capitalists to develop their power further.

By 1860, when Assaf Khater was born in Lehfed, a small village in Mount Lebanon, the recession of the silk industry was pronounced. Its effects were further heightened by rapid population growth. Unable to make a go of it on his tiny plot of land, Assaf was led to seek his livelihood outside of the village. So big a step was not taken lightly, for attachment to the land was strong among Lebanese peasants.

Like many of his compatriots in these years, Assaf eventually took ship for South America where he hoped to make his fortune as a trader. (The Arab trader, or "Turco," played an important role in the opening up of the South American interior in the nineteenth century.) Although Assaf's life resembles that of countless other Lebanese migrants of the period, it was not without some surprising twists—most notably the departure of Assaf's wife for Uruguay soon after his return to Lehfed.

The experience of the Lebanese can usefully be compared with that of the Greeks and Italians, other Mediterranean migrants to the New World. The biography of Assaf contrasts in interesting ways with the lives of the North African migrants profiled in this volume: M'hamed Ali, a Tunisian who worked in Germany in 1919, and Haddou, a Moroccan who works in today's Germany. —ED.

Assaf Khater was born in 1860 in Lehfed, a small village in Mount Lebanon. His parents were peasants who descended from a long line of peasants who had inhabited the village for at least the past two hundred years. If his parents had been asked to predict their son's future, they would have answered confidently that it would resemble that of any other peasant. At best, Assaf might dream of a return to a mystical past where work was the basis of equality and where people lived off their honest work without landlords, taxes, or invading armies. But 1860 and the years that followed brought about changes that set Assaf and many peasants of his generation apart from their parents and on a track that led them away slowly but surely from peasant life and dreams. This essay is about those new dreams and the new life.

Lehfed, with its 840 inhabitants and some 120 stone cottages, was a large village by contemporary standards. It is located about sixty miles northeast of Beirut, where it rests in one of the rare plains in the steep and rugged Lebanese coastal mountain range. From the north it is protected by a high cliff, called the *shir* in Arabic, which rises straight up for about 600 feet. By the southern part of the village rises a series of hills at a slightly gentler slope, and toward the back of the village, at its eastern end, a road meanders through the oak- and pine-covered hills, connecting Lehfed to other villages. Finally, to the west the village opens on a plain overlooking the Mediterranean. Its 3,300-foot elevation made it a historic haven from religious persecution for the Maronite community. Paradoxically, and with an irony that suffused the lives of Lebanese peasants, the village's altitude forced its inhabitants to deal with the outside world more than they might have wished. For at that elevation, and with what little soil covered the stony surface of the mountain, very few crops could be grown. Wheat, lentils, and beans were imported from Syria, and most of the livestock was supplied by the Arab bedouin tribes who migrated to the mountain pastures during the summer. Since the sixteenth century Lehfed, like many villages in the surrounding mountains, depended on trading the major cash crop—silk—for the agricultural and animal products it needed to survive.

The village was made up of three separate sections that divided the inhabitants geographically as well as socially. At the northeastern end of the village, on the highest hill, lived the rich peasants; on the opposite, southwestern, lower ledge resided the less wealthy families; and in the small stretch of valley in between, called Saqi Rishma'ya, were the houses of those peasants who had the least amount of land. The Khater family's two-room cottage was in this area. Its walls were made of stone cut from the rock, and the roof was made up of mud and thatch that had to be packed down by a stone roller after heavy rain and shoveled after every snowstorm. One of the rooms served as a kitchen and workroom. In the other, whose ceiling was charred by years of burning dried olive pits for warmth in the winter nights, the family ate, visited, and slept. The few animals—a couple of goats, some chickens, and a rooster—lived outside in a stone shack. It was in this house that Assaf was born and raised.

From the age of five and until he was ten, Assaf attended the village's school during the late fall and winter. There he and most of the boys in the village received a rudimentary education. In those times the girls could barely step outside the house, let alone receive a public education. Except on extremely stormy days, Assaf walked up the small hill to the 250-year-old church, where classes were held. It was not much of an education, especially since the Maronite priest who conducted the classes was barely literate himself and spent more time chastising the children than teaching them. This lackadaisical schooling did not give Assaf much reason to continue after he finished his elementary education, for it held no promise of any benefits or use for a peasant boy. Even if he had intended to go on with his education, it would have been difficult, because the nearest high school was thirty miles away at Aintoura. Anyway, his family could not pay for ten-year-old Assaf's education, nor could they afford to lose his labor.

So Assaf joined his family in tilling the one acre of land that they owned. David Urquhart, a European traveler who visited Mount Lebanon in the 1850s, could have been describing the terraces in that acre when he said, "Everywhere man has planted the land, in Mount Lebanon he has made it." Aside from "making the land" the family secured its livelihood from it. A small part of the acre was occupied by a plot where the family grew tomatoes, onions, garlic, lettuce, zucchini, and some herbs and by another plot where they grew some wheat. There was also one olive tree, which barely gave the family enough olives each year for pressing olive oil and for eating. But most of the land was occupied by about thirty mulberry trees, which were crucial for raising silkworms. It was this crop that provided the Khaters with a product for bartering and later with the cash desperately needed by the family of seven.

Raising silkworms was extremely time consuming and labor intensive. For the Khater family, as for the 60 percent of Maronite peasants who were engaged in sericulture, the whole process started in the middle of

April. Around that time the silkworm eggs were brought down from their storage at colder, higher elevations in the Maronite monasteries. The eggs had to be kept at certain temperatures for the first few weeks until they hatched. Once the worms had hatched, Assaf's mother, brothers, and sisters had alternately to feed and fast them. The family was kept busy all day long during late spring and summer, picking leaves, cutting them into small pieces, and feeding them to the worms.

When the worms began to weave their cocoons the pace of the work eased up for a couple of weeks. That time was occupied with tending to other chores that had been neglected. Finally, before the metamorphosed worms had a chance to break free, the family collected the cocoons and took them to the village *makhnaq* (literally, choker), where they were placed in a smoke-filled closed room. After boiling the cocoons in limewater to remove the glue that held them together, they stretched the thread (which could extend up to 500 feet) and laid it out to dry on the rooftop. Next the silk thread was spun and reeled by Assaf's mother and sisters on an old wooden spinning wheel that gave the silk an uneven look. Most of the silk was bartered to a traveling merchant who would take it to Damascus, where he sold it to the textile shops. In a good year some silk thread would be left over to weave a scarf for the dowry of one of the girls.

By the time Assaf was old enough to partake in that work—around the late 1860s—things had changed. Now the silk merchants were based in Beirut, and it was they who provided the silkworm eggs to the peasants on loan, using the land as collateral. Also, by the 1860s these merchants had become the representatives of major French silk importers and had more money available for loans. While it became easier for Assaf's family to get a loan, it was now imperative that the eggs matured into a profitable cash crop in order for the Khaters to repay the egg loan and its 20 percent interest, and keep their land. The Beirut silk merchants who bought the cocoons from peasants like the Khaters took them to the new mechanized silk factories. These factories, the first of which was built around 1862, took over the jobs of preparing the cocoons and reeling the silk, which was then shipped to Marseilles.

Also around this time Assaf's family began to sell their silkworms for Turkish *qurush* (piasters) instead of bartering them for wheat or lentils. The price of silkworms fluctuated depending on the demand in France, the competition from Japan and China, and the quality of silk raised. In good years, like 1867, a price of forty to forty-four piasters for one *oke* (1.28 grams) was not unheard of, and it was better than anything the villagers could have gotten from the traveling merchant. In bad years, like 1873, the price of silk plummeted to twelve piasters per *oke*, and the family had to go deeper into debt in order to survive the winter.

The constant price fluctuations were not the only thing that caused the family to go into debt. Increased income raised expectations of a better standard of living. Assaf and his family were no longer satisfied with the simple amenities of the old life. Textiles from Damascus were less in demand. By 1870, English cotton cloth was all the rage, and everyone strove to have a suit made out of the fancied material. Yemeni coffee, which the Khater family had previously consumed only on special occasions, was replaced in the 1870s by regular consumption of more expensive Brazilian coffee. The family seemed to be always trying to match up its income with its ever-growing expenses, and never quite making it.

In order to supplement the family income from silk and subsistence farming, the young boys had to work outside the house. At the age of fourteen, Assaf joined the older boys, who worked the land of a wealthier neighbor. Work outside the house took even peasant girls out of their traditional context. One of Assaf's nieces went to work as a reeler in a nearby silk factory in order to pay off the debt of her family. Since she had never worked in a factory or on a French reeling machine, she had to be trained by the French women supervisors who were brought there by the European owners of the factory. Thus she was exposed to French ways of behaving and thinking. Naturally curious, she gathered whatever glimpses and ideas from these French women that the language barrier did not block. Together with her experience as a factory girl this contact transported her beyond the village into a larger world, and she carried this vision back to her family and village community.

Assaf consequently grew up in an environment very different from his father's. The horizons of the village, while never hermetically sealed, were definitely expanding by the 1870s. Steamboats linked Beirut to Europe, and from there to the rest of the world. A railroad was built to link Beirut with Damascus, and roads were built into the mountains. Letters from emigrants, who began to leave for different parts of the New World in the early 1860s, arrived with descriptions of lands that held incredible wealth and of strange ways of living. French and American missionaries also arrived, bringing with them an education not only of the bookish kind but also about different life-styles and different worlds. Travelers from Europe came through more often, recording their impressions of "The Lebanon," while their mannerisms and habits were recorded equally by the locals.

Then there were the stories of peasants striking it rich in the silk trade and building immense houses of five rooms and a veranda—stories that were common lore by the time that Assaf was fifteen. By the age of eighteen he had heard many letters from emigrants being read around the *ayn* (spring) in the village square, right underneath the large old walnut tree. He had heard of Naim who had gone to Nayurk (New

York) and struck enough gold to send his father fifty *ithmaliyi* (golden Turkish sovereigns), a fortune that would buy a small farm in those days and leave some to spare. He also could not have failed to see the blush of riches on the roof of Abu Latif's old house as the mud brick was replaced with imported Italian red tile. By the time Assaf was eighteen, the old Lebanon was already much changed, and new opportunities beckoned.

Yet as late as the 1850s the way up was blocked. The shaykhs (landlords of the Mountain under the *iqta* system) were quick to enforce their control over the livelihood and life-style of the peasantry. So great was their influence that Assaf's father had to receive permission from Shaykh Butrus al-Khazin, who controlled the area, before getting married. By the 1860s, peasants were legally free, and no such permission was required for marriage. Nor, for that matter, was marriage as socially prescribed as it used to be. A "bag of gold" could, in the 1880s, replace the required lineage as a prerequisite for marriage; hence the expression "she married gold," which became popular in the 1880s.

The changing economic tides in Lebanon that affected Assaf's family were paralleled by significant political changes. The old political system in which villagers were governed by a shaykh, as the local representative of the feudal *amir*, came under severe pressure in the 1850s. In the past the shaykh had been the largest landowner in the village, and most villagers had worked as sharecroppers on his lands. With the assistance of his henchmen (*qabadayat*), he had administered local justice and imposed various quasi-feudal obligations on "his" peasants (including requiring gifts of honey, olives, olive oil, and chickens on particular occasions).

This peculiarly Lebanese variety of feudalism came to an end in the 1858–61 revolution. Initially a revolt of peasants and lower clergy against the higher Maronite clergy and feudal lords in the Kisrawan district, the uprising soon engulfed other Maronite villages. In a later phase, the struggle degenerated into a bitter sectarian battle between Maronites and Druze before French and Ottoman troops restored order. The old political system was overthrown. In its place a new order guaranteed by the European states was set up, and the rule of the *amirs* was ended in the Maronite districts of Mount Lebanon. One by-product of the settlement of 1861 of special importance to peasants like Assaf was that individual liberties were recognized, including the rights of peasants to move freely and of merchants to buy and sell unfettered by the old feudal rules.

Thus by the time Assaf was born many of the restraints that had kept peasants from leaving the land had been loosened. As a result, Assaf and his family were more exposed to the opportunities and pitfalls of a market economy. As we have seen, this change had tangible effects on the structure of the family, its economic needs and desires. When Assaf was old enough to contemplate the prospects of his future it was obvious to him that peasant life as it had been was no longer viable.

As Assaf was the youngest of three brothers and thus had little hope of inheriting any land, his prospects were in fact bleaker than those of many other young peasant men. This was especially so because the population had doubled since the 1820s, while the amount of arable land had remained more or less the same. Finally, silk, the only cash crop that could be raised in Lehfed, was no longer as profitable as it had been in the 1860s and 1870s, because of foreign competition and backward techniques of production. By the 1880s, Lebanese silk production was in free-fall, and by 1930 it was definitely defunct. As early as 1910 Lebanese farmers had begun to uproot their mulberry trees and plant orange and lemon trees, the latest in cash crops. In 1878 Assaf had to choose: either he would remain in the village eking out a hard living from the rocky land or he would have to move elsewhere in search of a better life. With the encouragement of his father he opted for the latter route.

Assaf's first steps outside the village took him only as far as Baabda, the seat of the Ottoman government in Mount Lebanon. There in 1878 he enlisted in the gendarmes, the Ottoman internal security force established in 1864. Despite the short distance he traveled, Assaf's trip was momentous. After all, a famous local proverb praised the bravery of Naimi's husband for going "to Damascus [a 100-mile trip] and coming back all by himself." So to go to Beirut (a 50-mile trip) was in itself an act of bravery on Assaf's part. For a peasant with deeply ingrained suspicions of the government, Assaf's decision was mentally an even more substantial journey. A more cautious alternative would have been for him to become a Maronite monk, but that would have meant a celibate and circumscribed life of some schooling and church service. For a man who was to marry twice and have his last child at age fifty-two, celibacy would not seem to have been a very appealing concept. So into the gendarmes he went.

After a few weeks of training in the barracks of Baabda, Assaf was assigned to the gendarme post in Jounieh. Part of his job was to maintain public security in Jounieh and the surrounding villages and to protect peasants traveling the back roads from brigandage. But in reality the gendarmes were there to assert the authority of the government against the landlords and their *shabab*. Assaf's job also included providing protection for the government tax collectors from the peasants in the surrounding villages.

When Assaf first joined the gendarmes he had hoped that his new job would open up avenues for advancement. But after twelve years of service he had not advanced beyond the position of corporal. The novelty of the uniform and police life soon wore off. The respectability that he had hoped would come with the uniform was not forthcoming, for most peasants still regarded the government and its agents with deep suspicion. Thus being a gendarme was not rewarding either psychologically or financially, and it was even less so socially. Yet for lack of a better choice Assaf stuck with it.

On one of his few visits to his village, in 1884, Assaf was approached by his father about marrying one of his cousins, Saydé. Assaf was then twenty-four, while Saydé was in her late teens. Assaf did not know Saydé well at all and had seen her only when she accompanied her mother to visit his mother. At first he resisted the idea, but his father was very insistent because he wanted to make sure that his son married someone from the village. Assaf's uncle was equally anxious to see his daughter married to one of her paternal cousins, so he added a small plot of land to her dowry to sweeten the deal. By the end of June the two cousins were married and living temporarily with Assaf's family. Assaf himself could not stay very long after the wedding, for he had to report for duty in Jounieh. Since he could not afford to have his wife live in Jounieh with him and since it was unthinkable for her to live in a strange town with her husband gone on duty most of the time, Assaf had to leave Saydé behind. Within a year of their marriage their first son was born, who was named Selim.

From the start times were hard for the young couple. Not only did the long physical separation inhibit the development of normal married life, but also their financial situation was difficult. Saydé worked hard on the plot of land that she owned as part of her dowry, and she also helped Assaf's mother with her work in the house in order to make ends meet. Assaf's salary of a few hundred piasters per year was not by itself sufficient to support them; even with Saydé's work it barely kept them out of debt. It was quite obvious, especially after their daughter Nessim was born, that the dreams of wealth and a better life that they had were not going to come true while Assaf worked as a gendarme. His stint in the gendarmes exposed him to the cosmopolitan life of Beirut, its new bourgeois manners, European clothes, and the French language. He could also see steamships cruising in and out of the port of Beirut—constructed in 1860 to facilitate silk exports to France—and streams of emigrants boarding them to make the crossing to what they anticipated was a better life. The twelve years Assaf spent in the gendarmes only made him less inclined to be a peasant and more interested in seeking other ways of making a living.

Upon the birth of his third child in 1890 (named Jirjis after his grandfather), Assaf decided to emigrate. But first he needed some money. He could either borrow, using his land as collateral, or sell the land. The second alternative was unrealistic. Despite his rejection of peasant life, ownership of land still conferred social status and economic well-being in his eyes. What he wanted was more land, not to farm himself, but to rent to a sharecropper; thereby he could enjoy the higher social status of a landowner. So Assaf mortgaged the land, sold one of Saydé's gold bracelets, and gathered their joint savings of ten Turkish gold sovereigns for his trip. With many good-byes and a few words to Saydé informing her that she was now responsible for their sons and the honor of their daughter, Assaf left his village for the second time to seek his fortune. With four of the gold sovereigns he was able to buy passage on a steamboat heading to Marseilles in late June.

Four days after leaving Mount Lebanon, Assaf arrived in Marseilles. Unlike most peasants who emigrated in this period, he had no relatives or acquaintances in the *mahjar* (land of emigration). Hence he did not have any definite ideas about where his travels should take him. On the ship from Beirut he became friends with other Lebanese peasants who were going to Uruguay, so he decided to join them. Together they set about trying to find a way to cross the Atlantic, and within a couple of days they had boarded a freighter in Marseilles heading to Uruguay. The month-long Atlantic crossing was a nightmare. He and his companions lived in the hold of the ship and were fed stale bread and brackish water. Used to feeling the ground beneath his feet, Assaf was terrified and bewildered by the way the ship's motion upset his balance. In the overcrowded conditions and stench and filth of the hold, disease spread easily. A few people even died during the voyage. That hellish experience left Assaf weak and ill upon his arrival in Montevideo, the capital of Uruguay. Luckily for him, the small local Lebanese community was quite helpful to new immigrants. He was taken into the house of the Sakaf family, who had originally emigrated there in 1880 from Zahlé, a town in the Biqaa Valley of Lebanon.

After a week of recuperating from his arduous trip, Assaf began to look for work. Since he had come to Uruguay with the intention of returning to Lebanon, Assaf had no desire to acquire land or to work as a farmer. In a place where industry was almost nonexistent, only one avenue of work was left for him: commerce. Traditionally this was the first line of work that new immigrants engaged in. Assaf filled his beaten-up old leather valise with the few items that he had brought from Lehfed, wooden crosses and worry beads made from olive pits, together with whatever he purchased or got on loan from already established Lebanese residents of Montevideo. Thus Assaf started his career as a peddler.

Although he knew neither Spanish nor any of the indigenous Indian languages, Assaf put together enough words to make up a vocabulary for merchandising. What he lacked in linguistic abilities he made up for with his clothes, which immediately marked him as an emigrant from the Holy Land and attracted customers. After a year he was comfortable enough with the trade, the language, and the country to venture into inland areas away from the capital. He spent several months at a time traveling the backcountry, bringing anything from lipstick to fans to the farmers (who were mostly of Italian extraction) and to the Indian peasants. Over the following two years Assaf traveled enough miles on foot and by boat to save money to purchase a small shop in Montevideo and to retire from at least the walking part of his newfound trade. After opening the shop, Assaf remained in Uruguay for eight years, until 1898.

Few Lebanese emigrants became wealthy, but like many others Assaf prospered enough to live comfortably and to send small amounts of money back to Lebanon, money that was invested in plots of land in Lehfed. The years of emotional and physical separation did not reward his family back in Lebanon with material comforts; if anything, times were more difficult for Saydé, who had to care for and feed the three children almost by herself. Assaf's income from the gendarmerie had stopped, and his trip had consumed most of the savings of the family. Moreover, Saydé's relationship with her in-laws was not very good. As a married woman living alone with her children, she inevitably set tongues wagging in the village about her morals, and this only added to the pressures with which she had to contend because of the absence of her husband. Although she did not starve to death, Saydé was hardly a happy woman during those eight years of separation.

Nor was she overjoyed when Assaf returned in 1898. It was difficult to pick up the pieces of a flimsy relationship that had been based for the past eight years on rare and short letters. The breakdown of their relationship was also accelerated by Assaf's changed behavior. While he did return to the village (unlike other emigrants who could not even face going back to the "old country" life-style), he could not fully bring himself to be integrated into the traditional village life. His desire to display the wealth he accumulated in Uruguay by spending large sums of money in the village's coffee shop did not sit well with Saydé. Things between them deteriorated slowly but surely, and his relations with his children fared no better. The oldest boy, Selim, was especially resentful of his father for leaving them for such a long time. The other two children did not even recognize him when he first came back, nor did they grow closer to him in the following years.

In 1900, two years after his return, matters got so bad between the married couple that Saydé took Selim and Nessim and left for Uruguay. Jirjis, the youngest boy, stayed with his father in Lehfed. This event was as shocking to the village as Assaf's sister going to work in the silk factory had been in the 1860s. Women rarely left their husbands to travel thousands of miles away, even if accompanied by a fifteen-year-old boy. Nor, for that matter, did most men allow their wife and children to leave them, let alone allow their wife to take over their business in the *mahjar*. In this particular case, the traditional social patriarchal controls had obviously been seriously weakened.

The Atlantic crossing was difficult for Saydé, who was pregnant and suffered from tuberculosis. A year and a half after reaching Uruguay, she succumbed to her illness and died, leaving Selim, then age sixteen, as the head of the family, which now included a baby boy, Khater, who was born upon their arrival in Montevideo. By 1902, when Selim started running the shop, the situation of the Lebanese immigrants had shifted from that of exotic newcomers to that of pariahs in the eyes of the indigenous population. Their practical monopoly of the market as well as their competition with the native merchants invoked feelings of antagonism. While tensions and conflict generally remained beneath the surface, in a few cases bad feelings led to violence. Selim's was one of those cases. His youth and inexperience translated into rash behavior that got him into constant trouble. Like the Syrian protagonist in Gabriel Garcia Marquez's novel *Chronicle of a Death Foretold*, Selim had an affair with the wife of an Uruguayan merchant. Business, honor, and nationalist feelings came together in a fight that broke out between the two merchants and later developed into a big street brawl. Selim lost the fight and was humiliated publicly. As he could not bear such a dishonor, the next day he went to the house of his enemy and shot him dead. Thus he landed in an Uruguayan prison at the age of eighteen, while his sister, Nessim, who was only sixteen at the time, was left to care for the house, the business, and five-year-old Khater.

The Sakaf family—who had helped Assaf get started—took the small family in and sent for Assaf to come and deal with the situation. In 1905, Assaf got on a boat and traveled to Uruguay for the second time. Once there he expended much time and money in getting his son out of prison. He succeeded in doing so but lost most of the money he had made in his previous, eight-year stay. Not wishing to remain in Uruguay nor to leave his second wife—whom he had married after Saydé died— and family alone in Lebanon, Assaf hurried back to the village in Lebanon. But he did so with the promised financial support of Selim, who remained in Uruguay with Nessim and Khater.

Upon his return to Lebanon, Assaf set about finishing work on his house and expanding his holdings. By 1914 he had purchased 100,000 square meters of land in Lehfed and another 2,000 square meters in Jubayl (ancient Byblos). After adding two new rooms and a veranda to the old house, Assaf looked for a different kind of investment. He bought a flour mill in Jubayl that would provide him with a more regular and immediate source of income in addition to what he received from the sale of apples that he grew on half of his land. His efforts to break his complete dependence on the land reflected the general mood of the peasant population of Mount Lebanon, who had learned after the crash of the silk market to diversify its sources of income. The lesson came in handy for Assaf during World War I, when Lebanon was plunged into economic hard times, and Selim reneged on his agreement with his father. Hunger and deprivation swept Mount Lebanon as the Allies tightened their blockade of all Ottoman lands including Lebanon. The basic necessities of life—such as flour, oil, and meat—disappeared first from the cities and towns and later from the villages. By 1919 about fifty thousand Lebanese had perished from the ensuing famine, and many towns were depopulated. Lehfed also suffered from shortages, and many tried to cross the mountains into Syria in order to buy sacks of flour and bring them back to Lebanon. Prices skyrocketed, and life became dear. Assaf did not venture over the mountains, but he was forced to sell his mill in Jubayl in order to feed his family and survive the war.

Assaf died in the cold winter of 1933. When he passed away he was what social scientists would call a rich peasant: a man who owned quite a bit of property and who employed others to plough and sow his land. He had started moving away from the peasant life when he first joined the gendarmes, and when he left for Uruguay in 1890 he definitely set himself and his two families on a trek out of poverty into material comfort. The political, social, and economic changes that Mount Lebanon was undergoing obviously shaped the boundaries within which Assaf operated. The dramatic changes that replaced the old quasi-feudal shaykhs with the new silk bourgeoisie also brought down some of the obstacles that had previously kept the peasants bound to their land. At the same time these changes made life off the land even more untenable than before the watershed year of 1860; thus many of the peasants had to move off their land and onto the roads, towns, and cities of Lebanon and the world. Assaf, among other peasants who emigrated from Lebanon, pushed the boundaries to the limit, and maneuvered his way to achieving the material goals he wanted for himself and his family. In the process he was slowly and subjectively transformed from a peasant into a member of a new amorphous class that was still too raw to be defined in any set terms. All that can be said with any certainty about Assaf, and men and women like him, is that he dreamt of, and toiled for, a better life. He succeeded to an extent; others did better, and still others failed. For Assaf, and for Lebanon as a whole, success meant the coexistence of traditional "Eastern" social relations with new relations based on "Western" materialism, juggling ways of life that sometimes flowed almost effortlessly, and at other times came crashing down with a loud bang.

## A NOTE ON SOURCES

The basic sources for this essay include the Khater family papers and personal reminiscences. Also helpful were recent works on the social and economic history of Lebanon. These include notably Dominique Chevallier, *La société du mont Liban à l'époque de la révolution industrielle en Europe* (Paris: Librairie orientaliste Paul Geuthner, 1971); Toufic Touma, *Paysans et institutions féodales chez les Druses et les Maronites du Liban du XVIII<sup>e</sup> à 1914* (Beirut: Librairie orientale, 1971); and Boutros Labaki, *Introduction à l'histoire économique du Liban: Soie et commerce extérieur en fin de période ottomane* (Beirut: Université libanaise, 1984). The authors would like to dedicate this essay to those Lebanese whose dreams, aspirations, and homes have been destroyed by the war and violence of the last fourteen years.

## SUGGESTIONS FOR FURTHER READING

For a basic history of Lebanon see Kamal Salibi, *The Making of Modern Lebanon,* and his *House of Many Mansions: The History of Lebanon Reconsidered* (London: I. B. Tauris, 1988). Roger Owen's *Middle East in the World Economy, 1800–1914* (London: Methuen, 1981) surveys the basic economic context. For the nineteenth-century social and political background see John Spagnolo, *France and Ottoman Lebanon: 1861–1914* (London: Ithaca Press, 1977). On the Kisrawan peasant revolt see Y. Porath, "The Peasant Revolt of 1858–61 in Kisrawan," *Asian and African Studies* 2 (1966): 77–157; and Samir Khalaf, *Persistence and Change in 19th Century Lebanon* (Beirut: AUB Press, 1979). On the silk industry, Boutros Labaki, *La soie dans l' économie libanaise,* 2 vols. (Paris, 1974). On the growth of Beirut, see Leila Fawaz, *Merchants and Migrants in Nineteenth-Century Beirut* (Cambridge, Mass.: Harvard University Press, 1983). On emigration see Elie Safa, *L'émigration libanaise* (Beirut, 1976); and the articles of Afif Tannous, notably his "Emigration: A Force of Social Change in an Arab Village," *Rural Sociology* 7 (1942).

# THREE

# Yishaq Ben Ya'is Halewi:
# A Moroccan Reformer

*Daniel Schroeter*

From earliest times, there was a substantial Jewish minority in North Africa, which lived somewhat intermingled with the indigenous Berber inhabitants. (El Kahina, a famous leader of Berber resistance to the Arab conquerors in seventh-century Algeria, was probably Jewish.) Jews played an important role in Islamic Spain and in North Africa under Islam. After the Spanish reconquest and the expulsion of the Jews in 1492, many Andalusian Jews moved to North Africa. By the mid-nineteenth century, the Jewish population of Morocco stood at about 3 percent of the total Moroccan population of approximately four million people. Most Jews lived in the cities in Morocco, though there were also significant numbers of rural Jews in some parts of the country.

Moroccan Jewish society was marked by deep cleavages between rich and poor. While the vast majority of Jews lived crowded together in the *mellahs* (as the ghettos in Morocco were called), a small group of extremely wealthy Jews lived in opulent bourgeois dwellings in the Muslim parts of the city. As *protégés* (business representatives of European firms in Morocco) the wealthy Jews benefited from legal extraterritorial privileges that exempted them from local justice and local taxes.

As Daniel Schroeter shows in this selection, Yishaq Ben Ya'is Halewi, a Jewish leader from the city of Essaouira (also known as Mogador to Europeans), was a complex figure. At once profoundly Moroccan and strongly cosmopolitan in his outlook, Halewi dreamed of reforming the lives of the Jews of Morocco. However, as a ne'er-do-well merchant, he lacked the social position to bring this about on his own.

The context in which Halewi operated was thus a delicate one. To preach reform was to collide head-on with the wealthy Jewish notables of the casbah, who had their own ideas of what was fit. To attack the government (known as the *makhzan*) for ignoring or encouraging abuses against Jews was to risk retribution directed not only against him personally but against Jews generally. As Schroeter argues, to be effective Halewi had to avoid a complete breach with

*44*

the Jewish elite while also making clear his recognition of the legitimacy of the Moroccan sultan.

Schroeter's portrait situates Halewi in the context of both nineteenth-century Moroccan history and Jewish history. His nuanced contribution thus serves as a corrective to two major interpretations of the history of Jews of Arab lands, one of which views the experience of Arab Jews as characterized by a racism as bad in its way as that experienced by European Jews, the other of which sees the Arab Jews' experience (in contrast to that of European Jews) as unmarked by systematic persecution.* Schroeter's ability to situate his subject in multiple contexts (including the cleavages between rich and poor that divided Moroccan society) helps open up the subject to a more deeply historical understanding. (For more on non-Muslim minorities, see the chapters by Akram and Antoine Khater, David Yaghoubian, Sami Zubaida, and Leila Fawaz.) —ED.

On the windswept north side of the town of Essaouira, where the often stormy sea crashed against the somewhat dilapidated ramparts, was the Jewish quarter where Yishaq Ben Ya'is Halewi lived. Halewi was born about the year 1850, when Essaouira (better known to European travelers and sailors as Mogador) had reached its heyday as an international port. The town was founded by the sultan Sidi Muhammad b. Abdallah in 1764 as the royal port of the capital, Marrakesh, where all foreign trade was to be centered. By making dissident tribes dependent on the commercial activities of the port, the sultan hoped both to derive revenues from custom duties and to gain political and economic control of southwestern Morocco. To facilitate trade, the sultan settled representatives of the leading Jewish merchant families in the town. Essaouira soon grew to be Morocco's principal seaport. The bustling enterprises of the elite Jewish families attracted many other Jews to seek employment. During the nineteenth century, the Jewish community swelled with immigrants arriving from all over Morocco. The majority came from the south, whence drought and famine propelled them north to the coastal town. In the latter half of the nineteenth century, nearly half of the town's approximately twenty thousand inhabitants were Jews, making Essaouira the second largest Jewish center in Morocco after Marrakesh.

*On the first see Bat Ye'or, *The Dhimmi: Jews and Christians under Islam* (Rutherford, N.J.: Fairleigh Dickinson University Press, 1985). On the second see Norman Stillman, *The Jews of Arab Lands: A History and a Source Book* (Philadelphia: Jewish Publication Society of America, 1979); and Bernard Lewis, *The Jews of Islam* (Princeton: Princeton Unversity Press, 1986). See also the recent debate in *Tikkun:* Mark R. Cohen, "The Neo-Lachrymose Conception of Jewish-Arab History," *Tikkun* 6, 3 (1991): 55–60; and Norman Stillman, "Myth, Counter-Myth and Distortion," *Tikkun* 6, 3 (1991): 60–64.

At least 95 percent of the Jews lived in the *mellah*, the term used for all Jewish ghettos in Morocco. In 1807, Jews were required by royal decree to move to the recently constructed *mellah*. Thereafter all new Jewish immigrants, except for the privileged merchants who were granted government premises in the casbah, had to live among their coreligionists, either in the main "old *mellah*" or in the more recently built enclosure known as the "new *mellah*."

The prosperity of the wealthy Jews failed to generate a decent standard of living for all of the residents of the *mellah*. By the late 1870s, overcrowding, disease, and poverty were widespread. By the late 1880s, there were reports of as many as three families being cramped into a single tiny, windowless room in the *mellah*. A major drought that began in 1878 led thousands of rural Jewish migrants to seek charity in the town. The number of beggars grew enormously, and in the 1880s and 1890s the needy numbered some three thousand individuals.

Efforts by the community to expand the living quarters outside the walls of the *mellah* were to no avail. Petitions were repeatedly sent to Marrakesh in the 1880s and 1890s imploring the sultan to build new living quarters for the poor. Each time the sultan gave a favorable response, but divisions within the community itself and the resistance of the local Muslim authorities prevented the project from ever being initiated.

As a result, the Jews of Essaouira had no choice but to build upward. Despite prohibitions against infidels building houses higher than Muslim residences, some surreptitiously added a third story to their dwellings. Little sunlight penetrated through the high buildings, which were tightly clustered together on the narrow streets of the *mellah*. The filth and the stench from the garbage strewn in the streets was so overwhelming that few outsiders would ever venture through the gate leading into the main thoroughfare of the *mellah*. Yet within these walls, amid the squalor, there was a thriving Jewish community, producing rabbis and poets, craftsmen and peddlers, of whom many by the end of the nineteenth century were becoming increasingly conscious of their miserable plight.

Yishaq Ben Ya'is Halewi was a vocal member of the *mellah* community and was well known for his erudition. In 1890, Halewi was barely forty years old, married with two daughters. As a modest merchant and bookseller of the *mellah*, he had little influence in the affairs of the community, nor could he expect to be heard by the Muslim authorities of the town. Halewi was well aware of these limitations and in a sense accepted his fate as a humble Jew. If any changes were to be made, either within the Jewish community or regarding the position of Jews in the town as a whole, only the powerful and wealthy elders of the community, resident in the casbah and living together with non-Jews, could effectively implement reforms. The Jews in the *mellah*, by contrast, were poor and isolated. Halewi, like the other Jews of the *mellah*, respected the community leaders, even though the latter did little to ameliorate the poverty of the *mellah*.

Though Halewi could have no direct influence on the authorities, he was nevertheless determined to agitate for social change. While not attacking the community leaders by name, Halewi could at least decry the exploitation of the poor by the wealthy and powerful. The vehicle of his protest was a weekly Hebrew paper published in Warsaw, *Hasfirah*. Obviously Warsaw was a long way from Morocco, and contacts with Poland were minimal to say the least. But for some years, a few Jews along the Moroccan coast had begun to receive a number of Hebrew newspapers published in Europe that were widely circulated in European Jewish communities. Essaouira in the 1890s was linked to Europe by a number of steamship companies, two French, two British, two German, and one Spanish. Several times a week a boat would make a call in the port. Almost all the traders of the town were Jews, many of whom traveled with frequency to Europe, and especially to London. Undoubtedly these links fostered the growth of a regular readership of the Hebrew newspapers. Halewi was known as an avid reader of the newspaper *Hasfirah* and had a large collection of Hebrew books published in eastern Europe on a variety of subjects.

In 1891, Halewi sent his first contribution to *Hasfirah*, probably prompted by an eastern European visitor to Essaouira the preceding year. He soon became a regular correspondent for the newspaper, writing almost weekly stories about life in Morocco entitled "Among Our Distant Brethren." As a native, Halewi provides rare glimpses of life in Morocco. His stories also reveal his ideology and beliefs and his hopes to see his community reformed. His main foci of criticism were the misappropriation of community funds, the poverty, the inadequate education, the lack of medical facilities and absence of a hospital, the prohibition against Jews building baths, and the need to expand housing for the poor.

Halewi's articles began to receive the attention of the casbah notables, some of whom derided him for criticizing the leaders of the community. To the traditional leadership, it came as a shock that a Jew of the *mellah*, without the power or prestige of being a foreign national, would dare publicize his criticism in *Hasfirah*. "But let the reader judge," writes Halewi. "Must one be a native of Paris or London to have the right to speak the truth?" Halewi became extremely sensitive to criticism of his contributions to the newspaper and at one point defended himself by asserting in *Hasfirah* that he was responsible only for those articles bearing his name.

At the time that Halewi began writing his articles, there was a crisis of leadership in the Jewish community of Essaouria. For some years, the community had been led by the Elmaleh family, first by Joseph and then by his son Reuben. Reuben Elmaleh wielded a lot of power in the community, dispensing both charity and patronage to rich and poor alike. His charity to the poor was praised as much as his avarice was criticized. As head of the Jewish community, Reuben Elmaleh ruled his coreligionists with an iron fist. No longer prospering in trade, due in part to the declining role of Essaouira as an international port, he turned his attention to speculation in real estate. In addition, Reuben Elmaleh, like his father before him, served as vice-consul of the Austro-Hungarian Empire. Although the empire had little interest in Morocco, the position of consular agent in Morocco gave Elmaleh additional clout. Not only was he exempt from submitting to Muslim law and paying certain taxes such as the *jizya* (the capitation tax incumbent on all Jews in Morocco), but he was able to extend consular protection to his own agents, who in turn would also be exempt from Moroccan jurisdiction.

The Elmalehs were not alone in enjoying extrajuridical privileges. By the 1880s, a new class of Jewish protégés, protected by the foreign consulates, had emerged in Essaouira and in other parts of Morocco. This had an effect on the very nature of authority in the community. It meant that the elders of the Jewish community, such as Elmaleh (who himself enjoyed foreign protection), began to lose their unquestioned hegemony, as some of these protégés began taking initiatives independent of the traditional leadership. *Mellah* activists as well seized on the opportunity and through their association with sympathetic members of the elite began pushing for a program of social reform. Halewi was a devoted participant in this group, expressing his sharp criticism in the pages of *Hasfirah*.

Much of the *mellah* activists' program for reform stemmed from the efforts of two Jewish philanthropic organizations, the Alliance israélite universelle in Paris and the Anglo-Jewish Association in London. Both organizations shared the aim, on the one hand, of giving a Western education to their "backward" coreligionists and, on the other hand, of seeking to end discrimination against Jews around the world. By so doing, as they saw it, Moroccan Jews would gain the benefits of "emancipation" and enter the modern, liberal era of tolerance and liberty. Between the 1860s and 1880s, after several setbacks because of the resistance of the traditional leadership, these organizations succeeded in founding Jewish schools in Essaouira. In 1889, the Alliance school opened its doors for a third time. From that date on it was there to stay. There were now three schools for Jewish children in the casbah: an English school for boys funded by the Anglo-Jewish Association, the Alliance school, and a school for girls run by Stella Corcos. A new generation of Western-educated youth was to be born in these schools.

Westernization was nonetheless mostly restricted to the elite of the new and the old casbahs, which numbered about thirty to forty Jewish families. Halewi believed that the schools should be in the *mellah*, especially the girls' school, since those from the *mellah* who attended had to cross through the Muslim quarter and be subjected to the mockery of the Gentile population. The Jews of the *mellah* were still, for the most part, educated in their traditional milieu, where school instructors lived in a state of poverty off the charity of the community. Under such conditions, pupils received little more than a superficial exposure to Western ideas. Halewi was among the best educated in the traditional milieu of the *mellah*.

The language spoken by the Jews, as all over Morocco, was Arabic, with a number of specific Jewish intonations and idioms. Most male Jews learned to read and write, and the medium used, as elsewhere in the Arabic-speaking world, was Judeo-Arabic. In Morocco, it was a kind of colloquial Arabic, written in Hebrew characters and used for all kinds of secular purposes. Hebrew as well was studied by most, read in primary schools, where learning was restricted to the memorization of passages from the Torah to prepare the Jew for his religious functions. For most, knowledge of Hebrew was therefore limited to reading the alphabet and memorizing passages from the Torah. There was really no study of grammar, nor were there any other sacred writings. Only those belonging to the class of religious functionaries (*hazanin* in Arabic, or *hachamim* in Hebrew), who, much like the ulama, performed religious functions and represented the erudites of the community, would use Hebrew outside of prayer. Legal documents—contracts, deeds, jurisprudence, etc.— were drawn up in Hebrew by a notary and signed by at least three rabbis; only affidavits were written in Judeo-Arabic. Religious poetry and scriptural exegesis might also be written in Hebrew. Halewi was among the few erudites of the *mellah*, with a solid foundation in classical Hebrew, and certainly the first to use Hebrew extensively for other than religious purposes.

In nineteenth-century Morocco, Hebrew was simply not used for writing about secular affairs, nor as a spoken language. In eastern Europe, however, the use of Hebrew for secular purposes had been rekindled, and a flourishing movement, known as the *haskalah* (enlightenment) gave expression to an outpouring of Hebrew letters. One of the principal mediums of literary expression was the blossoming Hebrew press of eastern Europe. Newspapers such as *Hasfirah, Hamelitz,* and *Hamagid* were outlets for this new movement. Halewi participated in the *haskalah* by sending articles to *Hasfirah,* and occasionally to *Hamelitz* and *Hamagid,* and by acquiring an extensive library of Hebrew literature. Halewi decried the fact that Hebrew was spoken by no one in Essaouira and was embarrassed about the general ignorance of the community regarding the ancient history of the Jews.

Until the end of the nineteenth century, Morocco had no Hebrew press. There were in the 1880s and 1890s several French- and English-language newspapers and one Judeo-Arabic journal in Tangier. But any scholarly works in Hebrew by Moroccan scholars were sent for publication to Europe or Palestine. In the early part of the century, Moroccan scholars sent their manuscripts to be published in Livorno or Pisa. Such was the case with some of Reuben Elmaleh's ancestors who were noted jurists. At the end of the nineteenth century, Moroccan men of Hebrew letters, such as Yosef Knaffo, started seeking publication of their works in the Hebrew press of London, Vienna, or Jerusalem.

In Fez, a society called Dovevai Siftai Yeshenim (meaning "moving gently the lips of those who are asleep," from Song of Songs 7. 10) was established for the purpose of raising money for unpublished manuscripts of Moroccan rabbis and sending them to a printing press in Jerusalem, for books were published only when the author could find a wealthy patron or a sufficient number of subscribers to cover publishing costs. Halewi as well did his utmost to assist in the publication of books. He coedited a book of religious poems (*piyutim*), which were published in Vienna in 1890. He also attempted to have a book by Rabbi Yosef Knaffo serialized in *Hasfirah,* although he died before the project materialized. Likewise, Halewi sought to import those books that were published by Moroccan rabbis, and thanks in part to his efforts many found their way into the Jewish community of Essaouira.

Apart from books pertaining to religious scholarship, Halewi was also keenly interested in the new literature of the *haskalah.* Such books, however, sometimes had to be imported clandestinely since they were censored by the rabbinical authorities, classified in the same category as heretical or satanical texts. When Halewi began sending his articles to *Hasfirah* in 1891, it was a radical break with the past. For the first time, a Moroccan was using Hebrew as a secular mode of expression. What is equally important was that Halewi was not part of the economic elite, nor was he a rabbinical authority, even though he was given the honorific title of rabbi. Halewi also established a secret society in the *mellah* for the regeneration of Hebrew as a spoken language. He was the first *maskil* (an enlightened person, derived from the word *haskalah*) in Morocco.

Among the society's noted members were Hananiah Aben Hayim, Aharon Bohbot, Dawid Alqa'im, and Dawid Iflah. Iflah was a leading *paytan*, a composer of religious poetry in the community. Dawid Alqa'im, known as the Leonardo da Vinci of Essaouira, was a noted artisan of fine carpentry, an artist, and a poet, whose compositions on Jewish exile increasingly in the early twentieth century gave expression to Jewish nationalism and millenarian Zionist hopes. His beautiful illustrated marriage contracts (*ketubot*) on fine parchment were particularly celebrated in the community, and the wealthy of the casbah would pay a high price for his artistry. But Alqa'im was also a militant advocate of reform in the community and a contributor to *Hasfirah* and *Hamagid*. These men, though not among the merchant elite, were nonetheless recognized in the *mellah* as active participants in the popular life of the community.

The *haskalah* in Europe was a product of the growing secularization of Jewish society. A degree of secularization also began to occur in Essaouira, but only among the Westernized elite of the casbah. For Halewi and the *maskilim* of the *mellah*, the secular use of Hebrew did not come at the expense of religious belief or practice. On the contrary, Halewi and his comrades were expressing their religiosity. Their aim was to purify the religious practice of the community, which they saw as being corrupted by local, Moroccan influences. Superstitions, the use of amulets and mysterious potions, and belief in the supernatural were widespread among the Jews of Essaouira. Halewi deplored such practices.

As in the Muslim society at large, the veneration of saints (*saddiqim*) and the belief in the miracles they performed was an integral part of popular culture. Visits to the *saddiqim* were believed to be a cure for disease, insanity, and infertility of women. On Friday afternoons before the beginning of the Sabbath Jews in large numbers would go to the Jewish cemetery outside of the town to visit the tombs of their deceased rabbis. South of Essaouira was the tomb of Sidi Madgul, a marabout, or Muslim saint. Pious Jews would also visit this tomb, which they believed was that of Rabbi Abraham Magduli, a rabbi from Palestine. In the late nineteenth century, many Palestinian saints were "discovered," appearing to women in dreams. These saints were believed to have been great Palestinian rabbis/emissaries who died in Morocco during missions to that country.

One such alleged saint, "discovered" in the 1870s, was Rabbi Nessim Ben Nessim of the Ait Bayoud, whose tomb, located less than a day's journey from Essaouira, became the object of an annual pilgrimage drawing Jews not just from Essaouira but from all over southwestern Morocco. This type of pilgrimage in Morocco was known as *hillula*, and among Muslims as *mawsim*. Halewi believed visiting saints' tombs to be a superstitious practice, alien to true Judaism.

Halewi's position regarding superstitions and saint worship closely paralleled the discourse of the Salafiya, a reformist Islamic movement that sought to return to what were perceived as the pure practices of Islam in its nascent period. Halewi's efforts to regenerate Hebrew can be seen in this light as a puritanical movement to restore the pure Judaism practiced in ancient times, when the holy language was still spoken by Jews. Such a utopian aim obviously had little chance for success, because it threatened the foundations on which traditional Judaism rested in Morocco.

Halewi also deplored antiquated beliefs that stood in the way of modernization, like opposition to vaccination against smallpox. He displayed a clear understanding of the technique of vaccination, probably from his readings of *haskalah* literature. Unlike some of his coreligionists, he had no qualms about its application. Impediments to vaccination became critical in the winter of 1891–92, when hundreds of Jewish children died in a smallpox epidemic in Essaouira. Some local Jews refused vaccinations because of their beliefs. Others tried to vaccinate their children with homemade serums, which usually led to death. At the height of the epidemic, the rabbis of the city sent a warning to the synagogues not to allow children to be vaccinated. Only through the forceful intervention of Reuben Elmaleh did a general vaccination take place. Halewi supported this effort, a rare time when we find the two men on the same side on a community issue.

Of more immediate consequence were Halewi's efforts at social reform. Since the 1880s, unrest had become apparent in the *mellah*. A group of native Jews educated in Europe began speaking out against poverty. With the support of the Alliance israélite universelle in Paris and the Anglo-Jewish Association in London, they initiated a program of reform. New charitable sodalities were established to assist the poor, sick, and uneducated. Through these efforts, poor *mellah* residents became aware that European Jews were concerned about their plight.

When the editor of the *Times* of Morocco, a Tangier-based English-language newspaper, came to Essaouira in November 1889, a delegation of about two hundred Jews implored him to assist them. Calling themselves the United Congregations of the Dwellers in the Jewry of Mogador, the delegation charged that casbah elders had misappropriated communal funds derived from a tax on kosher meat, the proceeds of which were intended for students, orphans, widows, and the poor. More seriously, they accused wealthy casbah landlords of opposing the expansion of the *mellah*, despite a major shortage of housing for poor Jews. Every time plans were made for new housing, the critics charged, the casbah oligarchy bribed *makhzan* officials not to proceed. Four years before, a delegation of *mellah* Jews had tried to bring the issue to the attention of the sultan but had been compelled not to do so by the casbah oligarchy. Reports on conditions in the *mellah* became a regular feature in the *Times* of Morocco thereafter. Halewi's articles in *Hasfirah* echo these concerns.

The splits in the Essaouira Jewish community widened in 1890, when a dispute erupted over the appointment of a chief rabbi to head the rabbinical court in Essaouira. When *mellah* activists and casbah leaders each named their own candidate a protracted debate ensued. With his authority under attack, Reuben Elmaleh put together a communal committee known in the Sephardic world as the *maamad*. As both its president and treasurer, he thought he was in a position to crush further dissent. When protests continued, however, he "resigned" his position on 8 January 1890. Simultaneously a letter signed by the two rabbis was distributed in the *mellah* threatening to excommunicate those opposing Elmaleh or forming societies without his authorization. Responding to widespread appeals from prominent Moroccan Jews, he withdrew his resignation in February.

In this context, Yishaq Ben Ya'is Halewi intervened. He was convinced that funds were being misappropriated and that the poor were being deprived of their charity. He accused the wealthy of intentionally opposing having cheap new housing built because they feared losing the exorbitant rents they charged their tenants. Halewi dreamed of a new community, in which leadership would be based not on wealth but on merit. (Here he probably had the French Jewish consistory in mind, where communal leaders were, in effect, government appointees, empowered to act impartially without interference from the wealthy of the community.)

On 13 October 1890 a large crowd of Jews from the *mellah* presented a petition to Moroccan authorities in Essaouira. Conforming to standard practice on such an occasion, they sacrificed a bull and several sheep to ensure that their appeal would be heard. Several weeks later, a six-man delegation led by Moses Lugasy went to present its demands directly to the sultan in Marrakesh. Lugasy was a native of Essaouira who had spent many years in England and who returned to Essaouira to take up the cause of social reform. In response, the sultan agreed to send a surveyor to inspect the proposed site for the new Jewish quarter.

Things did not rest here, however. On 5 December 1890, the *mellah* Jews called a meeting to establish a local branch of the Anglo-Jewish Association, with the declared purpose of fighting for social reform. Halewi and the other leading members of the secret Hebrew society helped Lugasy establish the branch. Fifty men attended the meeting and joined the new association. Moses Lugasy was asked to be president, while Halewi, Iflah, and Aben Haim became vice-presidents. Bohbot and Iflah were named honorary secretaries of the association. Within three months, Lugasy, Halewi, and Halewi's comrades were able to recruit 164 members, of whom 113 paid dues of five shillings each.

The founders of the AJA branch had several goals in establishing the organization in Essaouira. One was to fight against the oppression of Jews in Morocco. Shortly after the foundation of the Essaouira branch, Halewi, Aben Haim, Dawid Iflah, and Aharon Bohbot, all members of the secret Hebrew society, wrote to *Hasfirah* and *Hamagid* to report the murder of a Jewish itinerant trader in the territory of the Haha tribe. They also called for the expansion of the *mellah* and attacked the exploitation of poor Jews by the wealthy.

Their boldness was perceived as a threat by the wealthy of the casbah elders, who immediately declared the society to be illegal, since it had not received their approval. Lugasy's attempt to have the branch approved by the rabbis was turned down in February 1891. Under pressure from the casbah elders, Rabbi Abraham Sebbah, the rabbinical judge nominated by the *mellah* activists, withdrew his previous endorsement of the association.

Halewi complained that whenever a meeting was called on some matter of public interest by *mellah* Jews, Elmaleh and his coterie would bring five or six of his cronies, not giving the *mellah* Jews a voice or a vote. "Obviously," wrote Halewi, "they would not be able to in any way assist the *mellah* community." Clearly, then, the establishment of the AJA branch in the *mellah* was a direct challenge to Elmaleh's erstwhile unquestioned hegemony. "So what did they do?" asked Halewi. "They turned to Stella Corcos, the head of the girls' school, and with her help they gathered signatures and founded their own branch of the AJA in the casbah."

Rival branches of the AJA now confronted each other in Essaouira. Since no official Essaouira branch had been approved by AJA headquarters, Lugasy went to London to argue that it endorse the *mellah* AJA branch rather than its rival. However, the AJA central committee urged Lugasy to seek reconciliation with the casbah Jews instead. When he communicated this news to an assembly of the *mellah*, they accepted the proposal with joy and asked Lugasy to send a letter to Elmaleh, which he agreed to do. Lugasy's letter, which Halewi published in *Hasfirah*, was curt and merely suggested that he was acting at the request of the organization in London.

Three days later Elmaleh was elected president of the association for a year. The casbah leadership claimed that the association was a representative body, since it had been well attended by both the leading merchants of the casbah and a large deputation from the *mellah*. Four *mellah* members transferred their allegiance to the casbah group at this time. Although Elmaleh's purpose had been to frustrate the efforts of the *mellah* militants, Halewi left the meeting believing that the matter had been settled. He fervently hoped that Elmaleh would exert all his efforts to convince the sultan to expand the boundaries of the *mellah* or to allow Jews to move into the Muslim districts of the town.

However, the meeting was far from a success, for it failed to unite the two branches of the AJA. By this time, about 120 members were recruited to the casbah group, as opposed to about 180 in the *mellah* branch. Needless to say, Lugasy was not happy with the outcome of the meeting. Among other things raised in the meetings was Lugasy's demand that Stella Corcos's school be moved from the casbah to the *mellah*, an idea that Halewi also advocated in *Hasfirah*. The AJA in London, however, did not support Lugasy on this issue, and the school remained in the casbah. His demand for the establishment of a new school in the *mellah* under the auspices of the AJA was also turned down. It was agreed between the casbah, the *mellah*, and the AJA in London that the dispute between the two branches would be resolved by the British consul of Essaouira, Charles Payton. However, Lugasy refused, and the *mellah* branch still continued to function.

The AJA headquarters in London continued to insist that their interests would best be served if the *mellah* branch joined the casbah branch, under the presidency of Reuben Elmaleh. Halewi himself was impressed with the conciliatory words of Elmaleh and in December 1891 agreed in principle to unification. Through the concerted pressures of the casbah elders and the AJA and the co-optation of their *mellah* clients, the two branches of the AJA were formally amalgamated in the following year. This did not mean, however, that Halewi abandoned his agenda for social reform, and especially, to gain more housing for the *mellah* residents. But he nonetheless naively placed his faith in the casbah oligarchy to work for change.

Contrary to the image painted of the casbah elders by *mellah* militants like Lugasy, it is clear that the situation was not as polarized as they claimed. On the one hand, few *mellah* dwellers were willing to rise up against the casbah elite. On the other hand, the wealthy casbah Jews were sharply split over many issues, including oppression of the poor Jews of the *mellah*. Indeed, since all Jewish merchants in the casbah were protégés of foreign powers, their numerous squabbles can be seen as an extension of the imperialist rivalries of the European powers. Halewi recognized Elmaleh's efforts to alleviate the problems of poverty in the *mellah*. Even Dawid Alqa'im, the most recalcitrant member of the society, was full of praise for Elmaleh at the time of the bar mitzvah of his son. The whole town rejoiced, and charity was distributed to the poor. Like many such, the dispute over the AJA committees gradually petered out.

But the divisions in the community were deep rooted, and a new quarrel soon erupted. In March 1892, *mellah* reformers demanded that the Marseilles-based steamship line Compagnie Paquet make contributions to local Jewish charities as the British line Forwood did. When Compagnie Paquet equivocated, a group of casbah merchants decided not to renew their contract with Paquet. They formed a new company, the Salvador Steamship Company, Ltd. The *mellah* reformers were quick to see this as a stratagem of the casbah merchants to shirk their responsibilities. Graffiti immediately appeared on the walls of Essaouira, denouncing the members of the new company. The casbah Jews were quick to riposte. The chief rabbi excommunicated those responsible for the graffiti, and Dawid Alqa'im, a leading militant, was arrested and accused of the crime. When nothing could be proved, he was released a few days later, after the intervention of the French consul and the local agent of the Compagnie Paquet. The affair ended when Elmaleh arranged an agreement between the Salvador Company and the Compagnie Paquet, by the terms of which Salvador's monopoly on the Marseilles trade was recognized in return for a donation to the communal fund for the *mellah* poor. Halewi wrote in praise of the Salvador Company, which (not coincidentally) was controlled by Elmaleh.

Aside from his intervention in the politics of Essaouira on behalf of Jewish reform, Halewi was also a stout critic of the oppression of Jews by local Muslim tribal leaders and *qaids*. However, he carefully exempted Sultan Mawlay al-Hasan (1873–94) from his strictures, since he was regarded as "good to the Jews," while criticizing specific measures the sultan adopted. In 1894, the sultan ordered the governor of Essaouira to require the Jews of Essaouira to pay eighteen years' arrears in *jizya*, the capitation tax assessed on non-Muslims. Along with the rest of the Jewish community, Halewi protested vigorously (though interestingly he did not question the principle of the capitation tax). Negotiations then ensued, as a result of which the sultan agreed to allow the Jews to pay half the arrears at once, and the other half in installments over nine years. Thus protests were made, but there was no questioning of the legitimacy of the Sharifian state. Halewi invoked the guiding principle formulated by the sages of ancient Babylonia, that "the law of the government is the law" (*dina demalkhuta dina*), a time-honored concession to Gentile sovereignty that helped preserve the coexistence of rabbinical law with the law of the non-Jewish state.

In this, as in Halewi's behavior during the dispute between the *mellah* militants and the casbah elite, we see how much Halewi was rooted in Moroccan culture, and his deference to traditional sources of authority like the head of the local Jewish community and the sultan. Emissaries from Palestine, who came to Morocco to collect money for the Jewish institutions of learning in Jerusalem, Tiberius, or Safed, were equally venerated by Halewi. Yet his respect for the traditional leadership went hand in hand with his advocacy of modernization. Halewi constantly bemoaned the absence of the amenities of modern civilization, such as printing presses, factories, doctors, hospitals, technical schools, insane asylums, banks, a telegraph, and a national postal service. His untiring call for modernization in the early 1890s was little more than a lonely, despairing voice amid the poverty and ignorance of the *mellah* society in which he lived.

Halewi died on a Sabbath afternoon, 30 November 1895, in the *mellah* of Essaouira at age forty-five. He was buried in the recently acquired extension of the Jewish cemetery, adjacent to the now overcrowded old section by the seaside. His closest associates, Dawid Alqa'im and Dawid Iflah, eulogized him in the pages of *Hasfirah*.

By the time of his death, the controversies of the community had simmered down to a degree. But the members of the secret society still continued to be active in Essaouira. Lugasy departed again for London but returned in 1899 and established the first Zionist society in Morocco. The fact that he was more or less ignored by the Zionist establishment in London did not deter him, and he found some ready adherents among Halewi's clique, who no doubt were attracted to the millenarianism of the Zionist movement. Thus Halewi's secret society of *maskilim* was a kind of precursor to the Zionist movement. But the Zionist group, like the secret literary society that preceded it, never really got off the ground in Essaouira. Their utopian hopes, we can now see, reflected the deepening crisis in the community, engendered by the forces of change affecting Morocco as a whole.

Halewi is an interesting figure who stands astride two worlds, the world of precolonial Moroccan society and that of the liberal West. On the one hand, he was influenced by European ideas and attracted by the benefits of modernization. His writings display a knowledge of concepts and ideas alien to Morocco. (For example, he refers to notorious oppressors of the Jews as "anti-Semitic," a term that would not have been employed by a Moroccan Jew unacquainted with European Jewish liberal concerns.) However, the aim of nineteenth-century European Jewry was full acceptance in civil society, an idea that at the time had no meaning in Morocco. On the other hand, Halewi continued to defer to the traditional sources of authority, which determined the fate of his community, Halewi's program for reform, though a reflection of the disintegration of the old society, had little chance for success. It lacked the social foundations to become a major social force. While he was courageous in a local context, Halewi never fundamentally questioned the basis of power in his community or in Morocco as a whole. The irrevocable transformation of the Moroccan Jewish community was brought about as a result of the establishment of the French protectorate in 1912. It was a fundamental change in a different direction from any that Halewi had anticipated.

## A NOTE ON SOURCES

This story was reconstructed primarily from articles written by Halewi himself in *Hasfirah*. Other newspapers, such as *Hamagid*, the *Times* of Morocco, and *Réveil du Maroc* were also used. Reports found in the archives of the Alliance israélite universelle, the Anglo-Jewish Association, and the British Foreign Office and personal communications from the people of Essaouira were also used for this story.

## SUGGESTIONS FOR FURTHER READING

On nineteenth-century Morocco, see Jean-Louis Miège, *Le Maroc et l'Europe, 1830–1894*, 4 vols. (Paris: P.U.F., 1960–61). On the town of Essaouira see my *Merchants of Essaouira: Urban Society and Imperialism in Southwestern Morocco* (Cambridge: Cambridge University Press, 1988).

I have discussed the events described in this story in two articles: "Anglo-Jewry and Essaouira (Mogador): 1860–1900: The Social Implications of Philanthropy," *Transactions of the Jewish Historical Society of England* 28 (1984): 60–88; and "The Politics of Reform in Morocco: The Writings of Yishaq Ben Ya'is Halewi in *Hasfirah*," in *Misgav Yerushalayim Studies in Jewish Literature*, ed. Ephraim Hazan (Jerusalem, 1987). Also Ami Bouganim, *Les récits du mellah* (Paris, 1982). On the Hebrew literary movement in Morocco see Joseph Chetrit, "A New Consciousness of the Anomaly and the Language: The Beginnings of a Hebrew Enlightenment Movement in Morocco at the End of the XIX Century" (in Hebrew), *Miqqedem Umiyyam* 2 (1986).

The history of North African Jewry has been examined by André N. Chouraqui, *Between East and West: A History of the Jews of North Africa* (New York: Atheneum, 1973); Michael M. Laskier, *The Alliance Israélite Universelle and the Jewish Communities of Morocco: 1862–1962* (Albany: State University of New York Press, 1983); Haim Zafrani, *Mille ans de vie juive au Maroc* (Paris: Maisonneuve & Larose, 1983); and David Corcos, *Studies in the History of the Jews of Morocco* (Jerusalem: Rubin Mass, 1976).

On social change in another Moroccan community, see K. L. Brown, "Mellah and Madina: A Moroccan City and Its Jewish Quarter (Salé ca. 1880–1930)," in *Studies in Judaism and Islam*, ed. S. Morag, I. Ben-Ami, and N. Stillman (Jerusalem: Magnes Press-Hebrew University, 1984). On Moroccan-Jewish beliefs and practices, see Issachar Ben-Ami, "Folk Veneration of Saints among Moroccan Jews," in *Studies in Judaism and Islam*.

# FOUR

# Shemsigul: A Circassian Slave in Mid-Nineteenth-Century Cairo

*Ehud R. Toledano*

High up on the list of Western stereotypes about Middle Eastern societies is the slave woman in the harem. The very existence of such a figure of power-lessness and degradation is a continual challenge to Western cultural values (whether patriarchal or feminist). Accordingly, to be presented with a histori-cally existing slave woman and to seek to understand the world in which she lived and functioned is to undertake an unusual exercise in crosscultural time travel. And that is what the reader is called upon to do with Ehud Toledano's portrait of Shemsigul, a Circassian slave woman of mid-nineteenth-century Egypt. (The Circassians were a tribally organized people of the Caucasus who lived under Ottoman rule.)

By a kind of miracle, the police archives of Egypt contain documentation of a lengthy legal case brought by one Shemsigul, a Circassian woman who was purchased in an Istanbul slave market c. 1850 and brought to Cairo by Deli Mehmet, a slave dealer. The documentation contained in this file is all that is known about Shemsigul: but what is there constitutes a precious win-dow into the lives of a whole category of women, slaves in the elite households of the Ottoman Egyptian establishment.

Toledano's contribution consists of a translation of the text of the legal in-quest by the Egyptian authorities into Shemsigul's case, together with his re-flections on it in the context of what is known generally about the history of slavery and the history of women in nineteenth-century Egypt, as well as what is known specifically about the slave trade in Circassian women to elite Otto-man Egyptian households.

In Greek and Roman times, the joint household staffed by female slaves and retainers (known as the *gynaeceum*) was characteristic of elite families in the Mediterranean basin, where it constituted an important locus of women's work and sociability. The *gynaeceum* was also known in the Byzantine and Per-sian empires prior to the coming of Islam, as were the associated cultural practices of the seclusion and veiling of elite women. The institution of slav-ery was also well known in the ancient world.

Under Islam both the elite household and slavery (especially domestic slavery) flourished, both hedged about by culturally accepted and religiously grounded edicts that tempered to a degree their practice. Shemsigul's story comes to our attention because she was able to avail herself of the possibility for legal redress and was able successfully to bring the slave dealer who raped her and made her pregnant to justice.

In Toledano's reconstruction, the case of Shemsigul is surprising in more than one way. For example, his portrait of the slave dealers' guild, while replete with a Simon Legree figure in the person of the villainous Deli Mehmet, is one of a professional organization that was very conscious of its reputation. Shemsigul herself, far from being a downtrodden wretch, comes across in the documents as a woman with a healthy sense of her own worth and a remarkable ability to utilize the system to her advantage.

There remains much that we do not know: How common was this sort of case? To what extent did Shemsigul fall into or take advantage of rivalries between Deli Mehmet and the other slave dealers? What became of her thereafter? Toledano's biography, because it provides us with the text of the court documents complete with gaps and silences, can be read in more than one way, which only adds to its interest.

Little is known about Middle Eastern women's lives, and what little we do know is doubly suspect. Until recently most of our knowledge came from European observers, whose cultural presuppositions and prejudices often intruded. Moreover, almost all of the individual named women we do know about are twentieth-century elite figures. Things have begun to change, however, as a new generation of scholars has begun to write the history of Middle Eastern women, utilizing new questions and new sources.* The results are bound to overturn most existing stereotypes.

For portraits of other Middle Eastern women, see the contributions in this volume by Lila Abu-Lughod, Julia Clancy-Smith, Leila Fawaz, and Julie Oehler. —ED.

On 30 June 1854, a young Circassian woman named Shemsigul appeared before police investigators in Cairo and presented testimony about her life over the previous two years. For both its historical significance and human interest, the record of that testimony is a unique document. There, in the old pages of a police register at the Egyptian National Archives, in Ottoman Turkish, unravels a troubled chapter of a woman's life that began in a Circassian village in the Caucasus, continued in Istanbul, and ended in Ottoman Cairo. Through Shemsigul's testimony we learn much about the Ottoman-Egyptian elite harem and about the possibilities for legal redress available to women in Egypt.

*See, among others, Judith Tucker's *Women in Nineteenth-Century Egypt* (Cambridge: Cambridge University Press, 1984).

Shemsigul was born in the late 1830s or early 1840s in the Caucasus, which was then under Ottoman control. Slavery was still common among the tribal federations of Circassia, where a special class of agricultural slaves had existed for centuries. This was one of the few areas in the Ottoman Empire where agricultural slavery was practiced. Otherwise, free labor, local forms of serfdom, and small-scale leasing by cultivators prevailed in agriculture throughout the empire. Slave labor as practiced in the antebellum American South was virtually unknown to the Ottomans. However, for short periods of time and on a smaller scale, black slaves were used in cotton and sugar plantations in Egypt during parts of the nineteenth century.

The extreme poverty of Circassian slave families and the dire conditions among free members of the lower classes forced them to sell their young children to slave dealers, who carried them off to Istanbul and other urban centers. Parents who did so also believed that they were thus improving the chance of their offspring to attain better living conditions and an entry into the Ottoman elite. This traffic filled the ranks of Ottoman harems, a central institution of the urban governing elite. In the nineteenth century, the large majority of slaves imported from the Caucasus were young girls in their early teens. Many slave girls were subsequently socialized into the Ottoman elite. As we consider how they ultimately fared, we should weigh the loss of family and legal freedom (for those who had not been born slaves) against the possibility that they might thereby have gained access to a better life.

Born into a poor Circassian family, Shemsigul was brought to Istanbul by a relative or a slave dealer, who offered her for sale in the Ottoman capital, where the slave dealer Deli Mehmet purchased her. Deli Mehmet was based in Cairo and operated on the Mediterranean and Red Sea routes, as well as on the long-distance route to India. As we shall explain later, the Egypt that Shemsigul came to in 1852 was a tranquil and prosperous country, at peace with its neighbors and its Ottoman sovereign, the sultan, and recovering from a heroic and traumatic period that had ended in the early 1840s. It was also a society in which domestic slavery was widely known. In those years, there were between 10,000 and 15,000 slaves in Cairo alone, out of a population of about 275,000. About 5,000 slaves used to enter Egypt every year, most of whom were black women destined for menial work in Egyptian households. Shemsigul belonged to the relatively small number of white women who served in the Ottoman-Egyptian elite harems.

The portion of Shemsigul's life about which we have information begins when she came into the possession of Deli Mehmet, when she was in her mid- to late teens. It covers a little more than two years, 1852–54; the account of these years is found in the police records of the Egyptian

National Archives. The events contained therein took place in Istanbul, on a boat crossing the Mediterranean, in Cairo, and in Tanta, a market town in Egypt. The specificity and high quality of the documented chapter are rare in the historical record of individuals belonging to nonelite groups in the Ottoman Middle East. In order to reconstruct the undocumented chapters with reasonable confidence, we have to rely on what we know from other cases. We begin with the full text of Shemsigul's testimony, as given to police interrogators at the end of June 1854.

*Questions:* When did you come to Cairo? Who was the person who brought you? Where did you stay when you arrived? To whom were you given by the person who had brought you here?

*Shemsigul:* I came here two years ago. The person who brought me from Istanbul is the slave dealer Deli Mehmet. When I arrived, I was sold to the palace of Mehmet Ali Pasha [son of Mehmet Ali Pasha, governor general of Egypt, 1805–48].

*Questions:* Was the person who brought you over to Mehmet Ali Pasha's palace Deli Mehmet? How long did you stay there? Where did you go afterwards?

*Shemsigul:* The person who sold me to Mehmet Ali Pasha is Deli Mehmet. I stayed there for about five months. Afterwards, the aforementioned [Deli Mehmet] took me from the palace. I [then] went to the house of Mustafa [another slave dealer].

*Question:* Since Deli Mehmet had sold you to the household of Mehmet Ali Pasha, and since you stayed there for five months, why did he take you from there and why did you go to Mustafa's house?

*Shemsigul:* After I had stayed at Mehmet Ali Pasha's palace for five months, it was suspected that I was pregnant. A midwife was brought in to examine me, and she verified that I was indeed pregnant. So they summoned Deli Mehmet and returned me to him. He then took me and brought me to the house of Mustafa.

*Question:* By whom did you become pregnant?

*Shemsigul:* I became pregnant by Deli Mehmet.

*Questions:* You state that you became pregnant by Deli Mehmet. Where, then, did he have sexual relations with you? And, since you became pregnant, how come he sold you [this being illegal]?

*Shemsigul:* In the boat, on the way here, he forced me to have sexual relations with him; he continued to sleep with me until he sold me. Before the sale, I told him: "Now you want to sell me, but I have missed my period, and I think that I am pregnant by you." When I asked him later what would happen, he did not listen, but went away, brought back some medicines, and made me drink them [to induce an abortion]. Finally, he sold me to the palace.

*Question:* Your answer is [now] well understood. When they said at the palace that you were pregnant, they returned you, and you went to Mustafa's house. But now, you need to explain how many days you stayed there and what was the state of your pregnancy.

*Shemsigul:* When I left the palace, I went to the house of Mustafa and stayed there for about ten days. While I was there, Deli Mehmet's wife came to the house and cursed me, as she also did Mustafa. Finally, when she wanted to hit me, Mustafa's wife prevented her from so doing. When Mustafa saw the woman's rudeness, he sent me to the house of Deli Mehmet. As I got there, Deli Mehmet's wife brought in a private midwife and demanded that she would perform an abortion on me.

At that, the midwife said: "This [woman's] pregnancy is well advanced, and now there is a big child in her stomach [which] cannot be aborted." Having said that, she left, but the woman [Deli Mehmet's wife] insisted, saying: "I shall put an end to this pregnancy." Later, her husband, Deli Mehmet, came. She said to him: "Let us beat this slave and end her pregnancy," [to which] Deli Mehmet stated: "I am not going to beat [her]." But the woman would not stop. She fetched a clothespress, hit me with it several times on my stomach and back, and [then] beat me with a mincing rod.

At that point, one of the neighbors, a peasant woman, came to the house. When she saw the cruelty with which I was being treated by Deli Mehmet's wife, she pitied me and went to the house of Selim Bey. As she told [them] about the beating and the pain inflicted upon me, the wife of the said dignitary heard the peasant woman, got up, and came in person to the house of the said Deli Mehmet. When she saw my suffering, she had mercy on me and said to Deli Mehmet's wife: "I shall take her and perform the abortion." She then took me to her house, but left my condition as it was. When[ever] Deli Mehmet's wife would come and ask [about the pregnancy], they [the people at Selim Bey's house] would lie to her, saying: "We are giving her medicine [to induce an abortion]." I stayed there in that way for about three months.

When the child was expected to come into the world, Deli Mehmet's wife came and stood at the bedside. As he was born, she took the child to another room and passed him through her shirt to mark that she was adopting him. To me she said that he died. Later, she went to her house, brought in a wet nurse for the child, and gave [the baby] to her [care]. One day, Selim Bey's wife brought the baby [home] secretly and showed him to me.

After twenty days, I went to the house of Deli Mehmet and stayed there for about twenty days, but they did not show me my baby. Finally, they gave me in trust to Timur (another slave dealer) in order to be sold at the Tanta fair, so I went with him to Tanta [the Tanta fair was the largest in Egypt, attracting in the first half of the nineteenth century from 100,000 to 150,000 visitors]. A few buyers came and looked me over, but did not buy. Ultimately, I returned from Tanta and stayed at the house of Timur.

Deli Mehmet took me there and gave me to [name not clear], where I stayed for three months and about ten days. Later, he returned from India and brought me to the house of the agent of Yegen Ibrahim Pasha [to be inspected for sale by] an Indian who was going back to India. Since an agreement was not reached with the Indian, and Deli Mehmet wanted to go to the Hijaz, he took me again to the house of Mustafa the slave dealer, on the condition that he sell me to a foreigner [someone not living in Egypt]. He himself went to the Hijaz, and I stayed at Mustafa's house.

Because Mustafa had become aware of Deli Mehmet's position [regarding my having borne him a child], he did not show me to any buyers. When Deli Mehmet returned from the Hijaz, he took me [from Mustafa's house] and sold me to Timur. I stayed there [at Timur's house] for about two and a half months.

*Questions:* Did you, at any stage from the beginning [of the story], inform the slave dealer Timur, or anyone else, that you had been pregnant and that you were badly beaten? If you did not, why?

*Shemsigul:* As a slave, I was afraid to say anything about my suffering, so I did not tell Timur [or anyone else].

This testimony is revealing in more than one way. Not only do we learn about the world of the slave dealers in the Ottoman Empire and the life of the Ottoman-Egyptian elite harem; most significantly, we learn about the life of a female slave in a Muslim society in the 1850s. In the process, we are afforded a precious glimpse of a corner of Egyptian society about which we otherwise have little documentation. Shemsigul's story brings out not only her sufferings as a slave woman but also her determination and resilience. From the Egyptian police records it is possible to understand at least a part of Shemsigul's life, and thus of the situation of poor slave women more generally.

Before exploring in greater detail this corner of the social history of Egypt, it is important briefly to situate Shemsigul's story in the context of nineteenth-century Egyptian history. In those years, Egypt was recovering from the forced-march modernization policies pursued by Mehmet Ali Pasha, who had ruled Egypt with an iron fist from 1805 to 1848. The Ottoman Empire was then—despite all its internal difficulties—the strongest and largest Muslim power in the world, and Egypt was one of the wealthiest and most important provinces of the empire. Under Mehmet Ali Pasha, Egypt experienced a period of military and economic expansion. In order to realize his desire for independence, Mehmet Ali launched an ambitious, Western-oriented reform program that exhausted the country's human and material resources. When Mehmet Ali's ambitions threatened the integrity of the Ottoman Empire in 1840–41, his forces were pushed back from Syria, and his regional empire was dismantled as a result of European military and diplomatic intervention. After his death in 1848, his family, invested with the hereditary government of Egypt, pursued his reforms, but on a smaller scale and at a slower pace.

Thus the middle decades of the century during the reigns of Abbas (1848–54) and Sait (1854–63) Pashas were a period of economic and administrative contraction. With the exception of Egypt's participation in the Crimean War (1853–56) on the Ottoman side, it was a peaceful and prosperous period. It was to this Egypt that Shemsigul came in 1852 as a young slave woman and in which she spent her adult life. We must now turn to a consideration of the slave dealers' network and the people that brought her over, sold and resold her, and affected her life to a great extent.

Until its abolition at the end of the nineteenth century, the institution of slavery was an integral part of Egyptian society. Most of the slaves in Egypt at the time were black women serving as domestics, engaged in menial jobs in urban households. A small number of black male slaves worked as attendants in better families or as assistants to artisans, shopkeepers, and merchants. Male slave labor was occasionally used on large cash-crop estates, but slaves never rivaled the Egyptian free cultivators (the *fellahin*) as a work force. During times of increased agricultural activity, such as the cotton boom of the 1860s, the use of slave labor rose significantly. White female slaves, like Shemsigul, were a minority among slaves in Egypt at the time. Some of them served as domestics, but others entered the harems and were socialized into the Ottoman-Egyptian elite.

The harem system was one of the cornerstones of Ottoman-Egyptian elite life. The harem was the most private part of the Muslim household, where the women and children lived. It reflected the values of a sexually segregated society, in which women's accessibility to men who were not members of their family was restricted. Accordingly, the harem was separated from the public section, where male guests were entertained. The master's mother, or his first (and often only) wife, managed the life of the harem, attended by female slaves and free domestics. The concubines also lived in the harem. An active social network linked harems of similar status through mutual visits and occasional outdoor excursions. Especially large and wealthy harems employed black eunuchs of slave status to guard the women and supervise their contacts with the outside, male world. The prototype of the whole system was the Ottoman imperial household, which the other households attempted to emulate on a smaller scale, according to their means.

Life in the harem was often romanticized in contemporary travel accounts by European women. To many Western men, the mystery of the harem was a rich source of fantasy. For the women who actually spent their life there, reality was, of course, far more mixed and complicated. The women who came into the harem as slaves, many of them Circassians like Shemsigul, were taught and trained to be "ladies," with all the domestic and social roles attached to that position. As they grew up, they would be paired with the men of the family either as concubines or as legal wives. If they bore children, the children were legally free, the mother's sale became illegal, and she would gain her freedom upon her owner's death.

However, harem slaves' freedom of choice was rather limited, as was that of women in general in an essentially male-dominated environment. In the case of harem slaves, there was not infrequently the difficulty of resisting sexual harassment from male members of the family. It was to such a life that Shemsigul, the main character of our story, was destined when Deli Mehmet purchased her in Istanbul and brought her to Cairo. There she was sold into a prominent Ottoman-Egyptian household, that of the son of Mehmet Ali Pasha, former governor general of Egypt.

Most of the white female slaves living in Ottoman-Egyptian elite harems were imported from Istanbul by slave dealers, who used to cross the Mediterranean with small groups of slaves several times a year. This was a very profitable trade, and successful dealers conducted long-distance business also with India, the Hijaz, and East African ports. The dealers themselves were of various ethnic origins, but those who traversed the Ottoman world on a regular basis usually spoke Ottoman Turkish and were at home in Ottoman culture. Slave dealers in the various urban centers of the empire were organized in guilds. Guilds were professional associations linking practitioners under the leadership of an elder (the shaykh). Each guild had a strict code of ethics that was binding on the membership. In the Ottoman Empire, guilds were not free associations expressing the interests of their members. Rather, they operated under government supervision and formed a major element in the state system of urban control.

Dealers in white and black slaves were organized in separate guilds. Because it catered to an elite clientele and its business was more lucrative, the guild of the dealers in white slaves commanded greater social respect. It was, in fact, listed among the prestigious merchant guilds of the Cairo bazaar. The slave dealers were, of course, bound by the Islamic laws governing the institution of slavery, and the code of their guild reflected that. Thus, master-slave relations (and for that matter dealer-slave relations), concubinage, childbearing in slavery, and other matters were considered part of the intimate domain of the family. They were regulated by Islamic courts and enforced by the Ottoman state. As part of that system, the guild shaykh acted to ensure that members complied with the law-derived ethical code of the slave dealers' guild. Obviously, both the law and guild practice expressed Ottoman-Egyptian elite values and perceptions, which favored freeborn Muslim men. The story of Shemsigul demonstrates exactly how these mechanisms operated.

From a legal perspective, the slave dealer Deli Mehmet was the owner of Shemsigul and, as such, was allowed to have sexual relations with her. The law did not require the slave's consent, thereby allowing rape in case of the woman's resistance. The dealer was aware, of course, that when the slave lost her virginity, her market value automatically declined. Moreover, if the slave became pregnant, as indeed happened to Shemsigul, the law forbade her sale. Long-distance slave dealers spent a great deal of their time on the road, away from their families, and in the company of young female slaves with whom they were legally allowed to have sex. This often led to the situation described in Shemsigul's testimony, especially if the slave dealer intended to form a long-term concubinage relationship with a specific slave. Male slaves, too, were exposed to sexual harassment, abuse and rape by dealers and masters, although the Sharia strictly prohibited homosexual relations. Custom, however, was more lenient.

Although we have no information about whether Deli Mehmet or Shemsigul attempted to avoid pregnancy, it is clear that methods of contraception were known and practiced at the time. It is likely that sex partners, whether married or not, applied such methods in order to avoid unwanted pregnancies. Earlier and contemporary Islamic law books even discuss various methods of contraception. Thus, for example, coitus interruptus was condoned by the greatest Muslim jurist of the time. As we shall see, legal discussions of contraception and abortions reflect a male perspective that treats the well-being of the woman, if at all, as secondary. This is especially true in the case of female slaves.

Thus some legal authorities required the consent of both sex partners to the use of contraceptive measures, which seems to have been ignored when a female slave was involved. Other doctors of law mentioned the need for a reason to avoid pregnancy, procreation being strongly favored as a rule. Others considered contraception to be legitimate in the event of anticipated hazard to the fetus, such as might result from a long-distance journey or from danger to the would-be child, especially if the birth was expected to occur in a non-Muslim territory. If the husband intended to divorce his wife at some point in the future, attempts to avoid pregnancy were also legitimate.

From the legal perspective, once Shemsigul suspected she was pregnant, her legal standing changed. Deli Mehmet's legal freedom of action
was restricted, while Shemsigul's position was strengthened. As mentioned above, Islamic law stipulated that an owner, here the dealer, could
not offer for sale a pregnant slave carrying his child. Accordingly, if
Shemsigul gave birth, the child would be free and she would automatically be manumitted upon the death of Deli Mehmet. However, social
reality did not always follow the law, as happened in this case. The new
situation constituted a real threat to the status of Deli Mehmet's wife, especially if she had no children of her own, or if she had only daughters.
If Shemsigul's child was a boy, the threat would be greater still, given the
cultural preference for boys. Additional children would normally reduce
the share of the wife's children in the father's inheritance. Thus, beyond
jealousy and hurt, there were material reasons for the violent reaction of
Deli Mehmet's wife to Shemsigul's pregnancy.

Shemsigul's concerns and considerations are more complex; they led
her to struggle against the attempts to abort her fetus. It is certainly possible that she simply wanted to have the baby, not realizing that this
would tie her to Deli Mehmet for the rest of his life. On the other hand,
she might have come to see him as a lesser evil, fearing that new masters
might bring new and unforetold calamities. It is also possible that she
did not realize that as she was no longer a virgin, the chances that buyers
would be interested in her for marriage or concubinage leading to marriage were slim. That meant that she would rank low on the social ladder
of any harem and have a more difficult life. In any event, the revelation
of her pregnancy provoked the brutal, physical attacks on her by Deli
Mehmet and his wife. This brings us to the social and legal issue of abortion in mid-nineteenth-century Egyptian society.

Abortion was well known in premodern Islamic societies, and Ottoman Egypt was not an exception. From its inception, Islamic law dealt
with abortions, but, again, mostly from a male perspective. Jurists
tended to allow abortions during the first four months, or 120 days, of
pregnancy. They believed that before the end of that period the fetus
did not possess a human soul. The dissenting view maintained that there
was life in the womb from the moment of conception, and abortion was
not permitted at all. In such a position there was no room for the wish
or well-being of the pregnant woman. Some of those who consented to
abortion in the early months of pregnancy required that a sufficient reason be produced for allowing it. If, for example, a woman was believed
to be unable to breast-feed the child after birth, and if the man lacked
the means to hire a wet nurse, this constituted a legally acceptable cause
for abortion for some authorities. However, it seems that the consent of
the father was, generally, not required for abortion.

Shemsigul's story shows the importance of midwives in the women's world of the time. Midwives performed a major gynecological and social role during pregnancy, birth, and early maternity. In this story we note that a midwife was called to the palace to verify Shemsigul's pregnancy and that another midwife was later asked by Deli Mehmet's wife to perform an abortion on Shemsigul and refused because the operation would have endangered her. Until the early 1830s, midwives in Egypt acquired their knowledge through apprenticeship and experience. Mehmet Ali Pasha introduced modernized health services, which included women's medicine as well. A school for women doctors and midwives was established in Cairo in 1829, and the first class consisted of thirteen black slaves, since the idea was not readily embraced by the population and candidates were hard to recruit. It is clear from Shemsigul's story that midwives also played a role in police investigations of crimes against women.

We must now return to our story. The next witness summoned by the police on the same day, 30 June 1854, was Ali Efendi, head of the slave dealers' guild. The point to note in his testimony is the position and authority of the guild shaykh. In a way, this was what we might today call a preliminary hearing. The shaykh was empowered not only to listen to the parties but also to take action to redress grievances. The following is what he told his interrogators about the procedure he had followed.

*Questions:* How was the slave named Shemsigul—who had become pregnant by Deli Mehmet and bore him a child—sold to Timur? What offense was committed [thereby]? You must also make clear to the said slave where her child is.

*Ali Efendi:* On the morning of the third day of Bayram [a Muslim high holiday], Timur sent the slave named Shemsigul to my house. Later, he himself came and said: "The slave I had sent you is a slave who must be freed after her master's death [because she had borne him a child] and [therefore] her sale is illegal [according to Islamic law]. [But] having no previous knowledge of that, I bought her from Deli Mehmet and took a promissory note [in return]. [Thus,] there is now a [legal] dispute between us." [So] I sent for the said Deli Mehmet and had him brought in.

When I explained to him Timur's statement, he denied [all], claiming that the said slave [Shemsigul] had not been pregnant, nor was she entitled to the legal status of "mother of her master's child" [the child is considered free, and the mother, as mentioned above, cannot be resold and becomes free upon the master's death].

So I called in the said slave and asked her about the whole matter. According to her report, she had become pregnant by the said Deli

Mehmet and borne him a child. She [also] reported her suffering in this regard [from Deli Mehmet and his wife].

Nevertheless, Deli Mehmet denied everything. It was suggested to him to take an oath to that effect, at which he declared: "I swear [to it]."

The slave was then asked: "Do you have proof or witnesses that you were pregnant?" She stated: "Mustafa and his wife know that I was pregnant, and Selim Bey's wife and the servants of that household know that I gave birth."

It was then again inquired of Deli Mehmet: "Will you accept [the consequences] if the said Mustafa testified that the slave was indeed pregnant and gave birth?" Deli Mehmet replied: "[If so,] I shall manumit her."

Based on this declaration, the said Mustafa was summoned and interrogated about the matter. He corroborated the slave's assertion. As it became clear from Mustafa's testimony that [Shemsigul] had borne Deli Mehmet a child, I took the promissory note from Deli Mehmet, returned it to Timur, and detained the slave at my place [pending police investigation and likely manumission].

We now come to the main culprit, Deli Mehmet. His tactics changed several times, only exacerbating his credibility problem. At first he denied all; then he stated that he did not remember Shemsigul or the circumstances of her importation and sale; then he claimed that in Istanbul he had had a concubine named Shemsigul and that she had borne him a son who died a few months later and that she, too, had died since. Finally, he admitted that he had brought Shemsigul from Istanbul and sold her to the household of Mehmet Ali Pasha for sixty purses (about three hundred Egyptian pounds), and later to Timur for only half that amount.

Afterwards, in Deli Mehmet's words,

Shemsigul stayed at the palace [of Mehmet Ali Pasha] for about two months. Since the said slave was not on friendly terms with the harem ladies of the said Pasha, I was summoned to the palace, given back Shemsigul, and told to provide another white slave in her place. I took Shemsigul and, since she had misbehaved and claimed that she was pregnant, I asked her whom was she pregnant by. She replied that she had alleged to have been pregnant only to get herself out of the Pasha's house. Until the question of her pregnancy could be verified, I left her in trust at Mustafa's house, [where] she stayed for about a month. [It turned out that] she was not pregnant, and when she menstruated, the said Mustafa notified me. So, I removed her from there, and she spent some time at our house.

At one point, Deli Mehmet stated that if Mustafa confirmed Shemsigul's version, he would have nothing further to say on the matter. He then appealed to the mercy of the police, without, however, accepting responsibility for the offense attributed to him.

At another stage of the interrogation, Deli Mehmet was asked to produce the papers issued to him in Istanbul for traveling by steamer to Egypt. The police expected that, according to practice, the document would contain the names and sex of his family members and the number, type, and sex of the slaves he was transporting. But, perhaps not surprisingly, Deli Mehmet failed to locate the certificate among his documents at home. At that, a fellow traveler and slave dealer, Uzun Ali, was summoned to report that Deli Mehmet had on board approximately thirteen white female slaves and two white male slaves. The witness had not seen among them any female slave with a child. That testimony undermined Deli Mehmet's story about the "other" Shemsigul, the concubine he claimed to have brought with him from Istanbul with a child. The credibility of the witnesses and the compatibility of their testimonies led to one, clear conclusion, which police investigators did not fail to realize.

Thus on 11 July 1854 the police department concluded its investigation of the Shemsigul affair. In the report submitted to the administrative court, the police accepted Shemsigul's story and rejected Deli Mehmet's version. Mustafa's testimony was pivotal in forming the view of the investigators, who believed they had established the basic facts of what had happened. Their report concluded:

> The police department informed [Deli Mehmet] that he must abandon his deceptive assertions and tell the truth. When asked "How do you answer [now]?" he here [at police headquarters] affirmed: "I have no answers but those which I had [already] given."

On the following day, the report was forwarded to the administrative court, and, a week later, the court gave its decision. Although I could not locate the actual ruling in the Egyptian archives, we know from the police records that after the court ruling had been studied by the police, the matter was referred to the grand *mufti* of Egypt. In such cases, a legal opinion was usually solicited from the *mufti*. The probable outcome of a case such as Shemsigul's was that the slave would be manumitted and the slave dealer punished, according to circumstances. To enforce manumission, an Islamic court ruling was desirable, for which purpose, too, the case was probably referred to the grand *mufti*. It is also likely that Deli Mehmet received some punishment in addition to the loss of a valuable slave. It was rare for the court to rule against a police recommendation, especially after elaborate investigation backed by a lengthy report, as in this case.

How did this story reach the police and court? The circumstances are fairly clear, though the motives of the characters involved are not. Some two and a half months after the slave dealer Timur had bought Shemsigul, an unidentified man informed him that a while back she had borne Deli Mehmet a son. When Timur asked her about it, she confirmed the story. Realizing the legal situation, he immediately went to the shaykh of the slave dealers' guild. It was this official, after internal investigation, who turned the whole matter over to the police. At this point, we must consider Deli Mehmet's claim during the investigation that the whole affair was instigated by his competitors in order to hurt his business.

It is impossible to know what the motive of the unidentified man who provided Timur with the incriminating information was, but malice should not be precluded. Timur had to protect himself from possible litigation, so it is not difficult to see why he went to the head of the guild. The shaykh might have been able to resolve the matter inside the guild but chose not to. He might have wanted to show the authorities that he was loyal and honest or to enhance his own standing within the guild. It is also possible that he might have had it in for Deli Mehmet and seized the opportunity. We should note, however, that the risk of harboring the culprit and concealing the information from the police was considerable, given the fact that a number of people already knew about the situation. Shemsigul herself must have been made aware of Deli Mehmet's precarious position and could have used the story at one point or another to pull him down.

What happened to Shemsigul afterwards must be left to the imagination. In some ways, her manumission would make her less secure and more vulnerable to harsh economic and social realities. This is not to say that there was no element of oppression in harem life. Female slaves in an Ottoman-Egyptian elite harem were restricted in their freedom of movement, association, and choice of partners. In the power relations with the adult male members of the family, slave women did not have the upper hand, though they could sometimes negotiate a highly influential position within the household. While concubinage was hardly an ideal arrangement for women like Shemsigul, it was socially respectable and, if a child was born, also legally binding on the man. However, especially for women, but for men too, freedom had its own disadvantages, limited choices, deprivation, and oppression.

The act of manumission did not usually entail severance of master-slave relations. Rather, the mutual dependence would continue under patronage without bondage, and the slave would remain attached to the manumitter's household. Manumitted slaves, male or female, often remained within the family compound and were expected to render such services as were required of them. This they provided in exchange for the social and economic protection an elite house afforded. Patronage ties were often maintained even if the slave left the master's house, frequently in order to get married. Shemsigul was probably manumitted by court order with Deli Mehmet's reluctant acquiescence. Obviously, she could not expect any assistance from him. If she could not secure alternative patronage immediately upon manumission, she stood the danger of falling out of society's accepted frameworks for an unmarried woman, which could bring upon her want and destitution.

Shemsigul probably sought patronage from the house of Selim Bey, whose wife had offered her protection during the last phase of pregnancy and in whose house she gave birth. The women's world would then take her in and prevent her from drifting toward the margins of society. If she could secure patronage, she would probably live in the compound, perform services, and gradually negotiate her position in that milieu. It would be the patron's responsibility then to marry her off well and see to it that she settled down properly.

We shall probably never know how the story of Shemsigul ended. What happened to her depended on circumstance, but also on her resourcefulness. We do know that she was courageous enough to state her case and stick to it despite the pressures that were undoubtedly put on her. We also know that during her pregnancy, when she was most vulnerable and virtually defenseless, most women with whom she came into contact showed her compassion. And, not least important, although as a woman and a slave she belonged to a doubly oppressed social group, Shemsigul did ultimately receive justice in the courts. Given these propitious circumstances, there are grounds for cautious optimism that Shemsigul's story ended well.

## A NOTE ON SOURCES

The police investigation report on which this article is based is found in the Egyptian National Archives in Cairo. The report, numbered 13, covers pages 44–54 in Register L/2/67/4. An earlier, and quite different, version of this paper appeared in *Slavery and Abolition* 2, 1 (May 1981): 53–67. It did not contain the translated excerpts from the text that are cited above.

## SUGGESTIONS FOR FURTHER READING

The Islamic legal concept of slavery is summarized in R. Brunschvig, "'Abd," *Encyclopaedia of Islam*, 2d ed. (Leiden: Brill, 1960), 1:26–31. Slavery in nineteenth-century Egypt is discussed in Gabriel Baer, "Slavery and Its Abolition," in id., *Studies in the Social History of Modern Egypt* (Chicago: University of

Chicago Press, 1969), 161–89. On the Ottoman slave trade, see Ehud R. Toledano, *The Ottoman Slave Trade and Its Suppression, 1840–1890* (Princeton: Princeton University Press, 1982).

For insights regarding the family life of the Ottoman-Egyptian elite, see Emine Foat Tugay, *Three Centuries: Family Chronicles of Turkey and Egypt* (London: Oxford University Press, 1963). Accounts of Ottoman harem life by European women include Malik-Khanum, *Thirty Years in the Harem* (New York: Harper, 1972); Demetra Brown, *Haremlik* (Boston: Houghton Mifflin, 1909); Lucy Garnett, *The Women of Turkey and Their Folk-Lore* (London: D. Nutt, 1891); id., *Home Life in Turkey* (New York: Macmillan, 1909); and Grace Ellison, *An Englishwoman in a Turkish Harem* (London: Methuen, 1915).

One place to begin reading about nineteenth-century Egypt is Edward Lane's classic *An Account of the Manners and Customs of the Modern Egyptians* (1860; reprint, New York: Dutton, 1966). Concise and useful accounts of the political history are still P. J. Vatikiotis, *The History of Egypt* (London: Weidenfeld and Nicolson, 1980); and P. M. Holt, *Egypt and the Fertile Crescent, 1516–1922* (Ithaca, N.Y.: Cornell University Press, 1966).

A good introduction to Egyptian social history is Baer, *Social History of Modern Egypt;* and id., *Fellah and Townsman in the Middle East* (London: F. Cass, 1982). Women's history is treated by Tucker, *Women in Nineteenth-Century Egypt*, although the chapter on slavery leaves much to be desired. Cairo's urban history can be found in Janet Abu-Lughod, *Cairo: 1001 Years of the City Victorious* (Princeton: Princeton University Press, 1971).

The bureaucracy and administrative reforms in nineteenth-century Egypt are dealt with in F. Robert Hunter, *Egypt under the Khedives, 1805–1897: From Household Government to Modern Bureaucracy* (Pittsburgh: Pittsburgh University Press, 1985). See also Ehud R. Toledano, "Muhammad Ali," *Encyclopaedia of Islam* (Leiden: Brill, 1990) (with bibliography), on the early part of the century; and id., *State and Society in Mid-Nineteenth-Century Egypt* (Cambridge: Cambridge University Press, 1990).

On economic history, see Roger Owen, *Cotton and the Egyptian Economy, 1820–1914: A Study in Trade and Development* (Oxford: Oxford University Press, 1969); and id., *The Middle East in the World Economy, 1800–1914* (London: Methuen, 1981).

# FIVE

# Journeymen Textile Weavers in Nineteenth-Century Damascus: A Collective Biography

*Sherry Vatter*

It is not easy to reconstruct the lives of ordinary nineteenth-century Middle Eastern men and women. Not only are the sources cruelly lacking, for the most part we do not even know the names of ordinary people. This is, of course, especially true of rural society, where peasants and tribespeople, deeply suspicious of the state and its agents, kept largely to themselves. But even in the cities, where our sources are relatively more complete, it is rare that we know even the names of individual workers and artisans (though the elite of merchants and ulama are better known).

Given the state of the field, Sherry Vatter's portrait of journeymen weavers in Damascus in the middle of the nineteenth century is a considerable feat of the historical imagination. Because of the absence of sources, Vatter's collective biography (or prosopography, as it is sometimes called) is focused not on a single individual but on the social category of journeyman weavers as a whole. While the weavers remain anonymous, from her account we learn a great deal about the specific conditions under which they labored. We also gain a heightened appreciation of the possibilities and limitations of artisan life in Damascus, including insight into the impact of the Ottoman reform program and of changing economic conditions. Because of the importance of the textile sector in the urban economy of Damascus (it was the major employer and paid a big share of wages and taxes), the life of journeymen weavers is of general significance for understanding the impact of change upon society as a whole.

Beginning in the 1840s, the importation of growing quantities of European finished textile goods (especially cheap Manchester cottons) drastically undercut local production throughout the region. This was especially true in Syria and Lebanon, traditional centers of textile production. As Vatter's contribution shows, the impact of these changes depended a lot on the sector of the market for which one produced. Thus producers of expensive luxury cloth managed to retain their markets reasonably well, while producers of inexpensive cloth suffered intensely. Although the overall Syrian (and Ottoman) market expanded considerably during the century as a result of increased communications and rural security, and some did quite well, the producers of poor-quality cloth never really recovered.

Similar differences emerge if we examine the parallel fates of spinners and weavers. Some weavers did well, but many others were driven out of business by European imports. Nevertheless as a whole the craft survived. Spinners, on the other hand, were particularly hard hit by the importation of machine-wound thread and were virtually eliminated as a category. Since most spinners were female, the loss of income must have had a considerable impact on family budgets as well as on the life chances of large numbers of women. Little is known about this as yet. (See, however, the essay of Akram Khater and Antoine Khater for the Lebanon case.)

Even within the weavers' guild, there were important differences in income, working conditions, and status. As Vatter shows, merchants controlled operations to their own benefit, and masters, journeymen, and casual employees had varying fates depending upon their specific connections to the work process. Contrary to received opinion, indigenous traditions of protest were not absent. Vatter documents how under pressure from greedy master craftsmen in the 1870s, Damascene journeymen became involved in a wave of strikes and sabotage that persisted into the twentieth century. Struggling to survive, journeymen weavers sought successfully to protect their livelihood for over a generation. —ED.

Ahmad paused just inside the door of the dimly lit workshop. His friend Ali sat with his back to the door, interlacing the burgundy and blue silk mounted on the loom in front of him with a strand of red cotton thread.

Ahmad watched the shuttle make a full circuit, from the right side of the loom, behind Ali's body, to the left, and to the right once again, before announcing himself.

"Peace be upon you, Ali. Well done."

"God keep you. Welcome," responded Ali as he secured the shuttle and turned toward his visitor.

"Have you heard the news?" Ahmad queried.

"What news?"

"Wages have been cut."

"What? Not possible!"

"But yes. The masters will pay thirteen piasters per piece instead of sixteen."

"Where did you hear this?"

"In the market. Everyone is talking about it."

In the center of a small ground-floor room charcoal burned in a brazier, taking the chill out of the damp February air that intruded from the adjoining courtyard. Three young men huddled around it, giving vent to their indignation.

"Look at us. Sharing a room, and barely managing to survive at that."

"What kind of future do we have?"

"An unbearable one!"

"They should be ashamed."

In a neighborhood coffee shop, a cluster of men passed the evening around a table, sharing a *nargila* (water pipe) and sipping tea. In subdued tones they earnestly addressed the topic of the day.

"Shall we be martyrs to their greed?"

"Will we let them profit at our expense?"

"What shall we do?"

Conversations similar to these certainly were heard in Damascus in early January 1879, just before some three thousand journeymen weavers went on strike in protest of a wage cut against the master weavers who employed them. They brought all activity in the city's weaving workshops to a standstill. It remained so for four weeks. Militants ensured that all weavers honored the work stoppage by intimidating potential strikebreakers with threats and by cutting threads mounted on looms. The strikers won a resounding victory. Masters reinstated the old pay rates, and journeymen returned to work.

The journeymen weavers in this provincial Ottoman capital had engaged in a recognizably modern form of labor struggle. Their militant, collective, and disciplined confrontation of employers was characteristic of actions by industrial wageworkers against employers where capitalist relations prevailed. This style of industrial politics was new to Damascus. Up to the 1870s journeymen appear to have addressed grievances as individuals, one or two confronting the master who employed them. Conflicts were not resolved in a militant or collective manner, but quickly, quietly, and out of public view.

How did a group of Middle Eastern workers come to engage in a form of struggle associated with capitalist Europe and America? Were they imitating foreigners, or did their behavior have indigenous roots? If the latter, did they find models of action already available, or did they need to invent them? These questions are best addressed from the perspective of the individual journeymen who conceived of striking and participated in strike actions.

Unfortunately we are not yet in a position to write life histories of specific journeymen weavers. Even individuals at the forefront of change, those who first articulated a new vision of the journeyman's relationship with masters and strike leaders, remain unidentified. However, a reconstruction of the conditions under which the average

Damascene journeyman weaver lived and worked between 1820 and 1880, a collective biography if you will, promises to shed light on how thousands of individual journeymen came to engage in new forms of struggle.

Damascus had long been famed as a textile-manufacturing center. At the turn of the nineteenth century, this reputation rested upon luxury fabrics—silks, wools, and, above all, silk-cotton combinations made by interweaving silk and cotton thread, the most important of which was known as *alaja*. These fabrics were characterized by irregular tie-dyed stripes running through a solid background. The silk thread mounted on the loom, the warp, was tie-dyed one of a dozen or more two-toned patterns—red and yellow, blue and white, among others. The tinted cotton thread interwoven with it, the weft, was allowed to show through, contributing to the final effect.

Damascus's stature as a major textile-manufacturing center was not immediately apparent to the first-time visitor. Minarets rather than smokestacks defined the city's skyline. Its industry was not powered by steam but by people. At its heart were some five thousand handweavers working on prejacquard looms: Christians, Shii and Sunni Muslims, some master craftsmen, but mostly journeymen. All were men. Though women participated in the formal textile sector in nineteenth-century Damascus, the commercial weaving of luxury fabrics was a male profession.

The typical Damascene weaver was a Sunni Muslim journeyman employed weaving *alaja*. He labored in a small, dingy second-story room, cramped together with three other weavers—two journeymen and a master craftsman—their looms, and two apprentices, who assisted the weavers and ran errands for them. This workshop, like hundreds of others in the city, was located in a small *khan*, a building given over to diverse commercial and industrial purposes. Very likely two saddlebag makers cut and sewed in a workshop across the landing, and a second group of weavers worked next door. Downstairs several donkeys were stabled, a Baghdad merchant warehoused Persian and Iraqi carpets, a felt merchant stored wool that his employees unloaded from the backs of donkeys and rebundled in the unkept courtyard at the heart of the *khan*. A large wooden gate stood open, allowing easy access between the courtyard and the narrow, bustling commercial thoroughfare beyond.

When fully employed, the journeyman weaver worked a ten-hour day, six days a week. He would be in front of his loom plying the shuttle back and forth not long after sunrise and depart for home at sunset. On average he could expect to weave four to five pieces of *alaja* per week, complete a length of seventeen pieces every four weeks, and take a half-day break while the finished cloth was removed and the loom restrung with silk for a new one.

The pace of work was not set by clocks or bells but by the weaver himself. Work would be interrupted for mid-morning prayers, occasional forays to the market, and visits with friends who stopped by. Some days the journeyman ate a lunch of bread and cheese and took a nap on a rug rolled out in one corner of the workshop before resuming work in mid-afternoon. On others he went home for a more elaborate meal and rest.

The weaver did not work a fixed number of hours or follow the same routine year-round. As the month of Shawwal and the departure of the annual pilgrimage caravan to Mecca drew near, he would expect to work into the night seven days a week. This heavy workload anticipated the tens of thousands of pilgrims who descended annually upon Damascus, eager to purchase its fabrics. The weaver's opportunities tended to dwindle after the pilgrimage; he might go several weeks between jobs before conditions improved and full employment returned. Exports to North Africa, eastern Europe, and within the Ottoman Empire ensured a modicum of employment year-round.

Levels of employment fluctuated from year to year depending upon export demand but above all upon how many people traveled with the Damascus pilgrimage caravan. In years when a member of the Ottoman royal family planned to make the pilgrimage, greater numbers than usual would be expected, and the weaver would find more work than usual. In others, when the trip through the desert between Damascus and the Arabian peninsula appeared hazardous, the weaver might be underemployed much of the year. Such was the case when the pilgrimage departed during the dry summer months or when bedouin raids along the caravan route had been frequent. Political conditions might adversely affect the size of the caravan, as they did for much of the 1810s, when the Wahhabis turned back or imposed heavy duties upon caravans reaching Mecca, and in the 1830s, when the Egyptian occupation of Syria made Ottoman pilgrims reluctant to undertake the *hajj*.

The journeyman was not self-employed. He was a wageworker employed by a master craftsman. The latter engaged him on a piecework basis to weave a specified piece of cloth and paid him upon its completion. The journeyman depended upon the master for work space, materials ready for weaving (cotton and silk dyed appropriately and the silk mounted on the loom), and even the loom upon which he worked. If the journeyman roughly fits the profile of a modern wageworker, the master was not a typical capitalist employer.

The master was a workshop proprietor, but he worked alongside his employees. Moreover, his scale of operation was modest. Generally he managed a single workshop and employed two or three journeymen and one or two apprentices. Some masters owned workshops, but most rented theirs from a private landowner or *waqf* endowment on an indefinitely renewable basis. Renters were not propertyless. They owned looms and other equipment as well as the right to weave in the workshop. This right was restricted to specified commercial spaces and was bought and sold independently of the building in which a workshop was housed. Its purchase was deemed a prerequisite for operating a weaving establishment. Though the master weaver owned property, he was not a textile producer.

The textile merchant controlled the overall production process. He determined what would be woven and how much, provided the raw materials, and covered the expenses of production. The merchant did not own a factory but subcontracted work to a series of artisanal specialists who worked at home or in workshops throughout the city. Each in turn received materials, oversaw one stage in the manufacturing process, and was paid for his or her contribution. Masters, journeymen, loom mounters, spinners, and other workers involved in making textiles all depended upon the merchant economically. Only masters dealt directly with merchants, however. They engaged and supervised journeymen and paid them from funds provided by the merchant.

Production involved an elaborate division of labor. Before reaching the master weaver as dyed silk and cotton thread, cotton had been spun into yarn and dyed, and silk cocoons had been graded and unwound, twisted into thread, measured into skeins, tied with fabric to establish a pattern, and dyed one or more times. Before the weaver could begin his work, the silk had first to be mounted on the loom. For this purpose the master engaged two loom mounters. After the journeyman wove the cloth, the master turned it over to another subcontractor, who starched and pounded it to bring out its color and luster.

The journeyman, at the bottom of this distribution pyramid, had good reason to feel dissatisfied with his lot. He had little control over pay rates and the distribution of work. In slow periods the master might opt to keep the greater portion of work for himself or his relatives. The exploitative nature of the master-journeyman relationship was clearly visible. The master covered his expenses and made his living at the expense of the journeyman; he retained for himself a portion of the fee the merchant paid for the journeyman's work. The latter had reason to be dissatisfied not only with the master for whom he worked but with all master weavers.

Masters and journeymen belonged to a common professional organization, the craft corporation or "guild" (*sinf;* pl. *asnaf*) of weavers. The affairs of the weaving community—production standards, output, training of weavers, settlement of disputes—were regulated under its auspices. The guild provided weavers with a collective means of dealing with outsiders, negotiating subcontracting rates with merchants, and articulating grievances to the state.

The weaver's guild was not, however, a democratic institution. A small group of masters, the elite of the weaving community, monopolized power and exercised control over the journeyman's life in ways that the latter did not always find agreeable. Masters limited how many journeymen were promoted to their ranks. Since only masters were entitled to operate workshops, employ journeymen, and take on apprentices, they determined whether the journeyman became a self-employed small businessman or remained a wage employee for the duration of his career. The Ottoman state's use of guild structures to control and tax the urban population gave rise to other grievances. The authorities did not deal with weavers individually but as a group, through the head of the guild, the shaykh. This allowed the shaykh, in consultation with a few master craftsmen, not only to distribute the tax burden among guild members but also to place a disproportionate part of it on the journeymen.

If the guild structure embodied inequalities that fueled the journeyman's discontent with the masters, it also provided a counterweight. Its existence gave substance to the notion of collective identity and common interests. The rhetoric of craft solidarity and rituals buttressed the journeyman's feeling of solidarity with masters and downplayed differences. Ceremonies of initiation, for example, imbued potentially divisive issues with nondivisive meanings. By presenting unequal positions as sequential stages in a career, the professional hierarchy appeared to hold the promise of advancement rather than to be an obstacle to it. Thus the weavers' guild played a role in maintaining the journeyman's identification with the master who employed him and served to minimize conflicts between them.

The journeyman's perception of himself as a member of a corporate group united by common interests was not entirely illusory. It had a basis in social reality. As a rule, masters used their power to ensure that the textile industry remained competitive and that weavers had jobs. To this end they enforced production standards, protested increased financial burdens slapped on the industry by the state, and attempted to limit the number of weavers trained to compete for available work. Rarely did the guild masters flagrantly abuse their authority. Although bias against journeymen weavers in disputes and in the allocation of tax burden was pervasive, it was also well calibrated and subtle.

Even though the master profited at his expense, the journeyman made an adequate living. Paid eight to ten piasters per piece of *alaja*, weaving four to five pieces a week, the journeyman could expect to earn forty piasters a week in the 1820s and 1830s. In the Damascene context this was satisfactory, since bread, the staple of the workman's diet, was not expensive, and most journeymen weavers lived in inherited housing or paid low rents. Overall, the earnings of journeymen weavers compared favorably with those of other textile workers, such as silk thread twisters and loom mounters. Though slightly less than those of the best-paid skilled workers like shoemakers, blacksmiths, and carpenters, they were substantially more than those of unskilled laborers and domestic servants.

The artisanal character of the weaving profession made the master-journeyman relationship a personal and multifaceted one, not simply one of exploiter and exploited. Although at times he might see his master as harsh or even unjust, the journeyman identified with him and might be linked to him by feelings of affection and gratitude. The master was an employer but also a coworker. The fact that he left the journeyman to set his own pace of work, giving the journeyman some control over his work environment, put them on somewhat of an equal footing. Further, the master embodied the journeyman's hopes for the future. Since the master had moved up through the ranks from apprentice to journeyman to master, the journeyman might hope to do the same. These positive bonds between journeyman and master were reinforced by their relations beyond the workplace in the local neighborhood, where masters and journeymen jointly attended weddings, funerals, and other significant occasions and took up collections for weavers in need.

The complex structure of this relationship gave the journeyman good reason to acquiesce in less than satisfactory conditions—militant confrontations might jeopardize his social relationships and economic future. He depended upon the master for employment and would one day need his goodwill to be accepted into the ranks of master weavers and set up a shop of his own. Thus although the journeyman occasionally chafed at his powerlessness and exploitation, he tended to regard the master's exercise of power as legitimate and even beneficial. Disagreements between master and journeyman were expressed individually and resolved through the intervention of guild authorities.

The above portrait, true for most of the eighteenth century, was no longer accurate by the 1830s. In the late eighteenth and the early nineteenth century, the market for Damascene and other Ottoman textiles expanded rapidly, aided by the withdrawal of French competition and a burgeoning rural market. The number of weavers proliferated throughout the region. In Damascus, janissaries, textile merchants, and other nonweavers rushed to open workshops. Because of the boom conditions, these new shops, operating outside of the official guild structures, seem to have been tolerated. The unregulated expansion of the industry was to prove a liability, however. It meant that during downswings more weavers were un- or underemployed. By the 1830s normal fluctuations in market demand had eaten away at the journeyman's standard of living. Instead of owning his own loom, he now rented it from the master. This development undermined one of the most powerful bonds tying the journeyman to the master, his aspirations for the future. In theory a journeyman could escape this unequal and exploitative relationship by setting up his own shop. By the 1830s his prospects for doing so were poor. He was a wageworker who owned neither workplace, materials, nor tools of production. It was unlikely he would ever accumulate sufficient capital to rent a workshop, purchase a loom, or set up a business of his own.

The eroding position of the journeyman weaver was signaled by the fact that a declining number elected to pay for initiation into the craft corporation. As a result, a new category of skilled weavers began to emerge, trained within the corporate system, working in workshops run by master weavers, and in principle subject to decisions taken by the craft corporation but not formally entered in its rolls as journeymen.

Most of these "unofficial" journeymen failed to register because they could not afford the fees. They were not part of an organized movement, nor did they openly defy their masters. Their very existence, however, was troubling. It showed that some journeymen did not view the guild hierarchy as serving their interests or worth the cost of membership. Over time this was to drive a wedge between masters and craftsmen. Though most journeymen continued to opt for initiation, the sense of belonging to a community of journeymen and master weavers was crumbling.

In the 1840s journeymen weavers and the industry as a whole faced a qualitatively new challenge. *Moreas, printanières,* and other cotton fabrics that aped the patterns of the city's silk-cotton combinations but sold for a fraction of the price flooded Syrian and Eastern Mediterranean markets. Swiss *moreas,* for example, sold for 1.3 to 2 piasters per meter as against 8 to 9.75 for Damascene *alaja.* Sales of the latter plummeted as consumers rushed to buy the cheaper imports.

*Moreas* were not the first European imports to do well at the expense of Syrian textile products. The value of European textiles imported into the region had already jumped dramatically from less than a million francs annually in the 1810s to fifteen million in 1841. Most, however, were relatively inexpensive cottons—chiefly British-made longcloths, grey domestics, muslins, and nankeens—which did not compete directly with Damascus's silk-cotton fabrics. Imports made gains chiefly at the expense of good-quality cottons rather than the luxury fabrics, upon which the livelihoods of most of this city's weavers depended. The number of looms in use, for example, remained roughly constant into the early 1840s. Growing demand for less expensive fabrics, reflected in increased purchases of cottons, pressured producers of luxury fabrics to hold down prices in spite of rising costs of raw silk and cotton. The merchants achieved this by substituting British machine-produced cotton yarn for the more expensive and higher-quality domestic hand-spun yarn. Thus while the position of Damascene *alaja* weavers remained stable for the time being, large numbers of Syrian women spinners were thrown out of work.

By the mid-1840s it was the weaver's turn to experience economic dislocation. With influx of *moreas,* employment opportunities contracted, and the number of silk looms in use fell precipitously from five thousand in 1839 to one thousand in 1845, leveling off at two thousand by 1848–50. Faced with ruin, the master weavers moved to close down the new nonguild workshops in hopes of securing remaining work for themselves.

A case from 1842 illustrates this effort. In that year, the master weavers of Damascus sought to enforce their monopoly over weaving by getting the local authorities to close down the weaving workshop run by a merchant interloper named Mishaqa. Mishaqa, a British protégé, used the backing of the British consul to defy the order successfully. (Protégés were exempted from local taxes, laws, and civic obligations as part of the treaty rights granted Europeans and their local agents by the Ottoman government.)

The failure of the corporate leadership to eliminate unauthorized competition not only reveals the growing intervention of the West in Ottoman affairs but also demonstrates the declining effectiveness of guild structures. Even without European intervention, "illegal" workshops continued to operate in Damascus. Master weavers, despite the weight of corporate authority, were unable to close them down. Runaway shops had become too numerous and too much a part of the fabric of textile production to be easily done away with. By the 1840s the inability of guild members to enforce their exclusive control over jobs had become an industrywide phenomenon. For example, in 1847 loom mounters attempted, also unsuccessfully, to prevent newcomers who had taken up their profession twelve years earlier from exercising it or teaching it to their children.

By the 1850s the local textile industry entered a boom period, and conflict over enforcement of guild privileges diminished. The number of weavers employed in Damascus crept upward from 2,000 in 1848–50 to 2,800 in 1856, reaching 3,500 by early 1860. By the mid-1860s the number had reached 5,000, and production matched 1820 levels once more.

Four main factors contributed to the recovery of the 1850s. The first was the expansion of rural markets. In response to rising demand for agricultural products and higher agricultural prices, peasants increased production. They used a part of their greater cash incomes to expand purchases of textiles, both European and Damascene, thus boosting textile production and employment in Damascus. This trend intensified during the Crimean War (1854–57) and the American Civil War (1861–65), which heightened European demand for grain and cotton, respectively. A second factor was changing consumer preferences. In the 1840s the popularity of European imports was due to both their novelty and their low prices. The imports were of inferior quality, being made of lighter-weight, less durable cotton. By the mid-1850s many Syrians resumed purchases of better-quality local products.

Thirdly, competitive pricing by Damascene merchants aided the comeback. Between 1836 and 1860 the price of the least expensive and most widely marketed *alaja* remained basically unchanged. In the 1830s the price had been eighty-five piasters a piece. In 1856 it was eighty; in 1861 it was eighty-five, and a quarter-century later in 1879 it cost only ninety. Since the piaster lost two-thirds of its value over this fifty-year period, the ten-piaster monetary increase represents a dramatic fall in real terms.

Finally, the development of new products that responded to the demand for lower prices and shifts in taste also contributed to the recovery. Two cotton fabrics developed in Damascus in the late 1850s, *dima* and *mabrum*, were particularly successful. *Dima* was a cotton version of *alaja*, comparable to *moreas* but of better quality and only slightly more expensive—2.43 to 2.55 piasters per meter as against 1.3 to 2 piasters. Credit for developing a commercially viable version of this fabric goes to Hasan al-Khanji, a master weaver, who worked with the backing of a textile promoter, Abu al-Jayd al-Asfar. The technical problems of producing a competitive version of *mabrum*, a coarser cotton, the equivalent of British shirting, were also worked out in this period. When in the early 1860s these and similar fabrics proved successful, other merchants entered production, and many master weavers shifted their workshops from silk-cotton to cotton weaving.

Production statistics attest to the role these fabrics played in the recovery. During the 1830s 5,000 of the total 5,500 looms in use were employed in the making of silks, and only 500 for cottons. In 1860 most of the 3,500 in operation were still mounted with silk. However, by 1869 the number of silk looms had dropped to 1,600, those used for weaving *dima* had jumped to 2,000, and an additional, unspecified number were employed in the making of *mabrum*. By 1879 only 1,200 of a total 7,000 active looms were used for production of silk-cottons as against 2,500 for *dima*, and 3,000 for *mabrum*.

By the late 1860s, therefore, the typical Damascene journeyman weaver produced *dima*, not *alaja*. In spite of the shift to cottons, he still worked on a hand loom for a piecework wage, weaving tie-dyed yarn with undyed cotton. Capitalists still decided what would be produced, provided raw materials to be worked, and paid masters to engage and supervise journeymen. Even the fabric patterns of *dima* and *alaja* were essentially the same.

Despite appearances much had changed. The journeyman weaver's standard of living had fallen dramatically between 1820 and 1860. Stable prices for Damascene fabrics had been maintained by freezing the journeyman's wages at 8–10 piasters per piece. Over the same period, the cost of living had increased sharply. The journeyman paid .3 piasters for a kilo of wheat in the 1820s, .9 piasters per kilo in 1856–57, and between 3.2 and 5 piasters by 1862.

Journeymen might grumble about inadequate wages, but they refrained from demanding higher pay because they viewed their falling real incomes as part of industrywide sacrifices necessary to preserve their jobs. Both merchants' and master craftsmen's profits had fallen along with their wages, and tax farmers had gone along with this spirit of sacrifice and cut tax rates. Instead, journeymen weavers identified grain speculators as the chief culprits and complained that the government had not done enough to restrain them. They called on local Ottoman authorities to set maximum prices for bread.

By the late 1860s the crisis appeared to be in the past. With the industry out of acute danger, tax farmers doubled duties on fabrics, and merchants risked a price rise in an effort to restore profit margins. They increased the price of the least expensive *alaja* from eighty to eighty-five piasters. This confidence proved justified, at least in the short run. The number of weavers continued to climb, reaching a peak of seven thousand by 1879 before leveling off to five thousand, where it stayed until World War I. The merchant passed on some of his profits to the master weaver, who in turn passed on a portion to the journeyman in the form of a higher piecework rate.

Yet many journeymen were dissatisfied with the raise. The increase came nowhere near covering the losses they had sustained over the previous half-century. While the piecework rate rose from 8–10 piasters to sixteen for a piece of *alaja* between 1820 and 1878, the cost of living had tripled. To survive, the journeyman reduced his consumption of wheat and substituted cheaper and less desirable grains. Rising housing costs forced the unmarried journeyman to share rooms and delay marriage. Falling real wages and the rising cost of urban real estate had broader import to the journeyman than his immediate standard of living. Both mitigated against a journeyman whose father was not already a master accumulating sufficient capital to set up his own workshop. His prospects for the future were at stake. These were not the journeyman's only complaints. He had expected to benefit from renewed prosperity.

Indeed, in view of his sacrifices endured for the sake of the industry's survival he felt as entitled to recoup losses as any other group. Yet his gains were minor compared with those of others. The lion's share of the profits went to the merchants.

The journeyman had to contend with another adverse development in this period. This was the tendency of large merchants to bypass the guild structures altogether and to set up large workshops that they ran themselves. These employed more journeymen weavers in one place than did the old-style workshops, a dozen or more rather than three or four, with one master at good wages to supervise them. In this fashion, the merchant could dispense with the two or three additional master-subcontractors who would have been employed under the old system.

Because the new "factory" system allowed the merchant to benefit from economies of scale, it proved profitable. However, it was less satisfactory to the journeyman weaver, who found himself locked into the position of a wage employee with no possibility of becoming a master himself. Merchant-owned and -operated workshops made the guild increasingly irrelevant to the production process. Merchant capitalists replaced master weavers as the arbitrators of workplace conditions.

In these circumstances it would have been logical for the journeyman to identify the merchant as the source of his problems. Instead, the master weaver became the target of his anger. Master weavers increased the portion of the merchant's payment that they kept for themselves and decreased that paid to the journeyman. Since masters worked alongside journeymen, this profiteering was the more visible, and the more deeply resented. The craft elite's self-serving behavior outside the workplace was a further source of complaint. For example, when taxes increased in the mid-nineteenth century, the masters placed the burden of the new impositions disproportionately upon the journeymen, thus discrediting themselves as the journeyman's protectors.

The journeyman's dismal appraisal of his prospects for self-employment and a decent standard of living as well as his perception of the master as unable and unwilling to look out for his interests undermined the rationale for identifying with the master and for overlooking the unequal and exploitative aspects of their relationship. As a result, the journeyman gradually came to view his interests as separate from and antagonistic to those of the master. He felt betrayed—that the master had failed to honor obligations at the heart of artisanal ideology. The journeyman's antagonism toward the master intensified and found collective, public expression in the strikes by Damascus journeymen against master weavers over wage rates.

This new state of affairs was graphically illustrated by events in Damascus at the start of 1879. In January, a number of master weavers increased their percentage of what the merchant paid for piecework. They had instituted such increases previously but had timed them to correspond with an increase in fees received from the merchant. This permitted masters to improve their position while leaving the journeyman's piecework rate intact or even raising it. On this occasion, however, no such increase was forthcoming; they lowered the journeyman's wage from sixteen to thirteen piasters.

The journeymen responded with indignation. They maintained that they would have accepted the cut if it had been instituted in order to lower the market price of fabrics. Such a move promised to make Damascene fabrics more competitive and would translate into more work for them. But since the masters merely sought their own gain, it was not accepted. The journeymen's anger was fueled by the unilaterally self-serving nature of the masters' action, a flagrant violation of the masters' historic obligation to protect the journeymen's interests as well as their own. It is noteworthy that the journeymen's novel behavior did not reflect the eclipse of communal solidarity but was spurred on by a perceived betrayal of it.

The journeymen's outrage found expression in a citywide work stoppage enforced by activists. The latter cut silk threads mounted on the looms not only of masters who had announced cuts but also of those who had not, "owing to suspicions of collusion between master and workman." After four weeks, with three thousand journeymen weavers on strike, the masters agreed to rescind the cuts. Such strikes were not a flash-in-the-pan development. Common by the 1870s, they were still part of the Damascus landscape after 1900. Journeymen were not always as successful as in 1879, as their failure to prevent cutbacks in 1902 demonstrates, but with each successive strike, their alienation from and antagonism toward the master came into sharper focus.

The persistence of labor militancy might seem to foreshadow the emergence of a mass labor movement, all the more so since the strikers did not meet with the repression that marked nineteenth-century labor struggles in Europe and the United States. The Ottoman ruling class, still dependent upon agricultural and commercial rents, did not perceive its vital interests to be riding on the outcome of industrial struggles. Government authorities and other outsiders did not intervene, leaving masters and journeymen alone to sort out their differences. Unsupported, masters were in a position of rough equality with journeymen.

In spite of favorable political conditions a mass movement of journeymen weavers did not materialize. Strikes by journeymen weavers petered out after World War I. The French postwar mandate government, not journeymen, was responsible for establishing a union of hand-loom weavers, and it included masters as well as journeymen. In the long run a decline in the number of handweavers brought an end to their militancy. The competition of factory-produced textiles, both imported and domestic, and changes in taste and life-styles reduced demand for hand-produced fabrics. The number of employed hand-loom weavers fell from five thousand before World War I to the handful who still work in Damascus today. As the handicraft textile sector became economically inconsequential, the journeymen's bargaining power eroded. They found themselves in the same boat as their employers—struggling to survive.

How do we situate the journeymen weavers' experience in Syrian history? It is clear that their novel behavior and the consciousness it implied were not imports but products of Damascene society brought into play by external pressures. Responses by merchants and masters to a head-on confrontation with European competition provoked journeymen to innovate. The conflicts of interest that emerged were rooted in the indigenous industrial structure that subsumed artisanal production within a commercial capitalist nexus.

On no account should the journeymen weavers be treated simply as victims. They did not passively endure change but actively participated in defining its shape. Nor would it be accurate to view their response to the challenge of Western capitalism as a quaint episode removed from the mainstream of Syrian history. We can hypothesize a connection between the journeymen's disciplined collective action and post–World War I labor unrest by factory workers, massive popular resistance to the French occupation during the 1930s, and the political successes of Communists and Arab nationalists whose platforms addressed the question of class in the 1940s and 1950s.

While the import of the journeymen weavers' experience for the broader shape of Syrian history remains to be specified, there is little doubt that handweavers, pushed from the dying handicraft industry into other jobs, in other sectors, took a new consciousness and models for political expression with them and used them to help move Damascene society toward its future.

## A NOTE ON SOURCES

This portrait of journeymen weavers was taken piecemeal from Iliya Qudsi, "Notice sur les corporations de Damas," *Actes du XIème Congrès des orientalistes*, pt. 2 (Leiden, 1885): 7–34; *Qamus al-Sinaat al-Shamiyya*, vol. 1 by Muhammad Said al-Qasimi; vol. 2 by Jamil al-Din al-Qasimi and Khalil al-Azm; both vols. edited by Zafir al-Qasimi (Paris: Mouton & Co., 1960); Numan Qasatli, *Al-Rawda al-Ghana fi Dimashq al Fayha*, 2d ed. (Beirut: Maktabat al-Saih, 1982); John Bowring, *Report on the Commercial Statistics of Syria* (London: William Clowes & Sons, 1840); Dominique Chevallier, "Un exemple de résistance technique de l'artisanat syrien aux XIX$^e$ et XX$^e$ siècles," *Syria* 30 (1962): 300–24; as well as from unpublished primary sources in the British diplomatic archives housed at the Public Record Office (Kew), especially FO 371 (1878–79), vol. 70, pt. 2, Damascus, "Report by Vice-Consul Jago on the Trade and Commerce of Damascus for the Year 1879"; and from French diplomatic documents held at the Quai d'Orsay, notably "Requête des ouvriers ourdisseurs catholiques à Monsieur le Consul de France," 16 October 1846, encl. in Tippel to Guizot (35), 29 December 1846, Damascus.

More generally, see my doctoral dissertation, "A City Divided: Damascus, 1830–1860" (University of California, Los Angeles, 1992).

## SUGGESTIONS FOR FURTHER READING

Published works dealing with Damascus's handweavers prior to the twentieth century are few, those in English almost nonexistent. Relevant secondary sources in English are for the most part unpublished dissertations. For the structure of the industry in Damascus and Lebanon see R. Joseph, "The Material Origins of the Lebanese Conflict of 1860" (Bachelor of Letters thesis, Oxford, Magdalen College, 1977). For an overview of the textile industry and artisanal workers see Muhammad Said Kalla, "The Role of Foreign Trade in the Economic Development of Syria, 1831–1914" (Ph.D. diss., American University, 1969); and Abdul-Karim Rafeq, "The Impact of Europe on a Traditional Economy: The Case of Damascus, 1840–1870," *Economie et société dans l'Empire Ottoman (fin du XVIII–début du XXᵉ siècle)*, Colloques internationaux du CNRS, no. 601, 419–32. For industrial techniques see Dominique Chevallier, "Techniques et société en Syrie: Le filage de la soie et du coton à Alep et à Damas," *Villes et travail en Syrie du XIXᵉ au XXᵉ siècle* (Paris: G. P. Maisonneuve & Larose, 1982), 121–40.

Two general economic histories of the Middle East contain important information on the textile industry in the nineteenth and twentieth centuries: Charles Issawi, ed., *The Economic History of the Middle East, 1800–1914* (Chicago: University of Chicago Press, 1966); and Roger Owen, *The Middle East in the World Economy, 1800–1914* (London: Methuen, 1981). For a recent case study see Donald Quataert, "Machine Breaking and the Changing Carpet Industry of Western Anatolia, 1860–1908," *Journal of Social History* 9 (1986): 473–89.

On Syrian textile workers in the twentieth century see Elizabeth Longuenesse, "Etat et syndicalisme en Syrie: Discours et practiques," *Sou'al* 8 (1988): 97–130; Elizabeth Picard, "Une crise syrienne en 1965: Les syndicats ouvriers face au nouveau régime ba'thiste," *Sou'al* 8 (1988): 81–95. For handicraft weavers in twentieth-century Turkey, see Gunseli Burek, *Women Carpet Weavers in Rural Turkey: Patterns of Employment, Earnings and Status*, Women, Work and Development Series, no. 15 (Geneva: International Labour Office, 1987).

For the experience of Egyptian textile workers in the twentieth century see Joel Beinin, "Islam, Marxism, and the Shubra al-Khayma Textile Workers: Muslim Brothers and Communists in the Egyptian Trade Union Movement," in *Islam, Politics, and Social Movements*, ed. Edmund Burke, III, and Ira M. Lapidus (Berkeley: University of California Press, 1988), 207–27; and Ellis Goldberg, *Tinker, Tailor, and Textile Worker: Class and Politics in Egypt, 1930–1952* (Berkeley: University of California Press, 1986).

# SIX

# Ahmad: A Kuwaiti Pearl Diver

*Nels Johnson*

So rapid has been the transformation of the economy of the Gulf region (and, alas, of its ecology as well) that it is difficult to recall that just a generation ago many people gained their livelihood from fishing the region's waters. Ahmad, a Kuwaiti pearl diver, interviewed by anthropologist Nels Johnson in 1973 was one such individual.

Johnson's account conjures up visions of a world in which Arab dhows brought the spices of China, India, Southeast Asia, and East Africa to Middle Eastern markets. Later Chinese porcelains and Indian cottons, along with coffee, tea, and pepper, became the object of interest, helping to stimulate Vasco da Gama's voyage around Africa in 1498, which opened up the southern seas to European expansion.[*]

Given the hazards of the diver's craft and the appalling conditions under which most divers worked, it is astonishing that anyone would willingly take diving up as a way of life. As Nels Johnson shows, access to livelihood throughout the Gulf was structured by kinship and debt, and pearling was one of the few occupations open to nonkin. Pride in one's abilities, intense bonding with coworkers, and a gambler's love of high stakes attracted people like Ahmad to the diver's life and retained them, even when other opportunities were available.

Prewar Kuwaiti society boasted one of the world's highest standards of living. Its impressive systems of health care, education, and welfare have transformed the lives of ordinary people. When he was interviewed in 1973, Ahmad was still going to fish each morning as in the old days. Alienated from his children and consumed with nostalgia for the old days, Ahmad is left cold by the new Kuwait. Its ways are to him forever strange. So extensive have been the changes he has lived through, it is as if he suffers from a kind of sociological version of "the bends"—a disease that strikes divers who, failing to

---

[*]K. N. Chaudhuri, *Trade and Civilization in the Indian Ocean* (Cambridge: Cambridge University Press, 1986).

decompress, surface too rapidly. It is an understandable reaction, one shared, moreover, by many of his generation. (See the biographies of Mohand N'Hamoucha, Muhammad Ameur, Migdim, Abu Jamal, and Haddou in this volume.) —ED.

I used to fish from a derelict jetty in Kuwait in the early 1970s. I never caught anything, but it was there that I met Ahmad, the former pearl diver whose working life will be recounted here.

Ahmad used to fish, using seaweed as bait, from a nearby beach. He made his livelihood from the fish he caught, selling them to the local residents, for whom he had become a fixture of the neighborhood. It was hard to estimate his age: to begin with, he did not know himself. But from things that he said and major events he remembered, he must have been in his mid- to late seventies when I knew him.

We often got into conversations about his past, conversations made difficult by his Kuwaiti brogue, which often forced me to resort to a Kuwaiti acquaintance for help in sorting out his story. The main topic of our talks was *al-ghaws,* "the diving," by which he meant the pearling industry that is now dead in the Gulf region.

Ahmad's story is one with several facets. It is his version of a life and so is not necessarily "accurate" in all aspects. But its importance lies in the fact that it is his perception of the world in which he lived, an expression of his culture that is important to record and preserve. This is also the story of a system of work, with all its social, economic, and political facets. Ahmad provides us with insight into an industry that was exploitative to a high degree, and no matter what our sympathies are for the individual, it is the system that is in need of close scrutiny. For that reason it will be described in some detail.

Pearl diving was an economic mainstay of the societies of the Gulf before the discovery of oil. It was an ancient industry that had provided the world with valuable jewels for many centuries. The rewards of pearling were great for the entrepreneurs, middlemen, and boat captains who formed the elite of the industry. But for the divers who risked their lives and whose health was often seriously damaged in bringing up the pearl oysters, profits were few, and ironically the work often resulted in personal debt. To understand this we have to look briefly at the societies in which pearling flourished and the social character of the work itself. Ahmad was one of those who dove for years but had nothing to show for his efforts, and this situation was a direct result of the social system in which he lived.

The settled societies of the Gulf coast were, and to a great extent still are, characterized by the politics of kinship. That is, tribal ties defined the individual's status, obligations, and loyalties. The prestigious families within a tribe controlled and manipulated the politics and economics of the wider group. This was a form of rule that was less dictatorial than it was autocratic, in that the preeminence of certain families was a result of respect based on a history of long-term leadership, wealth, and patronage rather than on pure physical coercion or threat. Nonetheless, the elite's rule was rigid and brooked little opposition. Kinship was the language of power: one obeyed the wishes of the elite because they formed the wealthiest and most influential stratum of one's blood kin.

Pearling up and down the Gulf coast was controlled by these old and wealthy families. They mobilized the men of their clans and tribes, among others, to serve in the pearling fleets. The ties of kinship allowed them to pressure men to participate and then held them, through ties of debt, in their service season after season. This system of debt ties permeated the whole hierarchy of pearling and will be discussed more fully later.

Ahmad began diving in his mid-teens. He entered the work through the usual channels: poverty, the illusion of opportunity, and debt pressures. He belonged to a poor clan of one of the major tribes whose territories lay at least partially within the modern borders of the state of Kuwait. Most of his relatives were nomads in the vicinity of Kuwait Town, though they ranged farther north into what is now Iraq. His extended family eked out an existence herding sheep, and some combined this with working as independent fishermen, alternating herding with fishing. Neither form of life was entirely satisfactory in Ahmad's eyes.

Kuwait Town itself, until the advent of oil, did not provide much in the way of opportunity. The town, up until the 1950s really a large village, served as a small port for trade, a craft center supplying nomads and townspeople with everyday needs, a hub of the Gulf boat-building industry, a political seat for important tribal figures, and, most importantly, a locus for the trade in pearls. Of these only the last provided Ahmad and his kinsmen with any chance of improving their lives. Crafts such as gun smithing, metalwork, boat building, and the like tended to be controlled by families who guarded access to their crafts, usually shutting out nonkinsmen to protect their livelihood. Boat building, a highly skilled craft and one of great importance to Kuwait and indeed to the whole of the Gulf, was particularly difficult to enter. Ahmad at one point had attempted to find an apprenticeship to a boat builder but found the trade closed to him because he lacked the necessary family ties to the important craftsmen.

Pearling, then, was the only alternative open to Ahmad and others like him. But it was a gamble as an occupation. The profits of the season's diving were divided on a strict basis. Nobody was paid a salary, and so everyone from captain down to diver could count only on the chance of finding valuable pearls and sharing in the rewards at the end of the season. Shares had little to do with energy expended: the biggest shares went to the entrepreneur who funded the boat and to the captain who directed its operation. Shares were calculated only after the costs of the season's diving were deducted—leaving little to be doled out to the workers themselves. The divers and other workers had their food, water, and supplies deducted from their shares, and if the profits were so meager as not to cover those expenses, the diver found himself in debt to the boat captain.

The system of debt bound together all levels of the pearling system. The principle that ruled indebtedness was that a debtor had an obligation in traditional law to continue to work for the creditor until his debt was paid. Further, debts were heritable: a man's debt was not discharged on his death or disability but was transferred to his son or other close male relative, who was, in his turn, bound to work for the same creditor.

The weight of indebtedness fell on the divers and other workers on the pearling boats. Their shares in the profits, as mentioned before, rarely covered more than their supplies for the season. In addition, the workers had to borrow money from the captain or the backing entrepreneur in order to feed their families for the time they were at sea. Being illiterate, they could not ascertain whether the records kept of debts were accurate. The result was an ongoing debt to a captain or backer that could be paid off only in the unlikely circumstance that the diver found a remarkable gem, in which case his share of the season's profits was much greater than normal.

A diver was expected to appear ready for work at the beginning of the season. If he did not appear, his creditor would go in search of him. This was not a common occurrence simply because there were few hideouts for a runaway diver. I once asked Ahmad why he and others did not simply abscond and take up a new life elsewhere. He made it clear that the question was naive, if not downright foolish. Where, he asked, would he go? Running from a debt meant either going into the desert or taking ship, and both deserts and seaports were inhabited by people who took notice of strangers or, worse, already knew you and would be curious about your movements.

The system of debt was central to the maintenance of pearling. Traditional practice ensured this system by protecting the rights of creditors to the labor of their indebted divers and workers. Among these traditional practices was the imposition of stiff fines on those who gave refuge to an absconding diver, or a demand that the diver's debt be paid by his new protector. In fact, this system was so clearly tied to the pearling economy and therefore to the economic viability of the Gulf towns that in 1897 the British (whose sphere of political influence encompassed the

Gulf at the time) engineered a treaty between Gulf principalities that formalized the control and return of recalcitrant divers and stipulated the fines to be paid by any who harbored them.

Besides poverty and the faint possibility of wealth, the factor of debt played a strong role in Ahmad's entry into diving. One of his uncles had died owing debts for family maintenance to a prominent boat captain. He died with no heirs, and pressure was put on Ahmad to go pearling in order to make good the debts. This pressure was not of a threatening kind: no heavies made unwelcome visits to Ahmad or his family demanding repayment. Rather the pressure was moral, a question of honor. The captain was a fellow clansman, and all the pressures of shared kinship were brought to bear on Ahmad, as the oldest and nearest young male relative of the deceased man, to discharge the debt. It was put to him as a family matter; one could dodge the demands of outsiders, but a family debt had to be respected, otherwise, as he put it, his "face would be blackened"; that is, his honor would be in doubt. This combination of poverty, illusory riches, and debt pressures led Ahmad to join others on the pearling banks some time in the years just after World War I.

An estimate of the size of the Kuwait pearling fleet in the early part of the century puts the number of boats at around eight hundred. The boats themselves were large, elegant clinker-built sailing vessels known collectively in English as dhows, a word not known in Arabic, which refers to them by their specific styles (for example, *bum, baghlah*).

The boats left Kuwait in the hottest part of the year, when temperatures in excess of 110 degrees Fahrenheit in the shade were normal. The pearling banks lay relatively close inshore, and the boats anchored over them, moving when the captain felt that an area had been cleared of pearl-bearing oysters. The boats only came into shore occasionally, staying out on the sea for several months on end and coming in only briefly to reprovision.

Conditions on board the boats were difficult in the extreme. The first thing that Ahmad told me about the boats, which was confirmed to me time and again by other former divers, was the stench. The smell of rotting oyster remains—the detritus from opening dozens of shells a day—crept into everything. One old boat builder told me that he did not go into the port to work on the days when the pearling ended and the boats came straggling in; the smell was too much for him. Crowding was another major feature of life on board a pearling dhow. The boats held up to fifty men, and the decks were stacked with the gear needed for the diving itself, the personal possessions of the workers, the food and fresh-water provisions for the crew, and the cooking equipment and tackle used to fish for supplementary fresh food. The only shelter on board was a canvas canopy that shaded a large portion of the deck.

The occupants of the boat were divided according to their jobs. The captain (*nakhuda*) either rented the boat from a backer or owned it himself. He made the major decisions and so took most responsibility for the outcome of the season's work. It is worth noting here that the same system of debt ties applied to the captain as to the divers; if he fell into debt to his backers, he was bound to continue to work for them until it was paid. This, however, does not seem to have been a frequent state of affairs.

Ahmad began work as both a diver and a deck worker. The latter spent most of their time monitoring the progress of the divers and hauling them rapidly up from the sea bottom when signaled. Ahmad alternated these deck jobs with diving for the first few seasons and then gradually limited his activities to diving.

Diving was an arduous, exhausting business. The demands made on divers were extraordinary. The oyster beds lay at depths from fifty to one hundred feet, and the deeper they were, the less efficient the divers became. The dives were performed in precipitous fashion. The divers stood on a heavy weight attached to the boat, which was then released and rapidly dragged the diver to the bottom. This sudden descent caused frequent pressure injuries to the ears and eyes of the divers. Ahmad, in fact, had lost the hearing in one ear over a period of years of doing particularly deep dives. After groping in the murky water for oysters, the diver put his catch in a basket and then signaled to the tenders to haul him quickly to the surface. The whole process—descent, collecting oysters, and being hauled to the surface—took just a matter of minutes, depending of course on the length of time a man could hold his breath. A healthy diver in good weather would make several dozen dives a day. A diver's equipment consisted simply of a nose clip, a basket slung around his neck for oysters, a tool for prizing the oysters loose, and leather finger stalls to prevent cuts.

Divers were generally debilitated, exhausted, and often ill or injured by the end of the season. This was in the nature of the work; diving with modern equipment is exhausting enough, but doing so in this traditional manner was physically destructive. The divers' diet may well have contributed to this. They were put on limited rations during the day, in the belief that they worked better on little food. The main meal of the day was at night and consisted mostly of rice and dates with any fish that had been caught during the day.

The hazards of diving were legion. There were the occupational hazards, such as pressure injuries, skin afflictions stemming from prolonged immersion in salt water, wounds that would not heal cleanly for the same reason, parasites, malnutrition, and so forth. Natural dangers were also present. Sharks were a persistent danger, although Ahmad himself claimed that they rarely attacked divers, especially if they were submerged. In his years as a diver, he witnessed only one attack, and that was on a man who was clinging to the side of the boat and was not actually diving. Jellyfish were also a definite danger. The stings of the bigger jellyfish, especially over large areas of the body, could be paralytically painful and even fatal. This was a possibility because jellyfish often travel in shoals that can cover sizeable areas of the surface. Protection against their stings was provided by a crude cotton suit that covered the diver from head to foot, leaving the face exposed. (The equipment needed by the divers was generally supplied by the boat captain. Ahmad, however, provided his own. He said that the captain had no real interest in maintaining the equipment, and so it was better to supply one's own, especially the protective clothing.)

Ahmad continued to dive for over twenty years. In that time he married, had three sons, and fished for a living in the off-season. He managed to pay off his debts slowly, largely because of his skill at fishing. He would have continued to dive even after his debts were discharged, but the loss of one eye made it impossible for him to do so. This was something I could not understand; why would a man continue to risk his life working in an occupation that could put him back in debt? Ahmad's reply to my questions about this was that it was a gamble, but there was an element of excitement in it that could not be matched by doing the same job day after day, year in and year out.

The pearling industry died out in the Gulf rather rapidly after World War II. The reasons for this were many. Probably the major factor was the development of relatively inexpensive cultured pearls whose growth could be monitored and did not entail the risk of capital that was part of traditional pearling. The gradual pollution of the Gulf waters probably also contributed to the demise of pearling.

The whole of Gulf society changed in the 1950s with the advent of the age of oil. Citizens of the Gulf states shared in this wealth to varying degrees, depending on their social position and the nature of the government that ruled a particular state. But in any case, the vast majority of people began to live in great comfort and affluence, coddled by a welfare state that subsidized food, housing, education, and private businesses. Manual labor was carried out by immigrant workers—Palestinians, Egyptians, Kurds, Baluch, Afghans, etc. Such labor, never highly respected in the region, became despised, as it was increasingly associated with low-status outsiders.

There were exceptions to this pattern, however, and Ahmad was one of them. From our talks, it was clear that he was still married, his sons were very well off, but that he had as little to do with them as possible. Ahmad in fact had no respect for the new society and its affluence. He believed that people should work for their living, that there was nothing wrong with honorable labor, by which he meant skilled work such as his fishing. Unfortunately this attitude, which is why he continued to fish for a living, was an embarrassment to his family. His history as a pearl diver was equally embarrassing, and that phase of his life, which was so important to him, was considered shameful by his sons—so much so that the only audience for his life story was made up of other old divers and sailors and a chance-met anthropologist.

Ahmad found the wealth and consumerism of Kuwait corrupting. He repeated time and again that his family had so many useless possessions and so much time on their hands that they were impossible for him to understand. His sons had several automobiles apiece (one of them, he said, laughing, even had a Palestinian chauffeur). His wife had a large modern kitchen but continued to cook on a single gas jet, as she had done all of her life.

Through all this, he returned over and over again to the past times when diving, fishing, boat building, and herding were the everyday lives of "true" or "real" people. He clearly felt that his society was diminished by the passing of these things. He did feel that some things were better and often mentioned the state clinic that sat on the edge of his fishing beach as an improvement over the old Kuwait.

I could not understand this nostalgia for what seemed to me an oppressive system, especially in its use of debt to bind people to entrepreneurs and boat captains. I wondered why it was that the divers did not rebel. This was a question that I put to Ahmad and to elderly members of an old and wealthy Kuwaiti-Persian family who had been very active as entrepreneurs in the heyday of pearling. The question was one that puzzled them all. The answer was the same: people did not find pearling an oppressive occupation. All shared the dangers and the gambles, though they were different for the captain and backer from those faced by divers. And debts were debts; they had to be paid, and if a man inherited a debt from his father, well, it was only right that the son should honor it.

Ahmad was very much like many people, such as miners, who have spent their lives in an industry that objectively is exploitative and dangerous. They, however, still saw value in what they did, and their struggles gave them a sense of shared spirit with their fellow workers that is now lost. In the end, I suppose, it was the passing of this spirit that he really mourned.

## A NOTE ON SOURCES

The interviews on which this article is based were conducted informally over several months in 1973. I was helped on occasion with the difficulties of Ahmad's

Kuwaiti dialect by Hamad al-Mutairi, a student who was a local resident. My thanks to him.

## SUGGESTIONS FOR FURTHER READING

There are few sources in English on pearling, though a considerable amount has come out recently in Arabic. The best firsthand account is that by Alan Villiers, who spent a year sailing in Kuwaiti trading dhows in the mid-1930s. He spent several months observing the pearling season, and his account can be found in his book *Sons of Sinbad* (London: Hodder and Stoughton, 1940).

The best sociohistorical account of pearling can be found in a British government official publication, J. G. Lorimer's *Gazetteer of the Persian Gulf, Oman and Central Arabia* (London: India Office, 1915). See also Salih Gharib and Shawqi Uthman, "Adawat al-ghaws fi al-khalij," *Al-Mathurat al-Shabiya* 2 (1987):107–10 (photo essay on pearl-diving equipment of the Gulf); and Captain Rashid bin al-Fadil Bin Ali, *Routes of Guidance/Majari al-Hidaya: A Pearl-diver's Guide to the Oyster Beds of the Gulf,* ed. and trans. Fayiz Suyyagh (Doha, Qatar: Arab Gulf States Folklore Centre, 1988).

The wider historical context of this article can be found in two books by Dr. Ahmad Abu Hakima, *A History of Eastern Arabia, 1750–1800* (Beirut: Khayats, 1965), and *The Modern History of Kuwait, 1750–1965* (London: Luzac, 1983).

A melodramatic, but basically accurate, view of pearling is provided by a film whose inaccurate English title is *The Cruel Sea (Bass, ya Bahr).*

# SEVEN

# Mohand N'Hamoucha: Middle Atlas Berber

*Edmund Burke, III*

Pastoral transhumants, like the *thamazight*-speaking Berbers of the Middle Atlas Mountains in Morocco, were especially sensitive to the changes that affected the Middle East and North Africa in the nineteenth century. With one foot in the world of nomadism and the other in sedentary agriculture, they were racked by conflicting tensions. The Aith Ndhir of central Morocco were more exposed than many neighboring groups to these contradictory pulls, since their territory was near Fez, the capital city, and thus within range of the punitive power of the government (known to locals as the *makhzan*). The portrait of Mohand N'Hamoucha presented here may thus usefully be compared with those of other pastoralists in this volume. (See the chapters by Julie Oehler, Lois Beck, and Lila Abu-Lughod.)

There is a second context in which the story of Mohand N'Hamoucha must be situated—it is that of Morocco at the parting of the ways in the early twentieth century. Like Iran, Yemen, and Afghanistan, an independent Morocco survived into the twentieth century because of the rivalries of the European imperialist powers, as well as because of its lack of valuable resources and its forbidding topography. Between 1900 and 1912, the struggle for colonial possessions intensified, and the "Moroccan question" several times brought France and Germany to the brink of war. While a weak and indecisive Moroccan government dithered over how to respond to the French and Spanish colonial offensives, patriotic Moroccans sought to expel the enemy via direct action. Following the landing of French troops at Casablanca in August 1907, a powerful insurgency succeeded in ousting the incumbent sultan, Abd al-Aziz, and installing a coalition of urban notables and rural power brokers under the leadership of Abd al-Hafiz, the sultan's brother.

Mohand N'Hamoucha was involved in this rebellion and subsequently went on to play an important role in the efforts of his group, the Aith Ndhir, to oppose the modernizing policies of the government and the encroachment of the French on their historic pasturelands. His biography confronts contemporary Moroccans with the paradox of someone who was both a hero of Moroc-

can resistance and, subsequently, a French collaborator. We come to understand the reasons for his actions as we recognize the complex pressures he
and his group were subjected to and the sharply narrowing range of options
available to them. Mohand's perception of the challenges posed by colonialism
changed over time, and with it his survival strategy. (The responses to imperialism of other first-generation anticolonial resisters, like Ramadan al-Suwayhli
and Bibi Maryam, may be purposefully contrasted with the nationalists whose
biographies are to be found in part 2.) —ED.

The deep, sunken eyes are grey blue, steely, but touched with sadness, a
sadness that comes from having outlived one's time. At ninety-four still
spry and able to scramble up a hillside or sit cross-legged, drinking syr-
upy Moroccan mint tea, and talk by the hour, Mohand N'Hamoucha had
survived almost a century of changes that had transformed Morocco
from a quasi-medieval Muslim monarchy to a modern state. When I interviewed him in 1967, he still had the clarity of mind and physical presence of a man thirty years younger. His weathered and deeply lined face
was dominated by those eyes, impressively bushy eyebrows, a prominent
nose, and a decisive mouth. Beneath the hood of his grey-and-white-
striped *jallaba* he was still an imposing man, tall, angular, and wiry,
though no longer vigorous. As a young man, together with his brother
Haddou and other members of his tribe, the Aith Ndhir, he had waged
a twelve-year guerrilla struggle against the French invaders in the rugged Middle Atlas Mountains.

An authentic Moroccan patriot then, Mohand fought the French
army from 1908 until 1919, at first with optimism and some hope of victory, then in a series of gallant rear-guard actions that took him and his
small band of resisters from their accustomed pasturelands on the
fringes of the wealthy agricultural plain between Fez and Meknes to increasingly more remote and forbidding mountain hideaways under mer-
ciless pressure from French air attacks and ground patrols. Eventually,
their numbers badly depleted, their few animals starving, they surrendered to French authorities in 1919.

By this time, only isolated pockets of resistance remained—notably
Abd al-Krim al-Khattabi in the Rif Mountains to the north and the re-
doubtable Ait Atta in the desert fastnesses of Jabal Saghru. By this time
as well, the conquest of the Aith Ndhir and of "le Maroc utile" (the ag-
riculturally rich central plains of Morocco) was long since an accomplished fact. The tribal territory, especially the farmlands of the Sais
Plain, had by a series of legal subterfuges passed out of the hands of the
tribesmen. French settlers, attracted by the fertility of the soil, the mild

winters and warm summers, and the numerous streams, began to establish themselves there in numbers. The Sais Plain was indeed one of the best regions in Morocco for viticulture—to this day it produces some of the best Moroccan wines.

When Mohand and his companions surrendered in 1919, they did so only after having endured enormous privations in their desperate effort to stem the tide of history. Recognizing finally that Morocco had passed into a new historical phase and that further resistance was fruitless, they negotiated terms for their surrender. As a result of these negotiations, Mohand acquired land near Bouderbala not far from El Hadjeb, the chief town of the Aith Ndhir territory. He agreed to serve the French protectorate authorities as a *khalifa* to his brother Haddou, who was made a governor (*qaid*) of the tribe. Mohand's surrender evoked a few murmurs of discontent but no protests from other Ndhiris, who by this time had lost control of most of their best lands—and of their destinies as well.

Under the French, Mohand prospered. Eventually he owned a lot of property in the area. His sons grew to manhood under the French protectorate, went to French schools, and eventually found careers as doctors, lawyers, and architects in independent Morocco. In 1967 he recalled the past of the Aith Ndhir and of Morocco with a certain bemusement. Most of his contemporaries had disappeared. His sons, who are modern professionals, he regarded as *roumis* (Europeans). Their "French" ways are forever strange to him. By 1967, Mohand had become a living anachronism, misunderstood by his family, a remnant of the folkloric "traditional Morocco."

The career of Mohand N'Hamoucha poses a dilemma for Moroccans and for modern scholars. How are we to regard him: as a resistance hero or a collaborator? To understand him is to confront the complex decisions many rural Moroccans made as they contended with the shifting political and economic tides. A consideration of his career takes us into the changing world of a pastoral transhumant Berber tribe of the Middle Atlas Mountains in Morocco from the turn of the century till the mid-1960s.

Preprotectorate Morocco was a complex society marked by common allegiance to the Alawi dynasty and its corrupt and unreliable bureaucracy, the *makhzan*. Despite a superficial resemblance to the Ottoman Empire (both were Muslim-dominated agrarian bureaucracies governing ethnically mixed populations) nineteenth-century Morocco was not on the road to becoming a modern, centralized state with a powerful army and an efficient modern bureaucracy like Turkey. Instead, it resembled states like Ethiopia, Iran, Afghanistan, and Yemen, whose survival into the twentieth century owed as much to European diplomatic rivalries as to any real obstacles they might have been able to place in the path of a determined European takeover bid. As with these states, only the absence of significant resources, a rugged topography, and the combative reputation of its population helped Morocco deter eventual European conquest.

Compared with the much more ethnically diverse societies of the Middle East, Morocco was relatively homogeneous: the majority of its population were Arabic-speaking Sunni Muslims of the Maliki legal rite. About 40 percent of its estimated four million people spoke one of three major Berber dialects (though most adult males also spoke Arabic). There was also an important Jewish minority who made up about 5 percent of the total population. The topography of Morocco was dominated by mountains. To the north there was the Rif chain, which extended along the Mediterranean coast. Inland to the south and east, the Middle Atlas and High Atlas mountain ranges separated the relatively well-watered central plain from the pre-Saharan steppes.

Historically, from the tenth century on, Morocco had been the center of powerful empires such as the Almohads and Almoravids, whose territories embraced Algeria, Tunisia, southern Spain, and even Senegal, across the Sahara. By the nineteenth century, as a result of a long-term process of urban decline, shifting trade routes, and nomadic incursions, the *makhzan* had become weak and corrupt. The Moroccan interior from Rabat (the present-day capital) on the Atlantic coast to Fez inland was occupied by pastoral tribes, the great majority of whom spoke the *thamazight* dialect of Berber. The Aith Ndhir were one of these groups.

The Aith Ndhir were pastoral transhumants who migrated seasonally with their flocks and herds. In the late spring, they left their homes on the edge of the Sais Plain south of Meknes to move to cooler summer pasturage in mountains above Azrou. In the autumn, following the first snowfall, they returned to their permanent dwellings in the plain. Although the distances involved were not large (thirty to forty kilometers), these migrations were moments of great tension. They involved traversing the territory of neighboring tribes and could upon occasion lead to pitched battles between groups eager to preserve claims to water and pasturage.

The seasonal moves of the Aith Ndhir intersected those of other tribes, who also trekked with their animals. Indeed, these movements were complexly patterned into a kind of pastoralist game of falling dominoes. Middle Atlas Berber tribes took over pastures in summer that belonged in winter to their neighbors farther up the slope. In winter, the movement was reversed. Thus, for example, a section of the Igerwan tribe, western neighbors of the Aith Ndhir, summered in fields vacated by sections of the Aith Ndhir. These in turn occupied land that in winter belonged to the northern groups of the Aith Njild, who displaced other Aith Njild clans farther up the mountain, who migrated over the passes to pasturage below Timhadit.

Until 1914, when they were reorganized by the French protectorate administration, the Aith Ndhir were politically decentralized. No chief was able to exercise authority within the group, other than during the semiannual migrations to and from winter pasturage. (Although there were six *makhzan*-appointed *qaids*, or governors, in 1900, their power did not extend beyond the circle of their immediate kinsmen and allies.) Internally, the group was divided into ten quasi-autonomous clans, each of which had its own territory, which it jealously protected from all comers, including other Ndhiris. Feuding between clans (and even within clans) in competition for resources was common. A healthy suspicion of everyone not directly related by blood was an important feature of Ndhiri society.

Acephalous societies like the Aith Ndhir, in which authority was widely diffused, look unworkable when viewed from the outside. In fact, their democratic ethos did not prevent the emergence of wealthy individuals and families. Also, the difficulties of forging alliances outside the kin bond were mitigated by a host of crosscutting institutions. These included religiously sanctioned alliances known as *tada*, membership in Sufi brotherhoods (in Arabic, *tariqa*), marriage alliances, and personal business partnerships. As we shall see, Mohand utilized all of these relationships in building his reputation and in sustaining himself during the period when he was involved in resistance activities.

While the term *tribe* suggests that Aith Ndhir was a "natural" grouping that possessed a degree of moral and political independence, the Aith Ndhir clans (known as *arbaa*) had in fact been assembled by the *makhzan* from the social rubble left after it had crushed the Aith Idrassen confederation in 1817. While the exact circumstances of the creation of the Aith Ndhir remain obscure, it was connected to the effort of the *makhzan* to establish loyal auxiliary forces along the strategic Middle Atlas corridor. In return for providing military service to the *makhzan*, the clans were given lands upon which to pasture their animals and build their dwellings.

By the end of the nineteenth century this system had fallen into disuse, however. In the collective memory of the Aith Ndhir, the group had always been free. (*Imazighren*, their name for themselves in the *thamazight* dialect of Berber, means "free men.") In reality, they were an important block in the edifice of *makhzan* rule over the Middle Atlas through much of the nineteenth century. Only latterly, in the wake of the collapse of Hasan I's rule, did they become the fractious and unruly group described in the colonial sources. The historically contingent character of the Aith Ndhir may usefully serve to warn us of the misplaced concreteness of the term *tribe*.

Mohand's clan, the Aith Harzalla, had a reputation for cooperation with the *makhzan*. No doubt this was in part occasioned by the vulnerability of its lands in the fertile Sais Plain to *makhzan* pressure tactics. Because the Aith Harzalla and their neighbors the Aith Bubidman were situated nearer to Fez, they developed closer relations with the city and its government. This relationship was supplemented by economic and religious ties. Fez was an important market and center of Sufi activity, which radiated into the surrounding area. The influence of the city and the *makhzan* appears to have been a source of tension and occasional hostility within the tribe. Feuds would break out occasionally between the two main factions, usually over access to water, pasturage, or women. Both factions had close ties with the *makhzan* as well as with neighboring tribes.

These contradictions alone would not have been sufficient to propel Mohand N'Hamoucha into the leadership of the anti-French resistance of his tribe. To understand how this came about, we must see how his personal situation intersected with the changing fortunes of the Aith Ndhir over the period 1860–1912. Two main sorts of changes worked to undermine the old structures of Morocco: government efforts at centralization inspired by the Ottoman *tanzimat,* and the incorporation of Morocco into the world economy.

The impact of government rule on the rural populations of Morocco had traditionally been limited and dependent upon the balance of forces between the *makhzan* and the tribes. Tribes were jealous of their autonomy and refused to pay taxes or accept government-appointed *qaids* unless obliged to do so. Under Hasan I (1876–94), a politically astute and militarily powerful leader, this slowly began to change. Hasan embarked upon an ambitious program of reform that sought to develop a modern army and a modern state apparatus. Not surprisingly, this was viewed by the tribes as deeply threatening. By 1894, despite efforts to modernize his army and bureaucracy along Western lines (as the Ottomans had done in their *tanzimat* reforms), Hasan I's endeavor was crowned with failure.

Following the death of Hasan in 1894, the reform plan crumbled. With the strong sultan no longer in control, the tribes gradually adopted a more independent attitude toward the government and refused to pay taxes unless compelled. Hasan I's "modern" army, no longer receiving regular pay, melted away. By 1900, the reforms of Mawlay al-Hasan were but a memory. The stage was set for the tribes to seek to regain their autonomy. Under the regentship of Ba Ahmad, the court of the young sultan Abd al-Aziz resided at Marrakesh from 1894 until 1901. In that year a European-inspired modernization program was announced.

When the court returned to Fez in the fall, construction was begun on a railroad and telegraph line intended to connect Fez with the coast. Since the line passed through the territory of the Aith Ndhir, they became alarmed and attacked it, destroying the new installations.

During the reign of Hasan I, the international context was also changing. Following the Congress of Berlin in 1878, European imperialism was once again on the march. Tunisia and Egypt lost their independence in 1881 and 1882, and the scramble for Africa began. As a result of French annexation of the Algerian Sahara, existing patterns of trade that linked Morocco with Egypt and the Arab East on the one hand, and Timbuctoo and the Muslim African states south of the Sahara on the other, were drastically altered. It was just a question of time before Morocco itself became the focus of European acquisitiveness. By 1900, French Algerian settlers were agitating for a more aggressive policy toward Morocco, extolling the economic and strategic opportunities for France that would result from the establishment of a protectorate.

While the internal political situation worsened, a second sequence of changes was simultaneously transforming the society in other ways. Taking advantage of the vague provisions of the 1880 Madrid Convention, Europeans began to acquire land in Morocco, especially around coastal cities like Tangier, Casablanca, and Essaouira. Commercial agriculture spread from the Atlantic ports far into the interior. Even isolated villages found themselves entering the cash economy as they sold their grain, wool, and dates in order to be able to purchase Manchester cottons, Chinese tea, Belgian sugar, and French firearms. Far-reaching social and economic changes were set in motion that had already begun to transform the old agrarian structures and the ways of life they fostered.

By the 1890s the export of Moroccan wool to the international market was growing. As a consequence the flocks and herds of the Aith Ndhir, who had been accustomed to a substantially autonomous existence, began to pass into the hands of Muslim and Jewish merchants based in Fez and Meknes, whose wealth increased accordingly. Each autumn vast herds of sheep were driven from the Middle Atlas to markets on the French side of the Algerian frontier. A tribal elite also began to emerge and to acquire tangible signs of status, including Winchester repeating rifles and houses in Fez and Meknes.

Mohand also benefited from these trends. In the 1890s he entered into a sheep-owning partnership with Qaid Umar al-Yusi, a business arrangement that was sealed by his marriage to Umar's daughter, Miriam. (Also the pasha of Sefrou, Umar was the most powerful figure in the Middle Atlas at the time. He governed the Aith Yusi and several other tribes to the south and east of Fez. His influence also extended over the eastern clans of Aith Ndhir.) This connection was an indication of Mohand's increasing status, although he was too junior to have a major voice in deciding the affairs of the group at this time. The intersecting crises that burst upon Morocco after 1900 weakened the authority of the tribal elders and provided an opportunity for individuals like Mohand to play a greater role.

The gradually increasing involvement of Europeans in Morocco meant more opportunities for Moroccans to develop potentially useful ties to Europeans. From them might flow business deals, increased political clout, and perhaps, eventually, coveted status as a protégé (Moroccans who benefited from official treaty status, including tax and other exemptions). But Europeans were also perceived as enemies, their religion inimical to Islam and their ways alien and potentially harmful. The two sides of the European connection must have posed a dilemma for individuals like Mohand. Still more, given the direct threat to the tribes posed by *makhzan* reform plans, it must have been unclear until fairly late in the game which threat was primary: *makhzan* reforms or European imperialism.

The economic and political changes outlined above reverberated throughout Moroccan society, setting in motion complex and occasionally conflicting responses among rural groups like the Aith Ndhir, who sought to cope in an atmosphere of uncertainty and heightened political tension. In such a context, personal relationships often influence the choices people make. Such seems to have been the case with Mohand. By his connections to the family of Qaid Umar, as we have seen, he was drawn into the circle of rural leaders in the Fez region. Through his connections with Muhammad ibn Abd al-Kabir al-Kattani, he was gradually led to become involved in opposition to the protectorate.

A fiery preacher and prominent member of the Fasi ulama, al-Kattani was the head of a Sufi brotherhood that had a significant popular following both at Fez and among the nearby tribes. In late 1904, on the eve of the first Moroccan crisis, al-Kattani threw himself into opposition to a proposed French plan of reforms, which he claimed (not unreasonably) amounted to a disguised protectorate. While we do not know just when Mohand became a member of the Kattaniya *tariqa*, it is likely that it was around 1905 that he first became a *fakir*. Other, mostly younger Ndhiris from his own and adjoining clans located closer to Fez became affiliated with the brotherhood about then as well. (Other Ndhiris were affiliated with the rival Wazzaniya Sufi order.)

Despite German diplomatic opposition to French reforms in 1905 an international conference at Algeciras confirmed French claims to the country. The young sultan Abd al-Aziz was compelled to accept the Algeciras Convention, which granted French primacy in the modernization of Morocco. Following anti-European riots at Casablanca in 1907, he

also had to acquiesce in the landing of French troops "to restore order."
By the end of 1907, Abd al-Aziz's policies had provoked a major rebellion. It was led by his elder brother, Abd al-Hafiz, who opposed his acceptance of the Algeciras Convention and his passivity in the face of
French aggression. The revolt spread to northern Morocco in January
1908, and Abd al-Aziz was deposed by the ulama and people of Fez. After promising to uphold Muslim law (the Sharia) and to oppose the
French military forces in the Shawiya (the agricultural hinterland of
Casablanca), Abd al-Hafiz was proclaimed the new sultan.

Muhammad al-Kattani had played a central role in the deposition of
Abd al-Aziz and the enthronement of his brother at Fez. Early in 1908
he called for volunteers to go to the Shawiya to help oppose the French
expeditionary force. Fired with enthusiasm, Mohand joined the others.
His enthusiasm for *jihad* was soon deflated by the pusillanimous attitude
of the Shawiya tribes, however. The struggle was not going well, and his
group was not warmly welcomed. He and his companions returned
home dejected.

This was to be the beginning of a series of disappointments. No
sooner was he in power than Abd al-Hafiz began to back away from his
uncompromising positions and to seek a *modus vivendi* with the French.
In early 1909, he initiated a crackdown on his critics at Fez, firing several
officials and attacking the Sufi brotherhoods. On 19 March, matters escalated further when he sought to arrest his biggest detractor, Shaykh
Muhammad ibn Abd al-Kabir al-Kattani. Warned in advance, the
shaykh sought refuge among his supporters in the Middle Atlas. Late in
the evening of 20 March, al-Kattani reached the territory of the Aith
Ndhir. He came to Mohand's tent and, grasping a tent peg in a traditional appeal to Mohand's honor (*ar*), claimed the right of protection.
Since Mohand was a staunch member of the Kattaniya Sufi *tariqa*, this
was willingly granted. Soon, however, al-Kattani was again on the run,
due to the arrival of a search party of *makhzan* troops. Captured the next
day at the edge of Aith Ndhir territory, he was brought back to Fez, tortured, and executed at the orders of the sultan. The killing of al-Kattani
demonstrated the lengths to which Abd al-Hafiz was willing to go to re-
press inconvenient opposition. It also showed the extent to which he had
put behind him the patriotic oaths of 1908.

When Mohand and I discussed this episode in 1967, half a lifetime
later, his eyes still clouded with emotion at the memory of the betrayal of
his spiritual guide and leader. Yet he had been in no position to defend
his honor, let alone to exact revenge. On the contrary, by agreeing to
help him, he and the other Ndhiri followers of the Kattaniya had endangered the livelihood of the group as a whole. Abd al-Hafiz had threatened to burn every village in the tribe if al-Kattani were not promptly
turned over.

From the sultan's point of view, the fact that al-Kattani had been helped by the Aith Ndhir was a sign of their unreliability. To prevent the contamination from spreading, an unprecedentedly large *mahalla* of *makhzan* troops was dispatched to Aith Ndhir territory. The Aith Ndhir were ordered to pay a huge fine in kind and in cash immediately or suffer the consequences.

When the government forces were defeated in an initial skirmish in which Mohand was involved, it looked as though the Aith Ndhir might be able to avoid complying. But a reorganized *makhzan* army, supplemented by a French artillery officer, soon turned the tide. In response to this show of force most of the tribe sought safety in the hills for their families and their animals. The few who tried to stand and fight were crushed. Fearing a similar fate, the bulk of the group remained in the mountains. To counter this ploy, the *makhzan* force camped on Aith Ndhir land and began "eating" its way through the tribal grain reserves. By spring this economic pressure had accomplished its aims. The half-starved tribesmen were compelled to surrender on terms more draconian than those originally proposed, including not only payment of a punitive fine but also acceptance of a *makhzan*-imposed *qaid* and provision of a three hundred-man contingent to the *makhzan* army.

The consequences were severe for Mohand, who was one of the three hundred hostages whose induction into the army at Fez was intended to guarantee Aith Ndhir acquiescence. In the army, he became a *qaid al-raha* and acquired the rudiments of military discipline that he was later to put to use against the French. The arrival at Fez soon thereafter of reinforcements under the command of the grand vizier Madani al-Glawi, lord of the Atlas, consolidated Abd al-Hafiz's victory. In order to win al-Glawi's full support, the sultan granted him full control of the tribes around Fez and Meknes. During the following year al-Glawi turned loose his private army of black African slaves to pillage the region. More than fifty years later, the memory of al-Glawi's oppression was still enough to make Mohand angry all over again.

Early in 1911, things came to a boil. Goaded by the abuses of al-Glawi's henchmen and a misguided *makhzan* attempt to reorganize its army along the lines of the French Algerian *goum*, leaders of the Aith Ndhir began to meet secretly with those of other tribes of the region. They decided to take advantage of the Id al-Mulud festival to launch a rebellion. Traditionally at this celebration of the Prophet's birthday, delegations of tribesmen presented offerings to the sultan as a sign of their fealty. The conspirators decided instead to assassinate al-Glawi, capture the sultan, and expel the hated French military advisors.

Unfortunately the revolt fizzled when the Cherarda tribe rebelled prematurely in February. Changing their tactics, the insurgents instead laid siege to Fez in an attempt to compel Abd al-Hafiz to dismiss his hated grand vizier and the French military advisors. At first it looked as if they might succeed. But this was to reckon without the Machiavellian skills of the French colonial lobby, who capitalized upon the alleged threat posed by the siege to Europeans at Fez to obtain the dispatch of a French relief column. After a forced march, French troops under General Moinier reached Fez at the end of May and occupied the interior. Mohand took part in these events, in which his tribe was a major participant, though he does not appear to have been a leader.

In the aftermath of the rebellion, Moinier's troops occupied El Hadjeb and turned it into a permanent military installation. They hunted down suspected rebels and imposed heavy fines and back taxes on the tribe. With the leaders of the 1911 rebellion imprisoned and others of the old tribal elite badly compromised by their dealings with the French, where were people to turn for guidance? If his people were to have a chance of throwing off the French yoke, it would depend upon younger men. In this Mohand needed no encouragement. As a *qaid al-raha* and a participant in the 1911 rebellion, his military prowess was already established. In the winter of 1911–12, Mohand began to seek out like-minded individuals and to plan a major rebellion against the French.

Without the knowledge of the French, Abd al-Hafiz soon gave active encouragement to the rebels. In April 1912, he secretly convoked his *qaid al-rahas* (among them Mohand) and ordered them to prepare an attack. But before the rebels could act, *makhzan* troops at Fez mutinied, sparking a popular uprising within the city. Initially taken by surprise, the French were soon able to regain control, although the cost to their prestige was enormous. Suddenly Moroccans saw that France was not invincible. In the Fez region the tribes hastened their preparations for a major offensive. Rumors that the Fez mutiny had almost succeeded and that "Abd al-Hafiz had sold Morocco to France" soon brought new recruits flocking to join them. Under the leadership of the *sharif* Muhammad al-Hajjami, they planned a series of coordinated assaults on French posts in Fez, Meknes, El Hadjeb, and Sefrou.

On 24 May, French positions throughout the region came under Moroccan attack. At El Hadjeb and Sefrou, the *mujahidin* were led by Aqqa al-Bubidmani (though for the first time Mohand also was prominently featured). The coordinated uprising had caught the French off guard. At Fez, it was only after three days of intense fighting that superior French firepower eventually scattered the ranks of the attackers. At Meknes and Sefrou, the story was similar. Although the tribes were able momentarily to breach the French defenses, they were ultimately unsuccessful. Since Mohand's wife was a daughter of Umar al-Yusi, he was particularly motivated to take part in the latter offensive. Along with other bands of resistance fighters, he and his men continued to harass French patrols in the nearby hills until late summer.

After the relief of the siege of Fez, the focus of attention shifted in mid-August to southern Morocco, where another major insurrection threatened the French. Under the leadership of Mawlay Haybat Allah (known as El Hiba) Moroccan insurgents occupied Marrakesh, taking captive nine Frenchmen (including the personal emissary of General Lyautey and the vice-consul). Significantly, El Hiba presented himself as an opponent not only of the French but also of the corrupt rule of the lords of the Atlas. Mohand and his band of patriotic fighters were greatly encouraged by El Hiba's successes. But their hopes were dashed when the French succeeded in retaking Marrakesh in early September, expelling El Hiba and reestablishing the grinding quasi-feudal control of the great *qaids.*

Although the French were victorious, it was some time before French hegemony was secured. In the months that followed, French errors continued to provide an opening to Moroccan resisters. This was especially so in the Middle Atlas, where French policies took no account of the special character of Berber pastoralist society. The mixture of bribery and intimidation that had worked elsewhere to assure French control failed utterly when applied to groups like the Aith Ndhir, whose lack of identifiable chiefs and pastoralist life-style rendered them less vulnerable to such tactics.

With their greatly superior firepower and resources, the French were able to impose their control over the Aith Ndhir from their post at El Hadjeb. They established a local administration with the aid of opportunists like Driss Ou Rahu, whose corrupt and bullying ways soon made him detested by all. Mohand watched Ou Rahu's ascent with anger and disgust. Under the French, grievances continued to pile up. Allowing their local agents free rein was bad enough. But requiring the proud Aith Ndhir to recognize their submission to the *makhzan* was an intolerable humiliation. Prior to the defeat of El Hiba, Mohand had been a participant in some of the most dramatic moments of Moroccan history. In 1913 he emerged as a leader in his own right, a key organizer in his tribe of the struggle against the French.

One of the catalysts that propelled Mohand and his friends into action was the dramatic intervention of a hitherto obscure local *sharif*, Sidi Rahu. With a reputation for piety and probity already well established by 1912, Sidi Rahu was ideally placed to rally those who wished to continue the patriotic struggle. In late 1912, Sidi Rahu withdrew into the snowy forest above Ifrane and began a public fast aimed at galvanizing the conscience of the Berber groups nearby. Impressed by the *sharif's* resolve, Mohand began to seek allies.

As if this was not enough to encourage Mohand to take up arms, a second factor now intervened. Having earlier refused to help al-Hajjami's patriots or to join El Hiba in opposing the French, the powerful Zaian tribal confederation decided that the time had come for action. With their large numbers, cohesion, and weaponry the Zaian were able to intimidate smaller tribes like the Aith Ndhir, the Igerwan, and the Aith Njild. They threatened to prevent their access to summer pastures unless they immediately launched a major offensive against the French. Thus inspired and compelled, it did not take much for Mohand and his comrades to take up arms.

In March 1913, French complacency was shattered when a large force under Mohand's leadership launched a surprise attack on the French post at El Hadjeb. Other French positions in the region also came under attack at this time. Soon a full-scale offensive was under way, in which the French suffered significant losses. For a time it looked as though French control over the entire region might be overthrown, as other groups to the north of Fez also became active. It was several months before they regained the upper hand. Only the application of relentless military pressure, coupled with a drastic reappraisal of their policies, permitted them to reestablish their hegemony.

Even though his tribal homeland soon fell to the French, Mohand fought on for the next five years. With varying degrees of success, he and his group of 30 to 150 men continued the struggle in the mountains. Gradually his small guerrilla band had less and less scope for its activities. He and his men were driven ever deeper into the remote fastnesses of the Middle Atlas. Finally in 1918, discouraged and exhausted by the years of life on the run, Mohand surrendered.

Over the next thirty years the French protectorate consolidated its hold on Morocco. In the new circumstances, Mohand prospered. After Mohand surrendered, he accepted a commission in the native auxiliary forces of the protectorate (the famous *goum marocain*) and became a minor official. In his new guise as a supporter of the French protectorate, Mohand was able to acquire considerable land in the region and to become a privileged member of the Moroccan rural elite. But unlike such French collaborators as Driss Ou Rahu, Mohand continued to enjoy the respect of his people because of his years fighting the French. By the same token, his past as a resistance hero guaranteed that he was never really trusted by French authorities.

By 1967, when I interviewed him as a still vigorous ninety-four-year-old, Mohand had managed to survive the French protectorate. By then a respected tribal elder in newly independent Morocco, he wore his many years with pride. How he had managed to navigate the tricky shoals of the nationalist period, when French collaborators like himself were widely despised and distrusted by the eager young nationalists, I do not know. When I was introduced to him by the Moroccan governor of the Aith Ndhir, it was clear that Mohand was regarded with a mixture of respect and suspicion. As the *qaid* and I talked it became apparent that ironically, despite his advanced years, Mohand's past as an opponent of French rule, then as a cog in the protectorate machine, had tainted him as an oppositionist.

His survival a living testament to the complexities of the transition from precolonial times to the present, Mohand had become a living anachronism.

## A NOTE ON SOURCES

This account was written on the basis of several lengthy interviews with Mohand N'Hamoucha in August 1967 at his home near Bouderbala. In addition, I have drawn upon research in French military archives in Château Vincennes, Section d'Afrique, Maroc, Série C, D, and E; British foreign office political correspondence (notably the letters of the British vice-consul in Fez, James Macleod, preserved in FO174); and published and unpublished French ethnographic writings on the Aith Ndhir and the Middle Atlas region, of which the most important are Abès, "Monographie d'un tribu berbère: Les Ait Ndhir (Beni mtir)," *Archives Berbères* 2 (1917) and 3 (1918); and Edouard Arnaud, "La région de Meknès," *Bulletin de la Société de géographie du Maroc* (1916).

## SUGGESTIONS FOR FURTHER READING

The best ethnography of the Aith Ndhir is Amal Rassam Vinogradov, *The Aith Ndhir of Morocco: A Study of the Social Transformation of a Berber Tribe*, Museum of Anthropology, University of Michigan, no. 55 (Ann Arbor: University of Michigan, 1974). My *Prelude to Protectorate in Morocco: Precolonial Protest and Resistance, 1860–1912* (Chicago: University of Chicago Press, 1976) provides a general political history. For a discussion of many of the events mentioned here, see my "Tribalism and Moroccan Resistance, 1890–1914: The Role of the Aith Ndhir," in *Tribe and State in Northwest Africa*, ed. George Joffe and Richard Pennell (London: M.E.N.A.S., 1990). In French there are two excellent semifictionalized accounts of Middle Atlas Berber life: Said Guennoun, *La montagne berbère* (Paris, 1929); and Maurice LeGlay, *Chroniques marocaines* (Paris, 1933).

# EIGHT

# Ramadan al-Suwayhli: Hero of the Libyan Resistance

*Lisa Anderson*

Libya was the first Arab province of the Ottoman Empire to proclaim its independence and to establish a republic, yet its historical experience under Italian colonialism is little known. The suffering of the Libyan people, however, was very great: between 1911, when colonial rule began, and 1951, when an independent Libya was established, more than one million Libyans perished, many of them in concentration camps established by the Italian colonial rulers. Most of the urban middle class and a disproportionate number of the literate population were among the casualties.

The protracted resistance struggle produced its share of heroes and villains. The exploits of Umar al-Mukhtar, a Tripolitanian *alim* and guerrilla leader in the 1920s, have been immortalized in a Libyan-financed film, *The Lion of the Desert*, with Anthony Quinn in the title role.[*] Prior to the arrival of the Italians, Libya was a province of the Ottoman Empire, with its administration centered in Tripoli, a city not far from the Tunisian frontier. Ottoman rule was strongest in the few cities; it weighed more lightly on the countryside, operating through a system of alliances with rural elites. As Lisa Anderson explains, the 1908 Young Turk revolution and the Italian invasion in September 1911 changed all this, stimulating local nationalism and encouraging political unrest.

Ramadan al-Suwayhli, the subject of Anderson's contribution, was a member of a lesser notable family of Misrata, a city in the province of Tripolitania in western Libya. Following the Italian invasion, al-Suwayhli appears initially to have cooperated with the invaders. Subsequently, however, he organized the rebellion of a collaborating Libyan unit and defeated a large Italian force. Anderson explores the background to this reversal of loyalties, and the emergence of al-Suwayhli as an important resistance leader.

---

[*]On Libyan resistance see Ruth First, *Libya: The Elusive Revolution* (Harmondsworth: Penguin Books, 1974), 45–58; and E. E. Evans-Pritchard, *The Sanusi of Cyrenaica* (London: Oxford University Press, 1949), 159–73.

The microhistory of anticolonial resistance is just beginning to be written. Anderson's essay on Ramadan al-Suwayhli constitutes a significant chapter, however. The political rivalries within the city of Misrata, in which al-Suwayhli's family was embedded, constitute one. A second is the political world of bedouin factionalism in Tripolitania. Finally, there were the politics of the capital, Tripoli, and the elite factionalism that divided the elite into pro- and anti-Young Turks, pro- and anti-Italians, and Libyan nationalist groups. Nerves of steel and a sure touch were necessary in order to maneuver in such a complex environment. The relative success of al-Suwayhli and his ultimate undoing stem from his capacity to mobilize leaders and their clienteles in a context not only of resistance but also of societal breakdown and civil war.

This aspect of resistance has received more attention in North Africa than elsewhere in the region. As attention shifts to the politics by which the early nationalists were able to displace their rivals much the same sort of analysis can be expected to yield substantial insights. (On this topic, compare the chapters by Eqbal Ahmad and Stuart Schaar, Edmund Burke, Julia Clancy-Smith, Philip Khoury, Julie Oehler, and Abdullah Schleifer.) Until the advent of nationalism, the chief available cultural/ideological language for political mobilization was the Islamic tradition of *jihad*. —ED.


This is the story of a hero of the Libyan resistance against Italian imperialism in the early twentieth century. His biography illustrates many of the historical forces that buffeted the Middle East as the centuries-old Ottoman Empire gave way to European domination: the appearance of new elites, the growth of nationalism, the dreams of independence, the disappointments and recriminations of failure. Libya's experience was not typical. The Ottoman influence in the province in the first two decades of the twentieth century was unusually strong; the Italian colonization of the province was unusually brutal; the resistance was unusually fierce, and its failure unusually devastating. It did, however, suggest why so many of the regionwide developments seemed fraught with danger to the peoples of the Middle East and North Africa.

The hero of the story, Ramadan al-Suwayhli, did not live to see the final imposition of Italian rule in Libya. In a poignant illustration of the panic, bitterness, and confusion that prevailed during those years, he was killed by Libyan rivals fully a decade before the resistance was completely extinguished. Soon after his death in 1920, however, the Libyan war—once a powerful symbol of Ottoman and Muslim steadfastness in the face of Western imperialism—receded from world attention, overtaken by more momentous events in Europe and the Middle East.

Thus hardly anyone noticed that by the mid-1930s, when Italian control of the North African colony was finally uncontested, the Libyan population had been halved by famine, war casualties, and migration. Particularly devastating was the loss of almost the entire educated elite and much of the middle class. Indeed, when the country became independent in 1951, the population was about the same size as it had been at the turn of the century, while in the same period the populations of both Tunisia and Egypt had doubled, and the literacy rate of between 10 and 20 percent among adult men in Libya was probably lower than it had been fifty years earlier. Ramadan al-Suwayhli's generation in Libya was exceptional in many ways, not least of all for having been so completely destroyed; and it represented a response to extraordinary crisis, full of heroes and villains a little larger than life. Yet it was also very much a product of its place. Al-Suwayhli's story, both in its exceptional character and in its ordinariness, conveys a great deal about life in the Middle East and North Africa in the twentieth century.

Ramadan al-Shitawi al-Suwayhli was born during the second half of the 1870s in the region of Misrata, on the Mediterranean coast of the Ottoman province Tarablus al-Gharb, or what we now know as Libya. Misrata, which was then the second largest city of the province, after Tripoli, the capital, is about two hundred kilometers east of Tripoli, near the ancient Roman site of Leptis Magna. By the turn of the century it was thought to have between fifteen thousand and twenty thousand inhabitants, with perhaps as many as eighty thousand in the district as a whole. (The city of Tripoli was home to about thirty thousand people.)

Like Tripoli, Misrata was a town built around a group of oases; the rainfall along the coast, which was plentiful by the standards of Libya's largely desert interior, supplemented by underground springs, made unusually fertile agriculture possible. The town itself was dotted with lush vegetable gardens, and the surrounding countryside included not only fields of wheat and barley but palm and olive orchards. At the beginning of the nineteenth century, Misrata had been an important caravan entrepôt, and caravans bringing leathers, gold, and slaves from the southerly routes of the trans-Saharan trade routinely stopped there. In addition, the artisans of Misrata produced fine woolen carpets in an industry for which the town is still known locally. The city was endowed with a good harbor, though most long-distance trade was overland and the local merchants sent their goods on through Banghazi in eastern Libya to Alexandria in Egypt, whence they were shipped throughout the Ottoman world.

During the course of the nineteenth century, trans-Saharan trade declined as a result of the abolition of slavery and European encroachment in sub-Saharan Africa, and the role of the caravan trade in Misrata's local economy began to diminish. Instead of the seasonal markets associated with long-distance commerce, weekly, and even permanent, markets developed. The people of the countryside began to devote less time to pastoralism and provision of pack animals and guides for the caravans and more to agriculture. Nomads exchanged their tents for more permanent dwellings, and the local markets began to see greater varieties of produce. More and more people grew cash crops and relied on market relations to provide their household needs rather than depending on subsistence agriculture and occasional barter exchanges. As a result, Misrata saw considerable new construction during the latter part of the nineteenth century. A covered fruit-and-vegetable market and several new streets of shops were built, new district and municipal government buildings and new barracks for the local Ottoman troops were constructed, and a number of new Turkish-style houses were built by the wealthier families of the town.

There were a number of wealthy families in Misrata at this time. The notables, also known as the "great families," made their money in commerce and preserved it by working closely with the Ottoman provincial government. Among the most important of these great families were the Muntasirs and Aghdams, both of whom had extended families and economic holdings not only in Tripoli and Misrata but in the towns along the coast toward Egypt, such as Banghazi and Darnah, where their commercial travels often took them. The Muntasirs were of local Arab stock; the Aghdams were *kulughlis*, descended from Ottoman officers who settled in the province. The Aghdams had resisted the Ottoman central government's efforts to reestablish direct control over the province during the middle of the century—a policy that they correctly saw as threatening the unique position of *kulughlis*—and as a result had seen their fortunes wane somewhat in favor of the Muntasirs as the Ottoman government consolidated its control over the course of the century. Nonetheless, the Aghdams remained powerful, and at the turn of the century the competition between the two families for lucrative administrative appointments dominated local politics.

The ordinary urban dwellers participated little in politics, hoping simply to stay out of the sight of the conscription officer and the tax collector, and in the countryside, relations with the provincial authorities were also usually avoided. In the rural areas, however, local politics reflected not merely competition among families and clans but full-scale tribal affiliations and loyalties. Many of the local peasantry had settled only recently, and they retained much of the tribal identity that characterized the social organization of the region's nomadic pastoralists.

Ramadan al-Suwayhli's family was probably urban; neither his name nor his subsequent political following suggests an important tribal identity. Moreover, he is said to have been related by marriage to the urban *kulughli* family, the Aghdams. If he was a son of the city, however, al-Suwayhli was by no means a conventional urban notable. Although he was said to have had some formal education, what most struck his friends and foes alike was his superior horsemanship, and he was often said to have been descended from horse thieves. While his admirers dismissed this allegation as merely the rancor of those who did not forgive him his youthful pranks, al-Suwayhli certainly did have a criminal record by 1911, when his political career began. He had been in and out of prison more than once before he was accused (and, as far as can be gathered, convicted and quickly pardoned) of the murder of Abd al-Qasim al-Muntasir in 1910.

However much venality or passion may have figured in al-Suwayhli's early brushes with the law, politics probably played an important role well before he became a noted figure in Libya. The end of the nineteenth century was a time of considerable upheaval in the Ottoman Empire, and many of the empire's political and intellectual notables served time in prison. The Ottomans faced threats both from beyond their borders and from within their ranks. The French occupied Tunisia in 1881, and the British followed suit in Egypt the following year; by the end of the 1880s the European powers acquiesced in Italy's eventual seizure of Libya, the Ottoman Empire's last remaining territory in North Africa. Partly as a result, disenchantment with the reigning sultan, Abd al-Hamid, grew throughout the empire. Having suspended the newly promulgated constitution upon coming to the throne in 1876, Abd al-Hamid went on to prohibit expression of political dissent for the next three decades. This repressive domestic policy combined with the real threats to the empire from abroad to fan the fires of illegal political opposition throughout the realm. This dissatisfaction and worry among the empire's intellectual and political leaders filled the empire's prisons with its elite and eventually contributed to the Young Turk revolution of 1908.

Though important throughout the empire, the 1908 revolution had particularly profound reverberations in Libya. Abd al-Hamid's practice of exiling political agitators to Libya had meant that far from being an intellectual backwater the province was unusually knowledgeable about the political currents in the empire. The lifting of press censorship permitted the intellectuals of the province to air their concerns. Although they were preoccupied with many of the same issues that worried their Arab counterparts in the East—religious reform, government language policy, and the like—they were particularly adamant about the dangers posed by Italian inroads into the economy, recalling the European economic penetration that had preceded the occupations of Tunisia and Egypt.

At the same time, the provincial administration was thrown into up-heaval as supporters of the new regime undertook to rid the local gov-ernment of "reactionary" supporters of Abd al-Hamid. Not a few of these reactionaries were the economic elite of the province. Not only were they politically suspect, but many had also begun to profit from the new Italian interest in the province. The mayor of Tripoli, for example, held a large meeting soon after the Young Turks came to power and charged that the liberty they had proclaimed was a menace to Islam and the Arab people. The meeting ended with the adoption of a resolution calling for the abrogation of the constitution, the return of all Turks to Istanbul, and peaceful relations with Christians and Jews. In this last provision, the mayor's long-standing and profitable friendship with the Italian Banco di Roma probably played a part.

Supporters of the Young Turks made a concerted effort to under-mine the position of people like the mayor, and in Misrata, the Muntasir family soon found themselves in trouble. As Ahmad Dhiya al-Din al-Muntasir would later explain to the Italian authorities,

> the Young Turks came and because of their hatred of the partisans of Abd al-Hamid pounced on our family. First, when there were the elections [for the reopened parliament], I who was elected deputy . . . was not con-firmed by the government of the Young Turks on the pretext that I did not know the Turkish language well, while there were many others con-firmed who knew less than I. Then I was unjustly dismissed as *qaimamaqam* [local governor] of Tarhunah, and they hired some murderers to kill my brother Abd al-Qasim, who was barbarically killed on the street, after pro-tection had been promised to the murderer. . . . Fortunately for us, we came to know Italy had decided to occupy Tripoli. . . . We offered them our cooperation.

Ramadan al-Suwayhli's involvement in the murder of Abd al-Qasim, whether a killing for hire or a political assassination, suggests that he was among the early partisans of the Young Turks.

Times of instability and change often permit unusually talented indi-viduals to seize opportunities to rise beyond what would have been their lot ordinarily, and al-Suwayhli seems to have been a case in point. Apart from the Muntasirs, of course, and despite his checkered history, al-Suwayhli attracted the grudging admiration of even his many hostile ob-servers. The Italians, who were to put a price on his head during World War I, described him as "tall, slender, with a very attractive demeanor and imperious profile, an excellent horseman, accustomed to life in the trenches and fond of the exploits of war, domineering and daring . . . suspicious, very intelligent, generous and wealthy, . . . more feared than esteemed or loved . . . the classic brigand." The British concurred, say-ing in an official report: "He is an extremely brave man and has a reputation for great charity with money (which is almost invariably stolen, to judge by what is known of his habits)."

The upheaval occasioned by the Young Turk revolution was soon followed by another, and ultimately far more important, blow. On 26 September 1911, Italy sent an ultimatum to the Ottoman government announcing its intention to occupy Libya and demanding that within twenty-four hours the provincial forces be instructed to lay down their arms. The Ottomans refused, and Italy declared war on the empire, attacking the Libyan coast. The defense of the empire's integrity in Libya quickly became a popular political cause throughout the Muslim world, and Ottoman military officers soon began pouring into the province to organize the resistance. At camps throughout Libya, officers like Enver Bey, future Ottoman minister of war, his brother Nuri, Mustafa Kemal, later known as Ataturk, founder of the Turkish republic, Jaafar al-Askari, future prime minister of Iraq, and Aziz Ali al-Masri, future Egyptian chief of staff, established procedures for arming, clothing, and paying the local volunteers, known as *mujahidin* (fighters in a holy war).

In eastern Libya, a religious brotherhood, the Sanusiyah, coordinated the local resistance; in the western provinces, a variety of local notables, including al-Suwayhli, took the field and canvassed the countryside for volunteers. They had little trouble finding recruits, for their own commitment was obvious; al-Suwayhli himself was reportedly wounded several times. The Italians availed themselves of the latest military technology—the first military use of airplanes was in Libya as the Italians dropped bombs from the open cockpits of their early aircraft—but they nonetheless fared poorly, barely progressing beyond the coastal towns. Indeed, they did not even land at Misrata until June.

By midsummer, however, the Ottoman central government was growing worried about unrest in the Balkans, and the minister of war, who backed the Libyan resistance, had been replaced. Negotiations to end the war began in July, and shortly after war broke out in the Balkans in October, a peace treaty was signed. Significantly, although they agreed to withdraw their military officers and civilian officials, the Ottomans did not cede sovereignty of their North African province to Italy. Instead, the sultan granted his Libyan subjects "full and complete autonomy." Although the Italians reaffirmed their previously declared annexation of the province, it was not recognized either in international law or, more importantly, by the local resistance leaders. The Ottomans had agreed to withdraw their officials, but a number of Ottoman officers resigned their commissions to stay and fight as volunteers, and, of course, the Libyans who had been Ottoman officials stayed behind as well.

With the formal withdrawal of the Ottomans from the war, a division appeared between the resistance leaders who were willing to negotiate with the Italians and those who wanted to continue armed resistance. By and large, those willing to compromise were from the coastal areas already occupied by the Italians; the advocates of continuing the military struggle were from the still unsubdued hinterlands. For their part, the Italians hoped to avoid a military occupation of Libya that, as had already become clear, would have been fiercely resisted. They turned to negotiation—in truth, bribery—in what they called the *politica dei capi.* If they could win the provincial notables to their side, they would thereby win the province, or so they hoped.

Thus they opened talks with the Libyan leaders willing to negotiate, and, at first, the policy seemed to succeed. By 1914, the colonial officials could report that the southern province of Fazzan had been occupied and that many of the local notables were on the government payroll. The Muntasir family, for example, had aided the Italian occupation as promised; Abd al-Qadir al-Muntasir accompanied the Italian troops that occupied Sirt, east of Misrata, at the end of 1912 after a brief battle against Ottoman Libyan troops officered by Nuri Bey, Enver's brother.

Al-Suwayhli may well have voluntarily decided to cooperate with the Italians; after all, Misrata was under occupation. According to his supporters, however, al-Suwayhli's cooperation was extracted through duress. He was briefly arrested in 1914, and although he was released, he remained bitter about the experience, perhaps because the Italians required that he either assist them in subduing the remaining *mujahidin* or face exile in Italy. This was no empty threat; several of his brothers were deported to Italy.

Whatever the reason, by 1915, we find al-Suwayhli officering a column of "friendlies"—Libyan soldiers accompanying Italian troops—on a campaign to subdue the region between Misrata and Sirt. By that time, with World War I raging in Europe, Italian attention had been diverted, and the Italians began to suffer serious reverses in Libya. In November 1914, Libyan forces sacked and destroyed the Italian garrison in the capital of Fazzan, and poorly supplied Italian troops in the south began a mad scramble for the safety of the coast. By April 1915, when the Italians had already lost control of much of the province, al-Suwayhli put the seal on their humiliation, leading a revolt of the Libyan friendlies at the battle of Qasr Bu Hadi. The Italians lost over five hundred dead; and well over five thousand Italian rifles, several million rounds of ammunition, and a variety of machine guns and artillery went to the Libyan resistance. For the duration of World War I, which the Italians entered in May of 1915, the Italian occupation in Libya was limited to Tripoli, the coastal cities of Khums and Banghazi, and several smaller towns on the eastern shore.

The withdrawal of the Italians and their supporters, including the Muntasirs, from Misrata after the battle of Qasr Bu Hadi left al-Suwayhli, then in his mid-thirties and well known for his exploits—the Italians put a price on his head after the battle—among the most prominent figures in the town. He appears to have enjoyed widespread support across the town's traditional cleavages; at least at the outset, his was a genuinely popular following and not merely a revival of traditional clan rivalries. The Muntasirs, of course, remained his implacable enemies. The Aghdam family appears to have divided, some supporting him and some siding with their class allies but traditional rivals, the Muntasirs. Certainly al-Suwayhli was the hero of the lower classes in Misrata and among the peasants and nomads of the countryside. The disruptions of the Ottoman and Italian administrative bureaucracies in the region during the war allowed him to extend his own influence and administrative reach well beyond Misrata itself, and he soon controlled not only Misrata but most of the region between the western Fazzan and Sirt, the area that divides western Libya or Tripolitania from the eastern region, Cyrenaica.

Al-Suwayhli had important aid in establishing and administering this virtually autonomous government. Because of its good harbor, Ottoman forces and their German allies—both, of course, Italy's enemies in World War I—used Misrata as one of their major supply ports. German submarines landed men and supplies there throughout the war in an effort to weaken the Italian position in the southern Mediterranean, and al-Suwayhli was their favored local contact. Al-Suwayhli himself was more concerned with extending his own influence than with furthering Ottoman or German war aims, but for several years he and Nuri Bey worked together to strengthen Misrata as a safe haven for the Ottoman forces.

By the end of 1917 al-Suwayhli had been appointed local governor by Nuri Bey and accorded the title bey himself. His influence—and his tax-collecting powers—encompassed most of eastern Tripolitania, including the Warfalla region, where the local leader, Abd al-Nabi Bilkhayr, saw to his regret his own influence diminish. Misrata had become the headquarters of an elaborate administration that supervised tax collection and military recruitment, had its own ammunition factory, printed its own money, and ran its own schools and hospital. Although the Ottomans transferred considerable sums of money to al-Suwayhli in Misrata, their influence had begun to wane well before the end of the war. During the early months of 1918 Nuri Bey was recalled to Istanbul, eventually to be replaced later in the summer by the Ottoman prince Uthman Fuad. By October, when the empire signed the armistice agreement ending its involvement in the war, however, the British reported that "there was never any chance of Tripoli becoming once again a Turkish province. Even al-Suwayhli, the most Turkophile Arab in the country, was at the same time the most bitter opponent of Turkish rule, which could only mean a diminution of his influence."

In fact, as the provincewide administrative system left by the Ottomans began to weaken and disintegrate under the pressures of nearly constant warfare, competition among local notables for scarce resources heightened. The leaders who, like al-Suwayhli, relied on personal talents and administrative effectiveness rather than on the wealth or traditional status of their families or clans to sustain their following were particularly jealous of their prerogatives, and al-Suwayhli was vigilant in warding off challenges to his authority. Early in 1916, for example, the Sanusiyah made an effort to extend its influence and its taxing powers into Tripolitania. In part because al-Suwayhli had coordinated his actions in the battle of Qasr Bu Hadi with Sanusi forces, they apparently hoped he would be willing to recognize their supremacy. When Safi al-Din al-Sanusi, cousin of the order's leader, was sent into western Sirt to collect tribute from the populations there, his troops were met and defeated by those of al-Suwayhli. Safi al-Din withdrew into Cyrenaica, and the battle marked the end of genuine Sanusi influence in Tripolitania.

Toward the end of World War I a young Egyptian, Abd al-Rahman Azzam Bey (who was to become the first secretary general of the Arab League after World War II), arrived in Misrata to take up the cause of unity and resistance as advisor to al-Suwayhli. In April 1917 the Italians had signed an accord with the Sanusiyah granting the brotherhood considerable autonomy in Cyrenaica. The local notables in Tripolitania welcomed this development, interpreting it as a starting point from which to obtain self-determination. What they felt was needed was a broadly based organization to represent Tripolitanian interests. In the fall of 1918 the region's notables met and at the conclusion of the meeting announced the formation of the Tripoli Republic.

The choice of a republic—this was the first formally republican government in the Arab world—appears to have been less a reflection of the republican sentiments of its founders than of their inability to agree upon a single individual to act as head of state. The post had been offered to Uthman Fuad Pasha, but he declined it, and a council of four was established to act as the ruling body. The four were Ramadan al-Suwayhli, Sulayman al-Baruni, leader of the Berbers of the western mountains, Ahmad Murayid of Tarhunah, southwest of Misrata, and

Abd al-Nabi Bilkhayr of Warfalla. Abd al-Nabi was included, it is said, on the insistence of al-Suwayhli, who felt that his commitment to continuing the resistance needed encouragement. Azzam Bey served as the council's secretary, and a twenty-four-member advisory group was established, carefully selected to represent most of the various regions and interests of the province. The republic, which declared Tripolitania independent, attempted to organize the administration of the province—the Italians still had control of only Tripoli and a few other coastal towns—granting permission to the local population to trade with Tripoli on the condition that they paid a 30 percent tax on their profits from the sale of the goods they obtained.

The republic's announcement of Tripolitania's independence and its leaders' attempts to plead their case at the Paris peace conference was met by silence in the international community, but the Italians themselves nonetheless agreed to meet its leaders. The two sides met in April 1919. The republic leaders believed themselves to be negotiating for genuine independence; the Italians viewed their talks as inaugurating a system of rule through native chiefs. The misunderstanding was never resolved, but the negotiations led to the announcement of an agreement (and the lifting of the price on Ramadan al-Suwayhli's head). In June 1919, the Legge Fondamentale was promulgated, providing for a special Italian-Libyan citizenship and according all such citizens the right to vote in elections for a local parliament. These citizens were exempt from military service, and taxing powers rested with the local parliament. A council was established to supervise implementation and to make administrative appointments, and many of the republic's leading figures were appointed to this council.

The cooperation implicit in the Legge Fondamentale was a gamble for both the Italians and the Libyans. The Italians hoped to buy time in their colony while they attended to more pressing political problems at home. The leaders of the republic compromised their desire for complete independence in recognition of the exhaustion and straitened circumstances of the Tripolitanian population. As a British report suggested, "the leaders of the population in Tripolitania were possibly beginning to feel that they might lose control of the inhabitants, if their own people suffered further casualties in the fighting at a period when war had rendered the economic situation as bad as it could possibly be."

Although the provisions of the Legge were never carried out in Tripolitania—indeed, within weeks of its promulgation accusations of bad faith were traded by the Italian and Libyan leaderships—the republic reconstituted itself in September 1919 as the Association for National Reform. Ramadan al-Suwayhli was its honorary president, Ahmad Murayid its active president, and Abd al-Rahman Azzam its general secretary and actual manager. Under the editorship of Azzam Bey, the association published a newspaper, *Liwa al-Trabulsi* (*The Tripoli Banner*), and readers were kept informed about subjects as diverse as the prospects for an independent Anatolian republic under Mustafa Kemal Pasha, the fortunes of the nationalists in Syria, the appointment of a new British ambassador to Washington, and domestic politics in the United States.

Although the membership of the council that oversaw appointments under the Legge Fondamentale was nearly identical to that of the founders of the Tripoli Republic, neither the republic nor the Association for Natural Reform was formally recognized, and the Italians did not acknowledge the authority of the republic to administer the hinterlands autonomously. Thus, although the Italians appointed the republic leaders to provincial administrative posts, they did not permit local coordination of the finances they provided to the various leaders. On the contrary, the Italians used the reliance of the Tripolitanian leadership on Italian patronage to sow dissension in the ranks of the republic. The scarcity of resources and the desire of the notables for administrative posts and their attendant tax-collecting powers exacerbated internal disputes within the republican leadership. Ahmad Murayid of Tarhunah objected to placement of his district under the purview of Misrata, which was governed by al-Suwayhli, and he was soon embroiled in a similar dispute with Abd al-Nabi Bilkhayr of Warfalla, who also objected to al-Suwayhli's administrative superiority and claimed further that he had diverted funds sent from Istanbul during the war. As it was, al-Suwayhli was said to receive a large monthly off-the-book stipend from the Italians. His rivals were said to be in their secret pay as well.

Although the Italians tried halfheartedly to mediate the disputes between Ramadan and his rivals, who were, of course, at the time councilors of the Italian government under the Legge Fondamentale, by the spring of 1920 al-Suwayhli had expelled the Italian advisor sent to Misrata under the terms of the Legge, and the British reported that al-Suwayhli, "an austere, incorruptible, religious man of strong character and intelligence, rules independently [with] about 10,000 armed men." An Arabic newspaper in Tripoli, *al-Rakib* (*The Observer*), sent a correspondent to Misrata at the time who wrote admiringly of the order and security, the application of religious law, the suppression of strong drink. This he contrasted with conditions in the towns in Italian control, such as Khums, where the bars were squeezing out the mosques. The British agreed, reporting stories of al-Suwayhli's severity in Misrata in "enforcing the total prohibition of strong drink for Moslems." "If he succeeds in this," the report went on, "it will be a great change in the habits of the Moslem population of this coast."

By the spring of 1920 the Italians were tiring of al-Suwayhli's insolence, as they saw it, and Abd al-Qadir al-Muntasir, whose family was still unwavering in its support of the Italian cause and its hostility to al-Suwayhli, began pursuing "commercial interests" in the regions of Tarhunah and Warfalla. The long-standing feud between al-Suwayhli and the Muntasir family had reportedly been worsened by al-Suwayhli's hanging of two of the Muntasir clan in Misrata in 1917 and his sequestering of family property in the region. By June, after the Italians had sent several carloads of arms and ammunition to Abd al-Qadir al-Muntasir and to Abd al-Nabi Bilkhayr, al-Suwayhli felt obliged to launch a preemptive campaign against his opponents. His forces were defeated, and he took refuge in a government garrison in Warfalla territory. According to Italian press accounts, "his enemies entered the castle. Abd al-Qadir took al-Suwayhli by the arm and was conducting his prisoner away when the latter tried to escape. Then it was that shots were fired from short range at al-Suwayhli, and it is stated that some 150 bullets were fired at him." Although Abd al-Qadir styled himself the hero of the action at the time, and the Muntasirs would later sue the Italian government for compensation for the service rendered in killing al-Suwayhli, the British consul in Tripoli reported that it was widely believed that Abd al-Qadir had not arrived on the scene until well after al-Suwayhli was dead.

Although Ramadan al-Suwayhli's brother Ahmad was designated to succeed him, it was apparent that much of the momentum of the resistance was lost. Soon after al-Suwayhli's death, the republican leadership met and resolved that a single Muslim ruler be designated to represent the whole country, including Cyrenaica. Their representatives met in Sirt with delegates from the Sanusiyah and agreed on a proclamation announcing their intention to elect a Muslim *amir* to represent the entire country and to "unite against our enemy who is trying to seize our country by force." The Tripolitanians learned the Italian reaction to this development when they returned to Misrata: a new governor had attacked the town.

As Fascist power grew in Italy, the Libyan leaders concluded that renewed conflict with Italy was unavoidable. The head of the Sanusiyah, Idris, therefore accepted the amirate of all Libya—earlier viewed as too provocative a statement of unified resistance—and fled to the safety of Cairo, where he would remain in exile until 1943. Azzam Bey went with him and several years later was elected to the Egyptian parliament. Abd al-Nabi Bilkhayr continued the resistance—his defeat of al-Suwayhli had not made him any more amenable to Italian rule—and he reportedly died of thirst in Chad in 1930. Ahmad Murayid and al-Suwayhli's brother Ahmad settled in Egypt, acquiring land together in Fayum.

Within thirty years Libya would be independent. Although the Libyan resistance was eventually defeated, Italy lost the colony to British and French forces in the hard-fought North Africa campaigns of World War II. Unable to agree on a mandatory power, the European powers gave disposition of the territory to the new United Nations, which granted it independence under the Sanusi leader Idris as king in 1951. Few observers were optimistic about the prospects for Libyan self-rule. The vast majority of the people were poverty-stricken; there was virtually no middle class and not a single Libyan doctor, lawyer, or judge. As a result, government was heavily dependent on a few wealthy families to staff its ranks, families who, in order to retain their wealth during the Italian era, had collaborated with the colonial administration. Thus, in perhaps the final irony in the story of Ramadan al-Suwayhli, the first prime minister of independent Libya was Mahmud al-Muntasir, scion of the prominent Misrata family.

The hopes of Ramadan al-Suwayhli, the determined opponent of Sanusi influence in Tripolitania and bitter enemy of Muntasir domination in Misrata, seemed to have been definitively destroyed at the very moment that his other dream, Libyan independence, was realized. Yet he was not completely forgotten. Misrata remained a source of trouble for the government. Riots there over official tampering in parliamentary elections in 1952 contributed to the monarchy's permanent ban on political parties. More importantly, with the overthrow of the monarchy in 1969, Libyan historians turned away from simply recording the accomplishments of the country's elites to examination of the lives of ordinary people and how they coped with the upheavals of the twentieth century. Ramadan al-Suwayhli, champion and representative of many of the virtues—and vices—of the ordinary turn-of-the-century Libyan, was vindicated.

## A NOTE ON SOURCES

Ramadan al-Suwayhli has been the subject of an admiring biography in Arabic by Muhammad Fushaykha, *Ramadan al-Suwayhli: Al-batal al-libi al-shahid bikifahihi lilitalyan* (Ramadan al-Suwayhli: The Martyred Libyan Hero in His Struggle with the Italians) (Tripoli, 1974). Also Tahar al-Zawi, *Jihad al-Abtal fi Tarablus al-Gharb* (Holy War of the Heroes in Tripoli) (Beirut, 1970). It is a reflection of the fate of leaders of unsuccessful efforts to resist European imperialism that there is no account of his life in a Western language.

This essay has drawn largely on official contemporary accounts by local administrators and diplomats of the Ottoman provincial, British, and Italian governments that are now preserved at the Libyan National Archives in Tripoli, the Public Records Office in London, and the Archivo storico dell'Africa italiana in Rome. All of the observations quoted in the text are from documents in these archives.

## SUGGESTIONS FOR FURTHER READING

Enrico de Leone's *La colonizzazione dell'Africa del Nord* (Padua, 1960) is easily the best account of the Italians' contradictory and ultimately futile efforts to deal with the resistance and its leaders. See also Georges Rémond, *Aux camps turco-arabes: Notes de route et de guerre en Cyrénaïque et en Tripolitaine* (Paris, 1913); and Mabel Loomis Todd, *Tripoli the Mysterious* (Boston, 1912).

John Wright's *Libya: A Modern History* (Baltimore, 1982) provides a good overview of Libya in the twentieth century, though most of the book is devoted to developments after independence. E. E. Evans-Pritchard's classic *The Sanusi of Cyrenaica* (London, 1949) includes a good account of the resistance in Cyrenaica, although it is openly partisan in its enthusiasm for Idris, longtime ally of the British and eventual king of independent Libya. Claudio Segre's *Fourth Shore: The Italian Colonization of Libya* (Chicago, 1974) is a good account of Italian policy but has little about the resistance itself. Two works by the author of this essay provide more information about the late Ottoman and Italian periods in Libya: *The State and Social Transformation in Tunisia and Libya, 1830–1980* (Princeton, 1986); and "The Tripoli Republic, 1918–1922," *Social and Economic Development of Libya*, ed. E. G. H. Joffe and K. S. McLachlan (London, 1982).

# NINE

# Bibi Maryam:
# A Bakhtiyari Tribal Woman

*Julie Oehler*

Middle Eastern tribes have received the attention of scholars only when their actions have impinged on the national government. Otherwise their histories have generally been ignored. How much more is this the case for the role of tribal women in politics, which insofar as it is discussed tends to treat women as the appendages of male relatives, the better to deny the significance of their actions!

The Bakhtiyari are perhaps the best-known Iranian tribe. Luri-speaking pastoralists, until recently the Bakhtiyari migrated with their flocks and herds twice a year from summer pasturage in the cool valleys west of Isfahan to their winter grazing grounds near Ahwaz in Khuzistan on the other side of the rugged Zagros Mountains. Their seasonal migration covered over two hundred miles each way. Prominent contemporary Iranians of Bakhtiyari origin include Queen Soraya, the recent shah's first wife, and Shapour Bakhtiar, his last prime minister.

Julie Oehler's biography of Bibi Maryam provides a window on the changing world of Bakhtiyari elite women in the early twentieth century. The daughter of the *ilkhan*, or paramount chief, Bibi Maryam played an important role in anti-British politics in Iran during World War I in defiance both of the Qajar government and the leading Bakhtiyari *khans*. She conducted Wilhelm Wassmuss, "the German Lawrence," into the Bakhtiyari lands, where he sought to rally opposition to the British, who were defending their newly discovered oil fields in Khuzistan.

While little is known of Bibi Maryam beyond this, that little is tantalizing. By reading the known facts against the grain, Oehler argues that in response to the transformation of Bakhtiyari society in the preceding decades, the role of the *bibis* drastically altered. As she explains, in the nineteenth century the *khans* acquired vast estates and were drawn into the national political game, leaving their wives, the *bibis*, to manage their affairs. This they did with gusto, organizing carpet production and entering trade on their own. Previously little noticed, the *bibis* began to take up positions often at variance with their menfolk. Bibi Maryam's role in the Wassmuss mission is one example of this trend.

Bibi Maryam's story also challenges prevailing notions of the bimodal gender division of labor in the Middle East, in which the public role of men stands in contrast to the family sphere of women's activity. In fact, such generalizations, while having some basis, do not begin to account for the great variety of possibilities for action available to women depending upon their class, status, occupation, and residence. Thus, for example, rural women throughout the area have seldom worn the veil, except when going to town, and some women have been able to play an active role in the economy, buying and selling goods and property.

Other selections in this volume treat the lives of Middle Eastern pastoralists. One might compare Bibi Maryam's situation with that of Migdim, for instance, a contemporary Egyptian bedouin matriarch profiled by Lila Abu-Lughod. Lois Beck's portrait of Rostam, a present-day Qashqa'i tribesman, allows us to see how much has changed in the life of Iranian pastoralists since the early twentieth century. Finally, my essay on Mohand N'Hamoucha, a Moroccan Berber pastoralist contemporary of Bibi Maryam's, suggests interesting comparisons across the region. —ED.

In 1916, at the height of World War I, a force of Turkish soldiers, renegade Swedish gendarmes, and Persian nationalists undertook the hazardous journey from Ahwaz to Isfahan. Led by Wilhelm Wassmuss, a German officer later known as "the German Lawrence," its mission was to capture the recently developed British oil fields in the territory of the Bakhtiyari tribal confederation east of Isfahan. Wassmuss and his men were able to come undetected into the region because they were guided by Bibi Maryam, the daughter of the paramount chief of the Bakhtiyari, Husayn Quli Khan. Maryam assisted the force in defiance of the pro-British policy of the leading *khans*, as well as of a Qajar edict that anyone opposing the British or Russian war efforts would have their property and personal possessions seized and sold. Maryam's exploit required great personal strength indeed.

Why was a Bakhtiyari *bibi* (daughter of a *khan*, or tribal chief) traveling on this dangerous secret mission? In their discussion of this episode, Western writers always describe Bibi Maryam as "the strong-willed and independent" daughter of Husayn Quli Khan. This formula is convenient, for it simultaneously deprives Bibi Maryam of agency, by ascribing her actions to her father, while dismissing her leadership role as an aberration. Yet it helps to explain why a consideration of this brief episode of her life is potentially so interesting, for Bibi Maryam's behavior does indeed appear to defy the traditional role of women in Persian society. But how typical of tribal women was her behavior? Of tribal women of elite background? What were the possibilities for public action by elite tribal women in early twentieth-century Iran? Although the sources that mention Bibi Maryam are fragmentary at best, by reading the sources against the grain it is possible to see her actions as part of a larger response by elite tribal women to the rapidly changing social and political conditions in the early twentieth century.

Basically, what needs to be explained is not so much how or why one woman sought to outwit the system in which she found herself, but rather what circumstances led her to resort to such a dangerous deed. Accordingly we must examine the historic relationship between the Qajar government, the British, and the Bakhtiyari and its impact on the lives of the elite women of the tribe. As we shall see, the importance of the wives, mothers, daughters, and sisters of the leading *khans* changed as a result of the growing dependence of the Bakhtiyaris on alliances with the powers outside the tribe, first with the Qajars and later with the British. These powers, especially the British, sought to circumvent the traditional role of marriage alliances as the essential mediating factor in intertribal struggles for power.

Bibi Maryam was a woman of prominence among the ruling family of the Bakhtiyari tribes. Not only was her father, Husayn Quli Khan, the paramount chief of the Bakhtiyari tribal confederacy, but also she and her family played an important part in the country's nationalist struggles. Bakhtiyari involvement in Persian national politics began with the constitutional revolution of 1906–11. The revolution represented an effort by the intelligentsia, bazaar merchants, and ulama to limit the autocratic powers of the Qajar ruler and encourage a program of modernizing reforms. A protracted struggle ensued, one of the results of which was the intensification of the political contest between reformers and reactionaries in the country. By 1909, when Bakhtiyari tribal forces intervened at Tehran, the revolution had lost its way. For the next decade Bakhtiyari *khans* played a prominent role in Persian national politics. Among them were many of Bibi Maryam's brothers, uncles, and cousins. From 1911 to 1913, one of her brothers was prime minister, and others were key members of the new cabinet. Although after 1916 Bakhtiyari *khans* no longer served in the central government, several still held governorships of large districts throughout the country.

As is the case for most Middle Eastern women, we know very little about Bibi Maryam except those facts that relate to her role as wife and mother. These facts, however, reveal a great deal about the life of the women of her class and the changes that were occurring in the tribal structure. Bibi Maryam's social identity was derived from her birth and marriage, which provided her with the capacity for undertaking initiatives in her own right. In order to understand the complicated political world in which she maneuvered, we must first turn to a discussion of the politics of kinship and marriage among the Bakhtiyari elite, the strategy of alliances pursued by her husband's family, and the way that strategy was altered by the centralizing efforts of the Qajar government.

Bibi Maryam was one of twelve daughters and eight sons born to the Bakhtiyari chief Husayn Quli Khan. Her mother, Bibi Fatima, was the daughter of Ali Reza, the head of a rival branch of the Bakhtiyari known as the Chahar Lang. (Husayn Quli Khan himself belonged to the Haft Lang branch. More on these divisions below.) Bibi Fatima's marriage to Husayn Quli Khan sealed an alliance with Ali Reza and the Chahar Lang against the intrigues of other tribes or the Qajar state. Bibi Maryam and her sisters and brothers continued the practice of taking marriage partners from outside their clan as well as from among the children of their father's brothers. Maryam married twice; she was married first to Ali Quli Khan of her mother's clan; then, after he died, to her cousin Fatula Quli Khan. Murdan Khan, her eldest son by her first husband, became an important figure in Bakhtiyari politics in later years.

The position of noble women among the Bakhtiyari declined significantly within the lifetime of Bibi Maryam. Bibi Maryam's struggles and those of other women of her class took place against the backdrop of this declining power. Formerly, Bakhtiyari marriage alliances insured harmony among the members of a tribe. As mothers, daughters, sisters, and wives, tribal women served as mediators in disputes between the men. A man did not want to be faced with the prospect of fighting against the husband of his sister or daughter. In this way most divisions within a tribe were resolved before real trouble began. The preferred marriage for a woman was to her father's brother's son. But marriages to members of outside tribal factions began to occur more often as the Bakhtiyari sought to unite against the encroachment of the central state. During Maryam's lifetime, the tribal network of relationships based on blood and marriage greatly extended the power of her family. A consideration of the nineteenth-century experience will make this clear.

The Bakhtiyari were made up of loosely organized nomadic clans that considered themselves to be of either the Chahar Lang or the Haft Lang branch of a people who spoke Luri, the Bakhtiyari language, and shared biannual migration routes. For centuries Bakhtiyari pastoralists migrated with their sheep, goats, and mules across the Zagros Mountains in southwest Iran. In the early spring the tribesmen and their families braved the high trails and swollen rivers to move their flocks from the winter feeding grounds on the plains of Khuzistan to the cool valleys west of Isfahan. Again, in the autumn, before the first snows covered the passes, the tribes gathered at the tribal meeting place in one of the northern valleys to prepare for the return to the warmer lands of the south. Transit between the summer and winter feeding grounds was difficult and dangerous. The western town of Ahwaz at the mouth of the Karun and the city of Isfahan on the eastern edge of the Bakhtiyari lands were separated by several mountain chains where the trail reached altitudes of more than eight thousand feet. As the river wound its way down from the high peaks to water the fertile pastures on both the eastern and western slopes, it cut deep channels into the limestone rocks. Narrow suspension bridges spanned the high banks in a few places, but more often the herdsmen were forced to descend into the steep gorges and swim with their animals across the cold, swift waters that blocked the trail.

In the nineteenth century things began to change. The rivalries between the Chahar Lang and Haft Lang branches of the Bakhtiyari gradually gave way to a new political organization. The centralizing Qajar government played a crucial role in this transformation. In the 1820s and 1830s, Muhammad Taqi Khan, head of the dominant Chahar Lang faction, imagined that he and the Bakhtiyari could remain independent from the state. For several years he refused to pay taxes or to furnish troops to the government.

Fath Ali Shah (1797–1834), the Qajar ruler, was faced with an empty treasury and the threat of revolt among his troops. He feared Iran would be completely overtaken by the Europeans, after humiliating defeats resulted in the loss of the rich northern provinces to the Russians in the treaties of Gulistan (1813) and Turkmanchay (1828). When Muhammad Taqi Khan sought to withhold his taxes, and subsequently began negotiating a commercial agreement with the British, Fath Ali Shah became convinced a plot was afoot and ordered his arrest. He was put into prison in 1841, where he died ten years later. Relations between the Bakhtiyari and the Qajars continued to slide downhill in the years that followed. Nasir ud-Din Shah, who began his long reign as a liberal reformer in 1848, became increasingly reactionary after the British invasion of Bushire in 1857. British overtures to the Bakhtiyari, even in the form of commercial treaties, were viewed by the Qajars as an attempt to subvert the power of the crown.

Husayn Quli Khan, Maryam's father, was in a position to profit from the mistakes of Muhammad Taqi Khan. In keeping with a traditional Qajar practice of using rival factions to check the power of tribal leaders, the government used *khans* from the Haft Lang branch of the Bakhtiyari to help capture Muhammad Taqi Khan. Husayn Quli Khan was one of those *khans*. As a reward for his loyalty to the government, he was recognized as the paramount leader of the Bakhtiyari. Thereafter, he used his ties with the Qajars to increase his status among the tribal factions.

As a Qajar official, he was responsible for maintaining order in his tribal area, collecting the excess surplus from the peasants and furnishing tribesmen to defend the state.

For the next few years Husayn Quli Khan was left alone by the government and consolidated his wealth and power within the tribal area. He married wisely, formed alliances with neighboring groups, and successfully eliminated all rivals to his rule of the Bakhtiyaris. In 1867, Husayn Quli Khan was given the title of *ilkhan*, or paramount chief, by Nasir ud-Din Shah. He was also awarded what amounted to private ownership of large tracts of land that had once been held in common by the tribes, the proceeds of which he used to enrich himself and his family. On this occasion his younger brother, Hajji Imam Quli Khan, was designated as the *ilbeg* (second in command) of the tribes. Thus was consolidated a new administrative division of the Bakhtiyari into Ilkhani and Hajji Ilkhani branches. The central government retained the right to give or take both titles at will.

The temporary security of this outside alliance with the Qajar government ushered in several significant changes in the lives of the newly created Bakhtiyari nobility. The permanent positions of *ilkhan* and *ilbeg* and the subsequent land grants that went along with these titles required Husayn Quli Khan and his sons and brothers, along with their families, to give up the role of pastoral nomadic chiefs. There was little time for the annual migrations for the leading *khans,* who as landlords now owned agricultural land complete with peasants and villages.

By the 1870s the *khans* had settled down and built castles in the lush valleys of the summer pasture to the east of Isfahan. They began to invest their land rents not only in greater herds but also in the agriculture and small craft industries of the villages throughout the area. However, in spite of growing responsibilities at home, the *khans* were now required to spend more and more time in the Qajar capital in Tehran to give service to the shah and lobby for continued royal support. The Qajars often kept *khans* under virtual house arrest in the capital in order to insure that their tribal retainers would remain faithful to the royal house. The move from nomad chief to elite landlord and agent of the government substantially altered the life-styles of the Bakhtiyari. This change was nowhere more pronounced than in the case of the elite women.

The wives and mothers of the leaders found themselves administering the household and its surrounding estates during the long absence of the men. Estates often included entire villages, where the *bibi*, in the name of the landowning *khan*, was in charge of the decisions about planting, water allocation, harvesting, and distribution of the crops. The *khans* claimed a percentage of everything produced by the villagers, from the grain that passed through the mill to the handicrafts made by the peasant women. This required that elaborate books be kept by the *bibis,* most of whom were literate by this time. During this period a *khan* became increasingly dependent upon the opinions of his mother or wife of noble birth not only because of her blood connections but also because of her role as administrator of the estate. During these years of the *khans'* absence, the *bibis* also gained an economic independence not known to previous generations of tribal women. Life on the estates surrounded by peasants and village craftsmen gave this new class of elite women the chance to run small businesses that were separate from those of the *khans.* A grain mill or carpet factory was often owned and run by a leading *bibi.*

Carpet making became a particularly lucrative business for the noblewomen. Most of the weavers were wives and children of servants on the estate. The *bibi* supervised every stage of the preparation. She selected the best wool and watched to make sure it was properly washed and dyed; she weighed out and mixed the dye with her own hands to make sure of the quality. The short, colored threads of wool were then woven into the warp, which was wound on simple horizontal wooden looms. The number of women on a loom depended upon the size of the carpet. The weaving of one carpet was a long process, and the women were paid little besides their food. Money from the sale of the carpets went into the *bibis'* private funds, and several of the *bibis* began to accumulate wealth in their own right and did not have to depend completely on their husbands. In later years some of the *bibis* found it very profitable to switch from the traditional Bakhtiyari pattern carpet designs to the large flowers that were popular in England.

The increased independence of the women was one side effect of the changing Bakhtiyari society; there were others, however, that eventually came to threaten the position of the *bibis* as partners and power brokers for the *khans.* The necessary alliance with the Qajars was not without its cost. While leading *khans* found it increasingly necessary to seek the favor of members of the court, they soon learned that the Qajar family could not be trusted in this relationship. While the official ties with the shah allowed Husayn Quli Khan to strengthen his alliances within the tribal confederation, it did not eventually give him protection against the intrigues of other members of the Qajar court. His success attracted the jealousy of the crown prince, who was governor of the district of Isfahan and who feared the growing power of the *ilkhan* in the neighboring tribal lands. The prince convinced his father that the *khan* was preparing to side with the British in a growing dispute between the Qajars and the Europeans over trade in the southern part of the country, and in 1882 he persuaded his father to have Husayn Quli Khan killed.

The murder of Husayn Quli Khan began a new era for the ruling family of the Bakhtiyari. It demonstrated to his sons and brothers that although outside alliances were necessary, the Qajars could not be trusted. As *ilkhan,* Husayn Quli Khan was the Qajar representative in the tribal lands. He had worked for more than thirty years in the service of the shah, collecting the taxes and furnishing tribal troops, yet he was cruelly murdered when it was feared he was becoming too strong. After his death, his brothers and his oldest son were put into prison so they could not immediately assume tribal leadership. They were released one by one over a three-year period so the Qajars could actively manipulate the competition between the different factions of the family. The *khans* were forced to compete among themselves for the titles and the power and wealth that went with them. Any unity between the factions depended largely upon the security of the kinship alliances.

This conflict between brothers, cousins, uncles, and nephews was not a new factor in the tribal system in Iran. The absence of inheritance by primogeniture or of clearly defined rules for the passing of leadership roles had for many years made the ascent to power a matter of contention through the tribe. However, once the Qajar government became part of the alliance system through which the *khans* struggled for position, marriage ties became even more important in keeping peace among the leading families. The *khan* most able to form the strongest alliances, especially through marriage, would end up with the most important tribal roles. For although the Qajar shah had the right to grant the title to the *khan* of his choice, he almost always chose the leader with the strongest ties among his people. It would have made little sense to name an *ilkhan* that the tribesmen would not follow. The value and influence of the women of Bibi Maryam's class grew as the rivalry made their mediation essential to the peace and unity of the tribes.

By the time of the constitutional revolution of 1906–11, the ability of the women to mediate disputes had become even more important. The Bakhtiyari *khans* were drawn into the war between the royalists, who supported the absolute power of the shah, and the nationalists, who wanted the constitution restored. In 1906, a revolution had forced the Qajar monarch to agree to a parliamentary system of government. The shah died a short time later, and his son, Muhammad Ali Shah (1907–9), set out to revoke the agreement. The Bakhtiyari *khans* joined forces with the nationalists in 1909 to reinstate the constitution and force the shah to step down in favor of his young son, Ahmad. The efforts of the Bakhtiyari *khans* were successful, and they became known as the heroes who saved the constitution, in large part due to the efforts of the women.

As part of the plan to unseat Muhammad Ali Shah, the supporters of the constitution asked the paramount chief of the Bakhtiyari, Najaf Quli Khan, to march on Isfahan and take over the governorship from the Qajar prince who held the office. From Isfahan the Bakhtiyari tribesmen marched to Tehran and with the help of a tribal army from the north defeated the troops of the shah. The plan was almost spoiled by Khusrow Khan, a half brother of the *ilkhan*. Khusrow Khan had for years sought to persuade the shah to make him *ilkhan* in place of his half brother Najaf Quli Khan. When he learned of the plot to take Isfahan, Khusrow Khan reported it to the Qajar governor and asked the court to make him *ilkhan* if he, rather than his brother, succeeded in capturing Isfahan.

When it became known that Khusrow Khan had decided to mount a challenge to the authority of Najaf Quli Khan, the women stepped in to resolve the conflict. From her home in the tribal district of Chahar Mahal, Bibi Sahab Jan, the wife of Najaf Quli Khan, wrote letters to her powerful brother, Ibrahim, the oldest son of Reza Quli Khan, and also to the wives of several of the other *khans*, urging them to help her husband. By the time Najaf Quli Khan reached Isfahan, the city had already been secured for him by Ibrahim. Khusrow Khan was unable to gather tribal support for his cause, and he joined the *ilkhan* in the march to Tehran to depose the shah.

It is interesting to note that as long as the disputes were settled through kinship and marriage there was very little physical violence or loss of life among the families of the Bakhtiyari leaders. Khusrow Khan offers a case in point; even though he was a known troublemaker, his half brother did not long consider him an enemy. In the same way, another Bakhtiyari *khan*, Luft Ali Khan, of the Hajji Ilkhani branch of the family, fought for the royalist cause in the revolution, against the forces of his brothers and cousins who supported the constitution. When the fighting ended he was immediately accepted back into the family and was later named *ilbeg* and governor of the district of Kerman.

Throughout the constitutional revolution and civil war the ties of kinship, held together primarily by the women, were very effective in helping to settle disputes among the tribal factions. With the *khans* away from home, women's roles as partners of their husbands and power brokers for their sons had grown stronger. Many of the leading *bibis* followed the news of the nationalist movement in Iran with keen interest, because their husbands and sons were involved in the political struggles.

It is commonly acknowledged that the influence of the Bakhtiyari *khans* in Iranian politics reached its high point during the civil war. Not so well known is that the influence of their women also reached its apex during these times of nationalist struggles. The *khans* depended on kinship alliances to keep harmony in the tribal homeland. However, it soon became evident that blood and marriage ties would no longer be enough to check the growing disunity among the tribal factions. During the years just preceding the civil war a new element entered the alliance of the Bakhtiyaris. The British, who had been active in Iran on a limited basis for more than a century, increased their commercial and political efforts. They sought alliances with the tribal leaders, much the same as the Qajar shahs had done fifty years before. They hoped to be able to use the tribal *khans* to help make the southern part of the country safe for British commercial pursuits. The Bakhtiyari had sought to find a European ally for some years. Husayn Quli Khan had realized that a powerful outside ally, as well as extensive kinship and marriage ties, was essential to holding power within the tribe.

After the death of Husayn Quli Khan at the hands of his Qajar supporters, many of the Bakhtiyari *khans* began to look more closely at the possibilities of seeking support from a European power. They were well aware that the British had proven unwilling to help the Bakhtiyari leader Muhammad Taqi Khan in his dispute with the Qajars in 1840; however, British interest in the tribal lands stepped up after 1901, when the British began to drill for oil in the southern part of the country. In 1907 oil was discovered in the Bakhtiyari lands, and in 1913 the British navy converted all its ships from coal to oil. These developments increased Britain's stakes in Iran, and soon the British legation supplanted the shah's government as the most significant power in the tribal area.

In the early years of British commercial penetration, the European agents had worked through the Qajar government to try to insure the security of the trade routes in the south. This led to conflict between the Qajar shahs and the tribal leaders, and did not bring safety to the trade routes. After the oil drilling began, the British began to usurp the authority of the central government and signed separate agreements with the leading chiefs of the Bakhtiyari to guard and maintain the roads through the tribal lands; in return the *khans* were promised shares of the oil revenues and money to pay for the road guards.

The younger *khans* were also anxious to become part of the European commercial and political power. Contracts to guard the drilling sites and the oil pipeline as well as the roads leading to the fields created new wealth and status. At a time when many of the leading *khans* were away fighting for the nationalist causes in the capital, lesser *khans* were busy vying for the money offered by the British oil company. Rivalry and jealousy had increased within the Bakhtiyari noble family as the leading *khans* were given positions of authority as members of parliament and as governors of the provincial cities. The lesser *khans* left at home in the tribal areas felt that they were not getting a fair share of the wealth that these positions offered. The young *khans* saw the alliances with the British as a chance to move up in the power structure.

The Bakhtiyari leaders who were paid to guard the roads were unable to control the situation. The *khans* not only failed to stop the raids by rival tribes; they also lost control of the situation within the Bakhtiyari tribes. While some Bakhtiyari tribesmen acted as guards, others robbed caravans and cut off supplies to the British oil fields to the west of Isfahan, making it difficult for their leaders to collect the fees promised by the British.

The problem of tribal rivalry became more intense after 1913 when the leading *khans* suddenly ended their political role in Tehran. When the fighting was over, the Iranian nationalist leaders, who were anxious to use the tribal forces to overthrow the shah, found it difficult to deal with the Bakhtiyari *khans* once they became part of the government. After the parliamentary government was firmly established, the nationalist cause split along conservative and liberal lines. The Bakhtiyari approach to politics had always been pragmatic, and the *khans* were unsuited for the ideological struggles that went on in the Iranian capital in the years following the civil war. They withdrew from their positions in the parliament and returned to their tribal homes.

The return of the leaders to the tribal lands did not put an end to the disunity among the *khans* of the ruling family. The British at first found it to their advantage to continue the Qajar policy of causing dissension in the leadership by playing one *khan* against another. In this way they could force the tribesmen to work for less money. Later, however, they found that they could not control the chaos caused by the competition among the factions. Robbery and raiding by the group out of favor with the British made it impossible for the *khans* who were hired to keep peace in the area. From the period following the civil war to the end of World War I, the roads in the southern part of the country were shut down. Trade goods could not be carried with any regularity throughout the area. This served only to worsen the miserable conditions caused by a downturn in the world economy.

The Qajar government refused to help the British control the Bakhtiyari *khans*. The central government was suspicious of British efforts to recruit the tribal leaders as partners in their commercial endeavors. The Qajars were not strong enough to keep the Europeans out of the area, and they feared that separate treaties between the British and the tribal groups of Iran would exclude the monarchy from the economic picture. World War I exacerbated the problems of the Bakhtiyari tribal factions. Anti-British feeling ran high, as the European power was blamed for the poor conditions and anarchy in the south. German agents actively recruited among the southern tribes, and the leading *khans* were attracted by the prospect of help from another European power to block British dominance of trade and oil rights in the south. By the outbreak of the war, it was not certain which side the tribal leaders would support. Though the Qajar government declared the country neutral, several of the Bakhtiyari leaders openly gave aid to the German-led Turkish forces. Other *khans* remained on the side of the British. The split in tribal loyalties increased the already wide divisions within the tribal leadership structure. Ironically many of the Swedish officers who in 1911 had been brought to Iran at the urging of the British oil company chose to join the tribal factions who supported the German agents against the British.

The women were forced to watch the anarchy grow as the men of the Bakhtiyari were used by yet another group who sought to gain power in Iran. First the shahs, then the nationalist reformers, and finally the British made agreements with the *khans,* yet none were able to enforce the agreements. The divisions that came to the tribe after the discovery of oil were much more serious than any before. The women's roles as administrators and mediators became less important after oil was discovered on the Bakhtiyari land. The land rents and revenues collected on the estates were no longer the predominant sources of wealth. The large amounts of foreign capital involved in the oil fields altered forever the social and political conditions in the tribal lands.

The nature of the tribal conflict was altogether different after the British government, as outside enforcing power, claimed the right to name the *ilkhan* and *ilbeg* of the tribes. As has already been pointed out, before there was little violence involved in settling disputes, and even challenges like the one put forth in 1909 by Khusrow Khan were solved without bloodshed. In 1916, however, the *ilkhan* and *ilbeg* named by the British asked the Europeans for military protection for their trip back home, out of fear that the other *khans* would kill them. The conflicts by that time were far beyond the ability of the Bakhtiyari to settle through traditional kinship and marriage ties.

It is not improbable that many of the *bibis* hoped for a German victory in the war. A victory by the Central Powers offered hope of breaking the grip of British oil wealth that controlled Bakhtiyari society. In this context Bibi Maryam's actions can be understood historically.

Wilhelm Wassmuss did reach Isfahan in the fall of 1916, but he did not succeed in capturing the city or the British oil fields to the east. He continued to avoid capture until the spring of 1918, and many of the Bakhtiyari and other tribal people in the southern part of Iran joined the pro-German cause. Bibi Maryam, along with some of the *khans,* had her property seized, as had been threatened. It is not known where she settled in the years following the war. Her oldest son, Ali Murdan Khan, joined the Russians in the north and managed to come out of the war years with a respected position among the leadership of the Bakhtiyari, probably through his connections with the Russians.

The years immediately following the war saw the complete disintegration of order in the tribal territories throughout Iran. The roads were impassable because of lawlessness, particularly in the south. Disease and famine were especially serious, and many tribespeople died. The Qajars continued their downward spiral in the face of the growing foreign intervention. The Russians were forced to retreat from active involvement in Iranian economic and political affairs as a result of the Bolshevik revolution in 1917. The British, however, persisted in trying to work with the Qajars and the Bakhtiyari to protect the oil fields. The Anglo-Persian agreement of 1919 was rejected by the government, and nationalist anti-British feelings ran high throughout the rural and urban areas.

When Reza Khan seized power in 1921, he was welcomed by many Iranians, including some of the tribal peoples. The Bakhtiyari soon learned that he was no different than the Qajars. The settling of the tribes became a top priority of the new Pahlavi shah. Although Reza Shah used anti-British sentiment to secure power, once he was installed he allowed the new Anglo-Persian oil company to lease the Bakhtiyari lands. The tribesmen were ordered to turn in their rifles, and the migration routes were closed to nomadic herdsmen. These measures resulted in a revolt of both the Bakhtiyari and the Qashqa'i in 1929. This rebellion, known as the battle of Safid Desht, was quickly and brutally put down. A major hero of the battle of Safid Desht imprisoned and later executed in 1934 was Ali Murdan Khan, the oldest son of Bibi Maryam.

## A NOTE ON SOURCES

Bibi Maryam's life, like that of many Middle Eastern women, is little known. She appears briefly in Elizabeth N. Ross, *A Lady Doctor in Bakhtiari Land* (London: Leonard Parsons, 1921), and in Christopher Sykes, *Wassmus, "The German Lawrence"* (London: Longmans, Green and Co., 1936). In Persian, the main sources are Hajji Khusraw Khan, *Sardar Zafar Bakhtiyari* (Tehran: Intisharat-i Farhangsara, 1362/1983); and Iskandar Khan Ukkashah, *Zaygham al-Dawlah Bakhtiyari* (Tehran: Intisharat-i Farhangsara, 1365/1986).

## SUGGESTIONS FOR FURTHER READING

The history of the relationship between the Bakhtiyari, the Qajars, and the British has been fatally contaminated by the language of the nineteenth-century "Great Game of Asia," as I discovered in my master's thesis in history, "The Bakhtiyari, the Qajars, and the British in the Great Game of Asia" (University of California, Santa Cruz, 1990). There is much, accordingly, to redo.

For the British perspective see Edward G. Browne, *The Persian Revolution of 1905–1909* (London: Frank Cass & Co., 1910); id., *A Year amongst the Persians* (Cambridge: Cambridge University Press, 1926); George N. Curzon, *Persia and the Persian Question*, 2 vols. (New York: Barnes and Noble, 1892); David Fraser, *Persia and Turkey in Revolt* (London: William Blackwood and Sons, 1910); Hermann Norden, *Under Persian Skies* (Philadelphia: MacRae, Smith Co., 1928); Morgan W. Shuster, *The Strangling of Persia* (New York: Century Co., 1912); Percy Sykes, *A History of Persia* (London: Macmillan, 1915); Arnold Wilson, *S.W. Persia: Letters and Diary of a Young Political Officer, 1907–1914* (London: Oxford University Press, 1942).

On the history of tribes in southern Iran, see Gene R. Garthwaite, *Khans and Shahs: A Documentary Analysis of the Bakhtiyari in Iran* (London: Cambridge University Press, 1983); id., "Khans and Kings: The Dialectics of Power in Bakhtiyari History," in *Modern Iran: The Dialectics of Continuity and Change*, ed. Michael Bonine and Nikki Keddie (Albany: State University of New York Press, 1981), 159–72; and Leonard Helfgott, "Tribalism as a Socioeconomic Formation in Iranian History," *Iranian Studies* 10 (1977): 36–58. Travel and eyewitness accounts about life among the Bakhtiyari (in addition to Ross) in the early twentieth century include Paul E. Case, "I Become a Bakhtiari," *National Geographic*, (January–July 1946, 325–58, and the classic by Merian C. Cooper, *Grass* (New York: G. P. Putman's Sons, 1925).

For some anthropological studies of pastoralism in Iran see, among others, Fredrik Barth, *Nomads of South Persia* (Oslo: Universitetsforlaget, 1964); Lois Beck, *The Qashqa'i of Iran* (New Haven: Yale University Press, 1986); id., "Women among the Qashqa'i Nomadic Pastoralists in Iran" in *Women in the Muslim World*, ed. Lois Beck and Nikki Keddie (Cambridge, Mass.: Harvard University Press, 1978); Richard Tapper, ed., *The Conflict of Tribe and State in Iran and Afghanistan* (New York: St. Martin's Press, 1983); id., *Pasture and Politics* (New York: Academic Press, Inc., 1979).

On the political history of modern Iran, see Firuz Kazemzadeh, *Russia and Britain in Persia, 1864–1914: A Study in Imperialism* (New Haven: Yale University Press, 1968); Nikki R. Keddie, *Roots of Revolution: An Interpretative History of Modern Iran* (New Haven: Yale University Press, 1981); Ann K. Lampton, *Landlord and Peasant in Persia* (London: Oxford University Press, 1953); Robert A. McDaniel, *The Shuster Mission and the Persian Constitutional Revolution* (Minneapolis: Bibliotheca Islamica, 1974); and Donald N. Wilbur, *Iran: Past and Present*, 9th ed. (Princeton: Princeton University Press, 1981).

# PART TWO

# Colonial Lives

# TEN

# The Shaykh and His Daughter: Coping in Colonial Algeria

*Julia Clancy-Smith*

The vitality of popular religion in the Algerian countryside was one of the features of North African culture that was most noted by nineteenth-century European observers. The marabouts (in Arabic, *murabit*), as those of the popularly venerated saintly lineages were called, were the focus of devotion of large numbers of rural people, who saw in them repositories of charisma, or *baraka* as it is called in Arabic. The blessing of a saint was believed to cure illness, revive sinking family fortunes, or cause barren women to conceive a male child. Marabouts were of many different kinds. They sometimes combined their saintly status with claimed descent from the Prophet or with the headship of a Sufi religious brotherhood, or *tariqa*. Some had strictly local clienteles, while others attracted the devout from all over Algeria.

The marabouts played a leading role in resistance to the French during the period of the conquest (1830–71). They helped organize, inspire, and lead the various piecemeal efforts of rural Algerians to oppose French colonial rule. The most famous marabout was Amir Abd al-Qadir, who, although of urban origin, traded on his religious prestige and his headship of the Qadiriya Sufi *tariqa* to rally the support of the tribes in western Algeria. In the Tellian Atlas of the pre-Saharan steppe, where resources were scarce and charisma was plentiful, rural holy men played an especially important role in resistance activities.*

The end of resistance in the steppe zone in the 1860s and 1870s signaled a change of strategy by the marabouts, who were gradually won over to supporting the colonial order by the liberal distribution of honors and rewards. Their options for further resistance were few, given the superiority of French military technology and French administrative prowess. Among the early

*For a survey see Peter von Sivers, "Rural Uprisings as Political Movements in Colonial Algeria, 1851–1914," *Islam, Politics, and Social Movements*, ed. E. Burke, III, and I. M. Lapidus (Berkeley: University of California Press, 1988), 39–59.

learners of the new game was Muhammad ibn Abi al-Qasim, the shaykh of the *zawiya* of al-Hamil and a leader of the Rahmaniya Sufi *tariqa*.

As Julia Clancy-Smith explains in her contribution, the shaykh took care to keep the French at arm's length so as to avoid compromising himself too much. He also untypically placed a high value on the upgrading of agriculture on his lands, sought to fend off French land grabbers, and adopted an uncharacteristic attitude toward religion, preaching against the cult of the saints and extolling the pursuit of science.[†] In another context, Shaykh Qassam, a Muslim religious leader in Palestine with strong Sufi connections (on whom see the biography below by Abdullah Schleifer), evolved in a rather different direction. Palestinians are still debating how he is to be seen. —ED.

The oasis of al-Hamil is located some twelve kilometers southwest of Bou Saada and situated on the right bank of the wadi that funnels water to date-palm groves below. The village, constructed of dun-colored mud brick, sits amid the barren foothills of the Saharan Atlas, upon a great rose brown mountain. By the late nineteenth century, a Rahmaniya *zawiya* (Sufi establishment) dominated the village and valley below; like other desert Sufi centers of the period, it resembled a fortress more than anything else.

Al-Hamil's importance as a pilgrimage site was due to the presence of the Rahmaniya center, which by then boasted a well-known *madrasa* (theological college) and a fine library containing a number of rare manuscripts that represented a significant portion of Algeria's cultural patrimony. The *zawiya* had been founded in 1863 by Shaykh Muhammad Ibn Abi al-Qasim (1823–97), a venerated Muslim scholar, or *alim* (pl. ulama), as well as a Sufi (mystic) and *wali* (saint). Because of the shaykh's piety, erudition, and unstinting generosity, the al-Hamil *zawiya* commanded an impressive popular following in the region and elsewhere. Muslim pilgrims, scholars, students, and the needy from all over North Africa flocked to the *zawiya*, which provided crucial religious, cultural, and socioeconomic services.

Muhammad Ibn Abi al-Qasim died on 2 June 1897, and a bitter struggle soon erupted in al-Hamil over who was to be his spiritual successor. Despite the village's modest appearance and seeming isolation, the stakes were quite high. Not only did the al-Hamil *zawiya* claim the single largest group of Rahmaniya clients in the department of Algiers, but it also held in various forms property whose net worth was estimated at well over two million francs, not a small fortune for the time. In some

[†]For another such experiment, see Fanny Colonna, "The Transformation of a Saintly Lineage in the Northwest Aures Mountains (Algeria): Nineteenth and Twentieth Centuries," in *Islam, Politics, and Social Movements*, ed. Burke and Lapidus, 81–111.

respects, the quarrel was similar to other disputes over social and spiritual turf that periodically divided North African Sufi orders and elites, particularly after the death of a charismatic shaykh. Indeed, two decades earlier, another powerful North African Sufi brotherhood, the Tijaniya *tariqa*, had split into two warring factions in Algeria during the 1870s over the matter of headship of the order. Open discord among the Tijaniya Sufi elite had caused momentary distress to the French colonial authorities of Algeria since such struggles frequently compromised the country's tenuous political calm. The troubles in al-Hamil were viewed at first in the same light by officials.

However, the uproar provoked by Shaykh Muhammad Ibn Abi al-Qasim's death in 1897 differed in one significant way from other such contests for Sufi hegemony. Leading one powerful Rahmaniya faction centered at al-Hamil was a female saint and Sufi, Zaynab (1850?–1904), who was also the daughter of the deceased shaykh. Opposing Zaynab bint Shaykh Muhammad was her cousin, Muhammad b. al-Hajj Muhammad, who enjoyed the support of the minor Rahmaniya notables and Sufi brothers not allied with Zaynab as well as the backing of local French authorities in Bou Saada. The contest between the two factions eventually reached those at the pinnacle of the colonial hierarchy in l'Algérie Française, including the *procureur général*, the chief official at the Ministry of Justice, and even the governor general himself.

Sidi Muhammad was from the Awlad Laghwini of the Jabal Tastara in the Bou Saada region. His was a minor clan of *shurafa* (sing. *sharif*: those claiming kinship with the Prophet's family). Sharifian descent could be a potent source of socioreligious authority if parlayed in the right manner. In addition, members of Muhammad's clan were credited with founding al-Hamil, which represented another source of local prestige. According to popular lore, the town's existence was associated with a miraculous event that occurred several centuries earlier. Sidi Muhammad's ancestors had caused a stick thrust into arid soil to be transformed into a verdant mulberry tree. This was taken as a sign of the family's supernatural powers. However, the translocal authority the shaykh wielded later in his life was the product of his religious knowledge, good works, and the miracles attributed to him by his numerous followers.

Shaykh Muhammad's early education was quite typical of saintly Sufi figures in North Africa at the time. He studied first in a local *zawiya* and was beginning to learn the Quran by heart when the French army landed at Sidi Ferruch in July 1830. Further studies were undertaken in the Kabylia in northern Algeria at the *zawiya* of the Awlad Sidi Ibn Daud near Akbou, where he mastered Muslim law and theology. Sometime before 1848–49, the shaykh returned to the al-Hamil region, which had long been popularly regarded as a holy place. This part of Algeria was still outside of effective or direct French control, then mainly concentrated in the north, which made the small oasis all the more attractive.

In al-Hamil, Sidi Muhammad founded a *madrasa*, began family life, and was endowed with *karamat*, or the ability to work miracles. For North African society at the time, evidence of supernatural gifts operated both to create and to confirm holiness; thus the saintly personage was at once the cause and consequence of the miracle that he or she performed. Moral probity, *ilm* (knowledge, especially sacred knowledge), and personal piety, ratified by the Prophet's appearance, were virtues demanded of the holy person, who thereby became the object of collective veneration and popular support. By the middle of the past century, Sidi Muhammad was building up a clientele drawn mainly, although not exclusively, from the region of al-Hamil.

The years 1849–50 witnessed major political changes in the upper reaches of the Algerian Sahara and in the fortunes of various branches of the Rahmaniya *tariqa*, which by then counted followers and allied Sufi centers in much of eastern and central Algeria, both north and south. Between 1849 and 1871, many Rahmaniya leaders were drawn into armed confrontations with the French army; all ended in disaster. Humiliation, exile or imprisonment in Christian lands, forced emigration to neighboring Muslim states, and destruction of Sufi centers and property were the rewards of those who opted for collective struggle. During the 1849 uprising near Biskra, Bou Saada was besieged, occupied, and given a permanent garrison to protect the newly created French administrative *cercle* of Bou Saada. In this period, Shaykh Muhammad Ibn Abi al-Qasim remained largely unscathed by the larger, more ominous forces around him, although he obviously drew some important lessons from the experiences of his Sufi peers in the Rahmaniya network elsewhere.

In 1857, he left al-Hamil for the Rahmaniya *zawiya* of Awlad Jalal in the Ziban, located southwest of Biskra, which had just suffered "pacification" at the hands of the French military. There he studied under the direction of a regionally prominent Rahmaniya shaykh, Muhammad al-Mukhtar, who initiated Muhammad Ibn Abi al-Qasim into the order. By the time of Shaykh al-Mukhtar's death in 1862, Muhammad Ibn Abi al-Qasim had become his closest spiritual associate and the inheritor of his *baraka* (spiritual blessing) after his master's death. For a year he even ran the *zawiya*, until the opposition of Shaykh al-Mukhtar's family forced him to return to al-Hamil. There he established an independent Rahmaniya center, using the older *madrasa* as a nucleus. Soon it rivaled the *zawiya* in the Ziban.

Before long a collection of buildings—a family residence, library, mosque, guest house, elementary school, meeting room for Sufi ceremonials, and student lodgings—graced the town of al-Hamil. These attested to the ability of the founder-saint to attract a diverse following as well as the funds (largely in the form of pious offerings) needed to finance a multitude of social and religious services. In fact, Shaykh Muhammad engaged in financial operati. ns for the good of the local Muslim community. Individuals were able to deposit money with him at the *zawiya* for safekeeping, receipts were issued, and account books kept, which suggests the existence of a sort of primitive savings bank. However, in contrast to some other Sufi elites elsewhere in Algeria, there is no evidence that the shaykh ever solicited or received financial subsidies from the colonial regime. Until his death, he maintained his ascetic lifestyle and simple manners, a mode of behavior followed scrupulously by his daughter Zaynab.

For Shaykh Muhammad, one method of cultural survival was redemption through land use, although distance from the main nodes of colonial agriculture was the key element in the *zawiya's* survival. In the region of Bou Saada alone, some nine hundred hectares of land were farmed for the benefit of the al-Hamil *zawiya;* outside the region hundreds of hectares were placed under the *zawiya's* control in the form of pious endowments. Shaykh Muhammad's involvement in the rural economy went far beyond the cultivation of existing arable land. Revenues and offerings were employed to open up new areas for agrarian exploitation by peasant-clients in an era when Algerian cultivators elsewhere were suffering cruelly from the progressive loss of land to settler colonialism.

By the early 1890s several hundred students and scholars were involved in education at the al-Hamil *zawiya* at any given moment; it was visited by between seven thousand and eight thousand pilgrims annually. The curriculum of study offered was surprisingly eclectic, a blending of the "traditional" Maghribi religious education with what might be termed the "classical." In addition to *fiqh* (Islamic jurisprudence), *hadith,* the Quran, and Sufi doctrines, students learned chemistry, mathematics, astrology, astronomy, and rhetoric, subjects that had fallen somewhat out of favor in some rural North African colleges during the past centuries. Muhammad's intellectual prowess in the important discipline of *ilm al-nahw* (grammar) won him the sobriquet "*imam* of the grammarians." Yet his greatest contribution was to remind the community that the pursuit of science was a duty incumbent upon all Muslims, an attitude that harked back to the medieval Islamic era while anticipating the modern reformist movements of the early twentieth century.

Among the shaykh's numerous writings was a treatise that constitutes a remarkable critique of the cult of saints as then practiced in Algeria. In it Muhammad questioned one of the sources upon which his own authority and prestige in the community were based. This suggests that his vision extended beyond the mere maintenance of the cultural status quo to the more daunting task of social regeneration through the acquisition of knowledge.

The steady influx of visitors from all over Algeria and the Maghrib required a permanent staff of some forty-six people to oversee the day-to-day affairs of the Rahmaniya establishment. Once again, the general situation in Algeria in the period contrasts with that in al-Hamil, while also helping to explain the popularity of the Sufi center. From the 1860s on, the rural Muslim population was afflicted by drought, famine, and epidemics that made more precarious an economic existence already seriously compromised by massive land expropriations. At the same time, after 1871 the colonial bureaucracy passed fully into the hands of civilian administrators, who were notoriously parsimonious about extending financial assistance to the beleaguered Muslim population. Thus the relatively thriving state of al-Hamil and its clients offer a striking contrast to conditions elsewhere. Much of the credit for this was due to the postures and strategies adopted by Shaykh Muhammad toward the unpleasant reality of foreign occupation.

North Africans were not the only visitors to Muhammad's *zawiya* in this period, although aside from the presence of the military administration Bou Saada did not attract permanent European settlements. This was naturally a critical factor in Shaykh Muhammad's relative freedom to construct a social space where the impact of asymmetrical power relations was attenuated. The commandant of Bou Saada, however, periodically called upon Shaykh Muhammad. On one occasion in the 1880s, he was accompanied by a group of French ladies, motivated by a mild curiosity in things Muslim and Saharan. During this visit, Sidi Muhammad Ibn Abi al-Qasim showed himself to be a cordial host, displaying an equanimity in the face of European eccentricities that can only be described as remarkable. Not only did the shaykh open the doors of the very private women's quarters to the female visitors, but he also agreed to a formal sit-down luncheon *à la française* at the *zawiya*. One can only wonder at his thoughts as he was seated for two hours, with French women on either side of him for companions, before a table set with the curious culinary implements of European civilization furnished by the delegation. For the first time in his life the shaykh had to maneuver with silverware, sit with women while eating, and engage in polite dinner conversation through an interpreter.

His hospitality earned him the sympathy of the French visitors, thus reinforcing the benevolent attitude of the military commandant, who was a powerful figure in the region's affairs and in those of the *zawiya*. Of this Shaykh Muhammad was painfully aware. In an age when the *régime du sabre* had given way to the more corrosive system of civilian bureaucratic control and cultural conquest, a consummate diplomat like Sidi Muhammad could claim victory in wars waged far from conventional battlefields. Thus his survival was due in no small part to his temperament, which enabled him to deal patiently and skillfully with Europeans.

Nevertheless, in contrast to other Algerian religious notables in the period, Shaykh Muhammad refused to learn French; Zaynab was unversed in French as well. A lack of proficiency in the infidel's language created a subtle sort of cultural distance between the shaykh and those forced to work with him or through him to govern the local populace. Maintaining a balance between rapprochement with and distance from the conqueror was critical for highly visible social intermediaries like Shaykh Muhammad. An overly cozy relationship with the French might erode popular indigenous support, while remoteness could compromise the shaykh's proficiency in wringing concessions for the community from colonial authorities.

In addition, Sidi Muhammad Ibn Abi al-Qasim prudently refused to accept any formal office, honoraria, or even decorations from the regime. This public rejection meant that his reputation remained untarnished, thus assuring the continued support of his constituency. In this he differed from some other religious notables of the period. Seduced by the temptation of minor positions in the administrative system, they frequently saw their followers transfer loyalties to other religious leaders. After enjoying an official post in northern Algeria for three years, which earned him the opprobrium of his clients, a local Rahmaniya figure made the *hajj* to Mecca to atone for his sins and recapture some of his lost socioreligious prestige and popular support.

French authorities rarely indulged in gratuitous praise of Algerian Muslim leaders. Yet Shaykh Muhammad b. Abi al-Qasim was often described as of "great intelligence, vast knowledge, and pure of morals." "His authority," it was said, "stretches from Bou Saada, Djelfa, Boghar, and Biskra to the region of Aumale, Médéa, Tiaret, and Sétif." Such a far-flung spiritual following demanded that the shaykh travel periodically to visit the faithful, confer his blessings, and receive donations in kind or currency. In the places where he had stopped to rest, his clients constructed small shrines (*maqams*) commemorating his holy presence.

One of his last journeys brought him to Maison Carrée, outside of Algiers, in April of 1896. On this occasion Shaykh Muhammad was greeted by some five thousand Muslim Algerians in the course of a single day. During this particular trip Shaykh Muhammad performed one of his most widely publicized miracles—a demonstration of *baraka* that was at the same time a discreet affirmation of powers superior to those claimed by the French masters of Algeria. His followers swore that the shaykh had employed his supernatural gifts to stall the departure of the train in which he had been riding so that he might perform his prayers undisturbed; the mechanics had been powerless to move the train forward until the saint had completed his devotions.

Shaykh Muhammad could not have undertaken travels to visit his numerous affiliated *zawiyas* and followers without the blessing of the colonial regime. By this period many officials were frantic about the supposed threats to the French empire posed by pan-Islam and by politically active Sufi brotherhoods. These apprehensions led authorities to monitor closely the movements of Algerian religious notables. Written permits had to be obtained from the authorities in advance of travel, a privilege that was selectively conferred and frequently refused. Denial of travel permits to uncooperative indigenous leaders loosened the highly personal bonds between Sufi masters and clients, thus undermining Sufi networks that had always been deemed inherently subversive by the French.

The positive attitude of colonial officials toward the al-Hamil establishment and its director—indeed the very prosperity of the family Sufi center—was directly tied to Sidi Muhammad's conscious decision not to oppose France head-on. Outwardly, at least, he maintained an amiable, if reserved, stance toward the regime, eschewed direct involvement in either profane politics or maraboutic squabbles, and even attempted to defuse movements of violent protest, during the revolts of 1864 and 1871, for example. This may perhaps be explained by the fact that as a young man he had witnessed several disastrous rebellions supported or led by Rahmaniya leaders, most notable the Abu Ziyan uprising of 1849 and the subjugation of the Kabylia.

By the eve of his death, Muhammad Ibn Abi al-Qasim was clearly one of the most influential Rahmaniya figures in North Africa. His *zawiya* was rivaled only by an older establishment directed by Sidi Ali Ibn Uthman (d. 1898) in the small oasis of Tulqa in the Ziban (in the region of Biskra). Significantly, the Sufi clan controlling the Rahmaniya center in Tulqa had also opted for accommodation of the colonial order from 1849 onward, a stance that won it the benign neglect of French officials.

While steering clear of contests pitting Muslim against European, the shaykh of al-Hamil risked the disapproval of the colonial order on more than one occasion. The most serious case of mild but determined insubordination was the fact that his house was made accessible to all. Shaykh Muhammad openly provided asylum to refugees from French justice, among them former rebels and leaders of insurrections—for example, the Awlad Muqran and Ibrahim Ibn Abd Allah, implicated in the 1864 revolt. Asylum was traditionally expected of saintly Sufi leaders, whose centers were havens of protection and hospitality in North Africa. To refuse the right of sanctuary to fellow Muslims would have diminished Sidi Muhammad's prestige in the eyes of the community and attenuated his ability to exercise moral persuasion in shaping collective behavior.

For Muhammad Ibn Abi al-Qasim survival was more important than armed struggle. Or more precisely, survival for Muslim Algerian culture represented in and of itself such an immense struggle that violent confrontations with the colonial order gave way to subtler, perhaps more enduring, forms of resistance. Because he perceived the limitations imposed upon him and others like him, Shaykh Muhammad was able to work all the more efficiently within a colonial system of domination that was marginalizing large numbers of people while reinforcing the abusive powers of selected indigenous elites.

As Shaykh Muhammad advanced in years, unease regarding the question of his successor steadily increased in colonial circles. These fears were only partly tied to the internal affairs of the al-Hamil *zawiya* itself. Muhammad Ibn Abi al-Qasim appeared to be grooming his nephew, Muhammad b. al-Hajj Muhammad, for a future leadership role. This he did by presenting his nephew on several occasions to local French officials as well as to those in Algiers. Yet the aging shaykh declined to appoint publicly an associate to succeed him, despite French insistence. On the other hand, the individual most intimately involved in the *zawiya's* day-to-day management was his daughter Zaynab, although few anticipated her audacious behavior prior to 1897. In the eyes of military administrators, the relatively calm political climate prevailing in the area and among Muhammad's followers resulted from his spiritual authority and his public stance toward France. Would the new shaykh be equally well disposed toward the colonial order?

French worries about future trouble within the al-Hamil *zawiya* in the early 1890s can be understood only in relation to a whole constellation of imperial concerns stretching far beyond the Sahara, Algeria, or even the Maghrib. Visions of pan-Islamic plots haunted colonial administrators, both French and British, in Africa and elsewhere at the end of the century, as did older French obsessions with the inherently "dangerous" Darqawa and Sanusiya *tariqas* in Algeria. Since the leaders of the Darqawa and Sanusiya orders in the region sent their children to al-Hamil for education and visited there regularly, the French feared that a weak successor might fall under their influence.

By 1897 the issue of al-Hamil's spiritual direction was a matter of no small consequence, not only for the *zawiya* and its clients, but also for those whose administrative careers depended upon the maintenance of social tranquility and order in the Sahara. This then was the complex political legacy inherited by Zaynab bint Shaykh Muhammad. Zaynab, too, would fight to carry on her father's work. While her father had managed to avoid serious clashes, Zaynab chose to confront the colonial system directly to sustain the religious and social functions so vital for the community's well-being, if not its very existence. She therefore contested that system more vigorously than her father had deemed wise or even necessary.

Information about Zaynab's early years is scanty, and many things can only be posited or deduced from her father's biography. Most of our material comes either from European visitors to al-Hamil, who were often very sympathetic toward her, or from hostile colonial officials during the period of the contested headship of the *zawiya*. In some ways, Zaynab embodies the dilemma of women in other colonial societies structured not only according to gender and class but along "racial" lines as well. She was part of a social order that was doubly patriarchal—colonial and indigenous. Nevertheless, saintliness and the miraculous powers attributed to her after her father's death meant that Zaynab was an extraordinary person, at least in the eyes of the Muslim faithful. Sainthood and special piety placed her outside of the normal boundaries circumscribing female behavior and status in Muslim society. While the French obviously did not subscribe to the same cultural norms, they were reluctant to take any actions against Zaynab that might offend her partisans and lead to political unrest.

Although the exact date of her birth is unknown, it appears that she was born around 1850, soon after Sidi Muhammad had arrived in al-Hamil to found the religious establishment that later grew into a Rahmaniya *zawiya*. Zaynab spent most of her life in the oasis, although she may have been with her father during his years in the Ziban. Raised in the harem (private women's quarters) of the shaykh's residence, Zaynab was educated by Sidi Muhammad, who took his daughter's instruction very seriously. She attained an advanced level of erudition, being well versed in the manuscripts and books housed in the *zawiya's* library, and she later helped keep the accounts of the center's properties. Her erudition was admired by her father's followers and increased the already great prestige she enjoyed in the community as the shaykh's daughter.

Following the custom of endogamy among North African saintly Sufi clans, Sidi Muhammad had taken a number of wives from other maraboutic families; even divorced wives continued to reside in the *zawiya*. The harem housed at least forty women—the shaykh's mother, sister, wives, and a large number of females without male protectors who were entrusted to Sidi Muhammad's care. These women led secluded lives devoted to spiritual exercises, not unlike cloistered nuns. While she had many suitors, Zaynab took a vow of celibacy, a somewhat unusual action since Islam prizes matrimony and family life above all else. Yet for Zaynab, virginity was a compelling source of spiritual authority and social power. It permitted her to devote herself entirely to caring for the destitute, unencumbered by the burdens of domestic chores or child rearing. Zaynab's celibate state also conferred upon her greater freedom of movement in the community, for she was not afraid to show herself to others. Her frail appearance resulted from a lifetime of prayer, fasting, and other forms of asceticism that enhanced her virtuous reputation. One European visitor to the *zawiya* described Zaynab as "a saintly being whose face is marked by smallpox and small tattoos."

It is unknown whether Zaynab actually witnessed the somewhat humiliating departure of her father from the Ziban in 1863, although presumably she knew about the dispute in Awlad Jalal since she would have been thirteen years old at the time. To avoid a similar sort of dispute over succession, her father directed the *qadi* of Bou Saada to establish a family endowment in 1877 after Shaykh Muhammad suffered a heart attack. The document, which was akin to a legally binding will, alienated all of his personal property—houses, fields, gardens, flocks, a mill, the library's manuscripts, etc.—to Zaynab's benefit. Moreover, Zaynab was explicitly mentioned as receiving a part equal to any future male heirs of Shaykh Muhammad, although no sons were ever born (or survived to adulthood). All other female descendants would be accorded only the customary one-half of a male share of property. This departure from the usual inheritance practices dictated by Maliki law indicates the great love and respect accorded to Zaynab by her father. However, the fact that she had renounced the pleasures of marriage meant that she would have no heirs to complicate the matter of inheritance.

Some European sources claim that the shaykh had raised his daughter—in the absence of male offspring—to assume command of the *zawiya* upon his death. However, apparently under intense pressure by local officials, Sidi Muhammad had written a letter to the military command in Bou Saada only two months before his death stating that he had chosen Muhammad b. al-Hajj Muhammad, his nephew, as his spiritual successor. It is uncertain whether Zaynab knew about this letter at the time. She later used the letter as the main basis for her grievances against French authorities in Bou Saada.

No sooner had Shaykh Muhammad been laid to rest than his nephew aggressively asserted his claim to the headship of al-Hamil. Accompanied by several followers, Muhammad b. al-Hajj Muhammad was immediately confronted by a resolute and hostile Zaynab, who publicly refused to acknowledge his authority over the *zawiya*. She forbade the students and *zawiya* personnel from obeying her cousin's orders and denied him access to the center's library, books, and buildings, instituting a sort of lockout by taking possession of the keys. Loss of control over the *zawiya's* material assets signified that Muhammad b. al-Hajj Muhammad also forfeited the spiritual and social perquisites that accompanied that control. Of this, both Zaynab and her cousin were well aware. The confrontation degenerated into a series of brawls in which some of Zaynab's partisans were beaten. Moreover, Muhammad b. al-Hajj Muhammad went so far as to attempt to shut Zaynab up in the harem against her will. A desperate act by a desperate man, this unsuccessful stratagem only brought disgrace upon the pretender and caused Zaynab to go on the offensive.

The conflict soon widened. Zaynab sent letters to Rahmaniya members all over the Bou Saada region denouncing her cousin. She accused Muhammad b. al-Hajj Muhammad of putting forward spurious claims to succeed her father. She claimed that local French officials had forced her father to nominate her cousin as his successor at a time when his health was failing. She also informed the French authorities of her cousin's untoward behavior, demanding that they curb his injustice and thievery and reminding them of her father's "devotion to France and public order."

Zaynab's bold actions had repercussions not only among the numerous Sufi clients directly attached to her father's center but also among other independent Rahmaniya *zawiyas* in the Sahara. Several of the region's powerful tribes split into two groups—one was pro-Zaynab, and the other joined her opponents. While information is lacking about the bases of tribal support for either of the contestants, it should be noted that tribal groups customarily split into two factions whenever they were confronted by politico-religious struggles of this nature. In addition, the Rahmaniya shaykhs of the Tulqa Sufi center sought to gain some advantage from the quarrel by wooing religious clients away from the al-Hamil establishment, apparently with some success.

Finally, while some of Shaykh Muhammad's followers regarded Zaynab's cousin as an acceptable successor, their great respect for Zaynab prevented them from breaking with her. The shaykh's daughter bore a striking physical resemblance to Sidi Muhammad; her carriage and mannerisms recalled those of the deceased saint. More important, many believed that she had inherited her father's *baraka;* awe came to be mixed with reverence for her person. An uneasy stalemate ensued.

French officials were stunned and infuriated, since they had anticipated that Muhammad b. al-Hajj Muhammad would assume control of the *zawiya* unopposed. On the eve of his death, the shaykh had taken his nephew on trips to Bou Saada to meet with colonial officers. This was interpreted as a sign of his favor. When Zaynab's opposition to her cousin became known, officials strove to limit the damage done by the upstart daughter by offering their full support to her cousin.

Described by military officers as of "average intelligence yet ambitious, haughty, and prone to excess," Zaynab's cousin seemed the most amenable to manipulation by the colonial regime. Moreover, the lack of popular support for Muhammad b. al-Hajj Muhammad among the *zawiya's* numerous inhabitants and clients—he was regarded as avaricious—also meant that he needed the French to exert his authority. In turn, Muhammad b. al-Hajj Muhammad expected the authorities to force Zaynab to yield, something that officials were unwilling, or perhaps unable, to do. This diffidence on the part of those ostensibly in power alienated Zaynab's cousin from his would-be colonial mentors, further complicating the matter of succession.

Zaynab's unexpected behavior provoked a great deal of bitter frustration among local military officers. Dealing with a defiant Muslim woman was a novelty, although by then the colonial regime had rather effective methods for dealing with insubordinate Muslim men. Moreover, Zaynab was a saint and venerated mystic with her own popular following, which rendered the matter all the more delicate. Another element that placed colonial authorities in an awkward position was Zaynab's health. It was common knowledge among the local French authorities that she suffered from a grave nervous condition as well as from chronic bronchitis (perhaps tuberculosis). At first it was calmly assumed that these afflictions would render her more receptive to some sort of compromise. But Zaynab held firm.

The helpless rage expressed in official correspondence by some military personnel led them to evaluate the actions of "the rebellious woman" in a certain way. For example, Commandant Crochard, Zaynab's nemesis, portrayed her as the compliant victim of sinister intrigues within the *zawiya*. According to Crochard's reports, she was exploited by anti-French malcontents who perceived her cousin as hostile to their own political self-interest. "Among [Zaynab's] associates, there are no good men. . . . She is surrounded by people who are untrustworthy . . . capable of the worst excesses. . . . They know well that she can be manipulated," wrote Crochard. Thus her strength was interpreted as the product of female weakness. Such explanations, however, reveal the absence of colonial mechanisms for containing small-scale, nonviolent rebellions, particularly by Muslim women, and French military views of female nature in general.

Zaynab was serenely conscious of the advantages that seeming powerlessness confers, and in turn exploited this tiny breach in the prevailing system of domination. "She [Zaynab] knows that a woman is always treated with circumspection," an official report observed, "and she exploits this in order to embarrass and cause problems for the local [French] authorities whom she sees as favoring her cousin." By this time, her main adversary was Commandant Crochard, whose reports to his superiors became increasingly censorious of Zaynab's personality and behavior as his awareness of his own impotence grew.

With the French in Bou Saada against her, Zaynab cleverly petitioned those at the top of the colonial hierarchy for assistance. In August 1897, she hired a French lawyer, Maurice Ladmiral, to represent her interests in Algiers, and he brought the dispute to the attention of the head of the French judiciary, the *procureur général*. The latter, alarmed by Zaynab's accusations and the dimensions the conflict was assuming, contacted the French governor general and the commander of the province in October 1897. While Ladmiral does not appear to have been a key player in the clash—he and his associate met with Zaynab only on a few occasions—the mere threat of the semiindependent judiciary getting mixed up in the affair caused unease in Algiers.

In laying forth her grievances to those at the top of the political heap, Zaynab revealed a surprising familiarity with the administrative structure of colonial Algeria and its weaknesses. This appears extraordinary since prior to 1897 she had remained largely within the oasis of al-Hamil. However, Zaynab had access to three important sources of information: her father, who traveled often and widely and treated her as a confidant; the political refugees long residing in the *zawiya;* and the thousands of pilgrims and students from all parts of Algeria who had visited over the years, invariably bringing news of conditions outside of al-Hamil. This knowledge of how the colonial order functioned allowed Zaynab to pit French official against French official, thereby enabling her to pursue her father's work of cultural survival.

After the death of Shaykh Muhammad, Zaynab emerged more fully into the public sphere normally reserved for men, in part because of the very opposition of Commandant Crochard, the head of the Bou Saada office. However, it was not necessarily the dictates of gender boundaries that had kept her on the sidelines until 1897, but rather deference for the old shaykh's prestige and authority. Such deferential attitudes were also assumed by subordinate or junior male associates in Sufi orders toward highly respected, older shaykhs. Then too, Zaynab had always moved more freely about in the community due to her saintly status and celibate condition. In order to combat her cousin's claims to succession, Zaynab began to travel widely, visiting not only Rahmaniya notables and local Muslim dignitaries but also French officials, among them her lawyer. She also agreed to meet personally with her bête noire, Crochard, which resulted in several heated confrontations. Finally, Zaynab accepted pious offerings from the hands of the faithful in person, without recourse to a male intermediary, a sure sign that she intended to succeed her father in office.

Zaynab employed every means at her disposal to thwart Commandant Crochard's support for her cousin. The material stakes by this time were considerable, since they included control over the *zawiya's* substantial properties. Increasingly frank, the commandant portrayed Zaynab to his superiors in the following terms: "passionate to the point of hatred, bold to the point of insolence and impudence, very haughty and eager for deferential treatment, she displays in the worst way the qualities of her father; her charity is nothing but extravagance; she does not hesitate to lie or make false accusations to pursue the plan of action that she had in mind."

In concluding his vilification of Zaynab, Crochard gloomily predicted the ultimate ruin of the *zawiya* of al-Hamil and the end to its numerous social services due to the actions of a rebellious woman. Significant to note is that those qualities that were regarded as positive in Zaynab's father—philanthropy and largess, for example—were negative in a recalcitrant female. Crochard reveals his true apprehensions about the contested headship by lamenting that "this behavior of Lalla Zaynab has completely destroyed all that I had labored so hard to construct"—in other words, to arrange for a smooth, untroubled succession after Shaykh Muhammad's death. In late nineteenth-century Algeria, small defiant acts could be as threatening—and effective—as larger, more militant gestures of noncompliance.

Zaynab eventually defeated the combined forces of French officialdom and her cousin. When it became clear that Zaynab would never yield on the matter without the use of force, the authorities in Algiers ordered Crochard to desist; the hapless Muhammad b. al-Hajj Muhammad was relegated to the sidelines for the next seven years. In addition, Zaynab successfully fended off another assault upon her management of the *zawiya* in 1899 that assumed the guise of fraudulent financial claims against the center's assets.

Feeling secure in her position as shaykha, Zaynab had the mosque in al-Hamil rebuilt in 1898, calling in Italian masons to construct a completely new structure, perhaps as a symbol of her hard-won spiritual authority. In part, Zaynab's victory was the consequence of her own determination and tactical skills as well as French powerlessness when confronted by a refractory Muslim woman. The feckless and greedy nature of her cousin also contributed to Zaynab's triumph, since enthusiasm for him was at best lukewarm even among his small cohort of followers. Finally, the backing of colonial authorities may have eroded what little prestige Muhammad b. al-Hajj Muhammad enjoyed in the local community. Nevertheless, Zaynab's father played a role in resolving the dispute by performing a posthumous miracle.

When the struggle over succession was in its most bitter stage, Lalla Zaynab took refuge one day at her father's tomb. There she wept and prayed for hours until nightfall. Alarmed by her absence and emotional state, Zaynab's family and clients gathered at the cemetery and implored her to return to the residence. As Zaynab refused to heed their pleas, the old *imam* (prayer leader) of the *zawiya's* mosque raised his voice to heaven and cried out: "O Lord, come and help us; who thus has inherited your *baraka?*" Immediately all present heard Sidi Muhammad's voice issue from the grave, saying: "It is my daughter, Zaynab, who has inherited my *baraka.*" From that day on, Zaynab's popular following was assured, its ranks swelled by those who had previously been undecided or unconvinced.

There is, however, one more significant, if less articulate, force, in the matter of Zaynab's victory—public opinion and collective consensus—for it was as much Zaynab's clientele, whether from the local community or from the wider Sufi network, that really decided the issue of succession. As stated earlier, Zaynab had inherited from her father a fund of sociospiritual capital that she then enlarged upon through her own piety, chastity, and generosity. Moreover, because *baraka*—that ineffable substance that combined blessings, supernatural powers, and charisma—was highly "contagious" under certain conditions, the struggle between Zaynab and her cousin was in reality over the dead shaykh's *baraka*. It was public recognition of Zaynab bint Shaykh Muhammad's worthiness to inherit her deceased father's *baraka* that settled the dispute, together with the overriding colonial interest in maintaining "public order."

Contrary to French predictions that "the daughter of the marabout by herself will not be able to administer the *zawiya's* vast fortune and holdings dispersed over three Algerian departments," Zaynab's seven-year stewardship of al-Hamil was successful. Threats by the colonial regime to sequester those holdings and incorporate them into the public domain if she refused to relinquish the headship to her cousin remained just that. One knowledgeable European source from the period observed that "Zaynab directed the *zawiya* with a quite remarkable mystical vigor," despite her deteriorating health and the taxing burden of caring for several hundred indigent *zawiya* clients per day. By 1899, local military officials reluctantly admitted that under Zaynab's direction the fortune left by her father remained intact and "the gardens around al-Hamil are flourishing, the farmland cultivated, and the numerous flocks owned by the *zawiya* are in a prosperous state."

Zaynab was not only the undisputed administrative head of the *zawiya* but also its spiritual leader. As her father had done previously, Zaynab initiated members into the Rahmaniya *tariqa* with her own hands. The number of annual pilgrims to al-Hamil remained as high as in the pre-1897 period, and the *madrasa* continued to offer advanced instruction to hundreds of students at a time. When Muhammad b. al-Hajj Muhammad's attempts to rally support to himself failed miserably, he earned the derision of the Muslims and the snubs of the colonial bureaucracy. Finally, it was once more the *vox populi*—the public veneration of ordinary people—that confirmed Zaynab's steadily growing spiritual authority, which extended far beyond the *cercle* of Bou Saada, Wherever she paused to pray during her travels in the region, the faithful immediately erected simple shrines to commemorate her visit and mark off the sacred space, as they had done for her father.

On 18 November 1904 Zaynab succumbed to the disease that had progressively undermined her health. She was buried the next day with an immense crowd in attendance. Her body was laid alongside her father's in the family cemetery—still a popular pilgrimage site to this day. Her cousin could at last assume the long-coveted headship of the *zawiya* of al-Hamil—or so he thought. However, Zaynab died intestate, almost certainly intentionally, leaving neither an officially nominated successor nor a valid, undisputed will. The result was to postpone the succession for a year while complex judicial inquiry proceeded through the courts. Eventually the case ended up before the civil tribunal in Algiers, pitting the would-be Rahmaniya shaykh against fellow Muslim jurists.

When Muhammad b. al-Hajj Muhammad finally took over the Sufi establishment the worst had happened. During the lengthy court proceedings, the *zawiya* had lost control over a good portion of its land and flocks, thereby forfeiting some of its material assets and with these part of its sociospiritual prestige. By 1910 the economic situation of the *zawiya* was so precarious that the new shaykh petitioned the French government to borrow money from the Société de prévoyance, falling into the very trap that Zaynab and her father had scrupulously avoided—financial dependence upon, and by extension moral subjugation to, the European masters of Algeria. By the eve of the Great War, however, colonial officials were no longer terribly preoccupied with rural Sufi leaders on the edge of the Sahara, since the locus of popular protest had moved into the cities. Muhammad b. al-Hajj Muhammad's requests for credit advances were regarded more as a minor irritation than as an opportunity to influence the course of Muslim politics.

Viewed in the long term, Zaynab's victory was a Pyrrhic one. Fearing that her cousin would squander the *zawiya's* resources, she fought successfully to retain full management of al-Hamil's spiritual and mundane affairs. By dying intestate, she exposed the Sufi establishment to a debilitating legal quarrel that ultimately led to direct French intervention in the internal affairs of the *zawiya*. Yet it could be argued that al-Hamil's social importance would have declined anyway due to the emergence of new urban-based political and religious forces after World War I, among them the reformist ulama of Shaykh Ben Badis. Nevertheless, the Algerian nationalist movement and particularly the modernist ulama led by Shaykh Abdulhamid Ben Badis in the 1930s were, perhaps more than they cared to admit, the cultural heirs of people like the shaykh and his daughter.

## A NOTE ON SOURCES

*Archives d'Outre-Mer,* Aix-en-Provence, *Archives du Gouvernement Général de l'Algérie,* carton 16 H 8, "Notice sur l'ordre des Rahmanya," 28 June 1895, and the report of 1897; carton 16 H 61; and cartons 2 U 20, 21, and 22 of the newly opened *sous-série* 2 U, Fonds de la Préfecture, Département d'Alger, "Culte Musulman."

The work of North African scholars has also been most helpful: Muhammad Ali Dabbuz, *Nahda al-jaza'ir al-haditha wa thawratuha Al-Mubaraka* (Algiers: Imprimerie Coopérative, 1965), 52–75; Ahmed Nadir, "La fortune d'un ordre religieux algérien vers la fin du XIX siècle," *Le mouvement social* 89 (1974): 59–84; Youssef Nacib, *Cultures oasiennes, Bou Saada: Essai d'histoire sociale* (Paris: Publisud, 1986); and Muhammad al-Hafnawi, *Ta'rif al-Khalaf bi rijal al-Salaf* (Tunis: Al-maktaba al-'atiqa, 1982).

A different version of this paper will appear in Nikki R. Keddie and Beth Baron, eds., *Shifting Boundaries: Women and Gender in Middle Eastern History* (New Haven: Yale University Press, 1991).

## SUGGESTIONS FOR FURTHER READING

In addition to the author's dissertation, "The Saharan Rahmaniya: Popular Protest and Desert Society in Southeastern Algeria and the Tunisian Jarid" (Ph.D. diss. University of California, Los Angeles, 1988), the reader is referred to the following works.

On Sufism and popular Islam in colonial Algeria, Octave Depont and Xavier Coppolani's *Les confréries religieuses Musulmanes* (Algiers: Jourdan, 1897) is the classic work. Also Jamil Abun-Nasr, *The Tijaniyya, A Sufi Order in the Modern World* (Oxford: Oxford University Press, 1965), 77–81.

On Islam and resistance see the contrasting studies by Fanny Colonna, Julia Clancy-Smith, and Peter von Sivers in *Islam, Politics, and Social Movements,* ed. Burke and Lapidus.

Isabelle Eberhardt is an important source on al-Hamil. See her diary, *The Passionate Nomad: The Diary of Isabelle Eberhardt,* translated by Nina de Voogt and edited with an introduction by Rana Kabbani (London: Virago Press, 1987); and the biography by Cecily Mackworth, *The Destiny of Isabelle Eberhardt* (London: Quartet Books, 1977).

French policy is described in Charles-André Julien, *Histoire de l'Algérie contemporaine*, vol. 1 (Paris: P.U.F., 1970); Charles-Robert Agéron, *Histoire de l'Algérie contemporaine*, vol. 2 (Paris: P.U.F., 1979); Kenneth Perkins, *Qaids, Captains and Colons: French Military Administration in the Colonial Maghrib, 1884–1934* (New York: Africana Publication Co., 1981); David Prochaska, *Making Algeria French* (Cambridge: Cambridge University Press, 1990); Yvonne Turin, *Affrontements culturels dans l'Algérie coloniale, écoles, médecines, religion, 1830–1880* (Paris: Maspero, 1971).

# ELEVEN

# Izz al-Din al-Qassam:
# Preacher and *Mujahid*

*Abdullah Schleifer*

Until recently Shaykh Izz al-Din al-Qassam was but little known outside of Palestinian circles, although he was one of the first Palestinian nationalists and an early practitioner of armed struggle. This is because the historiography of the 1936–39 revolt has emphasized the central role of urban elite politicians in the politics of the period, notably the part played by al-Hajj Amin al-Husayni, the *mufti* of Jerusalem, in the revolt.

Al-Husayni was the head of the Supreme Muslim Council and of the Arab Higher Committee, two of the leading Palestinian organizations involved in the events of the period. In stressing the role of al-Husayni and other elite politicians, historians have implicitly argued that Palestinian nationalism was essentially similar to the secular nationalisms that emerged elsewhere in the Arab world in the interwar years. Thus the significance of al-Qassam was not well understood.

The focus has now begun to shift to the role of the peasantry in the 1936–39 revolt, and a much more complicated picture has begun to emerge. In the new picture, Zionist settlers, British officials, and Palestinian elite politicians share the stage with displaced and disgruntled peasants and villagers. The struggle between British imperialism, Jewish nationalism, and an emerging Palestinian nationalism can be seen as only one aspect of a complex pattern of conflict. Secular nationalist slogans, it now appears, had a limited audience among the displaced peasants and rural migrants who crowded the cities of mandatory Palestine. Peasant anger was fueled not only by Zionist land policies but also by the oppression of Palestinian landlords. Appeals couched in the language of Islam found a wider following among the quasi-literate Muslim peasants who formed the majority of the rural population.*

The life of al-Qassam helps to explain how many Palestinians came to be involved in politics during the interwar years. It brings together strands of

---

*On the evolving literature, see Ted Swedenburg, "The Role of the Palestinian Peasantry during the Great Revolt," in *Islam, Politics, and Social Movements*, ed. E. Burke, III, and I. M. Lapidus (Berkeley: University of California Press, 1988), 169–203.

Islamic radicalism grounded in the Salafiya Islamic reform movement, as well as political notions forged in the pan-Islamic politics of the late Ottoman Empire.

With al-Qassam we encounter an individual deeply imbued with what we might wish to call the Islamic social gospel and who was struck by the plight of Palestinian peasants and migrants. Al-Qassam's pastoral concern was linked to his moral outrage as a Muslim at the ways in which the old implicit social compact was being violated in the circumstances of British mandatory Palestine. This anger fueled a political radicalism that drove him eventually to take up arms and marks him off from the Palestinian notable politicians.

Abdullah Schleifer's biography makes clear that while al-Qassam has been claimed as a Palestinian secular nationalist hero, the Islamic dimension of his political life ultimately best explains his actions—but it does so in ways that make him less easily co-optable by today's Islamic militants. Because he was one of the first to elicit a deep response from ordinary Palestinians, al-Qassam's life can serve to illuminate the complex roots of Palestinian opposition to the British and the Zionists in the interwar period. —ED.


On 21 November 1935 a three-column front-page headline in the *Jerusalem Post* announced that a British constable had been killed and another injured in a battle near Jenin with Arab gunmen described as "bandits" and "brigands." According to the official statement issued by the British authorities and quoted in full by the *Post,* "among the bandits known to have been killed were: Shaykh Izz-ed-Din al-Qassam . . . who disappeared from his house in Haifa early this month and was the organizer of the band."

Both British and Zionist intelligence circles were in fact better informed. They knew Shaykh Izz al-Din was the president of the Young Men's Muslim Association (YMMA), a popular preacher at the Istiqlal mosque near the Haifa railroad yards, and a roving marriage registrar for the Haifa Islamic (Sharia) court. Al-Qassam had been under surveillance, had been brought in for questioning, and had been cautioned against his habit of publicly preaching *jihad* against both the British occupation and the Zionist colonization over the preceding decade. He was also suspected of having organized a series of clandestine armed attacks against Jewish settlers and British officials in and around Haifa beginning in the early 1930s, but for lack of evidence the authorities did not prosecute him.

Convinced that his arrest was imminent and that his capture could jeopardize the secret organization he had carefully built over the previous decade, al-Qassam moved up into the mountains near Yabud between Nablus and Jenin early in November. He took only twelve men from Haifa, those most openly identified with him. After one of his patrols had killed a Jewish policeman serving in the British force in an accidental encounter, he divided his group to evade the inevitable pursuit better. Nevertheless al-Qassam's group was discovered and surrounded by a large force of British police and soldiers. Called upon to surrender, al-Qassam told his men to die as martyrs, and he opened fire. Al-Qassam's defiance and the manner of his death (which seemed to stun the traditional leadership) electrified the Palestinian people. Thousands forced their way past police lines at the funeral in Haifa, and the secular Arab nationalist parties invoked his memory as the symbol of resistance. It was the largest political gathering ever to assemble in mandatory Palestine.

Five months later, a band of Islamic patriots (*mujahidin*), led by one of al-Qassam's companions in the flight from Haifa, ambushed a group of Jewish travelers in northern Palestine. In the weeks that followed, peasant guerrilla bands and urban commandos led by other Qassamiyun (as his followers were called) sprang up across Palestine. The 1936 Palestinian rebellion had begun.

The biography of al-Qassam serves to frame a story that enables us to understand better the political mobilization of the Palestinian peasantry and urban migrants who had been displaced by British policies, Zionist land acquisition schemes, and the depression.

Izz al-Din ibn Abd al-Qadar ibn Mustapha ibn Yusuf ibn Muhammad al-Qassam was born in Jebla in the Latakia district of Syria in 1882 (A.H. 1300). His grandfather and granduncle were prominent shaykhs of the Qadari Sufi order, or *tariqa* (pl. *turuq*), who came to Jebla from Iraq. His father, Abd al-Qadar, held a post with the Sharia court during Turkish rule but was better known as the local leader of the Qadari *tariqa* in Jebla. However, Shaykh Abd al-Malik al-Qassam, nephew of al-Qassam and the *imam* of a mosque in Jebla, says that Abd al-Qadar also followed the Naqshbandiya Sufi order, which played a noticeably militant role in resisting colonial conquest in nineteenth-century Syria, as well as in India, Turkestan, and the Caucasus, while reaffirming the religious orthodoxy of the *turuq*.

Al-Qassam, who followed the Hanifi school of jurisprudence, studied as a boy with a well-known *alim* (Islamic teacher) from Beirut, Shaykh Salim Tayarah, who had settled in Jebla and taught there at the Istambuli mosque. Shortly after the turn of the century, al-Qassam left Jebla for Cairo to study at al-Azhar. There he studied with the well-known Salafi teacher Muhammad Abduh. This was probably between 1902 and 1905 (though the exact chronology is obscure). During his stay in Cairo he also met another well-known Salafi, Muhammad Rashid Rida, like himself a Syrian. All reports agree that he returned as an *alim* from al-Azhar in 1909.

While a student in Cairo, al-Qassam became friends with a fellow classmate, Izz al-Din Alam al-Din al-Tanukhi, the son of a Damascus notable. Their friendship was to last until Qassam's death in 1935. Even at this time his piety and self-sufficiency were noted by fellow students. One example was related by al-Tanukhi in his reminiscences to al-Qassam's son some years later:

> We were studying in al-Azhar together, and we were short of money. I asked the shaykh, "What do we do now for funds?" The shaykh asked al-Tanukhi what he could do, and al-Tanukhi said he could cook *nammurah*, an Arab sweet. Al-Qassam told al-Tanukhi to cook the sweets, and he would sell them. Al-Tanukhi's father was visiting Cairo at the time, and, passing by al-Azhar, he saw them together selling the sweets and asked his son what he was doing. Al-Tanukhi answered with some embarrassment, "This is what al-Qassam told me to do," and his father replied, "He taught you to be self-sufficient."

The story is instructive, for it is among the earliest of many anecdotes in which al-Qassam practices and encourages self-sufficiency as one of the moral elements along with humility, courage, and asceticism for training in *thabit* (steadfastness). This was understood by his disciples to mean the willingness to sacrifice and the practice of moral-ethical behavior. Al-Qassam was sensitive to what he perceived as the backwardness and moral debasement of the Muslims of his day. He believed that the only way Muslims could liberate themselves from foreign occupation (which was to become all but universal after World War I) and to progress would be by the revival of Islam.

In 1909 al-Qassam left Cairo and returned home to Jebla. He brought with him a heightened sense of the threats that faced Islam and of the moral struggle necessary to preserve it. He began teaching at a school maintained by the Qadari *tariqa*, where he not only taught the mystical disciplines of the Qadaris but also gave instruction in the Quran, its commentary and jurisprudence. He also served as *imam* at the Ibrahim Ibn Adham mosque in Jebla.

Al-Qassam undertook an Islamic revival in Jebla based upon the conscientious practice of religious obligations and orthodox voluntary practices. The simplicity of his manner and his good humor marked him off from the beginning. One story that still circulates in Jebla is how an important official came to the town to meet al-Qassam only to find him, to his great shock, eating a simple lunch with the man in charge of stoking the fire at the communal *hammam* (public bath). Similar stories circulate about his later life in Haifa, where he lived simply and with the poor in

a society rapidly dividing along the strict class lines of a modern industrial city, although he was a salaried official of the *waqf*.

At Jebla, al-Qassam devoted himself to moral reform. He encouraged
the community to keep regular prayer, to maintain the Ramadan fast,
and to stop gambling and drinking. His campaign was so successful that
those among the townspeople who were not noticeably pious either reformed or began to conform to Sharia standards in public. Because al-
Qassam had acquired moral authority with the Turkish authorities responsible for the district, he was able to call upon the police in the case
of rare but flagrant violations to enforce Sharia standards within the
town. On a few occasions when he heard that mule trains were moving
alcohol through the district he sent out his disciples to intercept the caravans and destroy the contraband. The religious revival in Jebla allegedly reached such a point that the women would go to the market unveiled on Friday at noon, certain they would encounter no man on the
streets, since every male in Jebla was at prayer.

The family of his classmate al-Tanukhi had been exiled to Turkey by
the Ottoman authorities for suspected Arab nationalist activities, but
there are no indications that al-Qassam himself was ever involved in the
anti-Ottoman Arab national movement. His behavior and the Turkish
assessment would indicate that he was a loyal subject. In September 1911
the Italians invaded Tripolitania (Libya). This act of blatant imperialism
stirred up strong passions among Muslims in the Ottoman Empire.
They struck a special chord with al-Qassam, who was moved to preach
against the Italian invasion and to take up a collection in Jebla to support the combined Turkish-Libyan resistance. He also composed the following chant for the townspeople:

> Ya Rahim, Ya Rahman
> Unsur Maulana as-Sultan
> Wa ksur aadana al-Italiyan
>
> O Most Merciful, O Most Compassionate
> Make our Lord the Sultan victorious
> And defeat our enemy the Italian.

The governor of Jebla attempted to take control of the fund-raising
away from al-Qassam; when the townspeople continued to contribute to
al-Qassam, the governor accused the shaykh of plotting against the Ottomans, but an official investigation vindicated al-Qassam and resulted
in the discharge of the local governor. Exonerated by the authorities, al-
Qassam soon became convinced that fund-raising for the *jihad* against
Italy was not sufficient. In June 1912, while preaching the Friday ser-
mon at the al-Adham mosque in Jebla, al-Qassam called for volunteers
to go fight against the Italians. Many townsmen came forward, but he

only accepted those who already had received Ottoman military training. He also undertook to raise funds to finance the expedition and to provide a modest pension to the families of the *mujahidin* during their absence.

Accompanied by from 60 to 250 *mujahidin* (accounts vary), al-Qassam went to Alexandretta (Iskandarun), expecting the Ottoman authorities to provide them with sea transport to Libya via Alexandria. The same route had been used by Anwar Pasha, Aziz Ali al-Masri, and Abd al-Rahman Azzam, who had already made their way to Libya to participate in the fighting against the Italians in Tripolitania. This, however, was not to be. A new government in Istanbul, mobilizing to meet the closer threat of a war in the Balkans, abandoned the struggle in Libya and came to hasty terms with Italy in mid-October 1912. After waiting at Alexandretta for more than a month, al-Qassam and the Jebla volunteers were ordered to return home by the Ottoman authorities. Some of the money raised for the aborted expedition was used to build a school. The rest was put aside for a time when it would be needed.

When World War I broke out, al-Qassam volunteered for service in the Ottoman army. Although ulama enrolled in the Ottoman army were usually offered assignment in their local town or village to register recruits, al-Qassam refused this offer and requested a military assignment. He was sent to a camp south of Damascus, where he received his training and remained as a chaplain assigned to the garrison.

In the chaos of the Ottoman collapse in the Arab East, with British forces in Syria and a French buildup in Lebanon, al-Qassam returned to Jebla and initiated military training for every able-bodied man in the town. With the funds put aside from the Tripolitania *jihad*, the proceeds from the sale of his property, and donations from local landowners, al-Qassam purchased arms for the Jebla militia. At that time Jebla was part of the "Blue Zone" or "Occupied Enemy Territory North" set aside by the Allies for French occupation. From late 1918 through 1919 French forces moved into the zone and consolidated their positions, while the Arab national movement struggled on in Damascus to establish an independent Syrian kingdom for Amir Faisal.

The period 1918–20 was marked by much turbulence and confusion in the Jebla area. Encouraged by the French, bands of Alawites (a heterodox Shiite group who inhabited the nearby Jabal al-Nusayri) occupied the orchards and farmland outside Jebla as part of a destabilizing move against the Sunni communities in the Latakia district. They were opposed by the Jebla militia organized by al-Qassam. When the Alawites were driven out of the Jebla area, the French quickly moved in. Al-Qassam withdrew along with his closest disciples into the mountains and established a guerrilla base near the village of Zanqufeh on Sahyoun

Mountain. From there he was able to harass French forces and to train his men in military tactics and in the doctrine of *jihad.*

A Sunni notable in the district, Umar al-Bitar, had also taken to the mountains with armed followers to resist the French. He was killed in action, and his followers joined forces with al-Qassam's group. As the French consolidated their hold on the district several large Jebla landowners who had been supporting al-Qassam were pressured by the French to pay their taxes or lose their property. They began to question the wisdom of continuing to fight and eventually gave up. (This experience undoubtedly made al-Qassam much more cautious when years later he began recruiting followers in Haifa.) Finding himself increasingly isolated, al-Qassam abandoned his base and moved toward Aleppo, where he joined forces under the command of Ibrahim Bey Hananu, who had been raiding French forces in northern Syria since May 1920.

In mid-July 1920 French forces pushed past Hananu's fighting forces and occupied al-Shughur Bridge on the road to Aleppo. They demanded (among other conditions in an ultimatum to King Faisal) that the government in Damascus punish the "criminals" resisting the French advance, or they would march on Damascus. Al-Qassam decided to flee. He and his men made their way through French lines with false passports provided by al-Tanukhi and thence by boat to Tartous, Beirut, and Palestine in 1921.

Like many other exiles from French-occupied Syria and Lebanon, al-Qassam settled in Haifa, and joined the teaching staff of Haifa's Islamic school, the Madrasa Islamiya, which had branches throughout the city. Along with other Islamic institutions in the district, the Madrasa Islamiya was supervised and supported by the Jamiat Islamiya, a *waqf* (pious foundation). Supported and directed by Haifa's Muslim notables, the Jamiat was a vehicle for communal self-support and expression for the Muslims of Haifa and the surrounding rural districts. During the British Mandate period it became a meeting ground for Islamic and Arab nationalist opposition to the mandate.

Under its well-known principal, Kamal al-Qassab, an exiled Damascus notable, the Madrasa Islamiya became a radiating center of the Salafiya Islamic modernist movement and of Arab nationalism. Al-Qassab was a friend of Rashid Rida and Shakib Arslan, and he had played a major role in Faisal's short-lived Syrian Arab Kingdom. It was al-Qassab who rallied the Syrian National Congress to confront French claims in Syria directly in March 1920 and who inspired the people of Damascus to seize arms and confront French forces at the battle of Maysalun.

In the early 1920s al-Qassab and al-Qassam became allies in a controversy with some of the Palestinian ulama over the permitted ritual for Islamic funerals. They published a pamphlet denouncing the laxity of officially sanctioned practice and for their pains were denounced by the establishment ulama as Wahhabi heretics—a standard (but ill-founded) accusation in any polemic between the orthodox ulama and the Salafiya. Al-Qassam, who was the pamphlet's chief author, concluded his argument by reproducing Islamic legal opinions (*fatwas*) taken from leading ulama at al-Azhar and in Damascus condemning the practice. Al-Qassam was also opposed to other popular innovations in the practice of Islam, such as the pilgrimage by women to the shrine of Khidr in the foothills of Mount Carmel to sacrifice sheep in gratitude for the recovery of a child from illness or a son's graduation from school. After making sacrifice the women would perform tribal dances around the shrine. Al-Qassam preached in the mosques of Haifa against this superstitious practice, which was opposed to the Sharia.

In the early 1920s al-Qassam met the Algerian Muhammad bin Abd al-Malik al-Alami. Shaykh al-Alami was a special roving leader (*muqaddam*) of the Tijaniya Sufi brotherhood. In the early decades of the twentieth century he established branches of the Tijaniya throughout the Arab East. Al-Alami had a great impact upon al-Qassam and his closest disciples in Haifa. According to Hanifi, only al-Qassam, Hanifi himself, and three others were initiated into the Tijani *tariqa* by al-Alami. It was around this small inner core of Tijani disciples that al-Qassam would build the new movement of Islamic patriots (*mujahidin*).

Over time, some important differences appeared between al-Qassam and al-Qassab. Both shaykhs believed in the inevitability of *jihad* against the colonial occupation of the Muslim world. Where al-Qassab concentrated upon developing a following among middle classes who he believed would lead the masses, al-Qassam found himself more and more drawn to the uneducated working classes. They in turn responded to his warm and modest personality. Al-Qassam's preaching was enthusiastically received, both at the Gerini mosque and subsequently at the Istiqlal mosque. (The latter was built by the Jamiat al-Islamiya to serve the spiritual needs of the growing number of Muslims employed in the new industrial district growing up in and around Haifa's railroad yards.)

Because of his easy accessibility in contrast to that of many of the other ulama, al-Qassam would frequently be stopped on the street on his way to teach at the Madrasa Islamiya for advice and religious guidance, so he was frequently late for his classes. As director of the Madrasa, al-Qassab insisted that al-Qassam should keep regular hours, but since that was becoming increasingly impossible, al-Qassam resigned his teaching post.

In the late 1920s and early 1930s, al-Qassam intensified his contacts with the people of Haifa. He became an "outstanding personality" at the Mawlid al-Nabi festivals held according to Syrian custom whenever a family has some good fortune to celebrate—the birth of a child, his or her memorization of a portion of the Quran, a graduation, or a promotion. Al-Qassam would recite the *mawlid* ritual at such occasions, since in a spiritual sense such events were "the birthday of the Prophet."

Slowly, patiently, he built a large group of followers, all personally selected. He studied the men who seemed most concentrated in their prayer and invocations and most responsive to his preaching at his Friday sermons. Later he visited them in their homes for more discussion and more observation. When he was certain of them, he formed them into perhaps a dozen circles, each circle unknown to the other. He taught them to read, using the Quran as text. All the time he preached the duty and inevitability of struggle against the British and the Zionists. Invariably, his followers were men without formal education, illiterate workers, or former tenant farmers recently driven off their land by Zionist land purchases, the Arab labor exclusion policies of the Jewish National Fund, or their own inability to meet steadily rising rents.

In Haifa, the effects of sudden development and the peculiar characteristics of the settler-colonization of Palestine were compounded. Because it was the major port, railroad center, and (by the early 1930s) oil refinery for the Arab East, Haifa had a greater attraction for the drifting Palestinian labor force than any other city in Palestine. The increase in Jewish immigration in the early 1930s stimulated a boom in building and allied trades in Haifa. This further intensified its influence, drawing in still more unskilled labor from the countryside.

Palestinian workers were crowded into shantytowns and were largely ignored by the traditional urban Palestinian elites who were locked into an all-consuming political struggle between the big families for the leadership of Palestinian Arabs. Victimized by inflation that often required more than half the wages of an unskilled worker to pay the rent of a decent room, and thrust into a rapidly secularizing environment, the Palestinian worker found that his

> feelings were intensified by the spectacle of the handsome new boulevards erected in the more desirable parts of the towns by and for the [Jewish] immigrant population, and by the acres of Jewish working men's quarters erected by Jewish building societies. Sometimes too, he had the experience of being driven from work by Jewish pickets and he resented the fact that the [British Mandate] Government paid the Jewish workman double the rate it paid him for the same work. (Neville Barbour, *Nisi Dominus: A Survey of the Palestine Controversy*, p. 134)

The same process that led to the emergence of a new, displaced Palestinian Muslim working class was producing a Zionist-settler society and state. The traditional Palestinian elites were incapable of responding to either phenomenon. At worst, the avarice and petty political rivalries of the big family notables and the decadence of the religious leadership contributed directly to the settler-colonization of Palestine; at best, by opposing Zionist settlement while refusing to confront directly the British colonial authority protecting that colonization, the Palestinian elites limited the effectiveness of their opposition. Qassam differed from the nationalists both in his diagnosis of the problem and in the remedy he proposed.

Unlike the elite politicians, who focused on the impact of imperialism on Palestinian society and saw a strong secular nationalist movement as a solution, al-Qassam saw the situation in religious terms. The remedy he proposed was *jihad,* the moral and political struggle for justice in the path of God. Instead of organizing demonstrations or a political party as the Palestinian nationalists were doing, al-Qassam sought to prepare the ground for a struggle at once spiritual, political, and military. In so doing, al-Qassam placed himself within the tradition of Islamic thought that saw a spiritual dimension to holy war. For him, as for others in this tradition, *jihad* had to begin with the individual moral struggle against evil. Only when the individual had turned away from evil could he move to the next stage, struggling physically to bring about the reign of justice.

Al-Qassam explained to his followers that the true *mujahid* (holy warrior) has been chosen by God and that the perfect *jihad* requires the sincere perfection of all aspects of ritual duties, creed, faith, and submission to God's commands. For al-Qassam, the holy warrior was one who helped the poor, fed the hungry, comforted the sick, and visited his relatives. All of these good deeds must be crowned by constant prayer. The *mujahid* achieved this sincere perfection by practicing the "greater *jihad.*" This al-Qassam described as the *jihad al-nafs* (the struggle of the individual soul against evil thoughts and desires—as contrasted with the lesser *jihad,* or armed struggle).

Good character, al-Qassam taught, was more important than bravery for the *jihad.* When God praised the Prophet, it was not for his bravery but for his good character or ethical standards. A man of good character will never accept humiliation but will fight, he preached. Therefore the virtues precede bravery or militancy as a prerequisite to fighting; thus the greater *jihad* is greater than the lesser *jihad.* In some ways, the Qassamiyun resembles the medieval Islamic *futuwwa* organizations, a combination of artisan guilds and religiously inspired chivalric fellowships. In building his circles among the Muslim working-class population of Haifa's shantytowns, al-Qassam was thus intentionally or not renewing an age-old social form.

A central focus of the *jihad* was the need to combat the moral degradation of the inhabitants of Haifa's shantytowns. Al-Qassam had a deep concern for these rural migrants, who lived separated from their families under appalling conditions and who were exposed to all manner of vice. He believed it was important to facilitate marriage as a barrier to corruption, which meant some sort of subsidy to young men who could not afford the *mahr* (bride gift), as well as keeping the age of consent low. He was also aware of the plight of those left behind in the villages. There are reports that he encouraged the *fellahin* in the movement to set up cooperatives for growing and distributing their crops. When an individual joined the Qassamites he underwent a complete conversion experience, reintegrating himself into a world of moral purpose, ethical standards, and religious culture. This transformation took years.

In the earliest years, when a follower was inducted into the *mujahidin* al-Qassam would ask him to grow a beard, as a symbol of his dedication to *jihad*. This was a form of testing by which he could determine the depth of the disciple's religious devotion. When a follower decided to grow a beard, al-Qassam would appear at his house with other bearded Qassamiyun to "celebrate his decision." After the recitation of *fatiha* and other passages from the Quran bearing upon *jihad,* the new disciple was congratulated by the company and sweets were served. In later years this ceremony was replaced or supplemented by an oath, sworn over either a dagger or a pistol placed alongside the Quran. Because the first members of the Haifa circles were bearded, the group was known as *al-mashayikh,* "the shaykhs." It was by his name that the movement first came to the attention of British and Zionist intelligence. (After al-Qassam's death the *mujahidin* were to become increasingly known as the Qassamiyun.)

The *mujahidin* were instructed to carry a copy of the Quran with them at all times so they could read and recite the Quran whenever they found themselves unoccupied. Al-Qassam also encouraged them to practise the Sufi spiritual exercises of the Qadiriya, and he gave them simple invocations and chants to recite when about to perform a mission in the *jihad.*

As soon as a group of disciples had been formed into a secret circle al-Qassam would give them basic military training and order them to continue to train among themselves. At least one retired Ottoman officer was recruited by al-Qassam to train the disciples, contrary to the claim by some of his biographers that al-Qassam in principle never recruited outside of the working classes.

Al-Qassam was very strict in his training. One informant described his method and the degree of obedience he commanded as follows:

> He would take us for training and shooting lessons and asked us to walk barefoot, and he made us sleep outdoors in the cold weather when we trained in the mountains. And he was tough on the disciples, making us go without food or water to be able to endure hunger and thirst. He would

ask us to sleep once or twice a week at home on the floor on a straw mat and with a light cover, and he always insisted that we be secretive about our activities, so we were all in trouble at home with our wives and family because we couldn't explain why we were sleeping in this manner, and we would endure this because we were devoted to carrying out his orders.

At the same time the disciples were encouraged to return to their villages outside of Haifa, either on regular visits or to resume residence, to cultivate the support of their local village head and to prepare likely recruits for a visit by al-Qassam. Then al-Qassam would visit the village, accompanied by the disciples and frequently by other members of his particular circle in Haifa, and the slow process of preaching, observation, guidance, military training, eventual initiation of disciples, and the formation of new circles would begin again. At times, the shaykhs, as the members of the oldest circles were known, were authorized to initiate directly tribesmen and villagers in the countryside into their movement.

By 1923 al-Qassam had secured land in the Beisan Valley, and he sent Muhammad Hanifi there to farm in order to have an eventual source of income to purchase weapons for the *jihad* as well as a center of communication with all parts of Palestine. In the summer al-Qassam came to Beisan and helped Hanifi plant his crops; in the winter Hanifi would come to al-Qassam, and together they visited the villages on horseback. Hanifi served as al-Qassam's deputy and as treasurer of the group. He was entrusted by al-Qassam with the contacts to all of the circles. The head of each circle was called either *arif* or *naqib,* both titles drawn from the technical vocabulary of the Sufi organizations.

Because the *mujahidin* knew only members of their own circle, or at most members of their parent circle, the total number of adherents was never known. From interviews with Hanifi, who visited all of the circles and arranged the dispatch of communications from al-Qassam to the *arif* of each village circle by courier, it would appear that the number of trained and initiated *mujahidin* was more than a thousand. These were concentrated chiefly in the northern districts but included disciples and secret circles throughout most of the countryside, even as far south as Gaza.

Al-Qassam's position as president of the Young Men's Muslim Association provided him with an acceptable explanation for his frequent visits to the villages around Haifa where he was organizing branches of the association that became, outside of Haifa, the equivalent of a "front" or "cover" group for the local *mujahidin.* It also provided him access to the notables and to the younger and more radical Arab nationalists from the modern educated classes who were to coalesce around the Istiqlal party, a loosely organized, nonsectarian party focused upon secular Arab, rather than Islamic, identity, founded in the 1920s. Although the Istiqlal was radical in comparison to the traditional parties of the big families, it was nevertheless profoundly respectable. Al-Qassam's relationship with the Istiqlal thus helped protect him from his political enemies.

Since the Istiqlal party drew its inspiration from the Salafiya reform movement, and Arabism and Islam were associated in the popular mind, it colored its Arab nationalism with an Islamic rhetoric that employed such phrases as *jihad* and *sabil Allah*. There was thus the basis for an alliance of mutual respect. This vague approximation of rhetorical style was reinforced by the one basic political position shared by the Istiqlal and al-Qassam, that opposition to the Zionist colonization of Palestine could not be separated from opposition to the British occupation, since Zionist settlement was possible only by virtue of British protection. This position contrasted with the prevailing strategy among all the big-family parties, be they "moderate" or nationalist, to work politically, mixing cooperation and principles, to protest for a realignment of British policy in favor of the Arabs that would halt further Zionist encroachment on Palestine.

Al-Qassam's identity of view with the Istiqlal was limited to this one point, but from the perspective of Palestinian politics and their subsequent interpretation as secular history that identity of view was not only profound but inescapably reinforced by al-Qassam's continuous denunciation of the British in his sermons and less formal public talks. But al-Qassam shared this perspective with whoever else held it, and as late as 2 November 1935 the *Palestine Post* reports al-Qassam sharing the platform at a Haifa rally condemning Balfour Day with Jamal al-Husseini, leader of the Arab party, rather than in Nablus for the big Istiqlal rally organized by Akram Zuayter.

Al-Qassam's closest associate in the Istiqlal was the Haifa banker Rashid Hajj Ibrahim, a leading figure in the charitable society Jamiat al-Islamiya and the founder and first president of the Young Men's Muslim Association in Haifa. Hajj Ibrahim appealed to him several times to moderate his sermons, since it was becoming difficult for him to persuade the British not to arrest the shaykh, who several times picked him up for interrogation. Because of his association with the notables and young professionals (men like Hajj Ibrahim) of the YMMA and the Istiqlal, however, he was not taken with sufficient seriousness by either British intelligence or his Arab nationalist acquaintances. In fact, despite some shared values, few adherents of the Istiqlal or the predominantly middle-class Young Men's Muslim Association of Haifa ever joined his cause. For his part, al-Qassam appears not to have joined any of the existing nationalist political parties, although he was claimed by both the Istiqlal and the supporters of Hajj Amin al-Husayni, who as *mufti* of Jerusalem and head of the Arab Higher Committee was the leading spokesman for the Palestinians in the mandate period.

More secularly minded nationalists tended to misunderstand the profoundly religious context for the activities of al-Qassam and his followers. They could not see why the Qassamiyun refused to take food from the peasants if it was not offered to them. Nor could they understand why they told the truth to their enemies about their objectives, instead of lying to protect themselves. But from the perspective of the chivalric code of the medieval Islamic *futuwwa* organizations on which they were modeled, their behavior was impeccable. Both their Quranic sense of *shahid*, or witnesses against mankind, and their imitation of the Prophet, who "makes the truth victorious by the truth," then become understandable.

If al-Qassam and the products of his effort seem to defy even the best-intentioned modern Arab thinkers, it is because his life and thought—dedicated to *jihad* in all of its dimensions—transcended the identity systems and contradictions of modern Islamic political thought. He was capable of waging *jihad* in the contemporary milieu because he was able to absorb whatever of these conflicting schools filtered through his own traditional orthodox conscience, applying what he understood was compatible with orthodox Islam and rejecting what he understood was not.

Moving among jealous effendis, decadent ulama, and worldly religious reformers, a secret presence in the shacks of railroad porters and stonemasons, Al-Qassam—illuminated by those spiritual virtues that he and his disciples perfected so earnestly—opened their tawdry and doomed natural world to the presence of the supernatural. This, by his own doctrine, was his greatest and only enduring triumph, and it is precisely this sacralizing triumph that has been denied him by his modern biographers.

## A NOTE ON SOURCES

In writing this life of Izz al-Din al-Qassam, I have drawn upon interviews with many of his family, disciples, and acquaintances, especially Imam Abd al-Malik al-Qassam, Umm Muhammad al-Qassam, Muhammad al-Qassam, Shaykh Muhammad Hanifi, Shaykh Nimr al-Khatib, Zuhayr Shawish, Muhammad Izzat Darwaza, Farid Troublsi, Atif Nurallah, Rashid Ibu, Hajj Hassan al-Hafian, Abu Ibrahim al-Kabir, Abu Adnan Sursawi, and Shawki Khayrallah.

Also consulted were the following collections of personal papers, held at the Institute for Palestine Studies: *Tegart Papers, Zu'ayter Papers, Zuhayr Shawish Papers.* Memoirs and other works in Arabic include Muhammad Izzat Darwaza, *Hawl al-haraka al-arabiya al-haditha* (Sidon, n.d.); Ahmad Shukayri, *Arabaun sannatin fi al-hayat al-arabiya waal-dawliya* (Beirut, 1969); Abil Hassan Ghanaym, "Thawarat al-Shaykh Izz al-Din al-Qassam," *Shuun Filastiniya* 6 (January 1972); Subhi Yasin, *Al Thawra al-arabiya al-kubra fi filastin, 1936–1939* (Beirut, 1959); Ghassan Kanafani, *The 1936–1939 Revolt in Palestine* (Committee for a Democratic Palestine, n.d.).

## SUGGESTIONS FOR FURTHER READING

On al-Qassam see especially the author's "The Life and Thought of Izz-idi-din al-Qassam," *Islamic Culture* 5, 23, pp. 61–81 (from which the present chapter is adapted), and the following: A. W. Kayyali, *Palestine: A Modern History* (London: Croom Helm, 1978); Nels Johnson, *Islam and the Politics of Meaning in Palestinian Nationalism* (London: Routledge, 1982).

The standard political history of Palestinian nationalism in the mandate period is the two-volume work of Yehoshuah Porath, *The Emergence of the Palestinian Arab National Movement, 1918–1929* (London: Frank Cass, 1974) and *The Palestinian Arab National Movement: From Riots to Rebellion, 1929–1939* (London: Frank Cass, 1977).

For the perspective of a British Mandate official, see Neville Barbour, *Nisi Dominus: A Survey of the Palestine Controversy* (London: George Harrap, 1946); for an Arab perspective, George Antonious, *The Arab Awakening* (Beirut, 1969); for contemporary Zionist perspectives, Amos Elon, *The Israelis: Founders and Sons.*

In addition to the above, the following more specialized works may serve as an introduction to the substantial bibliography on the Palestinian mandate: Ann Mosely Lesch, *Arab Politics in Palestine, 1917–1939: The Frustration of a Nationalist Movement* (Ithaca, N.Y.: Cornell University Press, 1979); Philip Mattar, *The Mufti of Jerusalem: Al-Hajj Amin al-Husayni and the Palestinian National Movement* (New York: Columbia University Press, 1988); Muhammad Muslih, *The Origins of Palestinian Nationalism* (New York: Columbia University Press, 1988); Edward Said and Christopher Hitchens, eds., *Blaming the Victims* (London: Verso, 1987); Rosemary Sayigh, *Palestinians: From Peasants to Revolutionaries* (London: Zed Press, 1979); and Kenneth Stein, *The Land Question in Palestine, 1917–1939* (Chapel Hill: University of North Carolina Press, 1984).

# TWELVE

# Abu Ali al-Kilawi:
# A Damascus *Qabaday*

*Philip S. Khoury*

While the Ottoman *tanzimat* reforms and the opening of the empire to the
world economy stimulated a host of important changes, the social and cultural life of cities evolved at a slower rhythm. In Syria, it was not until the interwar period that many of the old ways were replaced by new ones, and then
under the auspices of the French colonial mandate government. In other
parts of the region much the same process can be observed, although the
pace of change differed.

As Philip S. Khoury explains in his contribution, the old ways were especially persistent in the urban neighborhoods, or quarters. At the popular
level, the quarters of Damascus possessed their own identities, distinguished
by traditions and customs. A prominent feature of life in the quarters was the
neighborhood youth gang and its leader, the *qabaday*, an individual reputed
for his strength, prowess, and honor. Endowed with a quasi-chivalric ethic,
youth gangs redressed grievances and defended the honor of their quarter in
ritual combat against the gangs of other quarters. These fights featured displays of prowess in horsemanship, wrestling, and swordsmanship and have
their roots in earlier Islamic history.* Through their alliances with local notables, *qabadays* and their gangs controlled the streets of the quarter and maintained the dominance of the notables into the twentieth century.

Abu Ali al-Kilawi, the subject of Khoury's essay, was one of the last of the
Damascus *qabadays*. His career is situated between the older notable-based
clientele style of politics and the politics of the new nationalist movements.
As a result of the failure of the 1925 insurrection against the French, the in-
adequacies of the *qabadays*, most of whom were illiterate, became increasingly
evident, and Abu Ali, despite his heroism, became virtually obsolete. From
this time on, the turn toward new political organizations and ideas became
irreversible.

*On the organization of the quarters in earlier times, see Ira Lapidus, *Muslims Cities in the
Later Middle Ages* (Cambridge, Mass.: Harvard University Press, 1965).

Not quite part of the underworld, but not entirely respectable, *qabadays* have largely disappeared most places today. With the coming of modernity, their place has been taken by more explicitly criminal elements and by other voluntary associations, including labor unions, youth groups, women's groups, and religious groups.[†] —ED.

The period of the French Mandate (1920–45) was a pivotal time in Syrian politics. The country was in a transitional phase, uncomfortably suspended between four centuries of Ottoman rule and national independence. France had occupied Syria and Lebanon in 1919–20 and imposed a new form of colonial rule known as the mandate system, which received legal sanction from the League of Nations in Geneva. The French constructed an administrative system that separated Lebanon from Syria and then divided Syria into separate units along religious and regional lines. These and other measures caused serious discontent throughout much of the country. The result was a national revolt that lasted two years (1925–27) but that was ultimately crushed. The failure of the revolt convinced nationalist leaders to drop armed confrontation as a strategy, and in its place they substituted a more gradualist approach to the nationalist goals of Syrian unity and independence that relied on a combination of boycotts, strikes, demonstrations, and diplomacy. The architect of this new strategy was the National Bloc, an alliance of traditional elites in Damascus and other Syrian towns that in the 1930s became the most important nationalist political organization of the French Mandate era. It would steer the course of the nationalist movement until independence was finally achieved at the end of the Second World War.

Although the Ottoman Empire had collapsed and new forms of social and political organization were available, there remained a distinctive Ottoman cast to Syrian politics and especially to Syria's urban elites. The foundation of Syrian political life during the French Mandate, as in Ottoman times, were the major towns, of which Damascus was the most important. The towns were characterized by deep cleavages between different religious sects and ethnic groups, between the rich and the poor, between the various trades, and between long-settled urbanites and recent migrants from the countryside. In some senses, the most acute cleavages were those between the different quarters, which were separated from one another by walls and gates, a reflection of their narrowly defined interests and desire for protection from outsiders.

Even though the quarters retained their distinctiveness and purpose throughout most of the French Mandate years, their cohesiveness had

[†]See, however, the Lebanese case: Michael Johnson, *Class and Client in Beirut: The Sunni Muslim Community and the Lebanese State, 1940–1985* (London: Ithaca Press, 1986).

already begun to be eroded by new social forces. This was the direct consequence of the structural changes that had been sweeping the Middle East since the early nineteenth century—changes in administration and law; in commerce, industry, and agriculture; in the movement of goods, peoples, and ideas. The towns of Syria, and particularly their quarters, were affected by all these changes. New patterns of trade and production hastened the impoverishment of some quarters and the enrichment of others. New concentrations of wealth, coupled with the spread of modern education, accelerated the process of class differentiation. New landholding patterns uprooted peasants and encouraged their migration to the towns, where they often settled in quarters vacated by the recently rich and educated or in impoverished suburban quarters.

Although the winds of change in Syria intensified after World War I, their impact on urban politics should not be exaggerated. For instance, the exercise of local political power was characterized by a remarkable degree of continuity, which was not disrupted by the substitution of French for Ottoman rule. For the most part, the men who were important in local affairs under the Ottomans were the same men, or their sons, who wielded political influence under the French. Political leaders, now grouped into an array of nationalist organizations like the National Bloc, continued to organize their patronage networks as they had in late Ottoman times. Urban leadership remained the basic building block of political influence in Syria. And at the heart of urban politics were the quarters, the traditional domain in which political leadership operated and from which it derived much of its support.

One figure in the quarters who could give the nationalist leader a decisive edge in competition for clientele during the French Mandate (1920–45) was the local gang leader, the *qabaday* (pl. *qabadayat*), or, in the patois of Damascus, the *zgrirti*. Probably no individual with independent influence in the quarters was closer to the common man than was the *qabaday*. He was something akin to an institution. Each quarter had its own set of historical figures who were glorified from one generation to the next. In time, an ideal type was formed, one that characterized the *qabaday* as strong, honorable, the protector of the feeble and the poor as well as of the religious minorities, the upholder of Arab traditions and customs, and the guardian of popular culture. He was hospitable to strangers, always pious, and lived clean. This image placed far less emphasis on the *qabaday's* darker side, his shady dealings, his preference for physical coercion, and even his "mortal" crimes for personal gain. The common people clearly differentiated between the *qabadayat* and the *zuran*, or hoodlums, who ran protection rackets (*khuwa*) in the quarters and bazaars, although in reality such distinctions were hazy.

A *qabaday* might eventually become fairly well-to-do, but what distinguished him from the dignitaries of the quarter were his significantly lower social origins, his general want of formal education, his outspoken preference for traditional attire and customs, and the much narrower range of his interests and contacts, all of which accorded him a less exalted status than that enjoyed by merchants or religious leaders. He survived best in the traditional milieu of the self-contained quarter with its inwardness and narrowly defined interests. There he was needed to provide physical protection from hostile external forces, and extralegal mechanisms for settling personal disputes. But by the time of the mandate, the *qabaday* had begun to feel threatened by the pressures created by rapid urbanization, the growth of a market-oriented economy, and the rise of new classes and institutions outside the popular quarters. This period was a transitional phase in the life of the Syrian city, and in the organization and functions of its quarters; the *qabaday* survived it, although not without difficulty.

A *qabaday* might rise to leadership in the quarter by several different paths, and it is difficult to separate myth from reality when tracing the emergence of any particular strongman. It is, however, possible to trace the career of at least one prominent *qabaday* of the mandate period in Damascus, his links to the principal national independence organization, the National Bloc, and his contribution to the independence movement.

Abu Ali al-Kilawi [al-Gilawi] claims to have been born in 1897, in Bab al-Jabiya, an old popular quarter situated near the entrance to the central commercial artery, Suq Midhat Pasha, and including the charming Mosque of Sinan Pasha. The origins of the Kilawi family are obscure. They seem to have first settled in al-Maydan, the southernmost quarter of Damascus, some time in the early nineteenth century, where they were engaged in the transport of wheat from their native Hawran to flour mills in al-Maydan. They may have belonged to one of the tributaries of the Rwala bedouin who roamed with the Rwala chieftains of Al Shalan before the mandate. The Kilawis also claimed descent from Abu Bakr, the Prophet's companion and the first caliph, and billed themselves as members of the *ashraf* (descendants of the Prophet), although the great religious families of Damascus did not recognize their claim. According to Abu Ali, the family's surname had been al-Bakri until the end of the nineteenth century. When his father died unexpectedly, the family dropped al-Bakri for some inexplicable reason and adopted instead the surname of Abu Ali's maternal grandfather. During the mandate, the Kilawis were not regarded as members of the aristocratic al-Bakri family of Damascus; however, they were very partial to the Bakris and especially close to Nasib Bey al-Bakri of the National Bloc.

Abu Ali had two older brothers. He happened to be much closer to the oldest, Abu Hasan, who assumed the leadership of the family upon his father's death and under whose wing Abu Ali grew up learning the ways of the quarter. Abu Ali attributed his rise to the status of a *qabaday* to several factors, all of which suggest that he did not inherit the title. One factor was his own physical strength, which he displayed early in life despite his slight build. The youth of Bab al-Jabiya and other quarters engaged in different forms of informal competition that helped lay the groundwork for the rise of a *qabaday*. Abu Ali, for example, excelled in wrestling (*musaraa*). To the beat of two drums, the youth of the quarter would congregate in an open field or garden, where wrestling matches were staged between boys dressed in leather shorts worn above britches. By the age of sixteen, Abu Ali was reputed to be the best wrestler in the quarter.

By this age the youth of the quarter had already begun to practice the martial arts and in particular swordsmanship. Wielding a long, silver-handled sword in one hand and a small metal shield (*turs*) in the other, two young men would face each other, twirling their swords through different orbits over and around their heads while interspersing blows against their own shields and those of their opponents in a complicated cadence. The boy who could handle his sword most adeptly and innovatively advanced in the competition, and the best five or six contestants were asked to form a troupe. This troupe would then have the honor of performing on all festive occasions in the quarter, such as weddings and the Prophet's birthday. In his day, Abu Ali was the leader of such a troupe of swordsmen, and from it he began to build his own personal following.

Horsemanship was Abu Ali's other forte. After their father's death, his brother, Abu Hasan, used his family's relations with the bedouin tribes south of Damascus to convert the Kilawi transport business into a horse-breeding and trading concern. The center for their new activities was a small stud farm that the family owned just south of al-Maydan. In time, the Kilawis became renowned horse dealers throughout the Arab East, purveying purebred show animals and racehorses to the royal families of Transjordan and Saudi Arabia and to other Arab dignitaries. By the time he was twenty, Abu Ali was considered to be the best horseman in his quarter, a reputation that soon spread throughout Damascus and the rest of Syria. By the mid-1930s, the Kilawi stable of show horses had become an attraction at all national parades, and Abu Ali always rode at the head.

Successful business enterprises helped to vault the Kilawi family into the social limelight of Bab al-Jabiya. Neighbors began to ask for favors or assistance, and in no time they built up a solid core of followers and clients from among the poorer elements of the quarter, some of whom were personally loyal to Abu Ali. The result was that Abu Ali was able to put together his own gang, composed mainly of unemployed youth and casual laborers.

In the early 1920s, as the Kilawis began to accumulate capital, they were able to purchase a fairly large apartment in the heart of their quarter, one with a special salon for entertaining. This salon also was used as an informal courtroom where the Kilawis, now much trusted in Bab al-Jabiya, served as administrators of extralegal justice, arbitrating or mediating disputes between individuals and families who for one reason or another were not comfortable going before the religious or civil courts. The Kilawis also lent their salon to poorer families for wedding parties and other social functions, and it eventually became one of the main political meeting places in the quarter. Abu Ali claimed that he and his brothers never asked for money or other material rewards for their hospitality and services. But they did expect personal loyalty to the family, which they acquired as the Kilawi network grew and the family name came to be mentioned with both reverence and fear.

One of the most prominent features of urban life in Damascus were the *arada*, or traditional parades, held in the quarter to celebrate some religious event such as a circumcision, the return of the pilgrimage, or the Prophet's birthday. These occasions allowed the youth of one quarter to compete with the youth of neighboring quarters in wrestling matches, sword games, horse racing, and the like. The honor of the quarter was always at stake in these events, as were specific controversies over turf and freedom on movement. Certain quarters were known to be long-standing rivals, most notably Suq Saruja and al-Salhiya, and Shaghur and Bab al-Jabiya. Yet another way in which Abu Ali al-Kilawi reinforced his status in the quarter was to lead his stalwarts in street fights against rival gangs of Shaghur.

By the early twentieth century, however, the parades had begun to assume secular dimensions as they came to mark political events such as the election of a deputy, the return of an exile, the Young Turk revolt of 1908, or the Italian invasion of Libya in 1911. This politicization accelerated during the mandate, and acts of defiance against the French and their collaborators highlighted the continued independence of life in the quarters. But, equally important, as political consciousness rose in the quarters, the fierce rivalries between them were transformed into an alliance of the quarters against the French. The narrowness and insularity of quarter life began to break down as the scope of political activity widened.

The Great Revolt of 1925 hastened the erosion of many of the traditional social and political barriers and rivalries between quarters and helped to bind them together in a common front against the French. There is little doubt that the many stories of individual heroism that quickly became part of the local history and mythology of the Great Revolt helped many a young man to enhance his reputation in the popular quarters of the city, enabling him to achieve the status of *qabaday*. In fact, there was a noticeable turnover of *qabadayat* at this time, owing to the emergence of new heroes during the revolt who replaced those who had been killed. Probably the most respected and esteemed *qabaday* of his day was Hasan al-Kharat, the night watchman of Shaghur, who led a rebel attack on French positions in the Syrian capital and was later killed by French troops. His elimination permitted another rising star of the revolt, Mahmud Khaddam al-Srija, to assert himself as the undisputed strongman of Shaghur.

Abu Ali al-Kilawi frankly admitted fifty years after his own participation in the Great Revolt that it also enabled his family to consolidate their position as the *qabadayat* par excellence of Bab al-Jabiya. When the revolt erupted, the Kilawis and their armed gang prepared their quarter for insurrection against the French. Abu Ali joined the rebel band of Nasib al-Bakri, whose family had patronized the Kilawis for some time. After the French regained control of most of Damascus in October, Abu Ali followed Bakri's forces into the gardens around the Syrian capital known as al-Ghuta. One particular episode contributed to his immortalization in the minds of future generations. Seriously wounded in a single-handed attempt to liberate his rebel comrades imprisoned in the Citadel of Damascus, he managed to flee on horseback, taking refuge among his traditional enemies in Shaghur. Two days later, a weak but determined Abu Ali al-Kilawi recruited some young men of Shaghur and rode back with them to Bab al-Jabiya, where he rounded up more followers and returned to the Ghuta to rejoin the Bakri band.

Like the great merchants and the *imams* of the local mosques, the *qabadayat* rarely joined the National Bloc or any other political organization. Rather, their affiliation and loyalty was to one or another of the Bloc chiefs. Abu Ali al-Kilawi's allegiance was to Nasib al-Bakri, not to the Bloc's executive council. The *qabadayat* were typically more important to a nationalist leader's political machine in the quarters than were the merchants or religious figures. The Bloc chief's resources were limited, especially when in and out of jail or in temporary exile; therefore the recruitment and maintenance of his clientele required considerable finesse. He generally preferred to devote his personal attention to winning and sustaining followings among the wealthier families of the quarters. With these he made certain that he was able to maintain regular personal contacts at all times. When the National Bloc chief began to distance himself from his ancestral quarter, he had to depend more heavily on intermediaries to dispense favors and services to the larger mass of poorer residents with whom he probably never came into direct contact. Merchants, whose status was based on wealth, philanthropy, and religious piety, were among those intermediaries who assumed this function for the politicians. But as class differentiation evolved during the mandate, merchants began to take less and less interest in the poor and their individual problems. They neither found time for, nor were they well disposed toward, the poor. Philanthropy itself did not require regular contact with the lower classes. Some members of the Muslim religious establishment also placed a greater distance between themselves and the common people. Others, however, including preachers in the popular quarters, actually strengthened their influence among the destitute and the illiterate. Although leading religious dignitaries and lower-ranking *imams* generally supported the nationalist chiefs, they also formed benevolent societies (*jamiyat*) that assumed a militant anti-Western and antisecular political character by the mid-1930s and eventually posed an unwelcome challenge to the authority of the nationalist leadership in the quarters.

The *qabaday*, in contrast, posed no such threat. He hailed from the common people, was under the protection of one or another nationalist leader (bey), was often indebted to him for loans and services, and, in any case, lacked the education, status, and statesmanlike qualities to reach the chief's level of political leadership. Thus, while the National Bloc leader, assisted by his personal secretary and family, policed the core of his patronage network, the *qabaday* looked after its periphery, servicing it directly whenever possible and guaranteeing its support when the bey required it.

Although some *qabadayat* were able to attract their own personal followings by performing such services as the mediation of disputes, the protection of the neighborhood, and small philanthropic activities, they had neither direct control nor access to large material resource bases that might have allowed them to build their own independent patronage networks. In the final analysis, they were beholden to the nationalist politicians in many of the same ways that other clients were. The only significant difference was that the *qabaday's* apparatus for recruiting and policing his chief's clientele gave him direct access to the bey's immediate entourage, in particular to his personal secretary. In this way, the *qabaday* could count on preferential treatment and a few more privileges than could the average client on the periphery of the chief's network. Although the scope for social mobility was not wide, a number of *qabadayat* managed to enrich themselves through connections with their patrons.

At any given time the residents of a quarter might refer to several individuals as *qabadayat*. A quarter could support more than one strong-man, although it was not uncommon to associate the *qabadayat* with a single family. Residents of Bab al-Jabiya referred to *awlad* al-Kilawi (the sons of al-Kilawi) as frequently as they did to any one member of the family. It was the family, through its connections, that provided protection and assistance to the quarter. Abu Ali did make a name for himself, in particular as the family rabble-rouser, the gifted equestrian, and the local enforcer. But he frankly admitted that his oldest brother, who had some education, made the family's major decisions, ran its business, and dealt with the National Bloc politicians and their deputies, was in charge. Abu Ali was in effect Abu Hasan's lieutenant, prepared to execute his commands. When Abu Hasan died, the leadership of the Kilawi family passed to Abu Ali (his other brother was regarded as a high liver and a playboy, which disqualified him), who had already begun to educate his eldest son to fill the role of family lieutenant.

Part of the mythology surrounding the *qabaday* was that he never took money from politicians or their secretaries, or from merchants in the quarter for carrying out various instructions, such as mobilizing the youth of the quarter to demonstrate or enforcing a strike or boycott. Abu Ali admitted that the National Bloc offered him money at various times and cited several attempts by merchants close to the Bloc to pay him to keep the general strike of 1936 going. Defending the ideal image of *qabaday*, he also claimed that to accept such offerings ran against his honor. He did not deny, however, that some *qabadayat* broke this code of personal honor and morality by accepting cash and other benefits for merely fulfilling their duties. For example, after the National Bloc took office in 1936, in the wake of the general strike and the Franco-Syrian treaty negotiations in Paris, Shukri al-Quwatli, the minister of finance and the national defense, saw to it that Mahmud Khaddam al-Srija, probably the most renowned *qabaday* of the 1930s in Damascus, received a regular stipend from a *waqf* (religious endowment) originally designated for the poor in his native Shaghur for services to al-Quwatli, the leading politician of that quarter.

Given the combination of resources that fed any National Bloc chief's political machine, the support that these leaders received from the quarters was uneven. A politician like Nasib al-Bakri was extremely well connected to numerous *qabadayat* like the Kilawis, the Dib al-Shaykh family of the Amara quarter, and to other veterans of the Great Revolt of 1925, in which he had featured so prominently. Bakri, who cut a much more socially and religiously conservative figure than did his more cosmopolitan Bloc comrades and who had the religious prestige of his family behind him, moved easily among the tradition-bound masses of the popular quarters. By contrast, Shukri al-Quwatli, Jamil Mardam, and Fakhri al-Barudi (the other major Bloc figures in Damascus) were all extremely influential in their respective quarters, and particularly with merchants, but could not claim large personal followings in other quarters, despite the respect they commanded. Unlike Bakri, however, they serviced much more diversified political machines: each had a significant following in the modern sectors and institutions of Damascus, especially among the educated youth and the emerging professional middle class.

Although the popular quarters remained important units of political and social organization during the mandate period, their importance to the independence movement gradually declined. The advancement of urban political life produced new focal points outside the quarters. These were the modern institutions that were closely identified with the growth of a professional middle class whose fundamental interests lay beyond the quarters. The dominant sentiments of this class of lawyers, doctors, engineers, educators, journalists, and other members of the intelligentsia transcended the narrowness of quarter life. Their primary loyalties were to city, state, and nation rather than to family, clan, confessional group, or quarter.

The National Bloc recognized that the newly educated cadres were in need of youth leaders who were more sophisticated than the tradition-bound and often unlettered *qabadayat,* leaders with whom they could identify socially, culturally, and intellectually; simply, the *qabadayat* were increasingly unappealing and ineffective as role models for the growing numbers of educated youth in the cities who found their anchoring outside the popular quarters.

Thus, while the *qabadayat* and others with influence in the quarters continued to be important political actors during the mandate, they were merely experiencing a temporary reprieve from political obsolescence. This could perhaps best be seen in the changing composition and character of demonstrations against the French in the 1930s. By then, educated young men organized by Boy Scout troop or by political party were at the head of these demonstrations. Everything about them seemed different, from their secular slogans denouncing French imperialism and invoking pan-Arab unity, national liberation, and (by the end of the mandate) even socialism to their European dress and modern uniforms. Many belonged to the rising middle classes and hailed from the wealthier or newer quarters of Damascus. But even those who did not preferred to march under the banner of their youth organization or school rather than alongside the traditional quarter bosses, the *qabadayat*. Moreover, their role models were a set of young leaders who were more ideologically motivated than the *qabadayat* and whose political bases lay outside the popular quarters in new, more sophisticated institutions and structures, such as the government schools, the university, and various youth organizations.

These new youth leaders regarded Abu Ali al-Kilawi and his fellow *qabadayat* as relics and obstacles to progress. *Qabadayat* like Abu Ali regarded them as party hacks, men whose highest commitment was to an elitist organization, not to the common people. Like Abu Ali, these new political personalities served as intermediaries, but more for the National Bloc organization as a whole than for any single individual in it. They operated in a milieu that ultimately proved to be more important to the future of the Syrian national independence movement and to urban politics in general. They clearly belonged to the future, while the *qabadayat* increasingly belonged to the past.

But these new urban youth leaders who supplanted the *qabadayat* in postindependence Syria were themselves destined for obsolescence. Profound structural changes in economy and society that had begun during World War II unleashed new forces with new methods and aims that were beyond the towns and outside the traditional framework of urban politics. Elements from the countryside now struggled against more established urban elements for control of the towns and of government. In the 1950s and 1960s dispossessed rural peoples belonging to Syria's compact religious minorities used the army and the major radical nationalist party (the Baath party) as their vehicle for social and political mobility and ultimately to seize control of government. In the process, they effectively brought an end to independent urban politics in Syria.

## A NOTE ON SOURCES

My account of the life and political career of Abu Ali al-Kilawi is based on several days of conversations with him and with several other *qabadayat* in the spring of 1976. It also draws upon his unpublished memoir "Thawra amma 1925: al-Faransiyyin fi suriyya." Also of help was Ahmad Hilmi al-Allaf, *Dimashq fi matla al-qarn al-ahsrin*, ed. Ali Jamil Nuaysa (Damascus: Wizarat al-Thaqafa, 1976). See also the published memoirs of several prominent Syrian nationalist politicians of the French Mandate era, including Fakhri al-Barudi, Abd al-Rahman Shahbandar, Lutfi al-Haffar, and Khalid al-Azm. Some of their private papers and those of other nationalist leaders are housed in the Center for Historical Documents in Damascus.

Other unpublished sources include René Danger, Paul Danger, and M. Ecochard, "Damas: Rapport d'enquête monographique sur la ville, 1936," found at Bibliothèque de l'Institut français d'études arabes in Damascus; the French Mandate collection (Al-Intidab al-faransi) in the Center for Historical Documents (Markaz al-Wathaiq al-Tarikhiyya) in Damascus; the French Mandate archives at the Ministère des affaires étrangères in Nantes; Série E. Levant: Syrie-Liban 1918–1940; the *mémoires de stage* pertaining to Syria in the Centre des hautes études administratives sur l'Afrique et l'Asie modernes (CHEAM) in

Paris; and the British Foreign Office files (FO 371, FO 226, FO 684) for the French Mandate located in the Public Record Office in London (Kew).

## SUGGESTIONS FOR FURTHER READING

On Syrian politics during the French Mandate, see Philip S. Khoury, *Syria and the French Mandate: The Politics of Arab Nationalism, 1920–1945* (Princeton: Princeton University Press, 1987). For comparisons with the Ottoman period of Syrian history, see Philip S. Khoury, *Urban Notables and Arab Nationalism: The Politics of Damascus, 1860–1920* (Cambridge: Cambridge University Press, 1983); and Linda Schatkowski Schilcher, *Families in Politics: Damascene Factions and Estates of the 18th and 19th Centuries* (Stuttgart: Franz Steiner, 1985). The best study of the postindependence era is Patrick Seale, *The Struggle for Syria: A Study of Post-War Arab Politics, 1945–1958* (London: Oxford University Press, 1965).

On the phenomenon of *qabadayat* and the challenges posed to them by new social and political forces in the twentieth century see Philip S. Khoury, "Syrian Urban Politics in Transition: The Quarters of Damascus during the French Mandate," *International Journal of Middle East Studies* 16 (November 1984): 507–40, from which this essay is adapted. Michael Johnson has studied the *qabadayat* of Beirut; see his "Political Bosses and Their Gangs: Zuama and Qabadayat in the Sunni Muslim Quarters of Beirut," in *Patrons and Clients in Mediterranean Societies*, ed. Ernest Gellner and John Waterbury (London: Duckworth, 1977), and his *Class and Client in Beirut*.

For a general interpretation of how urban politics changed in Syria in the nineteenth and twentieth centuries see Albert Hourani, "Revolution in the Arab Middle East," in *Revolution in the Middle East and Other Case Studies*, ed. P. J. Vatikiotis (London: Rowman and Littlefield, 1972). Also Philip S. Khoury, "Syrian Political Culture: A Historical Perspective," in *Syria: Its Society, Culture, and Polity*, ed. Richard Antoun and Donald Quataert (Albany: State University of New York Press, 1991).

# THIRTEEN

# M'hamed Ali: Tunisian Labor Organizer

*Eqbal Ahmad and Stuart Schaar*

An examination of the life of M'hamed Ali, whom Tunisians consider the founder of their trade union movement, reveals a complex personality who has undergone a wide variety of experiences and influences. M'hamed Ali reflected, as he shaped, the trends and forces that came together in Tunisia during the early twentieth century. His first known political activity, his support of Libyan resistance against the Italians in Tripolitania, exposed him directly to the pan-Islamic movement, whose nonterritorial, universalist ideology was later to mark Arab nationalism. (For other examples of the role of pan-Islam as a predecessor of nationalism, see the chapters by Lisa Anderson, Julie Oehler, and Abdullah Schleifer.)

During World War I M'hamed Ali was one of a small number of Tunisians who served in the Ottoman forces (in support of Germany and the Axis powers) as a way of opposing French colonialism in the Maghrib. The end of the war found him in Berlin, where he was exposed to the revolutionary currents of the German workers' movement. This experience made him a militant supporter of workers' rights.

After the war, a confused period in Tunisian politics ensued. The French protectorate government was opposed by a number of rival nationalist formations, notably the old Destour party and the Néo-Destour party. The Néo-Destour represented the rising younger generation, and the original Destour represented their parents. Class and regional elements also played a role in the split. (Such struggles can be found in many national liberation movements in this period.)

This conflict was paralleled and intersected by the three-cornered struggle over workers' rights. Here the French protectorate's labor policies were opposed by the Confédération générale des travailleurs (CGT), which was affiliated with the French Communist party and most of whose leaders were European, and by the nationalist Confédération générale des travailleurs tunisiens (CGTT), one of whose founders was M'hamed Ali. In the interwar years, the CGTT emerged as a leading defender of the Muslim working class and a strong ally (and sometime rival) of the Néo-Destour. M'hamed Ali participated in the major conflicts of the period, playing a decisive role. Sent into political exile by the French, he died in Cairo in 1927.

M'hamed Ali's biography allows us to reflect upon the always problematic relationship between nationalism and the labor movement in the Middle East. In Tunisia as elsewhere, a burning question was, Which should have priority—the national struggle or the class struggle? M'hamed Ali's analysis of the power of the colonial state led him to throw his energies into the national struggle. It was not an uncontested decision, and much of the debate in the 1920s (in which he played a central role) focused on devising the parameters of worker support for the nationalist movement.

In thinking about the Tunisian case, comparisons with Egypt and Morocco, both of which were marked by strong labor movements, are especially useful. Close readers may also want to note M'hamed Ali's peasant origins in seeking to gauge the roots of his militancy. Here Kenneth Brown's biography of Muhammad Ameur, another Tunisian peasant, is suggestive. (For other biographies of peasants in this volume, see the contributions of Joost Hiltermann, David McMurray, and David Seddon.) —Ed.

In the history of the modern Maghrib, M'hamed Ali, whom the Tunisians consider the founding father of their still influential trade union movement, is a unique personality. He lived during the formative years of Tunisian nationalism and reflected the trends and forces that converged in Tunisia during the early twentieth century. His first known political activity, on behalf of the anticolonial resistance in Tripolitania, brought him in direct contact with the pan-Islamic movement, which spearheaded early anti-imperialist resistance in the Muslim world. It also placed him in contact with the nonterritorial, universalist trends that have marked Arab nationalist movements.

In the 1920s, when Tunisian nationalism was being transformed into a mass movement, M'hamed Ali played a key role in creating a national federation of workers independent of the French Confédération générale des travailleurs, or CGT. In the process, he became a central figure in the rivalries and polemics between nationalists and socialists in colonial Tunisia, a political struggle that played a large part in shaping the ideological premises of Tunisian nationalism. Finally, as a member of the young, progressive wing of the Destour party, M'hamed Ali belonged to that generation of youthful, often rural, radical nationalists who later founded the Néo-Destour party and led Tunisia to independence.

Perhaps as a result of the many gaps in the historical record, the life of Muhammad Ben Ali Ben Mokhtar Al-Ghaffani, alias Dr. M'hamed Ali Al-Hammi, alias Titon, popularly remembered as M'hamed Ali, has given rise to much controversy. Even his date of birth is in question.

M'hamed Ali was born in a rural community where, until recently, births and deaths were for remembrances rather than recording, and it was common for families to say that a boy was younger than he really was in order to assure him a longer term of employment. Similarly, little is known about his life and activities in Germany at the end of World War I—an early testimony to the anonymity of migrant workers in Europe. His death in exile conforms to this pattern. Although patriots and scholars have researched the time and place of his death, his birth date, and schooling, few details are known. It is clear that the obscurities concerning his life and the controversies surrounding his politics are a direct result of his social and political origins.

We now believe that M'hamed Ali was born in 1896 in El Hamma, an impoverished village in southern Tunisia near Gabès. El Hamma has but few economic resources, chiefly date palms and a few carpet weavers. As a result, its hardworking people have been forced to migrate to the coastal cities, where they enjoy a considerable reputation as dockers and construction workers. The image of these rural migrants as sober, straightforward, and loyal workers has accounted for their popularity with the Tunisian and colonial bourgeoisie, whom they have served as porters, guards, chauffeurs, and butlers.

While he was still a young child M'hamed Ali's mother died. His father, a poor peasant, took the boy to the home of a sister in Tunis. There he studied Arabic at a *kuttab* (Quranic school). His first job was as an errand boy at the central market. Later he was hired as a domestic in the household of the Austrian consul, where he added a smattering of German to his Arabic and French. Most importantly, he also learned to drive an automobile, becoming the consul's chauffeur. As there were few Tunisian Muslims who could drive at the time, the possession of this critical skill was to provide him with many opportunities for personal advancement.

His political education came in the years prior to World War I, when after years of quiet the Tunisian political situation suddenly became inflamed. The emergence of the Young Tunisians, a small group of would-be nationalists who were the contemporaries of the Young Turks in the Ottoman Empire, was an important moment in modern Tunisian politics. M'hamed Ali was drawn to them because they aimed to reawaken Tunisian Muslims from their political torpor. The Young Tunisians called upon Tunisians to rid themselves of indolence and fatalism and "from all prejudices that shackle their evolution, destroy their faculties, and hold them outside the movement that carries humanity toward progress," as Muhammad Lasram, one of their number, put it.

The Young Tunisian weekly, *Le Tunisien,* was founded in Paris in 1907 and developed ideas on the future Tunisian state. About the same time the Young Tunisians also established a political party, the *Parti*

*évolutionniste.* Its aim was to bring about greater Franco-Tunisian cooperation and thereby to facilitate the emergence of a modern Tunisian
state in which all citizens would have equal rights. Their concern with
rights was a major source of the popular appeal of the Young Tunisians.
It was their willingness to address the racism that defined relations between them and the Europeans that attracted the attention of M'hamed
Ali. The normal tensions that existed in Tunisian society between
classes, and the class struggle that might have emerged in a noncolonial
setting, were submerged in conflicts between the foreign and indigenous
communities over racial issues.

In 1911 the Italians invaded Tripolitania. Then an Ottoman province
administered by a governor appointed by the Ottoman sultan, Libya was
the only North African province not yet conquered by European imperialism. Already France had occupied Algeria in 1830 and Tunisia in
1881, and 1882 had witnessed the takeover of Egypt by the British. The
invasion of Tripolitania by Italy provoked deep emotions among Tunisians and crystallized their discontent into bitterness and fear. This was
all the more the case because of the large numbers of Italian immigrants
in Tunisia, some of whom were known for their racism.

The Italian invasion challenged the premises of pan-Islamic propaganda, which was then ascendant in the Ottoman Empire. Pan-Islam
raised the hope that the Muslim people could be restored to their place
in history. The chief instrument of that restoration was to be the Ottoman caliphate. Revitalized as an ideological force by the Ottoman ruler
Abd al-Hamid (1876–1908) and used by the Young Turks as a tool of
policy, the caliphate was a symbol of Muslim unity. Italy's attack on
Turkish power so close to home threatened the dreams of ordinary
Tunisians, shattering their lingering hopes and producing a nervous
disquiet.

The invasion of Tripolitania prompted M'hamed Ali's first known political involvement. At the time he was in his early twenties and was employed as a chauffeur in the household of a wealthy Tunisian. In response to the Italian invasion, the Young Tunisians, led by Ali Bach
Hamba, had formed a committee of solidarity with Tripolitania. They
also began publication of a pan-Islamic journal, *Al-ittihad al-islami (Islamic Unity).* More practically, they took up a collection to send a medical
supply unit to assist the Ottoman forces in opposing the Italians. In order to transport the medical supplies to Tripolitania they needed an experienced driver. Someone who knew of M'hamed Ali's background as a
chauffeur suggested that he might be the right person for the job. Thus
in the autumn of 1911 M'hamed Ali embarked on a journey that took
him to Tripolitania, Turkey, the Arab Middle East, and Germany. In the
process, he was introduced to the pan-Islamic, reformist, and nationalist

currents prevalent in the Ottoman Empire, as well as to socialist milieux in turbulent postwar Germany.

In Tunisia the climate produced by the Turko-Italian war sharpened the conflict between Tunisians and the French colonial authorities. In November 1911 rumors of an alleged French plan to confiscate the venerated Muslim cemetery of Djellaz on the outskirts of Tunis spread among the Muslim population, sparking a major protest that soon spilled over into violence. The French authorities launched a full-scale attack to dislodge the Tunisians from the cemetery and established martial law. The resultant loss of life and heavy repression heightened political tensions. Three months later the accidental killing of a Tunisian child by an Italian trolley-car conductor provoked a recrudescence of political turmoil. It soon led to a boycott of the Tunis streetcar lines. Trolley-car workers also demanded equal pay for Muslim employees and better treatment for Muslim passengers. The episode marked the entry of Tunisian workers into national politics. General national grievances began to be expressed along with specific worker demands. This was to become a pattern for the future. While the Young Tunisian leaders did not originate the boycott, they supported it. On 12 March 1912, the police arrested seven of them and deported four, including their leader, Ali Bach Hamba.

While Tunisian politics were heating up, M'hamed Ali was involved in the Young Turk efforts to bolster the Libyan resistance to the Italians. As a result of his expertise, he was hired as the personal chauffeur of Enver Pasha, the Young Turk leader. Following the Italian victory in the Libyan war he accompanied his important friend to Istanbul, where he studied Turkish and perfected his literary Arabic. During World War I he claimed to have headed the servicing section in the Ottoman army's automobile fleet. In 1918, following the conclusion of the war, M'hamed Ali fled with Enver Pasha from Turkey to Germany. When his mentor moved on to the Soviet Union in 1919, he remained in Berlin. There he resided, except for brief trips to Tunisia in 1922 and 1923, before finally returning home in March 1924.

In Germany, M'hamed Ali moved in socialist and labor union circles. Between November 1921 and January 1924 he worked in an aircraft-manufacturing plant and intermittently studied political economy at one of several free universities in Berlin. Tahar al-Haddad, who cofounded the Confédération générale des travailleurs tunisiens (CGTT) with him, recalls his friend's enthusiastic references to the German labor movement. According to Haddad, it was the revolutionary zeal of German workers that inspired M'hamed Ali to devote himself to the betterment of Muslim countries. Whether or not M'hamed Ali obtained a degree at Berlin is uncertain. Although his enemies often asserted he had not, he himself would neither confirm nor deny it, though he allowed those who wished to believe it to do so. In refusing to confirm it, he implicitly denied the importance of status symbols. In laying claim to it (when arrested, for example) he used it as an instrument of struggle.

In 1924 M'hamed Ali returned to Tunisia, where he soon became a leader of the young, progressive nationalists, who included Haddad, Mahmoud Bourguiba, Othman Kaak, and the Algerian Ahmed Tewfik al-Medani. These young radicals sought a socially progressive and economically dynamic Tunisia. They explicitly opposed the so-called Old Turbans in the Destour, who spoke of Islam and Muslim culture with the tenacity of wounded devotees. M'hamed Ali and Haddad questioned their cultural heritage with the agonizing uncertainty of honest appraisers.

Unlike Destour party leaders such as Abd al-Aziz Talbi, author of *La Tunisie Martyre,* M'hamed Ali and his associates did not consider Tunisia simply a "martyr" of French aggression. On the contrary, they credited the French with jolting the Tunisian consciousness and with introducing Tunisians to modern techniques of economy and administration. To them, the subjugation of Tunisia to France was the result of internal weaknesses. They believed that meaningful emancipation could come only from a total reform of the society and the individual.

Instead of directing their energies toward dramatizing Tunisia's legal claims to independence and pinning their hopes for political reform on Woodrow Wilson, the League of Nations, and the French socialists, men like M'hamed Ali and Haddad insisted on looking inward. They placed a strong emphasis on self-improvement and self-reliance and on the search for the organizing principles of society. They also believed that it was necessary to root out the causes of backwardness, however sanctified by tradition they might be.

In the 1920s, direct contact with Marxists was commonplace among Tunisian nationalist and labor union leaders. A few liberals within the Destour party had joined the Socialist party during the war, when all other political groupings had been outlawed. Contact with the European Left in Tunisia pushed the nationalists toward the adoption of progressive positions. The French workers' organization, the Confédération générale des travailleurs (CGT), was affiliated with the union in France and had a great influence on men like M'hamed Ali and Tahar al-Haddad. It recruited Tunisians into a modern workers' organization based on progressive ideology. In this way Tunisian workers came to have admiration for the ideals of 1789, while deploring the colonialist excesses of the French government. Haddad acknowledged this debt when he praised the Socialists, who recognized the "injustices and inequalities within the working class" and in whose CGT branches "Tuni-

sian workers . . . participated in the strikes, in the organization and expansion of unions, and attended meetings." There, he went on, "they
heard leaders . . . proclaim the liberty and equality of man; declare that
the religion of the worker was his labor and his enemy was capitalism,
that neither race nor religion distinguished the workers from each other,
for these are the tools that capitalism employs in order to divide them
and to defeat their objectives."

Because of attitudes like these, Tunisian labor leaders had a dual view
of France. Although they resented being the dominated and scorned
majority in an ethnically divided country, they were attracted by the
Left's vision of liberty, equality, and fraternity, in a society in which race
and religion were transcended. At a time when the colonized were seeking to understand the causes of their subjugation, the European Left offered an interpretation of imperialism that was both satisfying and easy
to understand.

Still, the colonial situation was full of contradictions. The Tunisian
working class competed for jobs with a substantial number of privileged
European workers—some 44,000 out of 107,500 salaried workers in
1926. In effect they had become second-ranking workers in their own
country. Competition with Europeans was unequal, discrimination in
pay scales and wages galled many, and racist attitudes of European
coworkers could hardly promote human dignity. Haddad's contemporary description of the crisis of the interwar period brings out these
contradictions:

> Artisanal production has decreased; numerous professional people have
> gone bankrupt, and they have joined the ranks of the unemployed, who in
> turn are joined by the inhabitants of the southern infertile lands and by
> members of the tribes who are evicted from their lands by French colonial-
> ism. These are convenient circumstances for the grand French capitalists,
> who exploit the mining resources of Tunisia, who construct railroads . . .
> and factories such as limestone and cement works. These capitalists have
> been able to find by the hundreds, even thousands, an army of unem-
> ployed whose numbers increase with the passage of time. Capital recruits
> only as a function of its needs; it has been able to use the masses for hard
> labor at low pay, while others, and they are numerous, have to wander on
> the roads and in the towns, either begging or robbing.

M'hamed Ali, too, was deeply moved by the backward and miserable
condition of Tunisians. He described "the wretched condition of so
many of our people who live like animals." At night it was his practice to
walk in the *medina* (the old Arab quarter), indignant at the sight of the
poor, half-starved and seminaked, sleeping on sidewalks, receiving from
"heaven its gift of heavy rain," and yet satisfied with their *maktub* (fate),

while, he noted, "our leaders" sleep "in their fancy beds with their wives, their children and their golden dreams."

Despite M'hamed Ali's frustration with the Tunisian elite, the new order tended to bring Tunisian classes into closer, if superficial, contact. Before the protectorate, Haddad noted,

> important families abhorred labor, and they became high functionaries in the administration or they lived off an annual income from the exploitation of their lands by agricultural laborers. It is with the same disdain that they considered commerce, which for them was comparable to manual labor. Commercial activity meant that they would cater to a clientele to whom they would have to be nice. . . . They found that an unsupportable burden and a bit humiliating.

But the immigration of about 110,000 Europeans into the protectorate by 1900 led to the Tunisian notables—at times impoverished by their loss of function and land—to join the ranks of the old merchant families and new self-made people to form a local bourgeoisie.

Simultaneously the leaders of the European colony—mostly French—assumed the role of a new aristocracy. The lives of the Tunisian upper crust increasingly became filled with empty forms and ceremonies. Their dominance was significantly reduced; their way of life was threatened. European settlement accentuated this threat and compelled the Tunisian bourgeoisie to seek mass support in the emergent Tunisian working class.

Given these contradictory tendencies, M'hamed Ali concluded, as did Haddad, that conditions in Tunisia were not yet ripe for class struggle or a full-fledged social revolution. While accepting the general theory of class struggle, they denied its validity for colonial Tunisia, where the process of industrialization and class formation had been delayed and distorted. In their analysis, race took precedence over class in defining the major social cleavages in colonial Tunisia. The chief concern was not so much with the local class struggle as with getting rid of the European occupiers. While M'hamed Ali and his friends did not rule out the possibility of an internal revolutionary conflict in the future—at least Haddad articulated this position—in the organizational sphere M'hamed Ali stressed the need for Tunisians to bury their differences and unite in revolt against foreign domination.

World War I and the debilitating political and economic environment of the 1920s accelerated this potential for revolt. New disappointments accentuated old anger among increasingly larger sections of the population. Some 65,000 Tunisians had fought for France during the war, and of these 10,900 had died or disappeared. An additional 30,000 had worked on construction brigades in the metropolitan area. Therefore nearly a quarter of the active Tunisian male population had had direct contacts with the metropolis. Their sacrifice, loyalty, and service led them to expect rewards from France. Instead they returned home to face unemployment, high prices caused by inflation, and a fiscal system that violated basic social justice. The tax system hurt the already exploited Tunisians and gave settlers and French capitalists major privileges.

This crisis was exacerbated by major crop failures in postwar Tunisia. The 1919 crop was mediocre, and the 1920 harvest was one of the worst since the great famine of 1867. In 1921 it was a bit better, but from 1922 until 1924 less grain was harvested than was needed to feed the population. The French protectorate government was forced to import wheat at high prices. As a result, the cost of living rose by 29 percent between 1923 and 1924, and workers began to clamor for higher wages. The postwar economic crisis thus wiped out whatever profits Tunisians had gained during the war. In addition, Tunisian war veterans, like the workers who labored alongside the Europeans or the many who unsuccessfully sought work, were no longer ready to accept the status quo that treated them as inferiors. Inevitably, the national question came to seem the key to everything else.

In 1924 the political situation came to a head. With M'hamed Ali as the chairman of its management committee, the young nationalists launched a consumer cooperative movement in June and July, seeking thereby to expand the outreach of the nationalists and to impart new skills and a new sense of self-reliance among Tunisians. The management committee under M'hamed Ali had just started its work when Tunisian workers openly defied the orders of the leadership of the CGT. In August the dockers of Tunis and Bizerte, some of whom had grown close to M'hamed Ali through the cooperative movement, went on strike, demanding wages equal to those of French port workers. When the CGT leaders in Tunis advised moderation and calm, the workers formed an independent strike committee and solicited the help of the intellectual and youthful elements within the Destour party.

The striking dockers appealed for help to the leadership of the cooperative. M'hamed Ali responded to their call at the risk of exposing himself to charges of confounding objectives. Conflict, however, was inherent in the dual goals he set for Tunisians to achieve, namely, winning national autonomy and achieving social and economic progress for the masses. He had hoped to launch the cooperative movement to enhance the political strength of the nationalists, but he gave greater long-range importance to economic and social progress. Yet when faced with the critical alternative of abandoning the striking workers and thereby losing his potentially most important constituency, which favored the securing of his reformist program, he opted for political and syndical activism.

The dockers found ready support in the young Destourians, particularly M'hamed Ali, Tahar al-Haddad, and Tewfik al-Medani. After two weeks of peaceful picketing and an unsuccessful appeal to the bey and his prime minister, the strikers under M'hamed Ali's leadership appealed for help to the public. Popular street demonstrations, clashes with the police, and widespread support for the striking workers forced the Destour to endorse the workers' demands publicly. Under severe economic pressure, the maritime company in Tunis accepted arbitration. A compromise settlement was worked out by the terms of which some of the workers' demands were granted. On 6 September, the twenty-four-day Tunis dockers' strike ended, and that of the Bizerte dockers ended soon thereafter.

The strikes crystallized widespread discontent and set in motion a chain of events that was to lead by November to a permanent split in the CGT. The strikes had demonstrated the effectiveness of organized mass political action. They also revealed widespread and deep discontent among people who were willing to sacrifice heroically in order to win minor economic, but major psychological, battles against foreign exploiters. A propaganda committee under M'hamed Ali concentrated on winning popular support and the nationalist party's backing for the striking workers. Financial and moral support permitted a prolonged strike and ultimate victory. It also confirmed the young trade unionists' belief that a trade union could become viable and strong only with mass and party backing based on a nationalist appeal.

The initially hostile attitude of the French-dominated Socialist party and CGT further alienated the Tunisians from the metropolitan federation and intensified the move toward the creation of a national— and ultimately nationalist—labor movement. Arguments and debates started between the French socialists and M'hamed Ali's group. The split between Tunisians and European workers in the CGT eventually culminated in the establishment of a nationalist union, the CGTT, in November 1924. This development was the outgrowth of a protracted period of conflict and debate on the left. During the summer, striking workers, lacking the support of the CGT labor federation, established several autonomous local unions. In Tunis the dockers, textile workers, streetcar employees, cement-factory workers, and some traditional handicraftsmen formed their own unions. Workers in Bizerte and other coastal towns also left the CGT at this time.

The European Left vehemently opposed the formation of a nationalist organization on the grounds that such a labor union would be in-

imical to the principles of labor solidarity. They charged the union se-
ceders with racism, communalism, and negativism. The multiplication
of autonomous Tunisian unions alarmed CGT officials in France. Léon
Jouhaux, secretary general of the CGT, arrived in Tunis on 24 October
1924 and urged M'hamed Ali to help maintain workers' unity and solidarity. At a public meeting on 31 October, Jouhaux conceded that although the CGT rejected in principle any differences of race or color, in
practice the European workers in Tunisia had given the Muslims a genuine cause for complaint. But he warned that separatism would only
perpetuate evil practices and attitudes while intensifying divisions
within the working class.

The Socialist party (SFIO) in Tunisia presented a serious moral and
political challenge to the nationalist labor movement because it could
not be easily dismissed as imperialist, and its objections had to be answered and accommodated. The Socialists were as consistent in opposing the pretensions and the continued privileges of the settlers as they
were in objecting to what they regarded as the "narrow, communal,
counterrevolutionary" character of nationalism. The real issues, they argued, were neither national, racial, nor religious; the working class
should not permit fragmentation by dividing along such lines. European
and Tunisian workers faced common enemies: the dominance of capitalism and the clergy in an alliance of special privilege perpetuated by
the dead hand of tradition. The answer, they stressed, was to build a
movement, liberate humanity from superstition, instill a revolutionary
spirit in people, and build mass institutions to defeat imperialism. The
Left could point to their efforts in this direction. The Socialist party and,
after the December 1920 split, the Communist party were the only in-
terracial political institutions in Tunisia, and their unions were the only
ones in which both Europeans and Muslims were full members.

Not all Tunisian workers favored splitting the CGT. In response to
M'hamed Ali's proposal to establish a national Tunisian union federation, some workers, led by Ahmed Ben Milad and Mokhtar al-Ayari
(who nevertheless became a founder of the CGTT), at first opposed
him. They argued that the plan smacked of religious prejudice and violated the principle of universalism. M'hamed Ali pleaded with them:

> The creation of a Tunisian federation does not mean that we shall not be
> united with the workers of the world as a whole. France, Germany, and
> England have national federations. Why are we denied similar rights? The
> only reason for their [the European Left's] attitude is that they would like
> to consider us a part of France. Is not imperialism a denial of equality?
> Why such accusations from Socialists and Communists? Are they also de-
> ceiving us?

On the ideological level, nationalist labor leaders were placed on the defensive. They often took their cues from the CGT program and ideology and defined their goals in the moral, universal, and progressive terms that they had learned in the parent organization. In order to counter the harsh criticism from the European Left, M'hamed Ali and his comrades had to define their goals clearly and make distinctions between political exigencies and long-term objectives. In so doing they might win over Europeans who, like the Communists after their initial hesitation, could aid them to gain their freedom.

"If we achieve social progress, remove our internal weaknesses inherited from the past, and begin to view the world clearly and with a broad outlook," Haddad wrote,

> then we will be able to convince many Europeans that we deserve a free life. The Europeans do not trust our feelings; when we ask for freedom they think that we hate their presence among us, that freedom to us only means the license to wander aimlessly around the streets of our nation even if this delays industrialization and leaves natural treasures buried in the ground. They mistrust us. What they say seems true when matched by our immobility and our satisfaction in exposing only their injustices and our hatred.

When the CGTT was formally established in November 1924, M'hamed Ali was named its secretary general. He headed a provisional executive committee of twelve members, six of whom were veteran trade unionists. Initially the new federation made rapid gains. Its leaders demonstrated unusual organizing ability, and the masses proved ready for mobilization. After consolidating their position in Tunis they moved into the provinces. M'hamed Ali in the south and Mokhtar al-Ayari in the north registered unexpected successes. At its first congress in January of 1925 the CGTT publicly flaunted its achievement. A majority of employed Tunisians had gathered under its banner. For the first time, activists had tried and succeeded in mobilizing and organizing an important segment of the mass. For the first time a Tunisian militant, M'hamed Ali, had reached the grassroots by articulating concrete and specific demands. Yet its very success exposed the union to repression.

The protectorate authorities were alarmed when union organizers reached the farms of French settlers, and Tunisian workers began calling for land reform and speaking out against colonial exploitation. The French chief of police, who arbitrated labor disputes, called on M'hamed Ali to dissolve the federation and merge with the CGT. Instead, he responded by intensifying his efforts. He won over more affiliates, which only increased the ire of the Socialists, who then controlled the French government. Significant weaknesses soon appeared among the nationalists. The Destourian leaders who had hitherto supported the CGTT discreetly began to prepare to abandon them in return for reforms that they were negotiating with the French Socialist government. Only Communist leaders backed the CGTT, but this enthusiastic support further exposed the Tunisian workers to the red-baiting practiced by the settler lobby.

The contradictions within the nationalist camp added to those within the Left exposed to the CGTT to repression. Events did not cooperate either. Just as the CGTT was holding its first congress in Tunis, a wildcat strike broke out in a cement factory in Hammam-Lif on the outskirts of the city. Three days later, it spread to farm workers and limestone quarry workers at the *domaine de Potinville*, which was owned by the powerful French businessman Félix Potin. The CGTT leaders knew the risk they were running, but there was no alternative other than to support the strikers. The expected French crackdown was not long in coming. On 5 February 1925 M'hamed Ali, Mokhtar al-Ayari, and J. P. Finidori were arrested. Following protest demonstrations three other militants— Muhammad al-Ghanouchi, Mahmoud al-Kabadi, and Ali Daraoui— were apprehended and charged with conspiring against the security of the state.

The French authorities easily isolated the young leaders. A Destourian delegation to Paris led by its secretary general, Ahmed Essafi, had already negotiated the appointment of a Tunisian reform commission, and Essafi's group hoped for more political concessions. Charging that the nationalists were Communist dupes, French settler interests sought to sabotage the provisional agreement. French police raided M'hamed Ali's living quarters and found forty books in German, leading them to claim that he was a German agent sent to Tunisia to sabotage the French colonial enterprise. Destour leaders answered the anti-Communist propaganda with an equally anti-Communist declaration. A few days later, they repudiated the CGTT, abandoned its imprisoned leaders, and adopted the Socialist party position.

M'hamed Ali and the other leaders were placed on a ship destined for Naples and sent into exile. Soon after his arrival there, Italian authorities arrested M'hamed Ali and expelled him to Turkey, where he was also declared unwelcome by the authorities. Ten days later, he arrived in Port Said in Egypt. From there he set out for Morocco to join the Rifian revolt of Abd al-Krim. Before reaching his destination M'hamed Ali was again arrested in Tangier and deported to Egypt. There he was cared for by friends from Berlin until he moved on to Arabia, where, according to correspondence found in Shaykh Abd al-Aziz Talbi's papers, he died in 1927. After independence, the Tunisian government had his body transferred from Arabia to Tunis, where it was accorded a hero's burial.

## A NOTE ON SOURCES

An earlier version of this article appeared under the title of "M'hamed Ali and the Tunisian Labour Movement" in *Race & Class* 19 (1978): 253–76. Material used in this essay was initially collected during fieldwork in Tunisia in the early and mid-1960s. It also draws upon archival research in 1976 in the General Archives of the Tunisian government, series on the history of the national movement, especially carton 11. The authors would like to thank Mr. Moncef Dellagi, former director of these archives, for his invaluable assistance. Also consulted in the late 1980s were archives in the Ministry of Foreign Affairs, especially the series Tunisia 1$^{er}$ versement (Nantes) and the series Tunisia 1917–40 (Paris). French and Tunisian newspapers were also consulted.

## SUGGESTIONS FOR FURTHER READING

Three books are especially valuable in dealing with our subject. Tahar al-Haddad, *Al-ummal al-tunisiyun wa zuhur al-haraka al-inqabiya* (Tunis, 1927); Ahmed Ben Milad, *M'hammed Ali: La naissance du mouvement ouvrier tunisien* (Tunis, 1984); and Mustafa Kraim, *Nationalisme et syndicalisme en Tunisie, 1918–1929* (Tunis, 1976).

For works in English on this period of Tunisian history, see Eqbal Ahmad, "Trade Unionism in the Maghreb," in *State and Society in Independent North Africa*, ed. Leon Carl Brown (Washington, D.C., 1964); Jacques Berque, *French North Africa: The Maghrib between Two World Wars* (New York: Praeger, 1962); Charles Micaud et al., *Tunisia: The Politics of Modernization* (New York, 1964); Edouard Méric, "The Destourian Socialist Party and the Nationalist Organizations," in *Man, State and Society in the Contemporary Maghrib*, ed. I. W. Zartman (New York, Praeger, 1973).

1. Assaf Khater. Courtesy of the Khater family.

2. Mohand N'Hamoucha.
Photo by Lawrence Rosen.
Used with permission.

3. Shaykh Muhammad Ibn Abi al-Qasim of al-Hamil, Algeria. From Octave Depont and Xavier Coppolani, *Les confréries réligieuses musulmanes* (Algiers: Jourdan, 1897).

4. Shaykh Izz al-Din al-Qassam. From *Before Their Diaspora: A Photographic History of the Palestinians, 1876–1948,* with introduction and commentary by Walid Khalidi (Washington, D.C.: Institute for Palestinian Studies, 1984, 1991).

5. M'hamed Ali, a Tunisian worker. From Zin Abd al-Din al-Sinusi, *Kitab al-janat* (Tunis, 1925), p. 48, consulted at the French Archives, Nantes, 1er versement Tunisie no. 2171. Photographed and retouched by Roger Haile. Used with permission.

6. Hagob and Arshalous Hagobian and their son. Courtesy of the Yaghoubian family.

7. Migdim, a bedouin woman. Lila Abu-Lughod / Anthro-photo.

8. Mehdi Abedi and Michael Fischer. Photo by Susann Wilkinson.

9. Sumaya, a Lebanese housemaid. Courtesy of Sumaya.

10. Haddou, a Moroccan migrant worker. Photo by David McMurray.

11. Abu Jamal and his grandson Muhammad at Netanya Beach, 1986. Photo by Joost Hiltermann.

# FOURTEEN

# Muhammad El Merid:
# The Man Who Became *Qaid*

*David Seddon*

In 1921 the Spanish colonial rulers of northern Morocco were overwhelmed and decisively defeated at the battle of Anual by Rifian tribesman under the leadership of Abd al-Krim al-Khattabi. It was one of the greatest defeats a European army suffered by a colonized people—the Spanish lost more than twenty thousand men in this one battle.

The war in the Rif was one of the last episodes in the bloody conquest of Morocco by Spain and France, who in 1912 divided Morocco between themselves and established separate protectorate governments. The Spanish zone extended from the Algerian frontier to Tangier along the Mediterranean coast and consisted mostly of the mountainous Rif and Jabala districts. Most of Morocco to the south came under the control of the French. Moroccans put up a fierce struggle against both the French and Spanish colonial regimes. The Rif war was one of the most glorious chapters in the history of Moroccan resistance. It ended in 1925, when Abd al-Krim was finally defeated by the combined armies of both France and Spain.

Unlike most Rifians, Muhammad El Merid, the subject of David Seddon's contribution, was not tempted to join Krim's "Ripublik." His story is that of a wily opportunist who, seeing the chance to exploit the ill-defined borders between the French and Spanish jurisdictions, pulled off a spectacular land grab at the expense of the rest of the Zaio community, among whom he lived, and got the Spanish colonial authorities to underwrite his ambitions.

Individuals like El Merid certainly existed in goodly number not only in Morocco but throughout the region. Human nature being what it is, there is never a shortage of people willing to take advantage of misfortune. The colonial situation in this sense was no different from any other. Colonial regimes, despite their illegitimacy in the eyes of the local population, brought not only suffering and oppression but also economic opportunities and at times a more efficient, less corrupt government. Their seeming permanence and the fact that they also claimed implicitly to be on the side of progress led many Middle Easterners to try to make the best of a bad situation.

Where individuals drew the line varied depending upon their personal character and the particular context. From no compromise to opportunistic collaboration, individuals organized their lives as best they could. Some whom we have seen above, like Izz al-Din al-Qassam, portrayed by Abdullah Schleifer, refused to make any concessions. Others, like the shaykh of al-Hamil and his daughter, (about whom Julia Clancy-Smith has written), took pains to keep their autonomy while cooperating with colonial authorities on some matters. Indeed, some individuals could be by turns hero and collaborator (or indeed both at once), as both Edmund Burke's and Lisa Anderson's contributions show. El Merid's case is a useful reminder that despite some nationalist retrospective reconstructions of the colonial past not all individuals were heroes.
—ED.

Muhammad El Merid (El Merid means "the sickly") rose from humble origins to a position of *qaid* (governor) of the *qabila* (tribe) of the Ulad in Zaio in northeastern Morocco as a result of his collaboration with colonial authority. His life story reveals how colonialism made it possible for an opportunistic "nobody" to rise to a position of preeminence. The career of Muhammad El Merid, "the man who became *qaid*," involved him in a series of bitter disputes with his own people, particularly with those among whom he lived as a young man. These conflicts were to last even beyond his own lifetime, setting kinsman against kinsman and neighbor against neighbor.

To render the career of Muhammad El Merid intelligible, one must situate it in the complex and turbulent political context of early twentieth-century Morocco; especially against the background of the rivalries between Spain, France, and the Moroccan government in the northeastern frontier region, which provided the opening for self-made men like El Merid. From the time of its attempted *reconquista* of Morocco in the fifteenth century, Spain had gained control of a number of strong points in northern Morocco, among them the port of Melilla. Not until 1890, however, and largely in response to the European scramble for Africa and French, British, and German colonial ambitions in Morocco, did Spain develop imperialist dreams of its own in northeastern Morocco. These were opposed not only by local tribesmen loyal to the Moroccan government but by French interests based in colonial Algeria. While the government of Abd al-Aziz (1894–1908) sought to support local patriotic forces, both the French and the Spanish tried to find support among unscrupulous local Moroccan leaders. Since the status of the northeast was not settled until the establishment of the French and Spanish protectorates in 1912, the intervening years presented ample opportunities for would-be Moroccan entrepreneurs to set up shop. One of the more successful was Muhammad El Merid.

Northeast Morocco at the turn of the century was a patchwork of tribes, some reliant on cereal cultivation and small-scale agriculture, others dependent on livestock production and transhumant pastoralism. One of the smallest of the pastoral tribes was the Arabic-speaking Ulad Stut (Children of the Ogress), inhabiting the Sebra Plain and the hills to the west of the Moulouya River. The group of Ulad Stut called El Abbed occupied the southeastern part of the Sebra Plain and comprised four major clans: Daanun, Ulad Ali, Ulad Messaoud, and Juerba. They held land in common for grazing, although each of the four clans had a roughly defined territory within which it claimed rights to cultivate a little cereal and to pasture its sheep, goats, and a few camels. Some say that El Merid came to El Abbed to work as a shepherd. A young man of humble background, he crossed the Moulouya River from his home among the Ait Isnassen, a large Berber-speaking tribe that inhabited the mountains between the Moulouya and the colonial Algerian frontier. When Muhammad El Merid married Fatna Buabu of the Juerba clan of Ulad Stut some time in the first five years of the present century, he acquired a connection with the tribe. In the course of their marriage, she bore him several sons. Despite their father's Ait Isnassen origins, his offspring regarded themselves as Ulad Stut.

Muhammad El Merid was in his late teens or early twenties around 1902, when the Abu Himara rebellion erupted, setting in motion a chain of events that was to lead to the end of Moroccan independence and the establishment of the French and Spanish protectorates in 1912. At first Abu Himara was a staunch opponent of European imperialism as well as of the dynasty, which he accused of insufficient zeal in warding off the imperialist threat. Later he shifted. By 1903, no longer a direct threat to the throne, he moved to the region of Melilla, where without renouncing his earlier mission he gradually became a local power broker. Both Spain and France saw the rebellion of Abu Himara as an ideal opportunity to extend their interests in northeast Morocco. In 1907, with the help of French businessmen from Oran, Abu Himara established a munitions plant on the coast, southeast of Melilla. Abu Himara's involvement in the politics of the Moroccan northeast greatly exacerbated the tensions within the society and provoked much social turbulence. Some local tribes supported him, and others opposed him, while still others, like the Ulad Stut, were divided in their loyalties.

In 1907, no longer a serious threat to the Moroccan government and increasingly a nuisance locally, the rebel leader sold the right to exploit the iron mines west of Melilla and to construct a railway to transport the ore to Spanish interests. Following a change of ruler in 1908, a combination of the sultan's forces and growing local opposition obliged Abu Himara to leave the region. Spanish troops captured his munitions factory and began to build a rail link between Melilla and the iron mines to the west. Local tribesmen resisted these incursions, and a bitter struggle ensued, as a result of which the Spanish army suffered more than 4,000 casualties. After five months, however, superior Spanish organization and weaponry began to tell, and the tribes sued for peace. Spanish garrisons were established throughout the north of the region, including one at Selwan on the northernmost borders of Ulad Stut territory. To maintain its control thereafter, Spain kept a regular force of about 6,000 men and 210 officers in the region, together with a reserve of some 3,000 men based at Nador, just south of Melilla.

Since their occupation of Moroccan territory had not been sanctioned by the great powers who controlled international politics at the time, the Spanish authorities dared not seek to administer it directly but instead sought to work through local notables. They carefully deployed gifts and promises of personal gain to win loyalty and support. Late in 1910, after the king of Spain visited Melilla and reviewed the troops at Selwan, the governor of Melilla received deputations of local notables from several tribal groups, including the Ulad Stut, who signaled their general support for the Spanish presence.

In 1911, the Spanish governor of Melilla grew concerned about the possibility of French incursions across the Moulouya from the area around Berkane, where the French had established a military camp and a small European town as early as 1907–8. In May of 1911 the governor sent a force farther into the interior, up the Moulouya River itself, to safeguard the newly pacified territory. A military camp was set up at El Tumiat (later to be called Zaio) to the north of the Sebra Plain. A guard post was built at the southernmost extremity of the Sebra overlooking the river crossing Mechra Saf Saf. At the same time Spanish troops were sent westward to control the mountain areas of the Rif. After a year of fierce fighting and the death of a major leader of the resistance, Spain officially declared in protectorate over northern Morocco in 1912.

The Ulad Stut offered virtually no resistance to the Spanish penetration of their territory, and the Spanish had no fears of an uprising. However, the ill-defined frontier to the east and south of the Moulouya River came to mark the border between the Spanish and French zones of Morocco, though not without continuing Spanish anxiety about French claims on northeastern Morocco. After the division of Morocco into French and Spanish protectorates in 1912, El Abbed and other groups of Moroccans in the border area around Sebra began to sell their land to European settlers. The fact that some settlers were French further alarmed the Spanish, who feared a creeping annexation by land-hungry Frenchmen from Algeria. With their hands tied by the need to respect established diplomatic forms governing relations between the French and Spanish zones, Spanish authorities cast about for a stratagem to keep French speculators and would-be settlers at bay. Their chosen instrument was Muhammad El Merid, who must already have been known to them as a potential collaborator.

With the colonial context setting the framework, the career of El Merid thus revolved around protracted struggles over land in which it is not always easy to follow the thread of causality. Precisely what happened is difficult to determine, since family members, Spanish officials, and Moroccan cultivators of the land have different versions. The subject remained controversial as late as the 1970s. Disputes involving legal title to collectively held land are frequent in the annals of colonial North Africa because of the sharp contrast between capitalist notions of private property and the communal rights traditionally held by Moroccan cultivators. Land disputes were further exacerbated by the colonial context and the Franco-Spanish rivalry in northeastern Morocco. This was notably the case in northeastern Morocco, where in order to prevent French encroachment upon the Spanish side of the Moulouya River it was important for the Spanish to preserve their rights to the Sebra Plain and to find a way of contesting the legality of French land purchases in the region. Their success was due in no small measure to the existence of unscrupulous individuals like Muhammad El Merid, who were delighted to take advantage of the opportunities presented to them.

Typically there are a number of conflicting accounts of how the El Abbed land war began. According to one observer, El Merid

> was a *mokhazni* ("native" soldier) with the French in Berkane at this time, although his home was now with El Abbed. The Spanish heard of him and his willingness to help them, and they invited him to discuss the matter. They said that they would give him money to buy back the land; and this he did. In 1914, together with the Spanish authorities, he drew up a title, giving himself rights to half of the land concerned and a Spanish company rights to the other half.

His sons, by contrast, paint a rather different picture of their father. They claim that he married into the clan of El Abbed some time before 1910 and acquired full rights to a large tract of land in the southern part of the Sebra by purchase from other members of the group. This seems unlikely, as is shown in a Spanish report found in the local colonial archives in Zaio dated 11 August 1932. According to its author,

> the French wished to acquire these lands in our zone, and in order to prevent this a false purchase was engineered and registered retrospectively in the name of [Muhammad El Merid]. This avoided the danger that the land would pass into the hands of the French, and matters would then have continued as before, with each real owner continuing to work his

land, for in fact [those occupying the land] . . . had not ceded their property rights. But [El Merid] decided to make use of the registration in the registry office to establish private title. It was this appropriation of the land of . . . El Abbed as a whole that provided the basis of the [continuing] conflict [between El Merid and the other members of El Abbed].

How to make sense of this confusing tangle? The record shows that in 1916 Muhammad El Merid registered ownership of a large tract of land in the southern part of the Sebra, allegedly on behalf of the El Abbed community. On the basis of this formal registration he was able to have the title transformed from the French investors to himself in August 1916. Through a clever legal stratagem, the "collectively owned" land of El Abbed became the private property of El Merid. The Spanish authorities clearly intended this end. They regarded El Merid's registration as simply a way of preventing the alienation of collectively held lands to the French. Once this particular danger had been preempted, they expected that effective rights of cultivation and grazing would revert to the members of El Abbed as before. But this was to reckon without El Merid's cunning. In December of the same year, a further document was drawn up on the basis of the land registry document, witnessed by twelve notables of the Ulad Stut, and signed and authenticated by local "traditional" legal personnel. By it, Muhammad El Merid acquired title to "that portion of the land in front of Dar El Abbed."

Especially in areas where pastoralism was prevalent, collectively held tribal land came under dramatically increased pressure from land speculators in the early years of the Spanish protectorate. Spanish authorities must have vaguely apprehended the dangers of this situation, for in 1912 they published a decree forbidding the transfer of ownership of collective land between private individuals. However, this decree was systematically ignored. A further decree of 1914 set up a system of land registration whereby title to land could be established or confirmed. Many Spaniards, having bought land illegally from locals, now registered their new properties and thereby confirmed their legal title to the land. Few Moroccans registered private title to land in the colonial land registry. In 1916 a further decree confirmed that of 1912 regarding the inalienability of collective land by individuals, but since few of the collectivities registered their common ownership, their rights to the land in question were open to dispute under Spanish colonial law. Only a few Moroccans, like Muhammad El Merid, took advantage of the possibilities inherent in this transformation of property rights.

During 1916 further sales of land in the Sebra took place without the knowledge of the Spanish authorities. This time the legal formalities were carried out in Berkane in the French zone. In 1933 Spanish officials in Zaio who were trying to unravel the mystery reported that when the Spanish authorities learned that the land . . . had been sold to foreigners, the *commandancia general* of Melilla named Muhammad El Merid as ukil [*wakil,* or legal representative] to start proceedings against the purchasers, who represented French companies. After several meetings . . . he managed to restore to our zone the lands sold without due authorization, and the *commandancia general* of Melilla awarded the French purchasers, who had lost the case, twenty thousand pesetas as compensation. This accomplished, the representatives of the tribe took charge of the lands concerned and sold them once again, this time to a Spanish company, according to the evidence of the property register. This included a piece of land named Teniet el Khobs Yaglula, and the transaction was carried out in 1918.

According to still other documents, the local inhabitants claimed that it had been sold by the tribal "representatives" without their knowledge and that Muhammad El Merid, who had supervised the sale, was guilty of fraud. Other groups also contested the appropriation and sale of their collective land. To these charges El Merid responded that the land was not collective but privately owned land and that all he had done was to supervise a transfer of property from French into Spanish hands.

In contrast to the relative ease of their takeover of the Sebra Plain near Melilla, the Spanish attempt in the 1920s to impose their authority on the tribes of the interior of the central Rif mountains ran into major difficulties. A coalition of tribes under the leadership of Muhammad ibn Abd al-Krim initiated armed resistance against them. Disregarding warnings of the danger, a Spanish force under General Silvestre sought in 1921 to invade the heartland of the powerful Aith Warayaghar tribe, where Abd al-Krim had set up his headquarters.

The result was a series of crushing Spanish defeats, notably at Dahar Ubarran and at Anual, where Spanish forces were annihilated. By August the Spanish army had been thrown back almost to the outskirts of Melilla, and the Spanish settlers who had begun to colonize the eastern region left their land and fled from Abd al-Krim's advancing tribesmen. It was one of the greatest defeats inflicted upon a European army in the annals of colonial warfare. Despite the proximity of the fighting, there is no evidence that these heroics rubbed off on the Ulad Stut. The Sebra Plain remained quiet throughout 1920. Many even joined the Spanish army to fight the Rifians (and earn a regular wage). Even after the disaster at Anual in the summer of 1921, Muhammad El Merid was active in assisting Spanish settlers to escape across the Moulouya River to the safety of the French zone.

In February 1923 Abd al-Krim proclaimed himself the head of a Rifian "Ripublik," and it looked for a time like he might be able to wrest control of northeastern Morocco from Spain. But Abd al-Krim's success brought France into the war and shifted the balance of the struggle. By 1925 Krim was defeated, and the Spanish were able to reestablish their rule over the eastern region once again. News of Muhammad El Merid's efforts to assist the Spanish in their hour of need had reached the colonial authorities back in Zaio. With the prospect of continued fighting in the central Rif after the grueling military campaign of 1921, Spanish officials had been desperate to maintain law and order wherever possible through local intermediaries. Already familiar with Muhammad El Merid as a result of his role in the Sebra land recuperation scheme, the Spanish colonial administration in gratitude named him *qaid* of the *qabila* of Ulad Stut. The fruits of collaboration were finally harvested.

With the end of the Rif war in 1925, the eastern region of the Spanish protectorate was transferred to the civil administration of the Delegacion de asuntos indigenas (Department of Native Affairs). According to the new system of organization, the regional level was placed under the jurisdiction of an official called the *interventor territorial*, while subregional administration was the responsibility of the *interventor comarcal*. The subregional circumscription, or *comarcal*, was divided into *qabilas* (tribal units), each under an *interventor local*. The Spanish protectorate administration was paralleled by "native" administration descending from *qaid* to *shaykh* and *muqaddam*.

As the *qaid* of the *qabila* of Ulad Stut, Muhammad El Merid was the most powerful and influential of indigenous Spanish protectorate officials in Zaio. While in principle he was subordinate to the local Spanish officials, he was generally able to exercise considerable autonomous authority within his *qabila*. In fact, El Merid exercised effective day-to-day control over general administration and justice in the tribe. He was responsible for law and order and could call upon a small security force (*makhazniya*) for this purpose if necessary. The position of the *qaid* in the Spanish and French protectorates was very similar. The *qaid* was said to have "great formal powers and even greater informal powers, and legal authority was elusively located between [him] and the [European officials] in such a way that power was often uncontrollable and unchecked."

Once installed as *qaid* of the Ulad Stut, El Merid was able to consolidate his hold on the lands of the Sebra. He used his position to exact gifts and tribute from fellow tribesmen and to place his sons and clients in positions of authority. As he began to accumulate wealth, El Merid's newfound political status enabled him to make favorable marriages for himself and for his children and thus to enlarge his network of relations and supporters. By Fatna, his El Abbed wife, he had four sons: Mukhtar, Buaza, Huma, and Ramdan. As befitted the status of a member of the Moroccan rural elite, he married often. In addition to his first wife, he married four women: one from the Ait Abu Yahi tribe, one from the Banu Awkil, one from the Ait Isnassen (his tribe of origin), and another from El Abbed. In all he had seven sons and several daughters by his various wives.

El Merid's rise to power was, as we have seen, by no means uncontroversial. Indeed, by the usual criteria he had little to recommend himself. He was uneducated and could neither read nor write; he spoke poor Spanish, and Arabic with a Berber accent. He was, as many put it, *walu* (nobody). The Spanish authorities had apparently considered making Muhammad El Merid *qaid* as early as 1917, but more than half of the *qabila* opposed him when this was proposed by the Spanish authorities, and he was not appointed. Despite his success, he continued to be regarded by many of the Arabic-speaking Ulad Stut as an Ait Isnassen Berber interloper.

Among those particularly resentful of his power and authority were the members of the El Abbed community into whom he had married, among whom he had lived, and whose land, many felt, he had appropriated for himself. Some, like the Ulad Ali, had particular cause to hate him. While *qaid*, El Merid had ordered the houses of the Ulad Ali to be burned and the members of the clan expelled from the area. Only after Morocco gained its independence in 1956 and El Merid was fired as *qaid* did they return.

The affair began in May 1929 when several men from El Abbed decided to build houses on their pastureland, as more and more pastoralists were doing at that time. When El Merid caught wind of their intentions, he forbade them to do so, stating that the land on which they planned to build belonged to him and that he had written documents to prove it. The men protested to the Spanish authorities, and after some argument El Merid agreed to cede them five hundred hectares, while charging them for the cost of the survey involved. But an agreement was never reached, nor was the land surveyed, for the "beneficiaries" contested both his right to the land and the identification of the plots made within the property for the families concerned. El Merid appointed a lawyer to defend his rights to the land in the Sebra, and the dispute dragged on into 1930 and 1931. The Spanish colonial authorities, concerned by the virulence with which the men of El Abbed pursued their claims, supported the *qaid*. What was at stake is revealed in a report by the local Spanish administrator dated September 1932. In it, the *interventor local* argued that

> it was not possible to divest the *qaid* of his formal rights, even if the claimants were in principle in the right (for which there is no documentary evidence), and it was not possible to give them what they asked for, unless the *qaid* agreed to cede it to them or unless through some mistake of the earlier ruling they were able to secure an annulment of the registration made

in 1916. In the latter case, as the suit against the French was won precisely on the basis of this title, should the title be found to be invalid, then the French could renew their claims.

Like El Merid, the Spanish authorities were determined to uphold the title established by the registration of 1916, however fraudulent its basis. However, according to the same report, they did advise him to "be as generous as possible and do everything possible to reach an agreement."

By this time El Merid was in his late forties, and his older sons were married. His eldest son, Mukhtar (who was himself to marry seven times), had his first son, Mbarek, in 1930. Although El Merid was now a grandfather, he had younger wives himself. His fifth son, Abd al-Qadir, was born in 1934, to be followed shortly afterwards by Hamid. His position as *qaid* was assured, and his family was flourishing. It was a good time "to be generous," as he put it. In 1935, El Merid agreed to cede some fifteen hundred hectares of land in the Sebra to the aggrieved El Abbed families. In 1936 preparations were made to survey the property in question and identify the different claims being made. However, on 17 July 1936, Spanish officers stationed in the military garrisons of Tetouan, Ceuta, and Melilla rose in rebellion against the Republican government. The Spanish civil war had begun. Because of this, the land was never surveyed, let alone allocated. Many Moroccans, including the El Abbed claimants themselves, soon became involved in the war. A 1969 survey determined that twenty-six of forty-two heads of household interviewed in El Abbed had fought in Spain. Of the fourteen who had seen no army service at all, eight had been too young.

El Merid's sons, like those of most of the rich families of Zaio, avoided participating in the fighting. With hostility toward supporters of the Spanish Republic in the region running high, there was always employment for a select few as informers and spies. El Merid's son Buaza, who was especially hated by the local population, was a member of the Moroccan Fascists during the war years. The other sons managed to elude military service during the war and remained in Zaio. They were among the first non-Spanish to construct houses within the village of Zaio itself, although they also had houses in the countryside. By the war's end, El Merid and his family had become part of the local notability. The eldest son, Mukhtar, was made *khalifa*, or deputy, of his father, while another son, Hamid, was given the position of shaykh.

The Spanish civil war and World War II brought a succession of hardships for many in Spanish Morocco. The harvests of 1934, 1935, and 1936 were poor, and that in 1937 was even worse. In 1938 a reasonable harvest was followed in 1939 by a very good one; but 1940, 1941, and 1942 were all years of poor harvests, while 1945 was catastrophic. The cereal crop was negligible, and livestock losses were terrible. Imported goods were very scarce because of the war. The cost of living nearly tripled between 1936 and 1940 and doubled again over the next five years. The eastern region was one of the hardest hit in the Spanish zone. Areas such as Zaio, where livestock production remained important, suffered more than most. As their indebtedness increased, the poor sought to obtain money for basic necessities and were compelled to sell their lands. As some became impoverished, others (merchants and officials in particular) grew rich at their expense.

The war years were marked by at least one additional development that impinged upon the Ulad Stut. After years of inactivity, a joint Spanish and French commission began work in 1942 on a plan for the irrigation of the Sebra Plain as part of a larger irrigation scheme to include both banks of the Moulouya River. A committee was appointed by the Spanish authorities to discuss the legal problems associated with land-ownership in the new irrigation perimeter. Qaid El Merid, whose nickname suggests that he had to contend with frequent illness, was unwell and unable to participate in its deliberations. Certain groups of the Ulad Stut, taking advantage of his absence, were able to engage a local judge (*qadi*) to help them establish legal title to collective properties in the Sebra Plain. They had documents drawn up supporting their rights to land that they claimed had formerly constituted their traditional grazing grounds. This was unusual. Outside of Zaio most tribesmen had not sought to claim rights they possessed under Spanish colonial law.

Certainly there were ample grounds for confusion about the status of collectively held lands in eastern Morocco. Although a decree of June 1929 had required the registration of collective lands, it had not been properly applied, nor had the necessary investigation of claims to collective status been carried out. Also not implemented were the additional decrees of October 1930 and July 1935, which had respectively further defined collective property and ordered the registration of all collective lands. But in Zaio, with the prospect of irrigation enhancing the value of land in the Sebra, those groups with traditional collective rights in the plain had realized the importance of formal registration; hence their efforts to draw up the appropriate documents to support subsequent registration.

When he heard of the legal challenge to his control of the El Abbed lands, El Merid decided to take the matter directly to the *interventor comarcal*. The *qaid* claimed that this new attempt to define property rights was invalid and that the activities of the local land commission were suspect. The *interventor* urged him to be reasonable and to come to an agreement with the members of his *qabila*. But the *qaid* refused to accept the documents presented to the local commission as valid. He asserted that the members of the land commission had been bribed and had given false information. The land, he stated, was owned by himself or by the Spanish company to which individual members of the various groups concerned had sold it. Emphasizing that his title to the land in question had been established in 1916, El Merid demanded that the land be returned to him.

In the past, this maneuver might have worked. However, in the changed postwar context of the Spanish protectorate, El Merid found himself in a greatly weakened position. With the rise of nationalism, the Spanish authorities were less vulnerable to attempts to play them off against French interests. In the changed political climate they also relied less upon local Moroccan collaborators and were more solicitous of the views of other groups. After years of having his way locally, Muhammad El Merid was no longer indispensable.

In 1949, in response to a demand from his superior to define the limits of the native collective according to the requirements of the law, a "Sebra collective" was established by the *interventor comarcal* of Zaio. It looked as though El Merid's enemies had prevailed. But this would be to reckon without the labyrinthine intricacies of the law and the lengthy history of litigation of this issue; for despite the fact that El Merid lost that particular battle, he still retained effective title to the lands in the southern Sebra in the traditional grazing grounds of El Abbed. In 1950, the dispute over these lands was still unresolved.

Muhammad El Merid remained *qaid* of the Ulad Stut in Zaio until Moroccan independence in 1956, when he was replaced by a proven nationalist. Infirm and ill, the old *qaid* survived until 1958. His sons and grandsons remain among the most influential and wealthy members of the notability of Zaio to this day. The fruits of collaboration have been shared by all the family of Muhammad El Merid.

### A NOTE ON SOURCES

Much of Muhammad El Merid's story is based upon oral histories and personal recollections collected during my first period of fieldwork as an anthropologist in northeast Morocco between 1968 and 1970. I have also consulted documents in the local archives in Zaio and Nador relating to the Spanish colonial period. In addition, a number of secondary sources, mainly in Spanish and French, were used to provide background.

### SUGGESTIONS FOR FURTHER READING

The author's book *Moroccan Peasants: A Century of Change in the Eastern Rif, 1870–1970*, published by William Dawson of Folkestone, England, provides a detailed analysis of economic and political change in the eastern Rif of northeast Morocco over a period of about a hundred years, from the late nineteenth century to the late 1960s. Other studies of the Rif from an anthropological point of view include David M. Hart's two-volume work *The Aith Waryaghar of the Moroccan Rif: An Ethnography and History,* Viking Fund Publications in Anthropology, no. 55 (Tucson: University of Arizona Press, 1976); and Raymond Jamous, *Honneur et Baraka: Les structures sociales traditionelles dans le Rif* (Cambridge: Cambridge University Press, 1978). Hart's study examines the Rif rebellion of Abd al-Krim, as do David Woolman's *Rebels in the Rif* (Oxford: Oxford University Press, 1969) and the contemporary account by Walter B. Harris, *France, Spain and the Rif* (London: Edward Arnold, 1927). Other attempts to provide local histories of the early days of European penetration include Ross E. Dunn, *Resistance in the Desert* (London: Croom Helm, and Madison: University of Wisconsin Press, 1977). For a general overview of precolonial (early twentieth-century) Morocco, see Edmund Burke, III, *Prelude to Protectorate in Morocco: Precolonial Protest and Resistance, 1860–1912* (Chicago: University of Chicago Press, 1976).

# FIFTEEN

# Hagob Hagobian:
# An Armenian Truck Driver in Iran

*David N. Yaghoubian*

Hagob Hagobian was one of the survivors of the Armenian massacres during World War I. His life thus began with the crushing of hopes for an independent Armenia homeland in eastern Anatolia. Hagobian grew up in an orphanage in western Iran and through his ability to take advantage of the chances that came his way was able to establish a financially secure position in middle-class society in Iran before emigrating to California in the 1970s.

As told by his grandson, David Yaghoubian, the story of Hagob Hagobian is that of a self-made man. His survival strategy revolved around his ability to exploit kin and ethnic networks, as well as his intense desire to better himself and his family. His biography sheds light on Iranian society between the 1920s and the 1950s. Of particular interest is his membership in the truck drivers' guild, an indication that the old Islamic guild system flourished into the twentieth century and even showed a capacity to adapt to changing times. The fact that the truckers' guild included both Muslims and non-Muslims is also of note. The role of Armenians in trade and commerce in Iran is well attested.* Hagobian's involvement in this line of work would therefore not have been exceptional.

What emerges from the biography of Hagobian is the role of Armenians in artisanal trades, notably in the development of the trans-Iran trucking industry. Fakhreddin Azimi's biography of Amir Agha, who was also a long-distance trucker for a time (see below, part 3), provides an interesting point of comparison. For both Hagob Hagobian and Amir Agha, World War II brought rapidly changing circumstances: first destroying, then providing, remarkable opportunity. Since Iran was a crucial strategic crossroads in the support of the Russian front, long-distance trucking boomed for some and increased their personal fortunes.

---

*For a brief summary, see Philip Curtin, *Cross-Cultural Patterns in World Trade* (Cambridge: Cambridge University Press, 1988), chap. 9.

Although Hagobian's truck was confiscated, and he was deprived of his means of livelihood, he later regained his modest wealth and his former position through perseverance. In contrast, Amir Agha's business flourished, but he frittered his newfound wealth away and ended up worse off than before. Ultimately Hagob Hagobian was able to utilize his hard work, determination, and social networks to make a success of his life in Iran, before emigrating to the United States.

A number of other lives recounted in this book also feature migrants (see the contributions of Akram and Antoine Khater, David McMurray, and Sami Zubaida). A comparison of them can yield some important insights. In each case, the varying strength of family and ethnic networks, different strategies, and a different personality helped to shape a different response. —ED.

The frightened Armenian boy stood in the doorway of his family's home as his mother rushed past him in a vain attempt to protect her husband as he was being attacked by a band of Kurdish men. Following the violent struggle the Kurds quickly rode away, leaving his parents' bodies in front of the farmhouse. Although Hagob Hagobian was the oldest of three brothers, at the age of seven he was far too young to understand the enormity of what had happened. Seeking help, he sadly led his smaller brothers away from their farming village of Khan-Baba-Khan into the countryside of northwestern Iran. It would be many years before Hagob could begin to understand the political and ethnic ramifications of the violence that orphaned the young boys in 1916.

Intercommunal violence resulting in scenes such as this was widespread in eastern Anatolia and Azerbaijan during and after the First World War. The violence was in many ways the result of the Young Turk policies concerning Armenians living in the Ottoman Empire, who had been persecuted as a group since the reign of Sultan Abdul Hamid began in 1876.

Hagob and his brothers found refuge at the Near East Relief Orphanage in Tabriz, the provincial capital of Azerbaijan. An American-sponsored Presbyterian mission, it was home to them for the duration of their childhood. Orphaned children from other areas affected by the Armenian genocide and intercommunal violence arrived at the center almost daily. One such child, Arshalous Harutoonian, a baby girl believed to have been born in Baku, was brought to the orphanage early in 1917 and years later would become Hagob's wife.

The orphanage not only provided a safe haven and the necessities of living but coordinated its efforts with the local Armenian priest to educate the children. With the help of older orphans and adult volunteers from the Armenian community in Tabriz, the priest and orphanage staff instructed the children in the Armenian language and taught them about their rich cultural heritage, rooted in Christianity since the fourth century A.D. The boys and girls also attended classes in Farsi, English, mathematics, music, and handicrafts such as sewing and carpet weaving, which were taught by local craftsmen. While Hagob did not have much interest in his academic subjects, he worked for hours on end weaving carpets with other children. This activity produced revenue for the orphanage to reinvest after the items were sold in the bazaar and provided the children with job skills and a way to help pay for their care.

Reza Khan toured Tabriz in 1924 following his rise to power, and the children of the orphanage were gathered to sing for his welcoming parade. In 1925 Reza Khan had the last Qajar shah deposed and proclaimed himself shah and founder of the new Pahlavi dynasty. Soon after this event, Hagob moved into a sparsely furnished room with several boys from the orphanage who at fourteen were considered old enough to support themselves. Each boy occupied a *takht*, or wooden bed frame, and owned his own bedding and some clothing. A woven cotton carpet, or *zelo*, covered the bare floor in the room, which was heated on the coldest nights by a wood-burning stove. Bread, cheese, and sweet tea made up the customary meal, and when work was steady the boys bought heartier meals of rice, lamb, and vegetables.

At the age of fifteen, Hagob supported himself by working at small jobs, one of which was unloading goods from carts and the few trucks that made deliveries around Tabriz. Chosen for his capacity to work hard and his great interest in trucks, Hagob became an apprentice truck driver at sixteen. This was a prized position for a young man, as it provided some income, travel, and the opportunity to work around the rare and powerful vehicles that the master drivers piloted across the mountains to Tehran and then south to the Persian Gulf. Hagob Hagobian spent more than a year learning the specifics of the trade from his sponsoring driver in Tabriz. As an apprentice truck driver, he learned to perform daily maintenance chores, load and balance the cargo on the vehicle, and repair the vehicle under varying circumstances. Successfully completing his apprenticeship in 1927, he became a *shagaird-e-shoofer*, or driver's assistant, and began the actual driving portion of his training.

In order to become a master driver, or *arbob*, an individual had to pass a complicated and difficult licensing procedure in which he was judged on his truck-driving skills by an experienced government representative. One of the tests required that the driver maneuver the truck in reverse gear along a figure-eight-shaped path outlined by boulders. Once licensed, the driver proudly wore an insignia that represented his trade.

Hagob began his actual driving practice by alternating driving and resting shifts with his *arbob*, a fellow Armenian, on runs between Tabriz and Kermanshah. While on a layover in Kermanshah, he met a cousin from his home village of Khan-Baba-Khan who joyfully informed him that Hagob's maternal uncle and two of the uncle's five children, as well as a paternal aunt and her three children, had also survived the events of 1916. Fleeing south toward Baghdad through Azerbaijan and Kurdistan in western Iran, they had found calm and safety in Kermanshah, where, familiar with the language and customs, they began their lives anew. Hagob had fortunately found what remained of his family.

In 1933, after passing his driver's test and attaining the status of *arbob*, Hagob made arrangements for his marriage to Arshalous, who was now a young woman of eighteen living with a family in Tabriz, where she sewed to support herself. In a borrowed truck they drove together from Tabriz to Kermanshah, where she was introduced to Hagob's family. At the American Presbyterian mission in Kermanshah, they were married, with their best man, a fellow Armenian truck driver, and relatives in attendance.

Soon after the ceremony, Hagob and his new wife moved to the growing city of Tehran to be near the hub of the trucking and transportation industry of the country. Having no relatives with whom to share a home, as was customary in most Armenian families, Hagob and his wife made temporary arrangements to share rooms with friends from the orphanage in Tabriz who lived in Tehran. Before the birth of a son in 1934, the young couple moved into private rooms located on a narrow *koutcheh,* or alleyway, in an area of the city where some of their neighbors were other Armenian refugees from East Anatolia and Azerbaijan as well as Russian-educated Armenian professionals who had immigrated to Iran following the Bolshevik revolution. This small but growing Armenian community was affiliated with the local Armenian church. Churches became the locus of social interaction and cultural education for many in the Armenian diaspora.

Hagob began driving long-distance hauls between Tehran and the Persian Gulf and soon acquired his own truck through the assistance of his former employer. For an agreed-upon monthly payment made possible by their mutual trust, Hagob took possession of the truck immediately and repaid the debt through the truck's income.

Tehran and the Persian Gulf ports were the focal points of the country's economic activity. Agricultural goods and handicrafts were brought to Tehran from surrounding areas by animals, a small but increasing number of trucks, and Iran's single railroad line. From Tehran these goods were redistributed to other Iranian cities or moved south to the Persian Gulf to be exported or exchanged with goods and materials being shipped into the country.

In the nineteenth and early twentieth centuries, Iran's slowly growing economy was tied to the European and world markets through the export of cash crops such as cotton, tobacco, sugar, opium, pistachios, raisins, and grain, which were cultivated domestically. Commodities necessary for the development of Iran, such as steel, cement, and machinery, had to be imported from Europe and other areas. The Persian Gulf became the trading ground for these items as the raw agricultural goods were shipped out and traded for building materials and processed products. Iran's oil, which was granted in concessions to the British government early in the twentieth century, was not yet a major factor in the Iranian economy. It was decades before it began to play a major role. In the 1920s and 1930s the volume of import/export goods that required transport increased at a steady rate as Iran's economy and infrastructure were developed under Reza Shah. His goals were to move the country swiftly to industrialization and Western-influenced social change.

The economic, military, and political changes that had been occurring elsewhere in the Middle East in the nineteenth century, such as the *tanzimat* reforms in the Ottoman Empire and similar changes in Egypt, did not appear uniformly in Iran until nearly half a century later. There were several reasons for this. One was Iran's geographical distance from Mediterranean and European economic activities. In addition, major powers such as Russia in northern Iran and Britain in southern Iran pursued their own interests in Iran. The later shahs of the Qajar dynasty allowed spheres of influence to exist for the foreigners and independent tribal confederations within Iran. Iran's cohesive Shiite ulama were another challenge to the governing powers throughout the nineteenth and twentieth centuries.

The reign of Reza Shah (1925–41) can be seen as a turning point for the modernization of Iran, as the changes brought about during his rule, many of them a reversal of nineteenth-century trends, were indeed far-reaching and highly influential. The ideals surrounding the changes that took place were essentially threefold: a total dedication to the ideals of nationalism-statism; a desire to assert this nationalism by a rapid adoption of the material advances of the West; and an intent to break down the traditional power of religion with a growing tendency toward secularism, which would come as a result of the first two ideals. It was during this period that Reza Shah changed the name of Persia to Iran by decree.

In order to adopt the material advances of the West it was necessary for the country's interdependent economy and infrastructure to grow simultaneously; this became Reza Shah's main agenda during his reign. Because of Iran's large territory (628,000 square miles) and rough terrain, the country badly needed a modern system of transportation and communication. Reza Shah's regime turned to this vital task at an early date. In 1924 the government undertook a complete study of the country's transportation problems, and a list of priorities was drawn up and adopted.

Until this time neither Iran's single railroad line nor its extremely limited water transport system were sufficiently developed to handle the increasing transportation needs of the 1920s. Thus the moving of goods from place to place until the end of the 1930s was achieved through the widespread use of trucks, which replaced the ancient mode of land transportation, primarily animal-drawn wagons and beasts of burden such as camels and donkeys. To facilitate motor transportation, the government's main effort went into improving and maintaining the existing roads. By European standards the roads were considered well planned, but their surface conditions and grades were very poor. In 1925 alone the Majlis appropriated over 9,170,000 rials for road construction and repair. In 1926, registration and licensing of vehicles were introduced, with revenue from these measures being designated for road construction. An independent Ministry of Roads with wide powers and elaborate plans for expanding the country's highways was created in 1930. Apart from attention to roads, several steps were taken to encourage the use of motor vehicles. These included tariff exemptions for trucks and buses as well as reduced registration and licensing fees for transport vehicles.

The increase in miles of roads and numbers of available trucks greatly reduced the transit time, risk, and associated costs of motor transport. For instance in 1920 it cost two hundred dollars a ton and required two months to move goods from the Gulf ports of Tehran. By 1929 motor transport of goods was more prevalent, and the same trip took one to two weeks at a cost of fifty dollars a ton. The number of registered motor vehicles in Iran rose from about six hundred in 1928 to over twenty-five thousand in 1942. Miles of roads increased from two thousand miles in 1925 to fourteen thousand miles by 1942.


Hagob Hagobian and his fellow truck drivers independently contracted to deliver cargo. In addition to the paid cargo, truck drivers routinely carried any item that might conceivably be required on a trip. Thus a truck driver packed authentic and makeshift replacement parts, extra sets of tires, gasoline, food, water, and personal gear.

Trucks and their components were imported from abroad, and there was an acute shortage of all parts. United States–manufactured single-cab six-wheel trucks such as Hagob's 1934 International were the industry standard in Iran. The early trucks were especially vulnerable to the frigid air and ice of the mountains as well as to the desert environment, where heat and sand were brutal on the machinery. When trucks broke down, the men had to improvise ways to repair them, although they had

had no formal training. Up to two full sets of spare tires might be needed during one round-trip due to the ravages of the unpaved roads.

The hijacking of vehicles by bandits and associated violence were commonplace in the Iranian countryside in the 1920s. This continued to be of concern to Hagob and his fellow truck drivers even after Reza Shah largely suppressed such activities in the mid-1930s. Because of the many unpredictable dangers, truck drivers in Iran caravanned in groups, finding strength and security in their numbers. Driving in shifts, the truck crews of two, ordinarily the *arbob* and his *shagaird-e-shoofer*, alternated sleeping and driving eight to ten hours, with the driver at the wheel keeping the other trucks in sight.

The challenging nature of the truck-driving profession in Iran during this formative period necessitated a truck driver's involvement in a guild. The guild served a variety of crucial needs through a network of shared information and credit based on mutual trust. In the 1930s Hagob became part of a guild consisting of Armenian and Assyrian members, who maintained their ties for decades. He and the others proudly wore their guild's insignia, a jeweler's handcrafted replica of the front portion of a transport vehicle.

In addition to the physical protection that guild members found in the truck caravan, commercial bonds based on a member's spoken word were maintained, through which members could borrow money, parts, tools, and equipment. Vital information regarding the nature and availability of cargo at port, and road conditions, as well as basic communication between drivers and their families, was exchanged in an efficient network of verbal transmissions on the road. Further, guild membership served to limit and keep exclusive the truck-driving ranks and to guarantee the honesty of its members and the safety of the cargo to the cargo owners, thus establishing confidence with them. The guild was also able to help maintain a stable price structure.

Nevertheless, group involvement did not solve all of the problems associated with trucking in its initial stages. Perhaps the greatest danger of the job during an entire trip was the risk of an accident on the precarious mountain switchbacks that had to be crossed to get to and from the Gulf. Many Iranian truck drivers, including some from Hagob's guild, died as their overloaded or poorly serviced vehicles plunged down the mountainside after having made a crucial error on an ungraded turn.

A haven to which Hagob Hagobian and his driving colleagues could go for rest and some restocking of supplies was the rural teahouse, or *tchai-khaneh*. The teahouses, in effect truck stops, were the former caravansaries, which for centuries had been way stations for travelers and traders in camel caravans. Hagob and his fellow truck drivers paused at the shelters to eat a hot meal, buy supplies, and spend a night before beginning another grueling twenty-four-hour shift. If time permitted, the drivers would enjoy the common pastime of playing cards and *nardi* (backgammon) while drinking tea. Due to the unpredictable hygienic conditions of the *tchai-khanehs* and a general fear of disease and parasites, truckers rarely accepted the rooms and beds that were offered. Instead they slept in or on top of the trucks, using their personal sleeping gear. This practice also served the function of providing security for the valuable trucks and cargo, which were vulnerable to thieves if the drivers slept elsewhere.

Iranian truck drivers, predominantly Christian Armenians and Assyrians, enjoyed a unique status in the nation as the operators of novel and complex machines. The *tchai-khaneh* owners were Muslims, who, in Islamic tradition, provided a hospitable environment to every guest. Thus although they came from different religious backgrounds, the *tchai-khaneh* owners and truck drivers formed a trusting and enduring relationship that became an integral part of the transportation industry of Iran.

At a time when these multiple systems of support were becoming efficient, and trucking had become profitable, World War II created new troubles for Hagob Hagobian and some members of the Iranian truck-driving industry. As the transportation needs of the occupying forces took precedence over private ownership and private transportation, many large vehicles were impounded for war use. At the onset of the Allied occupation of Iran in 1941, Hagob's truck was being loaded by his assistant in Tabriz while Hagob was visiting his family in Tehran. Aware that trucks were being commandeered by Russian troops, some drivers and their assistants removed the tires and other crucial operating parts in time to avoid their loss. In Hagob's absence, his truck and its cargo were confiscated. His repeated appeals to the Soviet Embassy in Tehran were futile, and he thus lost his only means of livelihood; he never received compensation.

Further complicating his existing problems, Hagob became ill in 1942 with malaria. By mortgaging the family's Persian carpets to the state bank, a common practice in Iran, and with support from his relatives in Kermanshah, his family, which grew in 1943 to include a daughter, survived unexpectedly trying times. Hagob returned to his trucking activities in 1945 with the help of a loan from relatives that enabled him to purchase a dump truck. For the next several years Hagob transported construction materials to job sites in and around the growing city of Tehran in partnership with fellow guild members. By the early 1950s he had purchased a ten-wheel truck and again began more profitable long-distance hauling to the Gulf. This was becoming a quicker and safer journey with the continued construction of modern roadways.

Again earning a stable income Hagob repaid his debts and over the next few years began planning and saving for his son's higher education. He took advantage of a program offered by the Iranian government that paid half of the educational expenses for students who passed a qualifying examination and received an acceptance from an accredited university abroad. In 1956 Hagob sent his son to the United States to earn a university degree. In 1964, while still engaged in long-distance hauling from the Persian Gulf to Tehran, Hagob sent his daughter, accompanied by her mother, to the United States to begin her university education. A serious trucking accident near Kermanshah in 1966 necessitated his wife's return from abroad to care for him and forced his retirement. During the next decade, Hagob Hagobian and his wife were visited frequently by their adult children, who had established careers in the United States, but the continual separations were insufferable for a couple who had spent their youth as orphans. Therefore in 1975 Hagob and Arshalous Hagobian moved to the United States to be with their children's families and resettled in a California community in which Armenians in the diaspora had again established their churches, schools, and cultural centers.

## A NOTE ON SOURCES

This essay is primarily based upon interviews with Hagob Hagobian conducted between March and June 1989.

## SUGGESTIONS FOR FURTHER READING

For a general history of the Armenian *millet* in the Ottoman Empire, see Leon Arpee, *A History of Armenian Christianity* (New York: Armenian Missionary Association of America, 1946). On the role of the Armenian trading diaspora, Curtin, *Cross-Cultural Trade*. The emergence of nationalism is treated in Louise Nalbandian, *The Armenian Revolutionary Movement* (Berkeley: University of California Press, 1963). On the Armenian massacres and related intercommunal violence, Richard Hovanissian, ed., *The Armenian Genocide in Perspective* (Oxford: Oxford University Press, 1986). For a demographic perspective, Justin McCarthy, *Muslims and Minorities: The Population of Ottoman Anatolia and the End of the Empire* (New York: Columbia University Press, 1983).

For some general histories of modern Iran, see Ervand Abrahamian, *Iran between Two Revolutions* (Princeton: Princeton University Press, 1982); Amin Banani, *The Modernization of Iran, 1921–1941* (Stanford: Stanford University Press, 1961); and Nikki Keddie, *Roots of Revolution: An Interpretative History of Modern Iran* (New Haven: Yale University Press, 1981).

On Iranian economic history generally, see Charles Issawi, ed., *The Economic History of Iran, 1800–1914* (Chicago: University of Chicago Press, 1971); id., *An*

*Economic History of the Middle East and North Africa* (New York: Methuen, 1982). Also Malcolm Yapp, *The Making of the Modern Near East, 1792–1923* (London and New York: Longman, 1987).

On the development of Iranian roads and the advent of trucking, see Charles Issawi, "The Iranian Economy, 1925–1975," in *Iran under the Pahlevis,* ed. George Lenzcowski (Palo Alto: Stanford University Press, 1978); and Wilfrid Knapp, "The Period of Reza Shah, 1921–1941," in *Twentieth-Century Iran,* ed. Husain Amirsadeghi (New York: Holmes and Meier, 1977).

# SIXTEEN

# Naji: An Iraqi Country Doctor

*Sami Zubaida*

Like the Moroccan Jewish community discussed above by Daniel Schroeter, the
Jews of Iraq were predominantly urban and heavily involved in trade and
commerce. (In 1947 they numbered 117,100 and constituted 15 percent of the
population of Baghdad.) As in Morocco, a small minority of wealthy Jewish
merchants profited from its international connections and *protégé* status, while
the vast majority of Iraqi Jews lived in poverty—as did most Iraqi Muslims.
Through the Alliance israélite universelle, the Jews of Iraq were exposed
early to modern ideas and thus were able to benefit from the new opportunities that developed in the colonial state after 1919. Arabic-speaking and highly
acculturated, the Jews of Iraq were better integrated into their society. In contrast to Moroccan Jews, most of whom willingly sided with the French colo-
nialists, most Iraqi Jews, as most Iraqis, were apolitical. Some of the intelligentsia and craftsmen, however, were attracted to democratic and leftist politics;
many others had communalist feelings that translated into Zionist sympathies.
Some indeed were among the leading lights of the Iraqi Communist party.[*]

Dr. Naji, the subject of Sami Zubaida's contribution to this volume, was a
member of the Baghdadi middle class who was able to take advantage of the
British colonial presence to move into the modern professions. Through
Zubaida's biography of Naji we come to understand the extent of his integration into Iraqi society, his commitment to the people among whom he lived
and worked, and the personal ties and political affiliations that governed his
professional choices. Naji's medical career unfolded in a series of provincial
postings away from the capital. His upbringing, friendships, and talents
helped ensure him a successful career as a provincial doctor.

In Iraq, where large, tribally organized ethnic groups (including both
Kurds and Shiite Arabs) coexisted with an urban intelligentsia and a small but

---

[*]Hanna Batatu, *The Old Social Classes and the Revolutionary Movements of Iraq* (Princeton:
Princeton University Press, 1978).

radical working class, the ability of the British to play upon traditional interests gave a certain desperate quality to the anticolonial struggle. The fact that the bearers of nationalism, especially pan-Arabism, were Sunni Arabs, whereas the tribal populations were mostly Shiite Arabs (51 percent of the population in 1947) and Kurds (18 percent), no doubt further increased the stakes and gave a certain lurching quality to Iraqi politics.

By the end of the British Mandate, the marked tolerance of traditional Iraqi society had begun to erode. Not until 1968, when the political atmosphere shifted sharply following a Baathist coup, did things change decisively. A wave of political persecutions and ethnic attacks led to the violent suppression of the Iraqi Communist party and to the emigration of many Iraqis, including Dr. Naji. —ED.

Dr. Naji was a Jewish doctor who worked, often under adverse and difficult conditions, in the provinces of Iraq from his graduation in 1936 until the end of the 1950s. Naji was born in 1915, at the start of World War I. Many Jews, especially those educated and qualified, were conscripted. Naji's father, a pharmacist, played his part as an officer in the Turkish army. He was involved in the fighting that raged in southern Iraq between the Turkish and British forces, including the protracted Turkish siege of the British in Kut-ul-Imara. Demobilized after the Turkish defeat, Naji's father ran a canteen/snack bar for the British forces in Amara in the same region. The family was from Baghdad, where the Jewish community, long native to Iraq, inhabited particular old quarters of the city and established themselves as craftspeople, shopkeepers, peddlers, and service workers; there was also a tiny minority of prosperous businessmen, landowners, and bankers and professionals such as doctors, lawyers, and teachers. After the end of hostilities Naji's family moved back to Baghdad, where they found the population suffering from grinding poverty after the deprivations and shortages of the war years.

World War I was a major watershed in the history of the Middle East. Following the defeat of the Ottoman Empire in 1918, the political map was redrawn by the victorious Allies. The British emerged with control of Palestine, Transjordan, and Iraq; the French with Lebanon and Syria. Under the terms of the Versailles peace settlement, subsequently ratified by the League of Nations, British and French authority were given legal recognition. Under the terms of the British Mandate, the ex-Ottoman provinces (wilayat) of Baghdad, Basra, and Mosul were grouped together in the new state of Iraq. Between 1921 and 1932 the new entity was ruled by a "national" government headed by a monarchy, but under British supervision and control. In 1932, Iraq became formally independent, though still under British control and treaty obligations. Not until 1958 was the monarchy overthrown in a bloody revolution.

Under the monarchy, Iraq was ruled by King Faisal, who, having been displaced by the French as king of the Syrian Arab Kingdom in 1921, was installed by the British. In an effort to limit his ambitions and to provide a basis for his rule, the British promoted the power and interests of the heads of the large Arab tribal confederations. These local leaders, the *shaykhs,* had already come to possess as private property formerly tribal and state lands as a result of Ottoman policy, thereby accruing enormous fortunes. These landowners and their nominees became the main force in parliament. As a mandate Iraq was formally a democracy with an elected parliament. However, elections were generally rigged, and parliaments were often dissolved when they became awkward, allowing the country to be governed by decree. In the 1930s government revenues came increasingly to depend upon the control of the exploitation of oil resources under the control of the British-owned Iraq Petroleum Company. Tax evasion, especially by the wealthy landlord class, was endemic, and tax revenues were negligible. The regime was corrupt.

Iraqi society under the monarchy was thoroughly politicized, particularly urban society. The opposition especially targeted the corrupt regime and its British masters. There were two broad political streams: pan-Arab nationalism and "Iraqist" democratic forces. The chief force within the latter was the Iraqi Communist party, generally reputed to be the strongest Communist party in the Arab world. Arab nationalism found its chief support among army officers, who staged a series of coups d'état starting in 1936 that displaced particular cabinets or ministers but did not challenge the monarchy or British domination. The sole exception was the pro-Nazi Rashid Ali coup of 1941, which directly challenged the British by seeking German support. As we will see, this event and the British military intervention that it sparked gave rise to violent attacks on Jews in Baghdad and other urban centers.

Religious and ethnic divisions played (and continue to play) an important role in modern Iraqi politics. An estimated 18 percent of the total population of 4.8 million in 1947 were Kurds, whose struggle for national and cultural rights has constituted a dominant factor in the history of the country to the present day. The 80 percent of the population who were Arabic-speaking were divided along religious lines into Sunni and Shiite Muslims and included small Christian and Jewish minorities. Sunni Arabs, although a decided minority (possibly as small as 20 percent), have always been politically dominant. With the exception of the Kurds, who are Sunni, ethnicity in Iraq has tended to be ethnically coded by religious community. Most Arab nationalists have been of

Sunni origin, while most Kurds and Shiite have tended to support Iraqi nationalist solutions and groups. In the 1950s these opposition forces came together in a common front that cooperated with the Free Officers, who initiated the 1958 revolution. The ensuing regime of Abd al-Karim Qasim was characterized by struggles between Arab nationalists and Iraqists (the latter led by the Communist party). In 1963 Qasim was in turn overthrown by another coup led by a nationalist officer. From it the current Baathist regime of Saddam al-Husain eventually emerged.

This then was the Iraq into which Naji was born. There was never an exclusive "ghetto" in Baghdad itself, although a version of the Ottoman *millet* system had been maintained by the new state of Iraq for the autonomous corporate organization of Christian and Jewish communities. Naji's family settled in a predominantly Sunni neighborhood in an old quarter of Baghdad. Their immediate neighbor was a *mullaya*, a female reader/teacher of the Quran, and the young Naji memorized large portions of the holy book under her tutelage. He attributed his special strength in the Arabic language to this early training, although Arabic (with a peculiar Baghdadi accent) was the native tongue of Iraqi Jews. Later, the family moved to a house in Dahhana, a Shiite quarter. The family was well regarded in the neighborhood, with many friends on dropping-in terms.

Young Naji was sent to a Torah school to learn Hebrew and religion. He learned French at home from his mother, who had been one of the first batch of girls to go to one of the schools of the Alliance israélite universelle, which had opened schools in Baghdad and Basra in the late nineteenth century. These schools taught in both French and Arabic, as a result of which sectors of the Jewish community were incorporated into colonially related elites. (A parallel process also operated within the Christian community.) Nonetheless, in Iraq this did not lead to a separation into colonial cultures and languages with different political orientations, as happened elsewhere in the British Empire.

Eventually Naji was educated at a Jewish primary school close to his neighborhood. His school, like all others, followed a national curriculum. All pupils who remained at school until the appropriate ages took the government *baccalauréat* examinations at different levels. Some of those who finished school then proceeded to jobs and careers in government or in private employment, where they worked alongside people from other communities. Some went on to higher education in the newly opened colleges, most notably in medicine, pharmacy, and engineering, but also in law.

Naji enjoyed his childhood as a happy, harmonious period, with wide social contacts in school and in his neighborhood. This harmony continued into his secondary school experience at Al-Idadiya al-Markaziya, the central and most renowned government school in Baghdad, where

many of the later leaders and notables of the country were educated.
There, it would seem, the difference of the Jews was implicitly noted and
accepted by most pupils, who then made a special effort to emphasize
the equality of all in the new nation-state. Jewish pupils were defended,
for instance, against any hostility that might arise in the street or in the
schoolyard. Yet such hostilities, although sporadic, were still to be expected. A few students avoided or shunned their Jewish classmates, primarily out of religious prejudice.

Naji and his older brother graduated from secondary school in 1930
with very good marks in the official *baccalauréat* examinations, which
made them both candidates for entry into the Medical College, considered the highest achievement for graduates. The Medical College was
founded in 1927 by the British Mandate government under predominantly British direction and expertise but with increasing Iraqi participation. The intake of students in the early years of the college included
many Jews, a fact that led to unease in high quarters. Tacitly, a quota of
Jews was introduced. The fact that two brothers applied at the same
time was perceived as an undue share of the quota for one family, but
their father had connections with British medical authorities, and both
brothers were admitted.

Naji's college days in the 1930s were marked by an atmosphere of serious dedication to the fledgling Iraqi state among the educated youth
and by a sense of common purpose regardless of communal barriers.
But as the decade progressed, nationalist sentiments and agitation grew,
with an increasing awareness of the Palestine question and the Arab
struggles in that country. The development of militant nationalisms in
Europe, especially Nazism, was an inspiration to some Arab nationalists
in Iraq and elsewhere, especially insofar as it was directed against the
British. This accumulation of factors brought the position of the Jews
into question. These ideological trends were by no means universal, but
they affected an important sector of intellectuals and army officers; this
led to various attempted or temporarily successful coups d'état, which
were usually thwarted by British interests. Naji experienced changes in
the political and social atmosphere in his later years at college, with
some professors and students raising questions about the loyalty of the
Jewish students, sometimes in whispers and sometimes openly. But the
Jews also had their defenders, who maintained comradely relations and
held on to the ideology of common citizenship.

Naji graduated in 1936. There followed a period of training in different medical branches. This was marked by rivalry among graduates
for entry into the more desirable branches of the profession. Naji got on
very well with the British specialist in ophthalmic surgery, with whom he
spent eight months. During this time the surgeon came to rely on him a

great deal, both in the conduct of operations and in the organization of work schedules. This close relationship was resented by more senior doctors in the field, who agitated against such a young man being entrusted with serious responsibilities. When his patron went on leave for a few months, Naji's detractors took the opportunity to oust him from that department and push him into radiology, regarded as an inferior and undesirable specialty.

Naji did not settle there. The medical establishment seemed rather disorganized and lax, and Naji was able to frequent the department of general surgery, where he made himself useful and where the senior staff assumed that he was allocated to them. He would make an appearance in the radiology section for one or two hours a day, then slip into surgery. While doing this, Naji continued his efforts to be allocated officially to a desirable branch but failed. He approached another British eye specialist, who immediately asked his religion and discouraged him when he learned that Naji was a Jew. A Scottish bacteriologist was very welcoming but could not fulfill his promise of an attached post. When the training period was over, Naji was posted to his first appointment.

Admission to medical education in Iraq entailed a contract with the government for five years' medical service. The graduate doctor could be posted anywhere in the country. Baghdad and the other major cities held the most desirable posts, generally allocated to those with family connections and influence in the right quarters. The socially weakest and poorest, including most Jewish graduates, ended up in the remote country areas with the least amenities and entertainments and the most poverty and disease.

The Jewish country doctor became a regular feature of the Iraqi scene in the 1930s and 1940s. A number of these country doctors, including Naji, remained in this form of service long after their compulsory contracts expired. Many pressures kept Naji in government service. His ultimate objective was to travel to Britain for further training and specialization. Financial limitations and family commitments led to constant postponement of this action. Lack of finances was also an obstacle to setting up private practice in Baghdad. In the late 1940s, things became difficult, and the government sought to prevent doctors from leaving the service by issuing a decree forcing those who resigned to practice where they last lived. It was also thought at the time that an official position would provide exemption from arbitrary arrest and political persecution.

Naji's first appointment was to Hashimiya, a small town on the Euphrates near Hilla, about a hundred kilometers south of Baghdad. He was put in charge of the small public health center (*mustawsif*) there, manned by three medical orderlies/nurses (*mudhamiddin*). He felt utterly overwhelmed by the sheer magnitude of poverty, deprivation, and disease that he found among the tribal and peasant population. There was a great array of diseases. Naji reflected philosophically that working in a place like Hashimiya taught a young doctor more than many years of experience would in a wealthier environment. The most prevalent disease was chronic malaria. Another was bilharzia, which when left untreated led to terrible degenerations like cancer of the bladder. Naji examined so many cases of cancer of the bladder that he could diagnose it just by the feel of the particular spot when he pressed it.

Being the only doctor in the area, Naji also had to do police forensic work, such as performing autopsies. Given the tribal custom of the blood feud, which prevailed and was tolerated by the authorities, there were frequent occasions for such work. Naji was also required, in this and in subsequent postings, to supervise the other health centers in the district, which were operated under *mudhamiddin*. To that end he undertook regular tours, sometimes traveling in difficult terrain to places that could be reached only by horse or mule. Work had to be accomplished under primitive conditions, with poor equipment and inadequate supplies of even the most essential medicines, including anesthetics. Up to six hundred patients a day presented themselves for treatment. Yet there were no facilities for surgery, and even simple cases of hernia had to be referred to Hilla, the provincial capital, which had a hospital. Cancer cases were hopeless.

Poverty was the ally of disease. Naji wished he could feed his patients rather than just treating them. Most of the population were sharecroppers working the land of their tribal shaykh. The terms of their contracts left them with little to eat, and they were always deeply in debt. Public health measures were so rudimentary that Naji's duties included the supervision of spreading crude oil over stagnant water lagoons as a measure against malarial mosquitoes.

The terms of employment of a provincial government doctor allowed him to engage in private practice in his spare time. Under these conditions Naji had no spare time. He was still expected by local notables, landlords, and officials to attend to their medical needs, for which he may or may not have been paid. At this stage he could not open a private clinic, although he managed this later in his career.

Naji spent three or four years in the province of Hilla. He was temporarily transferred from Hashimiya to Hindiya to replace another Jewish doctor who had been drafted into the army. He returned to Hashimiya and then finally went to a permanent posting in Hindiya until January 1941, when he was transferred to the town of Hit in another region on the middle Euphrates.

As a government doctor, Naji took his place in the society of officials and notables of the town and the region. At the top of the hierarchy was the subprefect (*qaim maqam*) of the town. (The prefect, or *mutasarrif*, lived in the provincial capital.) While the doctor was responsible to the local health directorate, which in turn answered to the ministry in Baghdad, the prefectures had considerable say in matters of health policy, premises, and facilities, so Naji also had to deal with the local bureaucracy.

Officials, as well as professionals and technicians such as engineers, shared a particular status and social life in the province, centered upon the Officials' Club (*nadi-al-muwadhafin*). This is where those so inclined would meet afternoons and evenings, chat, play games, and drink. Naji was part of this circuit, although, he recalls, he had little time to engage in these diversions, and he did not gamble or drink. Local notables would hold banquets for the high-ranking officials, which would include the doctor: in terms of protocol, wherever the subprefect was invited, the doctor too would be included, on occasions ranging from public ceremonies on national days to weddings in notables' households. More routinely, a servant would cook Naji's meals or bring him cooked food from a local restaurant. For some of his time in the Hilla region, his brother, also a doctor, was posted in the nearby town of Diwaniyya, and he would occasionally spend the night there. On public holidays and leave periods he would go to his home in Baghdad.

Many parts of provincial Iraq included small Jewish communities among their populations. There were Jews in the Hilla province, mostly in Hilla itself. A few were merchants and landowners (although these latter tended to move to Baghdad and appoint managers to run their estates). Most were poor peddlers and craftsmen, while a few were teachers and local officials. Naji did not socialize with the local Jews. He had not made a conscious decision against it, but they were simply not his kind of people. He said of the Jews of Ana (a later posting) that they were like the local "Arabs." ("Arab" in that context meant bedouin or "native" and was used in that sense by all urbanites.) They dressed and talked and lived like other locals, and as such they were very different from Baghdadi Jews, especially the intelligentsia. As an educated man and an official, Naji had much more in common with Muslims and Christians like himself. The only provincial Jews with whom he had regular contacts were those employed by the health service, like Murad the Jew, who was the driver of the official car. Others included medical orderlies, nurses, and midwives.

Naji recalls a young Jewish girl who worked as a midwife in Hindiya. She was from a poor family, with a blind father, and it was her pay that kept them. Her mother would always accompany her on emergency calls outside the town. One night she and her mother accompanied Naji to attend to a difficult childbirth. They cleared all the people and the animals from the room but missed a lamb who was hidden in the shadows. Naji used forceps to pull out the baby, and as his head emerged the lamb bleated, at which the young midwife jumped in horror and shouted to her mother outside that the woman had given birth to a lamb!

Naji was an energetic and attractive young man, devoted to his work and patients, and he was warmly regarded by colleagues, subordinates, and patients, as well as by the local notables. He was a relatively high-ranking government official, and one on whom many people depended for their lives. Although he was Jewish, his professional persona and his personal qualities predominated. Shiite Muslims (the dominant religion in that region) observe certain taboos on contacts with non-Muslims, who are considered ritually unclean. Yet in the many years of his life in Shiite regions, Naji regularly treated patients, frequently shared people's food, and even slept in their houses, only encountering the observations of that taboo on rare occasions with unusual individuals. He was sought out, and occasionally entertained, by religious dignitaries as well as other notables. Once, during an epidemic, for example, Naji encountered difficulties trying to secure premises for quarantine. The landlord of the designated house tried to renege on the deal at the last minute. To obtain the key, Naji had to be very firm and exert his full authority, to the extent of slapping the man. This was not unusual conduct in the circumstances, but Naji was surprised at his own behavior: "I was a government official," he reflected. "I forgot that I was a Jew!"

Violence, like poverty and disease, was a regular feature of life in the provinces. The "code of honor" and the blood feud were prominent principles. This was recognized by the new Iraqi state in its enactment of a "tribal law," which embodied customary codes and as such was lenient regarding "crimes of honor." Naji recalled receiving hospitality from a shaykh, whom he found to be a most kind and genial person. When relating his impressions to some local people, they informed him that the same shaykh had the year before slaughtered all his four daughters, because he had heard that one of them had chatted and laughed with a young man.

On occasion, Naji was put under considerable pressure from powerful quarters to act against the regulations in ways that would leave him liable and vulnerable. This arose particularly over the issue of death certificates. In Hindiya a powerful local shaykh asked him to issue a certificate for one of his tribe who, he claimed, died of cancer. The shaykh would not present the body on the grounds that it was already on a train on the first lap of the journey to Najaf, where it was to be buried. (Shiite Muslims who are able to do so bury their dead in the holy city of Najaf.) Naji insisted on examining the body before issuing the certificate and persisted even after the intervention of the *qaim maqam* (subprefect). In the end the body had to be produced: the man had been shot at close range in the stomach. The story then was that the man had shot himself to escape the severe pain of his cancer. Naji, in his persistence, was mindful of the example of a Christian colleague in another area, who was similarly approached while gambling at the club. He had readily agreed to issue a death certificate without examining the body, only to be confronted later by relatives of the deceased who contested the specified cause of death and had the body exhumed to show that the man had been murdered.

While discrimination against Jews did not affect Naji in his daily work and life, at least not in the Hilla province, it was present in his official dealings with the Ministry and the Directorate of Health both at the provincial and central levels. As the 1930s progressed there was increasing discrimination against Jews. The Ministry of Health was more thoroughly penetrated by pan-Arab nationalists and, at that time, Nazi sympathizers than most other government departments. For Naji and other Jewish doctors, this meant confinement to the less desirable provincial postings, slow promotion in terms of salary increments, and almost a complete barrier against promotion to consultant or specialist ranks. This also meant barriers to any further training. Naji's great ambition was to travel to Britain for further training and specialization. The constraints of his contract, finances, and then the Second World War prevented the realization of this ambition.

While in Hindiya, Naji wrote numerous reports urging the establishment of a hospital in the town, and his campaign was ultimately successful. He worked hard at establishing the hospital and equipping it, but soon after he was posted to Hit, in western Iraq. This region was very important in the events of 1941. It is the part of Iraq nearest to Syria, which was the center of pan-Arab nationalism. Until the latter part of that year, Syria was governed by Vichy France, with a governor noted for his pro-Nazi sympathies. As such it was a center for Nazi propaganda and covert military aid to rebel movements with those sympathies. The predominantly Sunni Arabs of the western region were more open to pan-Arabism than their Shiite compatriots, since the rest of the Arab world is mainly Sunni. For all these reasons, the region was to be an important stage for the Rashid Ali revolt of 1941, which had distinct pro-Axis elements and culminated in a massacre of Jews in Baghdad. It was a dangerous place for a Jewish doctor.

Hit was another small town with a health center (*mustawsif*). Soon after arriving there Naji had to cope with an outbreak of smallpox in an outlying tribal area. He alerted the authorities and established quarantine around the affected areas, forbidding movement out of the boundaries, but the order was difficult to enforce. All infected persons were confined to a quarantine house, where they were treated. Inadequate facilities and medicines led to a death rate of about 30 percent of those affected. Naji embarked on a vaccination campaign around the area and ultimately succeeded in containing the outbreak. He did all this in addition to his normal duties. When the doctor in the larger nearby town of Ana was drafted into the army, Naji was ordered to take over there. He left the Hit center in the charge of a medical orderly and spent the months of the troubles in Ana.

The months of April to June of 1941 witnessed the height of the crisis in Iraq. The Rashid Ali government refused to extend the facilities for military movements that the British authorities claimed were required by treaty obligations. The British air base of Habbaniya was surrounded by units of the Iraqi army. The pro-British regent (for the child king) and his entourage left Baghdad. The British Middle East Command drew up plans for a military campaign against the "rebel" government. Hostilities broke out in May, leading to a brief and unequal war in which British air strikes played the decisive part. British forces reached the outskirts of Baghdad in the first days of June. These were the days of the breakdown of order in Baghdad and the unleashing of the anti-Jewish pogrom known as *farhud*, in which several hundred lives were lost and many atrocities committed. It ended with the reestablishment of order under a British-controlled government and the return of the regent. These were the most dangerous months for Naji.

At that time Ana was a town obsessed with the war and with the national struggle that became so firmly linked to it. Nazi sympathies were common among the intelligentsia and the notables of the town but had also spread to the common people. There were a few exceptions among people known as Communists or as British sympathizers. Anti-Jewish sentiments were common but, for the most part, restrained. The local Jewish community was well integrated into the bonds of neighborhood and custom of the town and was usually protected. All the same, one Jewish teacher in the town decided to go to Baghdad on leave.

Naji himself was received politely, but not always warmly. He received the warmest hospitality from traditional religious households, to the extent of being a regular guest at the Thursday night *dhikr* parties of one such house, where he enjoyed the Sufi religious ceremonial with music and chanting. His staff, nurses, and porter (*farrash*) were loyal. The *farrash* especially brought him intelligence as to what was happening and was generally protective.

The most vociferous protagonist of Nazism was a schoolteacher of Syrian origin. Naji would give the occasional lesson in health care at the local school, and on one occasion he received a visit from the teacher and his class at the health center. The attention of the teacher was attracted by a nail in the wall with a piece of string attached, which he proceeded to examine closely, telling the pupils that this must be a wireless device for transmitting intelligence to the British forces. Such suspicions and accusations were common during this period, and it was only the firm intervention of the *farrash* that prevented a hostile reaction. On another occasion Naji was called in the middle of the night to attend the body of a murdered woman. He found a young Jewish woman stabbed in the chest, her young child crying. The rest of the household had fled. Eventually the killer was arrested, a teenage boy from the school whose modern nationalist ideology had moved him to transgress the traditional neighborhood bonds.

One time six wounded guerrillas were brought to the health center for Naji's attention and had to be kept there until they had sufficiently recovered. Naji discovered that they were part of the volunteer force of Fawzi al-Qawuqji, a Syrian commander who was eventually killed in Palestine in the first Arab-Israeli war. He had brought his forces of Syrian, Palestinian, and Iraqi volunteers to the aid of Rashid Ali in his struggle against the British. With the imminent defeat of their ally they were retreating toward Syria when they were hit by British air strikes. Naji cared for them like he would have any other patients, maintaining a professional detachment. Eventually Fawzi himself came to Ana, and when visiting his men he hesitated visibly before shaking the hand of the Jewish doctor to thank him. Toward the end of this period, Naji felt himself to be under real threat. Sitting in a café one evening he heard a local police officer taunting his companions for tolerating a Jewish doctor in their midst and expressing mock surprise that he was still alive. Naji conspired with his *farrash* to steal the ignition key of the subprefect's motorcar as an emergency measure to facilitate escape in case of attack. Fortunately, the attack did not come.

In the meantime Naji was very worried about his family in Baghdad. Communications were difficult even at the best of times. The local post office manager, a keen supporter of Rashid Ali, was nevertheless sympathetic to the plight of the Jewish doctor and aided him in establishing telephone contact with neighbors of his family in Baghdad, who were unharmed. Naji's sentiments similarly blurred ideologies when it came to personal friends. After the defeat of the rebellion the restored government carried out retribution against rebel cadres. One such figure was a medical colleague and friend of Naji's who when pursued by the authorities received shelter in the Jewish doctor's quarters until the storm passed over and he was able to return to Baghdad.

Another of the dilemmas Naji had to face in Ana during this period was over the *mutasarrif's* (prefect's) attempt to requisition the premises of the health center for his own use. Fearing the threat of British air attacks, the prefect abandoned his quarters in Ramadi. Unable to reach Baghdad because of flooded roads, he took refuge in Ana, and he considered the health center premises to be the most appropriate for his temporary residence. Naji successfully resisted this attempted invasion of the busy center and the dislocation of patients and activities it would cause. But he was later to regret this victory. After these events, back at his post in Ramadi, the prefect punished Naji by sending him to a desert outpost on the Syrian frontier, Rutbah, where he was to stay until the end of the war.

Rutbah was a British army outpost guarding a crucial frontier crossing and the oil pipeline to Haifa. The garrison also supervised the construction of a military road to connect Baghdad to Haifa and included a depot for the servicing and repair of motor vehicles and tanks. It included two small hospitals, one military, one civilian (for the workers on the projects). Naji supervised the civilian hospital. The military hospital had British military doctors, but they were frequently shifted around in accordance with war needs, and Naji also worked there when required. Naji was responsible to the British military command as well as to the health directorate in Ramadi. He was given a small house near the civilian hospital but did not feel secure there, so he moved into a room in the hospital. He shared mess privileges with the British officers.

Naji felt isolated in this desert outpost, which had the added disadvantage of not providing any scope for private practice, a factor that was to become more and more important for his livelihood. At the same time, however, Naji found the British forces diverting and the company of British colleagues stimulating. He observed the interactions and conflicts between Sikh and Gurka troops with the local Arab population, and what seemed like the eccentric religions and customs of strangers.

In Rutbah, Naji had to cope with a typhus epidemic, to which he himself fell victim. The commanding officer decided to send him home to Baghdad, and provided a military car to take him there. After a difficult journey through the desert, sedated with morphine, he arrived home in a very weak state. He took to bed for several weeks in the care of his parents. When he recovered he felt weak and depressed and decided to resign his post. The director general of health in Baghdad called Naji to his office and cajoled him into withdrawing the resignation, giving him an immediate promotion in terms of salary grade, the first he was offered in all his years of service, and promising future posting to a more desirable center. Naji went back to Rutbah, but the posting to Ramadi, the provincial center, was not to come until near the end of the war in 1944.

In Ramadi, Naji was in charge of surgery at the hospital in addition to general medical duties. At first there was only one other doctor in the public service. Naji was under enormous work pressure but managed to run a private practice, which was a matter of increasing financial importance. At this point, Naji was contributing most of his income to the family budget, partly for saving but most importantly to support a sister studying medicine in Egypt and his elder brother, who was now studying in Britain for eye specialization. The idea was that both would return to work in Iraq and then be able to support Naji's further study in Britain. This was not to happen.

After World War II, political crises and popular upheavals followed one another in close succession in Iraq. The clique of politicians around Nuri al-Said, through whom the British had grown accustomed to rule, continued to dominate the official political life of the country. But it experienced growing difficulty in controlling an increasingly politicized society. Mounting economic difficulties, inflation, and unemployment at home were compounded by momentous events in the region that heightened national sentiment. In 1947–48 there occurred the United Nations partition of Palestine, the declaration of the state of Israel, and the first Arab-Israeli war. In 1956, following the failed tripartite intervention aimed at deposing Nasser and reestablishing British control over the Suez Canal, the prestige and appeal of Nasser reached new heights throughout the region. Through all of these events, the Iraqi government remained publicly loyal to Britain. Anti-British demonstrations on a grand scale erupted in January 1948 against a proposed military agreement with Britain known as the Portsmouth Agreement. Hundreds of demonstrators were killed by machine-gun fire. Faced with a near popular insurrection, the government fell, and the regent abandoned the treaty. Repression was intensified, including notably the public hanging of three prominent Communist leaders. Martial law was established later that year on the pretext of Iraqi participation in the fighting in Palestine. A further crackdown against the opposition was instituted.

The events leading up to the partition of Palestine and the foundation of the state of Israel in 1948 had negative consequences for the Jews of Iraq. There were threats of another *farhud*. Zionist societies and circles were eventually uncovered, which provided the pretext for unleashing a campaign of arrests and persecution of innocent Jews, on charges or suspicions of Zionism and Communism. The two were conveniently equated to facilitate the campaign against Communists and leftists at the same time. Jewish public servants faced added harassment, if not sacking. In 1946, at the beginning of this period, Naji received an order posting him to Rawanduz, a remote center in the Kurdish mountains of the northeast. On this occasion he was able to mobilize the intervention of a recent prefect of Ramadi who liked him, as well as that of the new British consul in Baghdad, an acquaintance from the Rutbah days whom he met by chance in the railway station in Mosul. The order was eventually withdrawn, and Naji returned to Ramadi.

The following years, from 1947 until the termination of his government appointment in 1955, were to be particularly difficult for Naji. In Ramadi, he had to work under an antagonistic Egyptian director of health. Jealous of Naji's success in private practice and exploiting his vulnerability as a Jew, the director wrote adverse reports on his work as well as inciting local thugs to harm him. All of this was reported to Naji by a patient, an Armenian carpenter working in the house of the director who overheard his machinations. On the night of the declaration of the state of Israel, Naji had to take refuge with friends in Habbaniya. The hostile director's efforts succeeded later in 1948, and Naji was posted to Abu Skhair, a small town in the south. The irony of the situation was that the same director of health was himself transferred to take charge of the province of Diwaniyya, where Abu Skhair is located, and Naji was again in danger. His petitions to the Directorate of Health in Baghdad eventually succeeded in getting him posted to another small town, now in the province of Amara, in the southeast.

The disadvantages of these small town postings were not only isolation but also loss of income from private practice. At this point Naji needed the money badly. Most Jews were preparing to leave Iraq under a policy by which Jews could renounce their Iraqi nationality and eventually travel to Israel. Jews who registered on this policy were to have their assets sequestrated under a new decree issued after they registered. The result of these events was the collapse of property prices in Baghdad as Jews scrambled to sell whatever they could. Naji's father had invested the family savings, including Naji's, in building a house, which was no sooner completed than it had to be sold at an enormous loss as part of the family's plan to leave Iraq. Naji was left penniless.

A combination of factors prevented Naji from resigning. There was a regulation, introduced shortly before, that stipulated that a doctor who resigns a public post can work only in the town to which he had been posted, in this case a small town with little prospect of work. At the same time, a government post, however precarious, was judged to provide some immunity against official persecution. Naji feared that were he to resign, he would be framed on some charge of Zionism and Communism and imprisoned. At this point he was also barred from travel outside Iraq, and his passport was withdrawn.

The Amara director of health, on a visit to Naji's outpost, realized his potential and offered him the temporary post of surgeon in Amara itself, a populous provincial center. Naturally Naji was delighted. He threw himself into work at the hospital and built up a thriving private practice. These happy days were to be short-lived, however, terminated by the appointment of another director who had been Naji's junior at medical college and who proved to be a dangerous enemy. The aim of this new director was to curtail or end Naji's successful private practice, which rivaled his own, and to try to get him transferred yet again to some small town. But in the meantime the director exploited Naji's vulnerability as a Jew for his own private profit.

The director forbade Naji to conduct any operations except at his order. He would then only authorize operations for which he had obtained an unofficial and illegal fee. He also contrived to put Naji on night emergency duty at the hospital continuously for six months, at the same time expecting him to perform all his other medical and surgical tasks. He attempted to drive Naji to resignation by withdrawing all the night-duty facilities: first food, then the bed, then other furniture. He then resorted to charging Naji with holding Zionist/Communist meetings at his house. Only the intervention of an honest prefect saved Naji from arrest and investigation. Finally he succeeded in having Naji transferred back to his previous small town outpost of Ali al-Gharbi, where he remained for one year. During that time, Naji enhanced his reputation further among the local population by performing difficult operations without hospital facilities, sometimes on the patient's own bed at home, with a high success rate.

Naji's final episode of public service was the campaign against a particularly virulent disease, Bejel, a kind of syphilis that is not sexually transmitted. Bejel had to be treated with penicillin injections. Naji was put in charge of the operation in the marshes region of southeast Iraq, centered in Amara, but spent most of the time traveling the desolate region by car, motorboat, canoe, horse, and donkey. This post was to occupy the years of the early 1950s until the termination of Naji's appointment in 1955 on a charge of being politically undesirable.

After that, Naji decided to spend a few weeks resting in Amara before traveling to Baghdad. During that time, he was inundated with crowds of private patients demanding treatment. He had acquired a reputation in the area of being a miracle worker. This induced him to stay in Amara until further troubles at the end of the 1950s forced him to go to Baghdad, where he conducted a thriving private practice until the next Arab-Israeli war in 1967. The aftermath of this war and the Baathist regime inaugurated by a coup d'état in 1968 combined to make life for the Jews very difficult. A wave of government terrorism spread in the country, and the Jews were specifically targeted. Mass arrests, torture, and public hangings (on spying charges) culminated in the exodus, legally or illegally, of the few remaining Jews via Iran in 1970 and 1971. Naji was among those arrested, but his reputation and contacts saved him from the violent fate of the others. Naji left Iraq in 1970.

## A NOTE ON SOURCES

This account is based primarily upon extensive interviews with Dr. Naji (not his real name), who is now living in London. They were corroborated and supplemented by interviews with other Iraqis who knew him personally or by reputation.

## SUGGESTIONS FOR FURTHER READING

The most important book on modern Iraqi history is Hanna Batatu's monumental *The Old Social Classes and the Revolutionary Movements of Iraq: A Study of Iraq's Old Landed and Commercial Classes and of Its Communists, Ba'thists and Free Officers* (Princeton: Princeton University Press, 1978). See also Peter Sluglett, *Britain in Iraq, 1914–1932* (London: Ithaca Press, 1976). On contemporary Iraq, Marian Sluglett and Peter Sluglett, *Iraq since 1958: From Revolution to Dictatorship* (London: Routledge and Kegan Paul, 1987).

For an anthropological study of the Iraqi countryside in the period, see Robert Fernea, *Shaykh and Effendi: Changing Patterns of Authority among the El Shbana of Southern Iraq* (Cambridge, Mass.: Harvard University Press, 1970). On the women of El Shbana, Elizabeth Fernea, *Guests of the Sheik* (New York: Doubleday Press, 1965).

For a history of the Jewish community of Iraq by one of its members, see Nissim Rejwan, *The Jews of Iraq: 3,000 Years of History and Culture* (Boulder, Colo.: Westview Press, 1985).

# SEVENTEEN

# Muhammad Ameur:
# A Tunisian Comrade

*Kenneth Brown*

The portrait of Muhammad Ameur provided by Kenneth Brown eludes easy categorization. By turns a nationalist, rationalist, skeptic, Communist, ne'er-do-well small farmer, and café philosopher, Ameur is an endlessly fascinating and opinionated individual. Ameur is by some standards a failure, though to describe him this way is misleading. His biography traces not the ascending curve of the successful peasant farmer, busily accumulating wealth and property; rather it follows a career made of great enthusiasms suddenly abandoned and of seemingly incoherent choices that nonetheless possess their own inner logic.

Through Ameur we are introduced to the bustling life of the Tunisian village of Ksibet. Located in the fertile coastal plain south of Tunis known as the Sahel, Ksibet is one of many similar small agricultural communities in the region. The Sahel was historically reputed for its wheat fields and olive groves. The numerous villages and towns of the Sahel also provided in recent times the chief base of support for the Néo-Destour party, which led the struggle for independence from France in 1956.

The experience of colonialism deeply affected Ksibet society. In this respect it resembled other Sahel villages. Ksibet derived its wealth in part from weaving and the production of olive oil for the market. Following the establishment of the French protectorate in 1881, the village economy was transformed by the establishment of a soap factory and a saltworks. These employed large numbers of workers, as a result of which many Ksibis acquired a precocious working-class consciousness despite their impeccably peasant roots.

Considering that Ameur had the distinct advantage of having attended a French school, it is in some respects surprising that he remained in his village. With this background, he might have gone on to become a petty official in the French protectorate government, or a member of the urban working class like many of his fellow Ksibet villagers. Instead, after the death of his father he took up residence in Ksibet to manage the family properties.

In the 1920s and 1930s Ameur became involved in Tunisian politics. Against the authority of the traditional religious authorities he became a supporter of the Néo-Destour party, the nationalist formation that replaced the earlier and more elitist and conservative Destour party. His political activism was not uncommon for the time. (Compare M'hamed Ali, whose biography by Eqbal Ahmad and Stuart Schaar is also included in this volume.)

In the 1940s (exactly when is unclear) Ameur broke with the Néo-Destour party and became a member of the Communist party. As late as the 1960s (well into the period of independence) Ameur presided over the local party cell, which was continually embroiled in debate with the Néo-Destourians. Brown speculates that this choice, which was far from typical, is at least partially to be explained by the reputation of Ksibet as perennially the home of oppositionists of all kinds.

This had been Ameur's personal itinerary when he encountered Brown in 1975: the lion of the local café scene, he was a man whose willingness to advance opinions on all subjects and zest for spicy anecdotes made him a noted village character. By then he had mortgaged much of his family olive grove to support his life-style. Yet it is also true by this time that as was the case for many small peasants throughout the Sahel old-style family farms like Ameur's had been left economically high and dry by changing economic fortunes.

The engaging portrait of Muhammad Ameur thus reveals much about the way Tunisians experienced the colonial period. It also helps shed light on the fate of the peasantry of the Middle East and may usefully be contrasted with the selections by Mehdi Abedi and Michael Fischer, Ashraf Ghani, Joost Hiltermann, David McMurray, Ahmad and Schaar, Abdullah Schleifer, and David Seddon. —ED.


Ameur, known as Mog and nicknamed al-Rafiq, was born from out of the sea. His village of fishermen, olive cultivators, and weavers lies along the Mediterranean coast a half dozen miles south of the town of Monastir in the region of the Sahel. It is called Ksibet el-Mediouni, which means "the little casbah [of Sidi Abdallah] from Mediouna," the name of a small town in Morocco. The name Mog was apparently passed on to him from his grandfather, who had served in the Ottoman army in the last half of the nineteenth century. It is the Turkish term (*mugh*) for magian, that is, a Zoroastrian priest, and in Ottoman Turkish had a scope of meaning that included fire worshiper, disciple, spiritual teacher, frequenter of taverns, innkeeper, vintner. Not a very complimentary term, and indeed a name by which people referred to, rather than addressed, him.

As for his nickname al-Rafiq, it means "gentle, soft, tender, gracious, courteous," and also "comrade" and "traveling companion." A Quranic verse (4.71) states: "And good, or very good, will be those companions after the journey of life, in Paradise (*wahasuna ulaika rafiqan*)!" A proverb widely cited in Tunisia cautions people to select their neighbor (or party companion) before selecting the house they will live in and to select their traveling companion before selecting the road to be taken (*al-jar qabl al-dar, wa al-rafiq qabl al-tariq;* literally, "[seek] the neighbor prior to the house and the companion prior to the road!") Ameur, as I shall refer to him, was my companion.

As an anthropologist doing fieldwork in Ksibet in 1975–76, I made the happy choice of Ameur as one of my informants. (Actually, to be honest, he selected me.) By then Ameur had been around some while. He was born in Ksibet on 15 April 1917, and sixty-eight years later, on 26 September 1985, he was to make it his final resting place. During the last ten years of his life we got to know and to enjoy one another through conversations and correspondence.

Let's begin with the chronological and the contextual: Ameur came into the world in 1917, thirty-six years after the French conquest of Tunisia in 1881 had transformed this more-or-less autonomous region, a beylicate of the Ottoman Empire, into a protectorate of France's North African empire. His grandfather Mog had been in the bey's army and perhaps played a role in pre-French days in the brutal suppression of the 1864 insurrection in the Sahel, an uprising in which Ksibet was one of the 52 villages of the Sahel region that joined the tribes against the government's policies of taxation and conscription. In a list of 180 participants in the insurrection, one finds the names of 40 Ksibis (as the inhabitants of Ksibet are known). It was among those places with the highest number of insurgents. At the time the bey was milking the peasants to feed and clothe his army and to pay interest on the public debt and to deliver over to European merchants vast quantities of olive oil for which he had already been paid in advance.

The Sahel, till then the country's richest region, paid dearly for the rebellion: the infamous general Zarrouk and his troops created ruin and hopelessness. The peasants had to sell most of what they had in order to raise the ransom demanded, including their homes, their olive trees, and their other possessions. So say the archives and historical records. Those too poor to pay ran away as far as Tripolitania and Egypt. The Sahel became depopulated and its cities deserted because of the repression and then, from 1866 to 1868, because of drought, famine, and cholera. It was probably about this time that Ameur's grandfather Mog built an impressive family house in Ksibet, and he managed to hold onto it. He may have been among the soldiers in Zarrouk's army who were said to have intervened on behalf of the Ksibis to lessen the exactions imposed.

Ameur's father, Salah, was also a soldier. He served in the French army during World War I and then became a customs official in the city of Sousse. His wife, Khaddouja Frigui, was the daughter of a local notable in Ksibet. Ameur was an only child. By the time he was old enough to go to school, in about 1922, a war veteran from the nearby town of Moknine who had the rudiments of a French education had set up a schoolroom in Ksibet to complement the Quranic school that had always been there. Most of the children in Ksibet learned Arabic and religious studies in the old Quranic school, and seven boys had gone on from there to study in the Zaytuna mosque-university in Tunis. Ameur was one of three or four boys in the village who got a primary education in French. (One of the others eventually became a member of the Tunisian Supreme Court.)

There was an additional incentive for modern education in Ksibet because of the presence since around 1900 of a factory owned by Eugenio Lombroso. Known as al-Merkanti (the Rich Man), Lombroso was a Tunisian-Italian Jew from the nearby town of Mehdia. The factory produced soap from the pulp of olives by means of a new process discovered in the late nineteenth century. Most of its sixty workers (fifty of them seasonal) were Ksibis, and they had already on occasion organized themselves in disputes over wages and working conditions.

In 1927 Ameur had moved to Sousse with his family and begun to study in the local primary school, where after four years he received the *certificat d'études*. He continued there in the Lycée Carnot, earning the *brévet* certificate in 1935. By then he had had his first taste of politics, participating in the strike and demonstrations at Sousse against the measures taken by the French resident general Peyrouton following the creation of the Néo-Destour party under the leadership of Habib Bourguiba and his allies in 1934. The party, founded in the town of Ksar Hellal near Ksibet, drew most of its leadership and early adherents from among the people of the Sahel, and Ameur, at the tender age of seventeen, counted himself among the initial activists. It should be pointed out that Ksibet already for some while had been a village whose inhabitants were politically awakened and motivated.

Ameur broke off his secondary studies in Sousse following the death of his father in 1935 and returned to Ksibet to manage a moderate-sized family property that consisted of a house and an olive grove of some five hundred trees. The population of Ksibet at that time must have been edging toward the 3,000 odd souls counted there in the 1942 census (there were somewhat more than 6,000 inhabitants there during my fieldwork in 1975–76), and that of Tunisia around 2.25 million (the estimated population at the beginning of the protectorate in 1881 was 1.5 million, that counted by the census in 1946 almost 3 million, and that of 1975–76 about 5.5 million). Ksibet in the 1930s (and still today) was a sort of cauldron, a place on the boil. The Ksibis themselves used the metaphor of the *berrad* (the small teapot in which they prepare the

strong green tea they endlessly drink) to speak of the intelligence, ambition, and cunning that were "brewing" among them and that were too
often frustrated and "burnt out" by lack of opportunity.

Ksibet was as cramped, poor, and introverted as the rest of the villages and towns of the Sahel among which it nestled, and like them probably between one-third and two-thirds of its active male population
gained most of their livelihood as weavers. The Ksibis had been weaving
cotton cloth since one of them, Ahmed Djbali, introduced the technique
in the 1920s. Djbali, who died in 1963 at the age of eighty-four, became
a kind of local hero and may be considered, at least to some extent, a
spiritual father of Ameur. He had been a member of the Aisawi Sufi order and sang in one of its musical troupes, was reputed for his folk wisdom and his knowledge of popular literature (especially *The One Thousand and One Nights*, which he was said to have read many times), for the
large number of women to whom he had been married, for his political
activism on behalf of the union of weavers, and for his belated membership in the Communist party (which he joined, people said, because of
the liberal availability of women and alcohol at the party conferences in
Sousse and Tunis).

The 1920s and 1930s in Tunisia were years of prolonged crisis, pen-
ury, and drought. The worst years had names like "the year of alfalfa"
(when one could eat nothing else), "the year of rice," or "the year of typhus." The period 1933–34, a year of drought and international financial crisis, was referred to as "the great misery": there was no grain, no
possibility of making bread at all, and people walked to Tunis in search
of work and food. In any year the months of March and April were particularly difficult because of the slowness of the market, and the weavers
and petty merchants headed the list of those who suffered most. Those
months were known as "the time of carrots," because people could afford to buy nothing else. Most everyone took any kind of seasonal work
available if they were lucky enough to find it. In Ksibet the alternatives
were limited to fishing, itinerant trade, work in l-Mkina l-Hamra—
Lombroso's red-brick soap factory—or in es-Subkha (the arid place),
the French-owned saltworks a few miles up the road beside the village
of Khnis.

The saltworks in Khnis had been founded by the French-owned
COTUSAL company in 1903. Its workers had already participated in a
general strike against their low salaries and dreadful working conditions
in 1904, and they had provided membership for the first Tunisian labor
union, the CGTT, founded in 1924, the year that grain prices rose 29
percent following the drought of the previous year. The Ksibis played an
important role in the saltworks, from which on the average 17,370 tons
of salt for the manufacture of saltpeter used for gunpowder and explo-
sives (almost one-quarter of Tunisia's total export of salt) were annually

shipped to France, Norway, Algeria, and the United States between 1934 and 1938. In the summer months, when most of the boats were loaded, between five hundred and six hundred workers were employed, and perhaps as many as half of them came from Ksibet. It was killing, poorly paid work, and the men were rounded up almost as if they were forced labor. Forty years later those who had worked there bitterly recounted the hardships and showed me their scarred hands. "There was no alternative then," they said. "People were so hungry they could die for the smell of bread alone."

The labor force in the saltworks was mobilized by two entrepreneurs—recruiter or boss might be a better translation for the Arabic term *tashrun*—who came from Ksibet. They had contracted with the company to provide the workers necessary to load the ships. These two men ran things in the village. Their personal itineraries were "rags-to-riches" stories. It is important to stress here that for Ameur and others of his generation in Ksibet the lives of these two entrepreneurs, nicknamed Yusuf et-Twil (Tall Joseph) and Hasan el-Mahrug (Bronzed Hasan), were considered paradigms of human nature, success stories in the struggle for survival. Yusuf and Hasan had formed a partnership as labor recruiters for the saltworks of Khnis in about 1918 after protracted gang wars between them and their followers for control of the contracts with the company.

In his youth Yusuf had been wild, to use a mild term: a robber, a roughhouse, and some said, the unidentified killer of the rich widow Kaka, whose gold and jewels disappeared at the time of her death and simultaneously with his extended absence from Ksibet. Later he returned and began to work for the French at the saltworks. Eventually he became, with Mahrug, the arbitrator of people's destinies in the village. Both men got rich. Mahrug invested his wealth in property and led a retiring life. Yusuf translated his profits into power. In the 1920s and 1930s he and those called by the Ksibis his allies or gang (*isaba*) ran things in the village, although in time he was said to have become calmer and more righteous, and a man of great generosity.

For Ameur, the position of Yusuf in Ksibet in those years was evidence of human nature as it expressed itself in society. Yusuf ruled Ksibet because he had wealth and economic power, Ameur explained to me, just as the United States ruled the United Nations and the world thanks to its economic power. The position of dominance is forced upon men and nations whether they seek it or not. People in Ksibet needed Yusuf just as the poorer nations need the United States. If he had not delivered the goods to people and resolved matters among them, someone else would have done so and in the process undermined his position. Because of his wealth, and because he was feared and respected, people came to him for jobs and loans, and when there were conflicts, they came to him to settle them. "That's how things are," Ameur informed me, adding a pithy Tunisian proverb to emphasize the point. "He who has no money will neither copulate nor embrace!" When I responded by citing the Moroccan variant of the same proverb: "He who has no money has unsweetened words!" my companion laughed and said, "Ah, but the Moroccans are so much more refined than we are!"

Of course, Ameur knew as well as I that Yusuf's domination in Ksibet was far from complete. There was too much turbulence in the country for the likes of Yusuf to go unchallenged. For example, there was Shaykh Muhammad Karkar, for whom the main street of Ksibet was later to be named. Karkar was a veteran of World War I, one of the 62,461 Tunisian soldiers who fought for France (of whom half were killed or wounded) and of the 24,442 workers (10,126 of them volunteers) who had been brought to France to work so that the French boys could be sent to the trenches of the Great War. Karkar seems to have been one of the latter, a farm worker, because we know that he was stirring up other Tunisians on farms in the south of France and got himself imprisoned in Montecristo's Château Dif as a political agitator. When Karkar returned to Tunisia after the war, he renewed the political activities that he had begun earlier as a student in the Zaytuna mosque in Tunis.

Shaykh Karkar was a student, a follower, and a friend of Shaykh Abd al-Aziz Talbi, a leader of the Young Tunisians (an early nationalist formation). Talbi was a follower of the Salafiya, a religious movement that sought to reform Islam. In 1904 he had been condemned to death by the Islamic law court of Tunis for his book *The Liberal Spirit of the Quran* and forced into exile. After the war and the establishment of the League of Nations he founded the Tunisian Liberal Constitutional party (more commonly known as the Destour party), the first nationalist party in Tunisia (later called the Old Destour, perceived as more stodgy in contrast to the politically more alert Néo-Destour). Thus Shaykh Karkar was a Destourian and a rationalist reformer when he returned from the war to his home in Ksibet. There he opened a modern school and began to put his ideas and his politics into practice.

However, Shaykh Karkar did not make himself very welcome in the Ksibet dominated by Yusuf et-Twil. The shaykh's reformist ideology went against the Sufi religious tradition that had roots and branches in the village, personified in the newly founded Sufi order of the Madaniya headed by Yusuf's charismatic, educated, and ambitious nephew, Shaykh al-Madani. The latter, who had also studied in the Zaytuna in the early years of the century, had taken another path—the Sufi one. He had gone to Mostaghanem in Algeria to learn the doctrine of the "modernist" order of the Alawiya. When he returned to Ksibet during or just after World War I, he established a lodge of the Alawiya there, which he subsequently transformed into his own brotherhood—the Madaniya.

When Karkar arrived, the Madaniya and its shaykh were flourishing not only in Ksibet but in many other places as well, especially among the bedouin of the Souassi region to the southwest, and all of this had the blessing and support of Yusuf, the local boss of Ksibet. Shaykh Karkar did not wait long to make his views on "superstitious maraboutism" and "retrograde saint worship" known. Before long he was perceived by Shaykh Madani and his uncle Yusuf as "an enemy of God." Within a short time, Yusuf had managed to maneuver Karkar into a situation where he could humiliate him publicly. When in the early 1930s the tough old man slapped him in the public square in the plain light of day, he decided to abandon the village to its vices and never to return there.

Shaykh Karkar moved to Tunis and became increasingly drawn into the nationalist movement. He established a school and an important cell of the Destour party, of which he became an executive member. In 1931, Karkar became the president of a group formed to protest the celebration of the fiftieth anniversary of French rule in Tunisia. That same year he became involved in the political campaign against the Eucharistic Congress sponsored by the colonial authorities at Carthage, which was considered by nationalists as an affront to their religion. In the face of the French opposition to the nationalists, he grew steadily more devoted to the political cause of the Destour party. In 1933, he organized a meeting in the Grand Mosque of Tunis that called for a boycott of tobacco, tramways, and the government-sponsored newspaper, *Al-Nahda*. Later that year he traveled throughout the Sahel to promote the establishment of a labor union of weavers.

Growing tensions between the young nationalists and the old Destour party culminated in the establishment of the Néo-Destour party in 1934 at Ksar Hellal. Thereafter the national struggle was increasingly led by the Westernized petite bourgeoisie of the Néo-Destour, headed by Habib Bourguiba. Shaykh Karkar remained loyal to his old Destour roots, a fact that Bourguiba and the new party were very slow to forgive. For the French, both Destour parties, old and new, were perceived as dangerous. In January 1935 Karkar was placed under house arrest at Matmata by the French. He died forty days later under mysterious circumstances and was buried in Ksibet after a massively attended funeral. (The French authorities had banned his interment in Tunis for fear of large demonstrations.)

This was the Ksibet in which Ameur grew up. During the general strike called by the Néo-Destour of 1938, Ameur was an active demonstrator in Sousse and had the experience of being clubbed by the Senegalese soldiers brought in to restore order. Later that year, at age twenty-one, he married Khadija Malak, a girl from one of the more respected families of Ksibet. His wife brought with her a parcel of land that adjoined Ameur's house, so there may have been some kinship links through marriage between their parents. Ameur was a member of the Umalda clan of Ksibet, while his wife was attached to the Qwadra clan. There were four or five such clans in the village, depending on whose account one accepted. Each of them claimed descent from one of the four or five male descendants of Ksibet's eponymous founder, Sidi Abdallah el-Mediouni, whose mausoleum at the side of the grand mosque was the main monument of the village.

Ameur's ideological point of gravity during the period from 1938 until the end of the war lacks consistency or clarity. He seems to have vacillated between adoption of Néo-Destour nationalism, flirtation with the occupying Axis powers, and adherence to the Communist party. He may even have been drawn to Shaykh Madani's brand of Sufism for a while, because he told me that at some time in his life he attended the shaykh's circle of adepts and found his lessons "very impressive, erudite, and moving" and that there were moments when he "wept from the emotions that those sessions with the shaykh awakened." Although he claimed to have participated in Communist party cell meetings in Ksibet from 1940, this seems doubtful, since the party was banned till 1943.

One witness of his evolving state of mind is a letter to the French authorities dated 24 January 1938, found in the Tunisian protectorate archives. It strongly protested the appointment of Shaykh Madani as *imam* of Ksibet's Friday mosque. Although the signature is illegible, judging from its style and content, it probably was written by Ameur. It illustrates the bitterness of the quarrel between Sufi leaders like Madani and the Néo-Destourians and the extent to which Tunisian society had become divided on the eve of World War II:

> The educated elite see this [i.e., maraboutism, the term for Sufi shrine cults] as a way of collecting money and don't want to have anything to do with a man who is adored by his followers and who enjoys the favor of the local authorities, because he belongs to no existing political party in Tunisia and indeed opposes them, claiming that he has a "politics" of his own. The educated have ignored him, but they have been amazed to see the local authorities falling into his trap and helping him to become *imam-khatib*. I don't want to pray behind an ignorant man who has made himself rich by his maraboutism. Though unattached to Tunisian political parties, he gives himself over to Mussolinian propaganda, receiving emissaries from Tripoli to plot against the French and the Tunisians. He is making a joke of our religion for political purposes, and he should not be appointed!

The war years were difficult times throughout Tunisia, popularly remembered as "the days of misery." At first their main impact was economic. In August 1942 the Axis powers invaded Tunisia. In November 1942 Allied troops landed in Morocco, and soon thereafter the war moved to Tunisia. On 14 January 1943, German and Italian troops moved into Ksibet, where they were to remain until 8 April 1943. Military headquarters were in the neighboring village of Benane, about a mile up the road and on the main railway line from Sousse to Sfax. A detachment of German troops was billeted in the local school in Ksibet. With the arrival of the Germans and the Italians, the economic condition of the country, or at least of the Sahel coastal plain, changed for the better. The occupying troops brought little with them, imports came to a standstill, and the local economy underwent a rebirth.

The period from 1943 until 1946 was called *waqt l-bund,* or the time of the black market. Army rations and commodities of all sorts were sold at handsome profits, and the local weavers did well, producing worsted-type woolen fabrics and cotton cloth for sale in the import-starved markets of the big cities. Until sometime in 1944, there were some one hundred weavers busily employed in Ksibet weaving cloth. In addition, the German troops needed coffee, tea, sugar, tobacco, and other basic goods and were prepared to pay high prices to obtain them. (A packet of cigarettes purchased by a Tunisian for seven francs could be resold to a German soldier for one hundred francs.) After the arrival of the British and Americans, the "golden days" of the black market came to an end, because they were plentifully supplied with their own notions.

Ameur spent these years in Ksibet and was involved in dealings with the Germans. Some people say that he flirted with Nazi ideas being propagated by Radio Berlin at the time. I would like to think that was not the case, but I am unsure of the truth. He told me that during the war and the German-Italian occupation he had been reported to the authorities as a Gaullist and was almost shot by the Germans. His friends from the neighborhood and from the Communist party had come to his defense, and he had been spared. His "crime" had been to listen to the broadcasts of Free France on the BBC, and his punishment the confiscation of his radio by the village shaykh. Later it came out that he knew a bit of German, and may well have been more involved with the Nazis than he at first claimed. He insisted that he had never had any illusions about the Nazis and knew that he was quite as much at risk as a Jew to Nazi racial policies. As for his knowledge of German, one of the funny stories that is told in Ksibet is that Ameur always claimed that it was exceedingly easy to learn German: you only had to put an *ich* before and after every word you said. Then he would give an example, pronouncing an Arabic sentence that stated that so-and-so in Ksibet was a big smoker of hashish and in which each word was prefixed and suffixed by *ich.* During those early months of 1943 there had been about two hundred Germans put up in Ksibet's school and some fifteen hundred Italian troops living in the olive groves in and around the village. The Germans, it was said, liked the Arabs and treated them with respect. Not so the Italians, who were unruly troublemakers.

It was the Italian troops who committed a major atrocity at Ksibet. The incident is seared into the memory of those who lived through the period. As pieced together from their account and from the pages of the Tunisian newspaper *L'avenir de la Tunisie* for 1 July 1944, what happened is the following: a group of drunken and bored Italian soldiers started knocking on the doors in Ksibet, asking for a "Fatma," that is, an Arab woman. Doors and windows were closed, women took fright and began to scream, neighbors gathered, and eventually two of the Italians got beaten, and the rest ran off. Later, however, a group of Italian soldiers returned. They began to shoot indiscriminately and to throw grenades into houses. Their "punitive expedition" continued into the night. Any Tunisian found outside was shot. People locked their doors or fled to nearby villages or tried to hide in Lombroso's factory. Not till the following morning did the Germans intervene and put an end to the massacre. By this time sixteen people had been killed, and dozens more wounded. After the war there was an investigation, and eventually some compensation was paid to the affected families by the Italian government.

After the Allied defeat of Rommel, the French reassumed control over the protectorate. Once again Tunisians found themselves in a period of economic crisis. Ameur's friend and neighbor Umar Lahwishi, a weaver, musician, and interpreter of dreams, remembered those days vividly. One day he was trying to illustrate to me how he went about the interpretation of dreams. In the grim days after the war, he told me, he had dreamt once about a donkey that was walking along the edge of the sea below Ksibet. Suddenly, out of the water jumped a fish, and it landed on the back of the donkey. The donkey continued to amble along. When Lahwishi awoke, he remembered the dream and consulted his books on the interpretation of dream symbols. He found that the donkey represented a Jew and that the fish represented gold. Then he knew that somewhere in his future a Jew and gold awaited him.

Times worsened. Lahwishi had a wife and several small children, and he was finding it increasingly difficult to feed and clothe them. So he went to Tunis and sought out Brahim Slama, a wealthy entrepreneur originally from Ksibet, to ask him for a job, but to no avail. He joined the ranks of the masses of unemployed in Tunis and became hungrier and more despondent. One day he went into a café in Bab Souika and asked for a glass of water because he could not afford tea. Tired and at his wit's end, he sat at a table, took out his penny whistle, and began playing. From the other side of the café, someone began to play a *darbouka* (small drum) in accompaniment. They moved together and continued to play. When they stopped, a few people gave them some coins. The dream had been realized: the Jew and the gold. The other man, similarly down on his luck, was a Jew from Zarziz. For the next few years they made the rounds of the cafés and streets of Tunis, playing their tunes, gathering in the coins, and managing to keep themselves and their families back at home from utter destitution. Then Lahwishi's Jewish companion went off to Israel, and Lahwishi found other work, returning eventually to Ksibet.

Ameur's itinerary during this period was different. On 10 November 1943, the official ban on the Tunisian Communist party was lifted. Activities of the party in the Sahel started up again, but they were controlled and counteracted by the authorities. According to police reports there were eighteen party members in Bembla, a nearby village about the size of Ksibet, in August 1944 when the local authorities banned a meeting there "to prevent public disorder." Not long afterwards, in February 1945, Ameur founded the first cell of the party in Ksibet. The meeting was held in a house in Ksibet with a large central courtyard and was attended by the leadership of the party from Sousse, who were, at least in part, Tunisian Jews—Lazar and Hayat are the names in my notes. French and Soviet flags hung from the roof, and about a hundred people attended. Soon after the meeting had begun, however, about twenty local youth climbed on the roof, tore down the flags, threw things into the courtyard, and yelled obscenities. When they were challenged, they ran off. In the process, they beat a young boy selling party newspapers outside the house and tore up his newspapers. Since the party had a permit to hold the meeting from the French authorities, they filed a complaint, though little came of it. Although the Communists continued to suffer harassment at Ksibet and were always outnumbered by the Néo-Destour supporters in the village, they were a constant presence on the local scene into the 1950s.

Ameur was somewhat reluctant to talk to me about his involvement in the Communist party. Still, though generally suspicious of others, he could not help talking. He had headed the local party cell for some years in the 1940s and regularly written in the party newspaper. He told me that he had quit the party about 1950 because he had reached the conclusion that it was engaged in a losing battle with Tunisian nationalism and that Bourguiba and the Néo-Destour would carry the day. Along with some others, he related, he had sent a letter of resignation that was published in the party newspaper, *Al-Amal*. Others related that he did not leave the party until it was banned in 1963 or that he remained a clandestine member until 1967. In any case, the authorities suspected him; he was regularly harassed, arrested, and imprisoned for belonging to "an association forbidden by law" until the late 1960s.

Another topic that was evoked in our conversations was the 1948 war between the Zionists and the Arabs. Although it can be assumed from the record that for most Tunisians the events of the Holy Land were relatively distant, physically and psychologically, such was not the case for at least some young men in Ksibet and, indeed, other parts of the country. In 1947 or 1948, a group of them volunteered to go off to fight for Palestine, and they actually got as far as the coast of Cyrenaica after various trials and tribulations. But by the time they got there the war had already ended, and they had to make their way back to Ksibet, where they have since been the object of a mixture of glamour and derision.

In the 1950s the Tunisian national liberation struggle began to heat up. In the fight for independence Ksibet was an important center of support for the Néo-Destour party, as was the rest of the Sahel region generally. By 1956 it had led to the establishment of an independent Tunisian state under Habib Bourguiba and the Néo-Destour party. In this period the village had its glorious and its sad moments. One of the latter occurred on 5 February 1952, when Ksibis awoke to find themselves surrounded by French troops. The French had a list of the names of fifteen political activists to be arrested. Though nine of those arrested were released soon thereafter, the rest remained imprisoned for four months. Upon their release, they were welcomed as local heroes. A less happy event was the murder of a Ksibi, a well-known and respected man who had served in the French army during the war, by *fellagha,* or freedom fighters, from a nearby town who suspected him of being a collaborator with the French. Ameur spoke of the man and his fate with immense sorrow.

During the struggle for independence, the debates that divided the Tunisian Communist party were bitter and acrimonious. Ameur seemed to accept the prevailing view, which held that the split was essentially between Muslim party militants, who favored an alliance with the Néo-Destour in support of the nationalist cause, and Jewish and European party members, who believed in internationalism. As a result of the turmoil and conflict within the party, many people resigned. (It was in this period as well that Stalin's crimes became public knowledge outside of the Soviet Union.) Ameur remained affiliated with the party nonetheless. Even after independence, Ksibet continued to have an important cell of the Communist party and a member on the party's executive committee. An acquaintance from Tunis remembered attending party meetings in Ksibet in the period 1958–63 in the courtyard of a house (maybe Ameur's) with about thirty men from Ksibet and the surrounding villages. All of them were dressed in the tunic of the Sahel and aged in their thirties. It was, he told me, an impressive sight to see these peasant party militants in the heart of the Sahel.

Throughout the 1940s and 1950s the French sought to keep the lid on the political process. In no way daunted, Ameur played an active role in local politics during the period. In 1943, just after the French had been reinstalled in power by the Allies, local elections were held throughout Tunisia for village head. In Ksibet Ameur was one of the five candidates. There was no nonsense about secret ballots: the men of the village were assembled in the town square by the French officer in charge and instructed to stand behind the candidate of their choice. Under the circumstances, it was clear to the villagers what they were supposed to do. On signal, they all stood behind the "official" candidate, Ben Aisha, who served as village shaykh until 1953. Upon his retirement in that year Ameur probably ran for shaykh a second time. This time the official candidate (and, it goes without saying, the winner) was Shaykh Hamza. Ameur's political activism was to involve him in two other losing battles in the 1960s on the local scene that embittered him: a campaign aimed at the dismemberment of the *habous* (pious endowments) and an attempt to wrest control of Lombroso's factory from Shaykh Hamza and his cronies in order to establish a workers' cooperative.

By the time I met him in 1975, Ameur had put all this behind him. He had become a fixture in the local café society, a philosopher, a master player of dominoes, and a fair hand at *belote*—one of those Mediterranean card games that fascinate the Tunisians and that were constantly being played and argued over in one of Ksibet's three, almost always filled, cafés. By then most of his fifteen children had grown up or were well into their studies. The eldest son had completed a higher degree in Tunisian history at a French university, was teaching at a Tunisian lycée, and had published several slim volumes of poetry in French. Two other sons were in France and England, working on French doctorates in English literature. All of his daughters were married—one of them to the brother of my landlord. Only the youngest remained at home, where she earned her keep by weaving carpets for sale to tourists.

Ameur had always seemed to me to have little visible means of support. Just how precariously balanced the family fortunes were I learned one day in October 1975 when he explained his finances. He said he had just sold sixteen of the two hundred olive trees that remained from his inheritance of five hundred. In the summer he lay in provisions for the year—wheat, garbanzo beans, olive oil, and dried vegetables. With these and around sixty Tunisian dinars a month (equivalent to sixty dollars at the time) he fed and clothed his entire family. What little money the family earned came from the sale of surplus olive oil from its olive grove, surplus produce from the garden, eggs, and the occasional chicken or lamb that the family owned, and from a portion of the profits from the sale of his daughter's carpets. In particularly tight circumstances, more could be obtained by selling a few olive trees or a bit of land.

Ameur was a man who could make ends meet. What really interested him, however, was not the material side of life, but the spiritual and the intellectual. To hear him hold forth in the café or in the evening over tea at his house or the house of his cousin, the barber Munji, or strolling with him through the streets and alleyways of Ksibet was an enriching and amusing experience. I often wondered whether to consider him a philosopher, a cynic, a fanatic disbeliever in revealed religious or pro-claimed secular truths, or someone troubled by religious doubt, or all of these at once. Clearly and certainly, I have concluded, he was a man without awe of the holy or fear of sin, and he was a fox who knew many things. Moreover, by the time I came to know him, he was, at the age of fifty-eight, old enough to feel relatively beyond the reach of favor or dis-favor in regard to others' opinions of and influence over him. What he sometimes said about Islam would probably have been considered blas-phemous by most of his countrymen.

One of the stories he especially enjoyed telling was that of the *muezzin* Fredj who had turned up once at two in the morning rather than at five to call the villagers to prayer. A group of old men who did not have watches or had not bothered to consult them had arisen and come to the mosque for prayer on the assumption that it was indeed time for *al-fajr*, the sunrise prayer. When they discovered the mistake, they became irate, and the police were called in. When questioned, the *muezzin* claimed that some of his friends had plied him with alcohol and that he had become drunk and had gotten mixed up on the time. He was locked up for a while, and then replaced as *muezzin*. Some of the Ksibis, and particularly Ameur, had a good laugh.

Ameur and his sidekick, relative and crony "Sir" Munji the Barber, were a mean pair. During the hot summer nights when they and their families gathered in the courtyard, their tongues wagged maliciously, and they would spin their yarns and minutely dissect local and global politics, reflect upon the universe and the nature of existence, etc. In the wee hours of the morning, when the cakes had been eaten and the younger children and the women had fallen asleep, they and the older boys would disappear from time to time to rinse their faces to reawaken in order to continue the *sahra*, the conversation, through the night. Munji was almost always a match for Ameur, but mostly his favorite audience and sounding board. A round little man with bright blue eyes brimful of memories and alight with wickedness, Munji was the perfect counterpart to Ameur's lean, narrow-waisted form and rounded, weather-beaten and youthful face and dark, luminous, sharp eyes full of intelligence and cunning.

Munji's barbershop, it should be mentioned, was a wondrous place. It included a collection of such objects as tools for repairing watches, pots and pans, stoves, bloodletting cups, and a faded photograph of Shaykh

Madani. Munji's antipathy to religion was mitigated by his insistence
that the barber's craft of bloodletting had been authorized by the
Prophet himself in Quranic verse. Munji, like Ameur, thought that
people were motivated chiefly by tyranny and greed, though education
offered a hope of overcoming these. Mostly the two of them liked to stir
things up and to create some "living theater" for themselves and others.

One of my last memories of Ameur comes from 1975, when he was
employed as an extra in Franco Zeffirelli's film *Jesus of Nazareth,* part of
which was filmed in a garrison in Monastir, done up to appear to be the
Temple of Jerusalem. I saw him on the set—one of thousands of Tunisians made up in biblical splendor with their weather-beaten faces and
greying beards. Extras earned three dinars a day and a can of sardines
and a loaf of bread for lunch. They often had spent their earnings in a
tavern before they reached home. Ameur looked at home on the set, at
times dejected and otherwise at once bemused and amused. Thus began
what was to become a modest acting career. Later he played several roles
in the Monty Python hit *The Life of Brian,* including the final scene,
where he sang the theme song "Always Look on the Bright Side of Life."
These performances were no doubt enlivened by his abiding natural gai-
ety and Solomonic wisdom.

## A NOTE ON SOURCES

This essay is based upon information collected in the course of fieldwork in Tunisia in 1975–76 supported by a grant from the Economic and Social Science Research Council (London). I have also consulted the Tunisian archives of the Dar
el-Bey in Tunis (Séries A, C, D, E, especially carton 150, dossier 5, in Série A)
with the support of a Hayter grant from the University of Manchester. French
and Arabic published sources were also consulted.

## SUGGESTIONS FOR FURTHER READING

For works in English on aspects of Ksibet history and society see the author's
"On the Appropriation of Surplus in Tunisia since the Nineteenth Century," *Di-
alectical Anthropology* 4 (1979): 57–64; "The Campaign to Encourage Family Planning in Tunisia," *Middle Eastern Studies* 17 (1981): 64–84; "The Discrediting of a
Sufi Movement in Tunisia," in *Islamic Dilemmas: Reformers, Nationalists and Indus-
trialisation,* ed. E. Gellner (Berlin: Mouton, 1985); and "A Tunisian Town: Internal Expansion and External Integration," in *Stratégies urbaines dans les pays en voie
de developpement,* vol. 2, ed. N. Haumont and A. Marie (Paris: L'Harmattan,
1985).

On Tunisia and the Maghrib during the period 1914–75, see especially the
following: Jacques Berque, *French North Africa: The Maghrib between Two World
Wars* (New York: Praeger, 1962); L. C. Brown, "The Tunisian Path to Modern-

ization," in *Society and Political Structure in the Arab World*, ed. M. Milson (New York: Humanities Press, 1973); Nicholas Hopkins, "The Emergence of Class in a Tunisian Town," *IJMES* 8 (1977): 453–91; and id., *Testour ou la transformation des campagnes maghrebines* (Tunis: Ceres, 1983). On contemporary Sufism in North Africa, see Martin Lings, *A Moslem Saint of the Twentieth Century* (London: Allen and Unwin, 1962).

# PART THREE

# Contemporary Lives

# EIGHTEEN

# Migdim: Egyptian Bedouin Matriarch

### Lila Abu-Lughod

Around 1800, bedouin pastoralist tribes constituted 5 to 10 percent of the population of the 3.5 million or so Egyptians. They inhabited a wide area, ranging from the Western Desert to the Nile Valley, even including portions of the Delta. The bedouin played an important economic role in the trade that linked Egypt with *Bilad al-Sudan* (Land of the Blacks) in the interior of Africa as well as with the Muslim states of the Maghrib. Powerful bedouin tribes like the Hawwara and the Hanadi were greatly feared by peasants and villagers for their depredations of agriculture.

During the nineteenth century as a result of the deliberate policy of Muhammad Ali (who ruled Egypt from 1807 to 1841 on behalf of the Ottomans) and his successors, the Egyptian bedouin were gradually sedentarized. Proud bedouin shaykhs were gradually transformed into a rural gentry owning vast estates, while their tribesmen became (not without some resistance) agriculturalists. A centerpiece of the changes introduced in the nineteenth century was the government-mandated switch from production of subsistence crops to long-staple cotton for the world market. The bedouin played an important part in the peasant revolts of the 1820s and 1830s against these changes. But by the end of the century, their violence curbed, the bedouin had become a somewhat discontented, but relatively docile, part of the rural population.

By the late 1970s, the life of the Awlad Ali, a bedouin people to the west of Alexandria, bore but a scant resemblance to that of the tent-dwelling pastoral nomads depicted in such films as *Lawrence of Arabia*. By then living in scattered villages along the coastal road that leads to the Libyan frontier, the Awlad Ali had long since abandoned their camels for Toyota pickups, although some remained herders until the 1950s, even to the 1970s. Yet as Lila Abu-Lughod shows in her portrait of Migdim, one of the Awlad Ali, the bedouin have not lost their sense of cultural identity. Because their sense of self is linked not to way of life but to genealogy and a code of morality emphasizing honor and modesty, their sense of themselves remains intact.

Most accounts of life among the bedouin are based upon the work of male anthropologists who because of the social conventions of bedouin society have lacked access to the private world of the family. The view they have provided us of bedouin society is inevitably limited to the public arena, of trade, politics, and religion. Yet androcentric views alone are clearly inadequate if we wish a fuller understanding. One of the great merits of Abu-Lughod's contribution to this volume is that it breaks with this tradition. Through Migdim, a bedouin matriarch, with whom Abu-Lughod lived between 1978 and 1980 and again in 1986, we acquire an understanding of bedouin life from a female perspective. It is a life full of surprises, one that breaks more than a few stereotypes about Arab societies and Arab women.

It is particularly interesting to compare Migdim's story with Julie Oehler's account of Bibi Maryam, another tribeswoman. (Other portraits of women are provided by Julia Clancy-Smith, Leila Fawaz, and Ehud Toledano.) If we keep the focus on tribal peoples, Migdim's life can be compared to Rostam, a Qashqa'i rebel portrayed by Lois Beck, and Mohand N'Hamoucha, a Middle Atlas Moroccan Berber profiled by Edmund Burke. —Ed.

On a quiet day toward the end of 1979, I asked Migdim whether she would tell me her life story. She said, "When you get old you think only of God, of prayer, and of the oneness of God. What happened has passed, you don't think about it. You don't think about anything but God." And she refused to say any more. Then, as now, the only decoration on the walls of her one-room house was a faded black-and-white photograph behind fingerprinted glass. It showed her as a younger, upright woman, standing proudly next to her eldest son, both wearing the distinctive white clothing of Meccan pilgrims.

She was busy in those days. Although she was bent nearly double and walked only with the help of a stick, she had the many social duties of a world where the mutual visits of relatives are the stuff of social relations. As the matriarch of one large family and the oldest sister of another, she was expected at many weddings, sickbeds, and funerals, as well as at feasts to welcome home those who had been released from prison or had returned from the pilgrimage to Mecca. Even when she was at home she was always busy with something—spinning, winding wool into thread, sewing burlap sacks together to patch the old summer tent, seeing to the goats, giving advice, or bouncing a grandchild on her lap.

By the time I returned in 1986, exactly seven years later, she could hardly stand up any more and could not walk except to go out to the bathroom or to do her ablutions for prayer. She had more time for me then, since her sons were gone most of the day and the women and girls in the camp had their chores and were not always free to sit with her.

When I asked her to tell me her life story or any girlhood memories, she said, "I've forgotten all of that. I've got no mind to remember with any more." But then she went on, "We used to milk the sheep. We used to pack up and leave here and set up camp out west. And there we would milk the goats and milk the sheep and churn butter and we'd melt it and we'd put the clarified butter in the goatskin bag and we'd cook wheat until it was done and we'd make dried barley cheese."

She laughed, knowing how formulaic this "story of her life" was, but that was all I got from my direct questions. Yet as we sat together over the next few months many tales of her life and the lives of those around her came out. For her, like the other women I knew in this bedouin community, the convention of "a life" with a trajectory made little sense. Instead there were memorable events, fixed into dramatic stories with remarkable details. I have put together some of these stories to try to convey some sense of both what her life has been like and how she constructs it for others, especially the daughters-in-law, nieces, and grand-daughters who surround her.

If there is any convention of telling women's life histories among the Awlad Ali bedouin I knew in Egypt's Western Desert it is the capsule summary offered when someone asks about a woman she has just met or heard about for the first time. Women say, "She's from such and such a family and a man from such and such tribe married her and she had two sons and three daughters." These three facts of a woman's life define some crucial circumstances: where she lives and what kind of support and standing she has in the community and, more important, who matters to her.

I have honored this convention in the stories that follow, stories about Migdim's marriage and her efforts to shape her large family's destiny. Her complicated relations with the sons so desired by women in patrilineal societies suggest the tensions between the ideals of a system and a woman's experiences over a lifetime. What she struggles over with them, as well as what she keeps alive through story memories, suggests to us too what the twentieth century has meant for a desert community that lived by herding sheep. Her life and that of her family have been shaped by how they coped first with the aftermath of the battles of European armies during the Second World War and then with the Egyptian government's land reclamation projects. A life, even a woman's life defined by marriage and children, is always located in time and place.

One of the most vivid of Migdim's stories was the tale of how she resisted marriages her father tried to arrange for her. I even heard more than once, almost word for word, the same account of how, over fifty years ago, she had ended up marrying Jawwad. I first heard it one evening that winter, in the presence of her sons' wives and some of her granddaughters. The first person to whom she was to have been married, she explained, was a first cousin. His relatives came to her household and conducted the negotiations and even went as far as to slaughter some sheep, the practice that seals the marriage agreement. But things did not work out.

"He was my father's brother's son," she said, "and I didn't want him. He was old, and he lived with us. We ate out of one bowl. His relatives came and slaughtered a sheep, and I started screaming, I started crying. And my father had bought a new gun, a cartridge gun. He said, 'If you don't shut up, I'll send you flying with this gun.'

"Well, there was a ravine, and I went over and sat there all day. I sat next to it saying, 'Possess me, spirits, possess me.' I wanted the spirits to possess me, I wanted to go crazy. Half the night would pass, and I'd be sitting there. I'd be sitting there, until my cousin Brayka came. And she'd cry with me and then drag me home by force, and I'd go sleep in her tent. After twelve days of this, my cousin's female relatives were dyeing the black strip for the top of the tent—they were about to finish sewing the tent I'd live in. And they had brought my trousseau. 'I'll go get the dye for you,' I said. I went and found they had ground the black powder and it was soaking in the pot, the last of the dye, and I flipped it over—pow! on my face, on my hair, on my hands, until I was completely black.

"My father came back and said, 'What's happened here? What's the matter with this girl? Hey you, what's the matter?' The women explained. He went and got a pot of water and a piece of soap and said, 'If you don't wash your hands and your face, I'll . . .' So I wash my hands but only the palms, and I wipe my face, but I only get a little off from here and there. And I'm crying the whole time. All I did was cry. Then they went and put some supper in front of me. He said, 'Come here and eat dinner.' I'd eat, and my tears were salting each mouthful. For twelve days nothing had entered my mouth.

"The next afternoon my brother came by and said to me, 'I'm hungry, can you make me a snack?' I went to make it for him, some fresh flat bread, and I was hungry. I had taken a loaf, and I put a bit of honey and a bit of winter oil in a bowl. I wanted to eat, I who hadn't eaten a thing in twelve days. But then he said, 'What do you think of this? On Friday they're doing the wedding, and today is Thursday and there aren't even two days between now and then.' I found that the loaf I was going to eat I'd dropped. 'Well,' he asked, 'do you want to go to so-and-so's [to seek refuge] or do you want to go to your mother's brother's?' I said, 'I'll . . . ,' but then it seemed as if there was an eclipse, the sun went out, and nothing was visible. I said, 'I'll go to my maternal uncle's.' I put on my old shoes and my shawl on my head and started running. I ran on foot until I got to my uncle's. I was in bad shape, a mess."

She complimented her uncle's wife, who had taken her in and explained to the man what the problem was. "May God have mercy on her, she was a good woman." But her uncle sent her back the next morning, with instructions to his son to accompany her and to deliver greetings to her father and to ask him to oblige him, as he had comforted his niece. If he were to postpone the wedding, perhaps she would come around. Migdim continued:

"So I went home. After that I didn't hear another word. The trousseau just sat there in the chest, and the tent—they sewed it and got it all ready and then put it away in their tent. And autumn came, and we migrated west, and we came back again. When we came back, they said, 'We want to have the wedding.' I began screaming. They stopped. No one spoke about it again."

Grandma Migdim continued her story with two more episodes of attempts to arrange marriages for her until she accepted one. When she remembered how her husband's family had come to ask for her hand, one of her granddaughters interrupted, "And Grandma Migdim, did you eat and drink at that engagement?" She answered, "Yes, I ate and drank." But then, as if to guarantee her virtue by assuring us that she had not had any special desire for this man, she continued, "Although I swear by my soul, that it wasn't in my thoughts nor was it in his. Not at all. It was his father who'd seen me when I was young. I was energetic and really smart. He'd say, 'That girl, if only my son could have her.' "

One of her daughters-in-law commented, "Bread and salt were running between you." She was referring to the notion that God wills certain people to share meals, that is, to live together. Migdim agreed, "Yes, it was bread and salt."

Migdim had seven children who lived, four boys and three girls. Her four sons and their families now made up the "camp" (once tents but now houses) that was her community. One daughter had married a neighbor and so also lived close by. The other two had married into other families and lived elsewhere, coming for visits on special occasions like weddings and illnesses and at the major religious feasts. Once as she watched from her doorway a group of her little granddaughters playing, Migdim sighed, "Little girls are nice. This one goes to get water, that one helps you. But in a week they can leave you, and their place will be empty. . . . Daughters aren't yours. When they marry that's it—they stay with their families and that's that. They leave you with nothing. But boys, they stay." Her daily life, as a result, revolves around her sons, their wives, and their children and even grandchildren.

Giving birth to children can be memorable, and Migdim had her own stories of childbirth to tell. There were no doctors around in her day, and she even maintains that, unlike most women, she did not like having other women around to help her when she gave birth. Of her fourth child, a son, she says, "I gave birth to him alone. I had no one with me but God. We were out west, inland from Alamein. That day I did the wash. I washed up everything. . . . In the morning I had washed my hair and braided it with henna and cloves. I cooked too—a pot of rice with yogurt sprinkled with some butter from the goatskin bag. . . . My sister-in-law and my husband's aunt were visiting, and they asked for lentils. So the other women started making some bread and cooking the lentils. It got to be sunset—the days were short that time of year.

"Jawwad had gone to sleep in the tent, taking the two older children. . . . I went to sit with the old women for a while as the girl cooked the lentils. My little boy fell asleep in my lap, so I said 'I'll go put my son to bed.' They said, 'Stay until we eat supper, then we'll all go to bed.' I said, 'I'll come back soon. But if I don't come, it means I don't feel like eating.' We'd had something to eat in the afternoon, and in those days people didn't used to eat much.

"I went off to put the boy to bed. I got three cramps while I was putting him down. Well, I didn't come back for supper. I circled around the tent, tightening the guy ropes. They called to me, 'Come have dinner, come have dinner.' The sun had gone down, and they called out, 'Come have dinner.' But I didn't want any. I scooped out a hole in the sand and went to sit by it. I brought out a straw mat and a donkey's burlap pack-saddle, and I put them down and sat on them, outside by the corner of the tent. When the labor pains hit me, I'd hold onto the guy rope's tension bar. One hand between my legs and one holding on to the rope above. The sheep came home after sunset, close to the time of the evening prayers, just as the child was coming out. . . . When the child broke through I lifted myself up by the pole, lifted my clothes up until the child dropped.

"When my sister-in-law came out to pee she heard. She ran into the tent and told the women, 'Migdim has given birth!' They came running. 'Where? Where?' they asked, and I told them, 'The child has a forelock [a boy]. The child with its forelock dropped.' So they lit a fire and wrapped the boy, and they moved me inside. They cooked a pot of asida [a special food for new mothers] that night and made tea. And Jawwad was sleeping near us, in the corner, and didn't wake up. The women had set up a compartment for me in the middle of the tent. He was sleeping with the children in the corner and didn't wake up.

"In the morning my mother-in-law slaughtered a chicken and was cooking it for me over by the hole I'd made. A woman neighbor of ours came over. 'Poor dear! When did she deliver? Why just yesterday she was doing the wash, and there was nothing wrong. Poor thing!' I tell you from the minute the old woman said, 'Poor thing'—God protect me, God protect me—I was seized by cramps. Something (may it be far away from you), something rang in my ears. And something covered my eyes so I couldn't see. I prayed, 'There is no god but God, there is no god but God,' until my mouth went dry. That was all the woman had said when they had to come running. Something blinded me, blinded me and knocked me out. My mother-in-law came and started moving my head, she made me sniff a burning rag. Well, I tell you, I didn't taste that chicken she was cooking. I never even saw it. I have bad cramps after I give birth. My cramps are bad then.

"I delivered my other children alone," she added. "I had no one with me but God." When I asked her why, she answered, "The women laugh and they talk and they bother you. You'll be as sick as can be, and they'll be making a lot of noise around you. I don't like them." When I asked if she would also cut the umbilical cord herself she said, "No, after the baby has dropped they come. They come and they cut the cord." Then I asked why they say that the woman who has just delivered is close to God. She laughed at my piece of knowledge. "Yes, they say it. By God it's difficult. Ask the woman who has given birth, ask her about death. She has seen it."

Death is not something people like to talk about. In fact, whenever women tell stories about bad things that have happened to people they interject phrases like "May it be far from you" or "May it only happen to enemies." Migdim was still sad about her brother's recent death. But she had lost other dear ones. Her husband, Jawwad, had died young. She connected his death to the death of his younger brother, killed by an exploding mine about seven years after what they knew as "the war between the Germans and the English." This kind of death was not uncommon after the battles of the Second World War had ended and the armies departed. In their desperate postwar poverty the bedouins had survived by scavenging scrap metal. They used the Arabized English term "to rubbish" for this activity.

Migdim did not like telling this story. When I asked one day how this younger brother-in-law of hers had been killed, her answer was brief. "We had migrated out west that spring. He went rubbishing riding on a donkey with a friend. I didn't believe he was dead because when he left the camp he had been heading east. And he had money—he had no need to go rubbishing. But he ran into friends who persuaded him to go. They came across a mound and found a bomb. The other man started taking it apart. My brother-in-law said, 'I won't work on it.' But instead of moving far away, he sat near him. The man kept trying to take it apart, but it exploded.

"The bomb exploded and killed the man. He flew, who knows where he landed. Who knows where it threw him. But my brother-in-law, all that came his way was a small bit, it landed (may it be far from you), landed in his chest. That year part of the family was camped near the train station at Alamein. They hadn't come with us. People brought him to them at night, in a car, and he died that night. They brought him in a car from the desert, from the camp of the man who had been rubbishing.

"We had all migrated from here and had set up camp way up in the desert south of Alamein. Someone soon came—the one who brought us the news came in the morning. He ran into the camp shouting his name, told us that he had died and was at the camp in Alamein. When he told us we jumped up and began running northward. My sons were young then, and they started running on foot, so I put on my belt and started running with them, wailing. We found everything in chaos. People came from everywhere. I found him all wrapped in a blanket and wailed his name.

"When Jawwad went in to see him, he shuddered. He told me, 'I trembled, and something pounded me from head to foot.' . . . He got sick, Jawwad, and he remained ill after the death. Ill for a year. And then a year after his brother had died, Jawwad died. And the old man, their father, died between them in the month of Ashura.

"My younger son wasn't very old then—he was still small. But he sang about his kinsmen who had died: 'He took away those around you, o eyes, despair hasn't been easy on you.' "

As her older son now describes it, this dangerous business of scavenging occupied many people after they returned to their territory from the camps in the Nile Valley to which the English had evacuated them during the war. He explains, "After they drove the Germans out, the English left. Then the Arabs could return to their territory. They went back as soon as they could. But they found that the armies had left the area of the battles covered with mines and bombs and big guns that had not gone off. We found hand grenades, some that had been tossed but had not exploded, some that were untouched. They had left everything: mines, broken tanks, cars, even whole garages with their dead in them. For six or seven years they were collecting their dead."

Migdim's niece tells the same story of those early days after the war. Their wells had been destroyed, they had lost much of what they had. And they had not been able to plant barley for their bread. They had nothing. "When the Germans came to Alamein the English stopped them. They pushed them back. So we came back to our land. We found the world in chaos. There were broken airplanes, ruined cars, and broken big guns. And big tins of biscuits. We used to find spoons and forks, rope, nice shoes, and burlap sacks from the sandbags. And nice bottles, nice little glass bottles. We used to collect them. White and green and red. Just lying around.

"The boys would collect them and sell them. And there were tires, you wouldn't believe the new tires! They used to carry them off on camels and go to sell them. Later there was the work in iron. The flints of big guns. They started gathering that, iron. And the copper, it was everywhere. They began collecting that. . . . But the bombs, they got aluminum from those. At the time it was worth a lot. So they started digging in the ground to get out the mines. They would collect four or five detonators, five or six detonators, and they'd take them far into the desert. Then they would light a fire and set them off. They would explode. When they'd cooled, they'd come and collect the stuff and sell it. Many of them got hurt. There are poems about that."

Migdim's son elaborated. "Dealers from Alexandria and Cairo came to buy the copper, one kind yellow and another red, and the gunpowder. . . . People would go into the desert in cars and on foot, any way they could. One time someone would pick up a mine, and it would explode in his hands. Another time someone would touch a bomb, and it would explode. Another time someone would try to undo a detonator to get out its cartridges or gunpowder, and it would blow up. Then five or six people would die together. It became like a war—explosions all the time. . . . A car would stray from the track, and a mine would go off and blow it up with whomever was in it. It was like a war." He estimates that at least twelve thousand bedouins have been killed through these accidents. To this day people and camels are being killed by unexploded mines they accidentally set off, even though no one works in scrap metal anymore. Reflecting on this period, he concludes, "Some people got rich. People got rich, but it destroyed families."

After the deaths of her husband, brother-in-law, and father-in-law, Migdim's sons found themselves forced to take responsibility for the family. They had to get themselves back on their feet after the devastations of the war. And as an important family, they had a reputation to uphold. There were many decisions to be made, and Migdim was usually consulted with or informed about family affairs. Her sons, when not traveling, spent their evenings with her, chatting together in her room by the light of a kerosene lantern. They also often stopped in during the day when they found themselves free. Her youngest son was the most affectionate in the days I was with them. Even as a forty-year-old man, he often came to sit close to her on the mat, stretching his legs out to tuck them under her blanket. Her sons were relaxed in her company, and as they had all gotten older, they were usually solicitous of her needs. They trusted her to run things in the household, among the women. She organized much of the work that needed doing, and she distributed the goods they brought home, from food to dress fabric.

Migdim, however, often complained about her sons. They sometimes made her angry—when they would not take her advice, when they put themselves in danger by getting involved in arguments with other families, when they made bad decisions about women. For example, she recounts that she had refused to sing or ululate at the marriage of one of her daughters. "I was opposed to it. It was against my will," she asserted. Her brothers had agreed to give her in marriage to her first cousin, although Migdim felt she was too young. And when the girl kept running away and hiding under a straw mat in the goat pen, her mother didn't tell the groom's family where to find her. The marriage ended in divorce after a few years and no children.

She also often got angry with her sons for their behavior toward their wives. Her daughters-in-law often came to her with their grievances. If she thought her sons were indeed treating them unfairly or poorly, she would speak to the men. On the other hand, her daughters-in-law praised her for being discreet about conflicts that arose between women of the community; she was careful not to involve the men in these. Most of her daughters-in-law recognized how often she took their side and looked out for them in situations in which they had little say.

As her sons got older and wealthier, they began to take second and even third wives. In her day it had been rare for men to have more than one wife. It was still unusual except for those who were rich and important. She yelled at her sons each time they decided to marry again, even as she recognized that men wanted to marry women so they could have more sons, men to make the family strong. One evening when one of her sons half-jokingly remarked that if death did not beat him to it, he would build a new house and get another wife, she had a fit. "You idiot! Bringing together many women is no good. Look at your household. Everything is left spilled, everything's a mess. That's because you have too many women. Each one says, 'It's not my responsibility. I won't pick it up. Let someone else do it.' " She had objected to his decision to marry a third wife and had even done her best to discourage the woman from marrying her son. She did not succeed that time, although she had managed earlier to dissuade the parents of another girl her son had wished to marry. She had told them he was a difficult man and that he already had two wives and too many children.

Her youngest son married a second wife after his first wife suffered several serious illnesses and miscarriages and was forbidden by the doctor from having any more children. When he started spending time at the household he set up for his new wife, away from his mother, she complained to everyone about how miserable she was. She moaned that it was terrible to be alone, not to have a man in the house any more; no one to say good morning to, no one to say good night to, no light in the men's guest room. But the women teased her about this. How often, they demanded, had her own husband, Jawwad, slept at his mother's house?

It was not just because her sons paid less attention to her when they married new wives that she objected. She was protective of the mothers of their children, the women who had been there for years, and of the children themselves. This complex mixture of jealousy and protectiveness toward her daughters-in-law and grandchildren figured clearly in a conflict Migdim had with her sons in the summer of 1987—a conflict over land.

A small family that had lived in their community for over thirty years wished to build a new house. The head of the household, now an old man, had come originally to help herd their sheep and goats but had since saved up for a sizeable herd of his own. He and his wife, who was the strong one in the family, had a modest house built on the property of their host family, quite close in fact to Migdim's small house. It seems they wanted a little more land to build on, and they wanted title to the land so they could feel secure that their sons could remain there.

Trouble simmered for weeks as the younger generation of boys and young men, Migdim's grandsons, worried about giving away family land that would become scarce. There were at least thirty boys in the family— where would they all build when they married? She supported them in this. When her sons came to consult her, she told them not to give over the land. Yet they went ahead and tried to beat up their own sons for threatening one of the old shepherd's sons. Migdim was furious. The day after it happened she ranted about her older son. "He's not my son, and I'm not his mother! . . . My son should respect my wishes. . . . He's my son. He came out of me. What could be closer to me? Yet he goes and signs it over to that family when I said not to. By the Prophet, isn't that wrong? Seeing how I said not to?"

This was obviously not just an argument about a piece of land. Nothing in this community can ever be an isolated incident, not when everyone has lived together so closely for so many years. For Migdim, this matter concerned the women's community, and particularly her relationship to her neighbor, the shepherd's wife. About eight years earlier, the woman's youngest daughter had become Migdim's eldest son's third wife. Just a few weeks before the incident over the land, this young woman had decided to go against the usual arrangements for the sharing of domestic work among the wives, grown daughters, and daughters-in-law of the household. Her husband had agreed that she could separate from the others and begin to cook and bake just enough for herself and her five small children. She claimed the work load was too heavy for her and that it was unfairly split. Her withdrawal had been discussed a lot in the women's community, defensively by the other two wives, who feared being blamed for having been unfair, and angrily by Migdim and the mother and sisters of the man's senior wife (who was also his first cousin), not to mention the other women in the community, who took sides with the older wives.

Migdim had been opposed to the marriage in the first place. When she was informed that he had arranged the marriage while she was away visiting her sick brother she blew up, insulting her son and calling him names. His first wife was his first cousin. She had not wanted to marry him yet had stayed and produced a line of sons. She was like a sister to him, and they had long since ceased sleeping together. His second wife was someone he had fallen in love with, the daughter of a shepherd's family that had lived near them for a while. He had longed for her. As his mother reminded him one day when he was complaining about the lousy bread she baked, he had raved, in the days before he married her, about how delicious her bread was—and that was before they had white flour, when they used only coarse brown barley. Migdim sympathized with both these wives, but especially with this good simple woman. Her son was mistreating her by not buying her a proper gift of gold to match what he had gotten for his new bride. That is a senior wife's due.

A couple of months after he had married this eighteen-year-old girl, he stopped by his mother's house, trailed by several of his little children. They played with him, but he soon tired of them and sent them off. Migdim complained about the number of children in the community. She criticized her son because his children had just accidentally killed a small goat they were playing with and she had only barely rescued a lamb from them. Four of them had climbed on its back to get a ride. She counseled her son, "A holy man said the man with many wives will go to hell. If he doesn't treat them exactly alike, if he brings something to one and not the other. Even if he looks at one and not the other. It's a sin, sin, sin."

Her son just laughed and said, "No, it's the one with only one wife who's going to go to hell." But his mother was just getting started. She went on to complain about the amount of gold he had bought for his new wife. "The old woman just buys, and you pay." The least he could do was buy his senior wife a little ring or something. "Shame on you," she said. Again he laughed and said, "Gold isn't everything." Then Migdim started in on the problem of having so many children. Who is going to feed them? Where will they all live? Her son responded with a religious line: "He who created them will provide for them. Every being on this earth is born with his God-given livelihood. God will provide for them." She muttered and grumbled, but her son just laughed.

If the conflict was over loyalty to kin versus generosity to longtime friends, over new wives against old, and exacerbated by the jealousy of an aging matriarch steadily growing weaker, the crisis was also one about land itself. Land was becoming scarcer and more valuable now that the Egyptian government had begun to reclaim desert land through irrigation projects. What had been good only for growing rain-fed barley or for grazing sheep could now be planted with other crops, especially fruit orchards, which were beginning to bring in much more money than herding. The government had also decreed that all the land held by Awlad Ali bedouins had to be purchased formally in order to secure title. It was now all becoming private property and the disputes over it had riven the whole bedouin community. The trouble with land, unlike a herd, is that it does not increase. That is why Migdim's grandsons were so worried.

By the late 1980s, Migdim's sons, like most wealthy bedouin, had shifted almost completely away from herding sheep and into other economic activities, including agriculture. These changes have had many consequences for the community, especially for women's day-to-day lives. When Migdim reminisces about what the area was like for most of her life, she is nostalgic. All of it, she describes, was sown with barley and wheat, so that in the spring, if there was rain, it turned green, and there was no place to set up the tents. They would leave to migrate west to Alamein with the herds. There they milked the sheep and stored up enough butter to last the whole year. Speaking of the past generation, she commented, "The old ones had been blessed, really fortunate. They were happy. They had camels and sheep. They lacked nothing. . . . My sons, though, they say the old ones did the wrong thing [by sticking with herding]. But all that we have is due to them. The government came and took their land, and so these young men had to buy it from the government. This business of agriculture they're now in, may God release them from its troubles."

They had planted their land slowly. Migdim had brought a few cuttings from her father's olive trees (he was one of the few in the area to have planted olive trees, following the advice of and taking cuttings from the local British administrator). They had watered them, and they grew. But the olive orchards that now take up much of their land were planted around 1960, when an Egyptian man who worked for the government came and told them he wanted the land to build a house on. They didn't want to give up what they considered their land, of course, and they heard that if the land were planted, no one could seize it from them. So day and night they worked, digging holes in the daytime and planting trees from Migdim's father's orchard by night. In fifteen days they had planted the whole orchard, with the help of many neighbors, relatives, and friends, and had surrounded it with high posts and barbed wire. When the government people came to inspect the land they found it all planted and so said the man could not have it. Migdim remembers that day well. The man left in his car, and Migdim's sons, on horseback, followed him all the way back to town, firing their guns into the air in celebration of victory. It was the first time a bedouin had won a land claim against the Egyptian government.

Migdim's one-room house sits, like most of the rest of the "camp," on a ridge that affords a wide view of these olive orchards, their new fig and guava orchards, and the scattered clumps of houses that extend to the horizon. There are so many people and houses now. She remembers when it was empty; nothing between here and her relatives' houses. This crowding means that the girls no longer go off to gather firewood—because there isn't any—and their trips to get water are short because their kinsmen worry about the girls passing by so many houses of people from outside their tribe and encountering at the tap so many others who are strangers. Migdim and the other older women bemoan this loss of freedom for women.

When she gets together with other women, she often rails against the younger men of the community for being so strict about the movements and behavior of their young sisters, cousins, and wives. "The boys are terrible now," she began one such conversation. Her daughter agreed, "The boys are terrible. I swear by my father we have one son who's black in word and deed. And he's so young." A visitor added, "Why, when we were young, remember, we used to go off to herd the goats on our own. Not any more!" Migdim's daughter continued, "Yes, that's how things were, may God have mercy on past generations. They weren't like this new generation. . . . The men now are awful."

Migdim's attitudes are contradictory. She defends her granddaughters and grandnieces and even her daughters-in-law when the young men, and sometimes the older ones, criticize them or accuse them of talking to men or going places away from home. But then she complains that the young women of today have no modesty. When she was young, she claims, they used to veil with heavy black shawls, not today's flimsy pieces of cloth that do not even hide women's faces. When a great-granddaughter of hers comes in crying because she has lost her hair clip, Migdim scolds her: "It's shameful for girls to wear hair clips. Why do you want a hair clip? Are you wanting to get married?"

Yet the world she remembers is one in which behavior that would now be considered scandalous was perfectly accepted. For example, Migdim thinks wedding celebrations have lost their appeal. She tells her newest daughter-in-law that they used to celebrate weddings for a week with evenings of singing and dancing. "Weddings now are like a shrunken old man," she comments. At weddings in the past, young women, including her husband's sisters and nieces, had danced veiled, in front of semi-circles of young men who serenaded them. Young men and women had always exchanged love songs at these weddings. "Stuff that couldn't happen now!" they agree, thinking of the sex-segregated affairs that weddings have become since they settled into houses.

Traces of that older world are kept alive in the women's world, with the older women remembering together and the younger ones listening to these tales of what would now be scandalous. Most of Migdim's time is spent with women. If she is feeling all right, able to sit and to eat, she always has the company of the members of her household—the two daughters-in-law whose husbands no longer sleep with them, and their children, including one young man who has recently married his cousin and had a son. Her great-grandson is a joy to her. Whenever he comes into her room she greets him warmly, as she does all her little grandchildren and great-grandchildren, "Welcome, welcome, welcome!" A chubby blond boy, he has become steady on his feet and wanders around her room getting into things.

One of her favorite games is to call out to him, "Come here, my little Kafy. Come gimme some snuff. I want to sniff some snuff. Where's the wild parsnip?" He toddles over to her, lifting up his robe so she can pretend to sniff his little penis. She pretends to sneeze, the way one does when one has taken snuff. This is outrageous behavior, but old women can do what they want. A visiting granddaughter is shocked. "What a black scandal!" she says. She teases the toddler, "Go put on your underpants!" But Migdim laughs and does it again. She sings to the boy, too, holding his hands in her own, wrinkled and tattooed, teaching him to clap. She often sings old lullabies to him, songs about little boys who grow up to ride horses, carry guns, and become tribal leaders. These are songs the younger women do not know.

Migdim is getting old, and her health is not good. She is diabetic but does not know what to do about it except to avoid rice and fried foods. When she has a fever, cries because her head hurts or her eyes burn, loses her appetite, or is unable to sit up, everyone in the community comes to see her. Sometimes her daughter moves in with her, to bathe her, feed her, and wash her clothes for her. As she feels better the mood lightens. All day her room will be packed with women and children who disappear or go quiet when one of her sons comes in. Otherwise, even if her grandsons or great-nephews stop by to chat, things are lively.

The conversations, especially among older women, can get quite bawdy. Once when I was there with my tape recorder, the women entertained Migdim with old folktales about the sexual desires of old women.

They laughed at the shamelessness of such women, and perhaps at themselves, these women with grown sons, mostly widowed or divorced. There is something disturbing in the hostility between mothers and sons these tales convey, something that hints at the ambivalence of that important relationship.

I missed the beginning of the first story Migdim's daughter-in-law was telling. "A man asked his elderly mother, 'Mother, do you want me to get you a husband?' She said, 'No, no, my son. That would be shameful. No, that's shameful.' But he said, 'No, no. He'll keep you company.' So she said, 'May God grant you success if you do. If you do it, may God bless you.' "

The storyteller laughed and went on. "He went off and killed a hyena. He killed the poor thing and wrapped him in a white shroud. And he brought him to her—she was blind—and he put him down next to her and said, 'Mother, be careful. His name is Hasan. He's sleeping now. Don't wake him up, he was up late last night. Let him wake him up on his own first. And don't move him. Let him sleep until he's slept enough.' And he put him down next to her and left.

"She started shaking him, trying to wake him up—her son was nearby, even though it was evening, and she assumed he had gone—she tried to wake him up. She said to him, 'Hey handsome! Hey handsome! Sit up, handsome. Look, here's a jar and here's another jar. There are some more as well that are hidden.' She was talking about jars she had filled with gold and buried. She had buried them all over, and she was showing him, the hyena, as her son watched!"

This reminded Migdim of another story; she called up a few lines from it, and Migdim's daughter-in-law picked it up. "She would always say, 'May God grant you success, if only.' Anytime he talked to her she said, 'May God grant you success, if only.' He went and asked someone, 'Why does my mother only say, "May God grant you success if only." What is this "if only?" ' He was told she wanted a man. 'If only' means only if you bring me a man."

Migdim laughed hard as she listened to the story. It continued, "So he went to her and said, 'Mother, I've gotten you a man, and he says you should come. I'll take you to him.' She said, 'Fine, let's go.' He went and put her in a hyena's lair. It was rainy and cold. He put her in the lair and left her there. When she heard the wind in the night whistling and going *oooh* and *rrrr*, she thought it meant that this was the night of her wedding and that she was going to get married. Soon her groom would come to her.

"Well, he came to her. The hyena wanted to eat her." Migdim interrupted, "Yes, he started eating her." Her daughter-in-law continued in a high voice, imitating the old woman but laughing as she tried to finish,

" 'Ooh! By God, by God, the groom is licking and stroking, licking and caressing me.' He was actually tearing her apart."

As they all laughed, one of the young women listening, Migdim's granddaughter, burst out, "Damn these bedouin stories!" Again imitating the old woman, her mother-in-law repeated the old woman's words, " 'The groom, he's licking and caressing!' He tore at her and bit her until he ate her up! (May it be far from you!) She assumed he was really her bridegroom, curse her! He came in the morning, her son, and found her dead."

Her daughter-in-law went on, "Shame on him." Migdim filled in the beginning of the story. "Her son had gone everywhere with her and done everything for her, but still she would never say to him, 'May God grant you success.' All she'd say was 'If only.' So he put her in with the hyena. 'I'll bring you an old man,' he said. 'And here is his house.' 'His house?' she'd said, 'God grant you success my son, God grant you success.' " At this point Migdim remembered my little tape recorder, resting discreetly near her, and laughed, "Lila's machine is working now, taping our words." Then she chanted a rhyme to it:

> A pity, you who this cap belongs to
> A pity, you who this cap belongs to
> A pity, you who this cap belongs to
> They said you were a man among men
> He died without me laying eyes on him
> A pity, you who this cap belongs to.

The caps of red felt were the standard dress of the older generation of bedouin men. Migdim explained the story that went with this rhyme to the excited questions of the women gathered there. They had never heard it. "Here's what it means. The old woman is lamenting the old man. Her son is a joker! He was teasing her. He said to his mother, 'I found'—what he found was a cap, a cap in a room on the floor—and he brought it to her and said, 'I found you a husband, but as we left the market he dropped dead. This is his cap!' " The other women exclaimed, "What a bastard! A joker!" Migdim laughed too as she finished, "So she started lamenting: 'Woe is me, such a pity . . . ' "

My tape went on for a while, recording the laughter and repetitions of the rhyme, the comments on the son that he was a bastard, a real joker, and one woman's comment, "Hey, if he'd said the old man was alive, she would have gone off to look for him!" One by one, the women sighed, chuckled, and got up to leave. They had things to do—cooking, baking, weaving, washing, taking care of children.

Migdim is almost blind now, despite the eye operation she had many years ago, and she always has to ask whether it is time for prayers. When

I am there I tell her by looking at my watch. "Yes, it's after three o'clock, time for afternoon prayers," I say now. She positions herself to face southeast, unrolls her prayer rug in front of her, and without standing, because she cannot, she begins her prayers. When she finishes she feels around under her blanket until she finds her prayer beads. She starts counting off on them the names of God. As she folds up her prayer mat she ends, as she often does, with "Praise be to God. Praise be to God. May God keep evil away from us. May God keep weddings going forever among Muslims. May God always bless Muslims with celebrations."

She is happiest at the weddings of her many grandsons. Whatever disappointment or anger she sometimes feels toward her sons seems to disappear as she sings songs praising them as fathers of these boys. At the last wedding in the community she sang a song that placed her where she wanted to be: at the center of her family—

> May they always be blessed with happiness
> the sons of my sons with me in their midst.

## A NOTE ON SOURCES

This life story has been adapted from my forthcoming book, *Writing Women's Worlds* (University of California Press). Migdim (a pseudonym) was one of several women I came to know well over the years I lived, visited, and did anthropological fieldwork in a small Awlad Ali bedouin community in the Egyptian Western Desert. My initial fieldwork in 1978–80 was funded by the National Institute of Mental Health; subsequent long stays in 1986 and 1987 were supported by a Fulbright Islamic Civilization Award and a National Endowment for the Humanities Fellowship for College Teachers. I am grateful for this support as well as for the generosity of the bedouin families who took me in.

## SUGGESTIONS FOR FURTHER READING

Those who would like to know more about the Awlad Ali bedouin community of which Migdim is a part may read my book *Veiled Sentiments: Honor and Poetry in a Bedouin Society* (Berkeley: University of California Press, 1986) and more recent article exploring the transformations it is undergoing, "The Romance of Resistance: Tracing Transformations of Power through Bedouin Women," *American Ethnologist* 17, 1 (1990).

There are several good studies of the bedouin in other parts of the Arab world, but very little specifically on bedouin women. Yet the excellent and fast-growing literature on Middle Eastern women touches on many of the issues raised by Migdim's life and especially her complex relationship with her sons. A good place to begin is Hilma Grandqvist's *Marriage Conditions in a Palestinian Village* [AMS Press, 1935]. Fatima Mernissi's *Beyond the Veil* (Bloomington: Indiana University Press, 1988) offers a harsh view of the effects of these mother-son dynamics in urban Morocco; Daisy Dwyer looks at male-female relations in Morocco through folktales in *Images and Self-Images: Male and Female in Morocco* (New York: Columbia University Press, 1976). Compare Margery Wolf's work on Chinese women's lives: *Women and Family in Rural Taiwan* (Stanford: Stanford University Press, 1972).

For other narratives of women's lives in the Middle East, see Nayra Atiya, *Khul Khaal: Five Egyptian Women Tell Their Stories* (Syracuse: Syracuse University Press, 1982); Fatima Mernissi, *Doing Daily Battle* (New Brunswick, N.J.: Rutgers University Press, 1988); Erika Friedl, *Women of Deh Koh: Lives in an Iranian Village* (Washington, D.C.: Smithsonian Institution Press, 1989); and Elizabeth Fernea and Basima Bezirgan, eds., *Middle Eastern Women Speak* (Austin: University of Texas Press, 1977).

On women and gender issues in the Middle East there is increasing literature. One article worth singling out is Deniz Kandiyoti, "Emancipated but Unliberated? Reflections on the Turkish Case," *Feminist Studies* 13 (1987): 317–38. More easily accessible are collections like Lois Beck and Nikki Keddie, eds., *Women in the Muslim World* (Cambridge, Mass.: Harvard University Press, 1978). Also Soraya Altorki and Camillia El-Solh, eds., *Arab Women in the Field: Studying Your Own Society* (Syracuse: Syracuse University Press, 1988).

# NINETEEN

# Amir Agha: An Iranian Worker

*Fakhreddin Azimi*

The twentieth-century history of Iran has been marked by two major revolutions—the constitutional revolution of 1906–11 and the Islamic revolution of 1978–79. The political balance has swung first one way, then another. At the same time Iranian society has undergone unprecedented changes. From a predominantly poor, rural, and illiterate society with a rudimentary army and bureaucracy, Iran has evolved into a modern state. The Iranian population has risen from about 5 million in 1900 to more than 40 million today, and standards of living for most people have improved greatly, including health and education.

The biography of Amir Agha by Fakhreddin Azimi provides a glimpse of the ways these enormous changes were experienced by many ordinary Iranians. Through Amir Agha, we are afforded a privileged look at life in a provincial Iranian town in the twentieth century. Amir Agha was born in 1921, the same year that Reza Shah took power and inaugurated the Pahlavi dynasty. Because of his family's precarious fortunes, like many other working-class youths, Amir Agha had to quit school early to work in his father's shop. Consequently he remained illiterate. By this time the family trade, saddle making, was in decline, and Amir Agha's father had become an opium addict. It was only through the intervention of a family friend that he found a job as a truck driver's assistant.

Amir Agha's life is a chronicle of dreams continually thwarted. Marked by the death of his mother and an abusive father, Amir Agha struggled hard to achieve a modicum of economic ease. During World War II he profited from the demand for experienced truck drivers to achieve a precocious success. But the economic hard times that followed and his own lack of providence combined to drive him out of the business. In order to survive he worked on road construction projects far from his home and family. When he was first encountered by Azimi, Amir Agha was running a modest business in used auto parts.

In view of the general image of Iran's highly charged political climate, one of the more extraordinary revelations of a reading of the life of Amir Agha is his remarkable allergy to politics. According to Azimi, Agha twice found himself under heavy pressure to become involved in politics. Both times his innately cautious nature led him to draw back. In the midst of the struggle over the nationalization of the Anglo-Iranian Oil Company in the early 1950s, many of Amir Agha's friends tried unsuccessfully to get him to join the Tudeh party (Communist party of Iran). In the late 1970s, a similar mobilization occurred in the lead-up to the Islamic revolution. Both times Amir Agha remained aloof. His avoidance of politics suggests the limits of political appeals for many Iranians, and the strength of basic conservative instincts in the working-class culture of Iran. Radicalism has always coexisted with its opposite even in the midst of the most turbulent actions.

It is interesting to compare the life of Amir Agha with those of other workers profiled in this volume (see the contributions by Eqbal Ahmad and Stuart Schaar, Joost Hiltermann, Philip Khoury, and David McMurray).

Amir Agha's life can also be effectively contrasted with those of the other contemporary Iranians included in this volume: Mehdi Abedi, Hagob Hagobian, and Rostam. Most interesting, perhaps, is the contrast with Hagob Hagobian, also an Iranian truck driver, but one of Armenian origin. How much does ethnicity appear to have played a role in shaping the destiny of each man? How much personal character? —ED.

Early on a cold and blustery autumn evening as darkness was falling on the town of Simab-shahr people hastened home to insure that they had enough kerosene for their lamps. Poor families with no other means of heating their homes dispatched their sons to the public bath to collect burning embers from its wood fires. The embers were placed in the *korsi*, a large box about four foot square placed on top of a small metal container filled with burning embers or charcoal lightly covered with ash. A quilt, sometimes enough to cover a whole room, was placed over the wooden box, and entire families would sit and sleep around the *korsi* during the cold months, huddling under the large quilt.

Amir was especially anxious to get home that day because his mother, who had been ill for several months, had begun to shiver in the early afternoon. When he entered the house he saw that the whole family had gathered in the small room where his mother, Batul Khanum, lay beside the *korsi*. She was almost unconscious and looked frighteningly pale. Hakim Musa, the bespectacled Jewish herbal doctor who had succeeded his father as the only "doctor" in the town, was administering a homemade concoction to the semiconscious woman.

Amir's father, Agha Sayyid Habib, sat outside, unable to conceal his tears or to speak. The old women prayed. One of them ordered Amir out of the room. A little while later, Hakim Musa left hurriedly, nervously clutching his briefcase and black *chapeau*. The screams of mourning arose from the room, and the perplexed child knew that his mother was dead. He rushed from the house, in hot pursuit of the fleeing Hakim Musa, hurling abuse at him and throwing stones.

Amir's mother was barely thirty-five years old when she died. She had been ill for several months, having fallen prey to a mysterious illness that left her weak and increasingly feverish. Hakim Musa had come almost every day, each time assuring the family that she would recover and each time demanding payment in money or goods, such as a chicken, eggs, butter, etc. The local *mullahs*, some of whom were related to Amir's family, competed with the Jewish doctor to help the sick woman. Prayers were said at the local shrine; supplications to the Imam-e Zaman, the Lord of the Age, the Twelfth Imam, believed to be in occultation, were enveloped in parcels of mud and cast into the streams. Quranic verses were written on the shells of eggs, which were then circled around her head and broken into a bowl in order to ward off the evil eye. The services of many soothsayers, who laid claim to every kind of skill, had also been sought, but to no avail. Amir's mother had died, and no one knew why. Was the disease infectious? Was anyone else in the family going to suffer a similar fate? Above all, why had it happened to Batul Khanum, who was a young woman, a devout Muslim, and a kind person? Had spells been cast by their enemies? Were there people determined to cause them further suffering? These were the questions that lurked in the minds of Amir's family and others in the neighborhood.

With the death of his mother, Amir's happiness seemed to have come to an end. Little did he realize that in that moment he had left his childhood behind and that he would have to face the adult world alone. His elder brother, only five years older than he, had left the town the previous year and made his way to Tehran, while his father's tenderness fell short of his cruelty. Amir's father was a skilled saddle maker who had found the demand for his craft declining and who, like many other men of his generation, had become an opium addict. His most immediate concern was to cater to his addiction. Amir's relatives were numerous but too poor or preoccupied to show any genuine concern for the ten-year-old boy, who, in any case, was not generally popular, having lost most of his hair as a result of a common skin disease contracted in early childhood.

Amir returned to work in his father's workshop in the old bazaar shortly after his mother's death, waking early and working until dark, as he had done since he was barely six years old, helping as apprentice, cleaner, tea maker, and errand boy. He soon stopped attending classes at the traditional elementary school (*maktab*), which he had begun on his mother's insistence two years previously. There he had begun to read and write, as well as to learn basic arithmetic and recite the Quran. Now his mother, the only person in the world who had really cared for him, was gone and Amir had no one to whom to turn. Feeling increasingly lonely and neglected, Amir found his only solace and distraction at the local *garage*, which he frequented at every opportunity. A gas station, parking lot, and bus terminal, the *garage* was an old caravansary. Fascinated by the sight of the trucks and buses, Amir took refuge in his daydreams, imagining himself traveling to distant cities and boasting about them on his return. He would earn lots of money, bring back exotic and luxurious presents, and become someone of significance.

A picturesque town of some ten thousand inhabitants, Simab-shahr was set apart from the villages in its vicinity both geographically and linguistically. Situated in a valley in the foothills of high mountains, it was bitterly cold in winter but enjoyed pleasant summers. When viewed from a distance no buildings could be seen, only an expanse of shades of green from the many trees. The town was watered by numerous mountain springs and by the age-old *qanats*, an elaborate network of wells interconnected by underground irrigation canals. The town was renowned for its vineyards and orchards, which produced fine grapes and delicate sweet apricots, peaches, pears, and several varieties of apples. A labyrinth of narrow alleys ran between the houses, and beyond them lay the gardens and courtyards. Throughout the summer the heavy-laden branches of fruit trees hung over the garden walls within the reach of passersby, and the aroma of fresh mint, basil, tarragon, and ripe apricots filled the air. Simab-shahr was divided into several quarters, each with its distinct communal attachments. These attachments resulted in intense competition during the mourning ceremonies of the month of Muharram, in which the martyrdom of Imam Husayn, the Third Imam of the Shiites, is commemorated. And yet, when confronting inhabitants of other towns, the Simab-shahris were all unhesitatingly chauvinistic.

The town was a marketplace for the nomads from the surrounding areas to sell their rugs, sheepskins, purified butter, yogurt, etc., in exchange for sugar, tea, cloth, soap, matches, and the like. Amir's father had his workshop in the bazaar beside the shoemakers, wool dryers, potters, carpenters, and blacksmiths. The local artisans, however, were not as successful as the shopkeepers who traded in raw materials for manufactured goods. The older inhabitants of the town remembered at least one major famine that had killed many among the poor, while the rich had not suffered greatly. The richer merchants, far from becoming the objects of envy, continued to enjoy great status. Traditionally deferential toward the rich, the poor lagged far behind in social prestige, while their self-esteem was also low.

Once noble but now impoverished, renowned for jealously guarding the honor of their womenfolk, Amir's family members were widely believed to be *sayyids*—descendants of the Prophet—and these attributes partly compensated for the erosion of their social prestige brought about by impoverishment. The staple diet of the townsfolk was a kind of meat stew cooked with chick-peas, which was eaten with large quantities of bread. Eating rice was a luxury that only the notables could afford, and yet at least one of Amir's four uncles, and sometimes even his father, while economizing on other essentials, would often eat rice and grilled lamb, behavior that baffled many of their neighbors, making them suspect that the family had hidden wealth. There were no hidden riches, however, and Agha Sayyid Habib's income from saddle making was, in fact, declining, since horse-riding notables increasingly turned to motorcars, which also threatened to draw away his apprentice son.

As time passed Amir's dream of being employed by a truck driver dominated his thoughts more and more, but how could he fulfill this dream? The older women in the family advised him to turn to the local shrine, pay the mendicant *sayyids*, and consult the fortune-tellers. Eventually it was his father who helped him. An old family friend who had recently acquired a rather primitive truck was persuaded to accept Amir as his apprentice. Amir took up the task with dedication and enthusiasm. He had often fascinated other children by making his own toys, particularly handcarts, and his inventive mind and curiosity about all things mechanical and technical were of great help in his new job. He soon knew much more about how the truck worked than its owner-driver.

However, Amir quickly became aware of the precariousness of his position. He could be dismissed at any moment. It was common for subordinates to be treated with contempt and exploited, and his ill-tempered boss was no exception, behaving as if he were a feudal lord. He demanded complete obedience and beat Amir frequently. Amir, however, was determined to endure any hardship and persevere. Because he was partially bald, he always had to wear a hat. Still, he was invariably tormented by others. And yet, ironically, his baldness saved him from being pestered to provide sexual favors for the truck drivers, as many apprentices were forced to do. His apprenticeship lasted eight years, during which time he worked for several drivers and visited all the major cities and ports in the country.

Amir was born in 1921, the year of Reza Khan's coup. Four years later Reza Khan founded the Pahlavi dynasty and assumed the title of shah. Reza Shah was an ardent modernizer, and Persia (or Iran, as Reza Shah later insisted the country be called) soon became the scene of great social transformations. Of particular significance to Amir as a long-distance truck driver was the building of roads and bridges. Under Reza Shah's authoritarian rule brigandage was virtually eliminated and armed tribesmen were controlled with the help of the new army and the strengthened rural police (known as the gendarmerie). However, the new regime also demanded that young men of Amir's age perform military service. Amir succeeded in evading his "national duty" by paying the local gendarmerie the money he had painstakingly saved, and eventually secured himself a certificate of permanent exemption.

Amir passed his driving test on the eve of the Second World War. Following the German invasion of the Soviet Union in 1941, the Allies deposed Reza Shah and occupied the main cities of Iran and took over the routes of communication. To support the Russian front, a massive supply effort was initiated by road from the Persian Gulf to Russia. There was a great and constant demand for drivers, so Amir had no problem in finding employment. He drove a massive ten-wheel American military truck, by far the most sophisticated and powerful machine he had driven. His salary was above local standards, and he did not have to tolerate an individual, often miserly, truck owner.

Occasionally, he would break his long journeys between the Persian Gulf and the Soviet border in northern Iran and pay his hometown a visit. His father was truly proud of him. He felt that the whole town shook as his son's truck approached, and looked on with satisfaction as large numbers of people gathered to look at the huge machine. Amir's considerable earnings insured his father a regular supply of opium and meant that his own standing in the town improved greatly. Amir looked impressive in his good secondhand American clothes and leather shoes, with his bushy eyebrows and thick brown moustache. A scar on his left cheek gave him a forbidding air. He became renowned for his generosity. Respectfully referred to by everyone as Amir Agha, he would pay for all his friends when they ate at a restaurant or visited a teahouse or a public bath. Porters competed to carry his suitcase and the boxes of fruit and other presents he would bring on his return from his journeys. For the beggars his return meant rich pickings. Although a nonpracticing Muslim, from time to time he arranged for a lamb to be slaughtered and the meat distributed in the neighborhood. He also paid to have the Quran recited in his mother's memory and for local preachers to pray for him.

While Amir benefited from the Anglo-Soviet occupation of Iran, the country as a whole suffered. Basic foodstuffs and other commodities, and in particular bread, mainstay of the people's diet, as well as kerosene, tea, and sugar, became scarce and expensive. Bread riots broke out in the cities. As law and order deteriorated, nomadic tribesmen robbed and harassed travelers. As a driver Amir had to deal with the occupying

Russians and British, both of whom treated the native population with disdain. He also found his American employers insensitive and arrogant. In the areas not directly under Allied occupation, he had to cope with inefficient and corrupt gendarmes and local officials who no longer had Reza Shah and a repressive central government to fear.

Amir began to look back on the years of Reza Shah's rule with some nostalgia. He was convinced that Reza Shah's natural authority and vigor were the qualities that the country needed in a ruler. He recounted stories of Reza Shah's decisiveness and brutality as though he had witnessed them himself. He saw Reza Shah as a man who had been genuinely devoted to improving Iran's socioeconomic conditions as well as its image. Perhaps he subconsciously saw Reza Shah's rise from humble origins to immense power and success as a sublimated embodiment of his own desires.

Amir's travels took him to various parts of Iran, so that Iran was for him not an abstract idea but a tangible reality. He had witnessed many changes and improvements in the country as they happened, and now, having been exposed to foreign occupiers, he had become even more conscious of his identity as an Iranian. If he had been literate, he might have been better able to articulate his strong patriotic beliefs.

After the war, the British and American forces left the country, soon followed by the Russians. The economy consequently suffered, and unemployment soared. Amir lost his job as the driver of an oil truck for the Anglo-Iranian Oil Company, and he resigned himself to a period of austerity. He was forced to move into the house where his brother, a mechanical supervisor in a construction company, also rented rooms with his family. After several months of hardship, during which he hung around his brother's job site, Amir one day was asked by the manager to drive one of the dump trucks. He had a job at last, although he knew that he would be retained only as long as he was needed. The meager wage he received was barely enough to meet his basic needs and repay the debts he had incurred, but each day he returned home relieved that he had worked another day.

In this social climate the Tudeh party (Party of the Masses) was established. It claimed to represent and articulate the demands of the oppressed. Formed in the immediate wake of the Allied occupation in 1941, the Tudeh initially appeared to be social democratic and independent in orientation, but it soon emerged as radically socialist and pro-Soviet. Many of its slogans intrigued Amir. Yet the alleged godlessness of its proponents offended his attachment to popular Shiism, while his deferential attitude to property and wealth made it difficult for him to understand why the party denounced capitalists as exploiters and parasites. Amir did not see what was wrong with being a capitalist or wanting to become one and found it difficult to stomach the Tudeh's obvious liking of the Russians, with whom he believed he was familiar from his own experiences. Many of the party's idioms and arguments were also unintelligible to him. He knew that there was widespread injustice in the world, but he believed that it could not be effectively remedied. He was skeptical as to whether collective action and labor unions could do much to improve workers' conditions.

Amir's political views were not untypical or unusual. While some of his friends (particularly Armenian and Assyrian drivers radicalized by the worsening conditions and inspired by Tudeh ideas) argued with him, he refused to concede that they might have a point. Still, Amir's beliefs were not as rigid or as developed as they appeared. He confided to his brother that if only he could be certain that things would improve or at least not worsen, he would be a tireless activist. Given the uncertain state of affairs, however, he feared the consequences of involvement in unionism or politics. He wanted to live his life without interference or unnecessary complications. He was neither consistent in his views and behavior nor fully aware of the inconsistencies: he resented his poverty but considered hierarchy and rank as part of the natural order of things; he himself was contemptuous of people of low social origin but expected courtesy and respect from his superiors; he was a fatalist who deeply believed in the preordination of his fortunes, and yet he expected and worked toward change for the better.

When his job as driver showed signs of lasting, he began to give some thought to the question of marriage. He was under pressure at home to marry, especially from his father. Amir's sister-in-law, a charming and kind, though wily, woman, did her best to introduce him to various eligible female relatives. It soon transpired, however, that Amir had harbored an affection for a distant cousin in his hometown, which pleased his father greatly. A young girl with a moon-shaped face and a gentle manner, Surayya had caught his eye since childhood, and so Amir's father and uncle went to ask for her hand on his behalf. The girl's father, a dour and unsmiling *mullah,* was opposed to his daughter marrying a truck driver who was reputed to drink alcohol and whose job involved him being away from home for long periods. He also did not wish to forge connubial ties with a "desert driver" (*shoofer-e biyabani*), as truck-drivers were deprecatingly called. Surayya's mother, however, favored the match. A kindly woman, she had watched Amir grow up, and knew the hardships he had endured since the death of his mother. Despite the wishes of the girl's father, the wedding was a festive occasion at which local entertainers provided music and Amir's guests sang, danced, and discreetly drank alcohol to the obvious dismay of the bride's relatives. After the wedding, Amir's new bride continued to live with her family for another year until he could afford to rent a larger room in Tehran. Only then did his young wife join him.

These changes in Amir's life coincided with the election of Dr. Muhammad Mossadeq as premier in 1951 and his campaign to nationalize the Anglo-Iranian Oil Company. Amir supported Mossadeq, as he believed that the nationalization of oil and other measures that Mossadeq championed would benefit ordinary people like himself. From his journeys in the south he had seen firsthand the extent of British privilege and influence in Iran and held them responsible for most of the ills that had befallen the country. He therefore thought that Mossadeq's opposition to the British was a courageous step.

Just at this moment he was fired from his job at the construction company. Once again he became a member of the idle crowds of unemployed men who filled the streets of the poorer quarters of south Tehran. The streets and teahouses had become unprecedentedly politicized. Tehran, with a population of almost half a million, in many respects still resembled a provincial city. However, it was the nerve center of the country, where the political forces unleashed by Mossadeq's National Front dominated the political scene. While the royalist and pro-British opponents of Mossadeq bided their time, the Tudeh party led street demonstrations against Mossadeq, whom it accused of seeking to replace British domination with American imperialism. Amir could not fully grasp the increasingly convoluted rhetoric employed by the Tudeh party and remained deeply suspicious of its aims.

Every morning Amir would begin wandering from street to street in search of employment, seeking the help of acquaintances and frequently calling on middle-ranking officials from his hometown for help, only to return home in the evening more disheartened than before. Despite his need, he refused to take jobs he felt to be socially demeaning or unsuited to his skills. His natural prudence kept him from involvement in politics, despite almost daily appeals to participate in demonstrations. Even if Mossadeq's policies were responsible for his unemployment, he was not prepared to take part in anti-Mossadeq demonstrations, even though it might have enabled him to meet and ingratiate himself with people who could secure him a job.

Amir was daunted by the additional responsibility of having to support a wife, who although she had adapted herself to their frugal and sometimes austere life, still had her needs. Much to his regret, they were soon forced to begin to sell much of her dowry: two large engraved copper trays, an antique samovar, some porcelain plates and bowls, and most important of all, a small carpet that Surayya had woven herself. He also had to borrow from whoever was prepared to make him a loan. An additional stroke of bad luck befell Amir when one day he found that his most prized possession, a Swiss-made watch, a souvenir of his onetime prosperity, was missing. With unflagging perseverance he spent two whole days scouring every shop window in the street where secondhand watches were bought and sold. Miraculously he found the watch and retrieved it, although only after a bout of fisticuffs with the shopkeeper. He cheerfully rushed home to tell his wife, feeling that the incident had heralded better times ahead. His wife used the opportunity of his momentary joy to announce that she was pregnant.

Although the news was not unexpected, any pleasure Amir felt on hearing it was overshadowed by anxiety; he simply could not face the prospect of fatherhood and continued unemployment. Amir decided that his wife should return to their hometown. She was silently resigned to her fate but was heartbroken that so far her marriage had brought her little joy or comfort. She prepared herself for the humiliation of returning home to face the reproaches of her less than forgiving father. Fortunately, on the recommendation of a member of parliament who represented Simab-shahr, Amir was offered a job in a road construction company operating in western Iran, which soon took him far from Tehran, from his home, and from his expectant wife.

Four years later Amir returned home. He had gained some weight, and his cap had given way to a gray *chapeau,* but he was otherwise little changed. During his absence, he was able to send money regularly to his wife and father. During her husband's absence, in addition to raising their child alone, Surayya had also had to pay constant attention to her father-in-law. The somber welcome she accorded Amir on his return also had other reasons: she had heard rumors that he had married another woman on a temporary basis while he was away. Although such temporary marriages were sanctioned by Shiite Islam and were common practice for men in Amir's circumstances, Surayya could not forgive him for it. Amir vehemently denied the rumor, insisting that he had simply employed an old woman to cook for him and wash his clothes, having had no other choice. Their relationship was never the same again.

Soon after his return, Amir persuaded two shopkeepers to become his partners in the purchase of a truck, of which he would be the driver. He worked hard to pay the installments on the truck but found it difficult to cope with two partners whom he regarded as petty and parsimonious. If he stayed more than two days with his family after returning from a journey, they would raise objections. One of them often accompanied him on his journeys to make sure he did not sleep too long or eat expensively. When they did the books, quarrels always ensued. The short-tempered Amir found the situation wholly uncongenial, and yet, although perhaps able to buy a truck of his own in installments, he did not feel sufficiently self-confident to do so. More practically, at a time when an insurance policy was virtually unheard of, he firmly believed that the hazards of owning a truck should always be shared.

The socioeconomic changes that had begun to sweep Iran in the late 1950s had also affected Simab-shahr. An inevitable hallmark of the official policy of modernization was the construction of broad new streets, which required the destruction of many old buildings and orchards. Amir's own family home, with all the bitter and sweet memories that it evoked, was one casualty. This situation was aggravated by the fact that virtually no compensation was paid by the authorities. Amir was forced to rent two rooms in order to accommodate his family and his father, and he worked even harder to pay the additional costs incurred. His father, however, could not easily forgive or forget the destruction of his home, which he had partly built with his own hands. Heartbroken, he often refused to eat, said very little, and smoked more opium. While Amir was away on one of his journeys, his father died.

Amir's father had expressed the wish that Amir build a house of his own. His wife, who found their situation humiliating, also cherished this dream. She therefore willingly parted with all her remaining gold and other valuables to help finance the rebuilding of the family home in what remained of the courtyard of the old place. It took over a year to finish the two-story brick house, with its high ceilings and large metal-framed french windows. By the time of its completion, Amir was heavily in debt. But he had realized the dream of owning a small house, which was a great morale booster. He only wished that his father had been alive to see his achievement.

Having overcome the challenge of Mossadeq and the National Front, Muhammad Reza Shah consolidated his rule and embarked upon a program of reforms known as the White Revolution. The Iranian economy entered a sustained period of growth, and the long-distance transport of goods from Tehran to the Persian Gulf boomed. Until the mid-1970s, Amir prospered. He now had four children, two of whom were attending school, and was able gradually to repay his debts.

Simab-shahr, once a sleepy provincial town, was transformed. Electrification was introduced in the mid-1950s and became a major catalyst of change. However, there was much more to come. The Simab-shahris, who had never seen an unveiled woman in public, became accustomed in the late 1960s to the sight of American girls in hotpants accompanying their boyfriends who were serving in the American Peace Corps in many parts of the country. Middle-class Iranian tourists dressed in T-shirts, jeans, and miniskirts also began to arrive. The shops were filled with luxury consumer goods, and almost every household possessed a radio and television. As communications improved, some Simab-shahris began to move to Tehran in search of greater opportunities. At the same time, the poorer classes felt increasingly threatened by the intrusion of ideas and fashions that offended their religious and moral sensibilities. Amir welcomed many aspects of these changes. In partnership with a relative of his wife, he purchased a new Mercedes truck. He worked hard to pay the installments on it, as well as to ensure that his children went to school and that all their needs were met. Though his work often took him away from home for extended periods, he was pleased to see his children better fed and dressed than those of the bazaar merchants.

By this time driving a truck had ceased to be a relatively respectable occupation and had even acquired a certain stigma. Since Amir had been one of the pioneers in the field, however, he was not barred from "respectable" company. A friend of his who had started as a truck driver owned a *garage* in Simab-shahr and had become a wealthy man who looked and behaved like a senator. He had a coterie of friends, consisting chiefly of the heads of local government offices, who met in the large office of his *garage* to chat about local, as well as national, politics over endless glasses of tea and, occasionally, bowls of ice cream. Whenever in town, Amir was a keen participant in these gatherings, often taking along his eldest son, who received the same respectful treatment as himself.

One day, after a number of years of relative comfort and prosperity, Amir's truck was involved in a head-on collision with another truck and wrecked. Fortunately, Amir's injuries were minor. Although the vehicle was insured, protracted wranglings with the insurance company came to nothing. He was ruined. How could he support his wife and their six children? His oldest son, who was at the university and whose views carried a great deal of weight in the family, agreed with his mother that Amir must be prevented from returning to truck driving, whatever the cost. Amir surrendered to their arguments and agreed to open a shop selling secondhand vehicle spare parts. This barely enabled him to earn enough to cover the family's basic needs. Even though his older children began to support themselves, the family experienced a decline in their living standard. Moreover, succumbing to the boredom that an uneventful sedentary life at home entailed, as well as to the anxieties that followed the change of occupation, Amir began to quarrel more with his wife. He had always behaved in a domineering and jealously restrictive way toward her and the children, though he always regretted his impulsive spells of anger later.

To keep his shop well stocked, Amir had to travel frequently to Tehran and Isfahan. Now he hardly recognized Tehran: it was no longer the small, compact city of the 1950s. It had expanded haphazardly in all directions, with spacious modern villas in the north accommodating the nouveau riche, and a densely packed honeycomb of small houses in the south providing shelter for the numerous rural migrants who poured into the city in search of riches. Because of the stifling atmosphere of unease and tension, he found Tehran unbearable. It was not difficult to imagine that the simmering popular discontent there would one day result in a violent eruption.

Isfahan, which he visited more often, was even worse. American servicemen and businessmen ran their own network of Vietnamese prostitutes, heedless of the offense to local sensibilities. Everywhere he felt that there were almost deliberate efforts by the authorities not only to disregard existing problems but to aggravate them. The shah's image deteriorated at home as his arrogance grew. In an attempt to realize his vision of the promised "Great Civilization," he created a totalitarian political party, Rastakhiz, which all were required to join. He abandoned the Islamic calendar in favor of the pre-Islamic one marking the beginning of the Iranian empire. These issues became real for Amir when his daughter was called up for compulsory military service. In order to secure her exemption, he had to pay a large bribe.

By 1978 the widespread popular discontent resulted in large-scale anti-shah demonstrations. During the year they grew in intensity. In February 1979, after the shah's flight into exile, the Islamic Republic was established. Neither a royalist nor a revolutionary, Amir remained aloof from street demonstrations and politics. Yet the revolution had an effect on his business.

The disruption caused by the revolution interrupted the flow of goods into the country. As a result, Amir's auto parts business improved slightly for a time. As the revolution continued, however, the economy declined further, and a plethora of arbitrary new revolutionary committees soon made daily contacts with the bureaucracy of the new order increasingly cumbersome.

In the "old days," before the revolution, the tree-lined streets of Simab-shahr would be sprinkled with water each day to keep the dust down. Groups of well-dressed young men would stroll through the town or congregate in the well-kept squares. Now the dust permanently settled everywhere, and shabbily dressed, unshaven, and unsmiling men roamed the town. The white and red brick walls of the houses were covered with incomprehensible slogans in which the word "death" appeared all too prominently. Bearded young gunmen in four-wheel-drive vehicles were a ubiquitous and intimidating presence. Amir found the fact that *mullahs* had become ministers, members of parliament, and governors unalterably strange. Moreover, their inexperience and incompetence contrasted unfavorably with the relative competence of the former government. Amir certainly saw no reason to believe that the promised reign of virtue had begun.

Ironically, money counted for as much, if not more, than it had done previously, and Amir and his family had little of it. Amir did not qualify for the privileges extended to the "disinherited," that is, the rank-and-file supporters of the revolution, and was not surprised to be classified as a member of the "arrogant" classes, but he found himself increasingly haunted by a daunting sense of insecurity. What if serious illness struck? How would he cope with becoming dependent on his children, who were not even fully capable of supporting themselves? Whenever he spoke about his anxieties, he was invariably told by his older relatives that there were millions far worse off than he and that he should be grateful to be alive and indeed not even more badly off. Comments of this kind suited Amir's stoical character, yet he often wondered whether it was not more appropriate to compare oneself not with the unfortunate of society but with the better-off.

## A NOTE ON SOURCES

The above account is based on interviews with Amir and his family and on additional information that they generously provided. In accordance with their wishes, names, including that of the town, have been changed. The rest of the account, as far as it could be ascertained, is factual and authentic.

## SUGGESTIONS FOR FURTHER READING

For an introductory account of modern Iran, see Nikki Keddie, *Roots of Revolution: An Interpretative History of Modern Iran* (New Haven: Yale University Press, 1981). Also Ervand Abrahamian, *Iran between Two Revolutions* (Princeton: Princeton University Press, 1982). For an imaginative work that chronicles the life of a *mullah*, see Roy Mottahedeh, *The Mantle of the Prophet: Religion and Politics in Iran* (New York: Pantheon, 1985).

There are a host of more specialized studies. Among them the following are notable. On Reza Shah's reforms see Amin Banani, *The Modernization of Iran, 1921–1941* (Stanford: Stanford University Press, 1961). On the Tudeh party, see, in addition to Abrahamian's work, Sepehr Zabih, *The Communist Movement in Iran* (Berkeley and Los Angeles: University of California Press, 1966). On labor unions see Habib Ladjevardi, *Labour Unions and Autocracy in Iran* (Syracuse: Syracuse University Press, 1985). On the background to the oil nationalization movement and the government of Mossadeq see Fakhreddin Azimi, *Iran: The Crisis of Democracy, 1941–1953* (London: I. B. Tauris, 1989); and James Bill and William Roger Louis, *Musaddiq, Iranian Nationalism and Oil* (London: I. B. Tauris, 1988). On the 1979 revolution, see, in addition to the works of Abrahamian, Keddie, and Mottahedeh, Shaul Bakhash, *The Reign of the Ayatollahs: Iran and the Islamic Revolution* (New York: Basic Books, 1984); and Farhad Kazemi, *Poverty and Revolution in Iran* (New York: New York University Press, 1980).

In contrast to scholarly accounts, many works of modern Persian literature closely reflect the lives of common people, but few of these have been translated into English. See, for instance, Sadeq Hedayat, *Hedayat: An Anthology of Short Stories*, ed. Ehsan Yarshater (Boulder, Colo.: Westview, 1979); and id., *Haj Agha: Portrait of an Iranian Confidence Man*, trans. G. M. Wickens, Center for Middle Eastern Studies, Middle East Monographs, no. 6 (Austin: University of Texas, 1979); see also Jalal Al-e Ahmad, *The School Principal*, trans. John Newton (Minneapolis and Chicago: Bibliotheca Islamica, 1974).

# TWENTY

# Rostam: Qashqa'i Rebel

*Lois Beck*

What is the place of national minorities in the contemporary Middle East?
The question is important, because many Middle Eastern states include large
ethnic, tribal, linguistic, and religious minorities. In Ottoman times, religious
minorities were afforded a measure of protection as *dhimmis* by Muslim doctrine, while ethnic, tribal, and other minorities could exist as fellow Muslims
without threat to their way of life as long as they accepted the authority of
the sultan.

In an age of nation-states this social complexity was later found to be vexa-
tious. Here the nationalist fiction of ethnically uniform societies clashed with
the protean complexities of the real world. Homogenizing national education
programs, which sought to turn all citizens into Moroccans or Iranians or into
Turks or Arabs, were perceived as a threat by minorities who were attached to
their own traditions. But the plethora of potentially competing nations within
each of the Middle Eastern states constituted a possible challenge to the national unity and was therefore perceived by governments as subversive.

Anthropologist Lois Beck's portrait of Rostam, a Qashqa'i tribesman of
southwestern Iran, poses the question sharply. Beck's intimate knowledge of
the Qashqa'i spans more than two decades, including two periods of research
among them since the 1978–79 revolution. Her encounter with Rostam provides us with an understanding of the fluid and sometimes conflictual relations between the Iranian state and the tribal minorities and with a glimpse of
the shifting alliances of underground and exile politics in the 1970s.

The youngest son of a Qashqa'i nomad, Rostam found himself propelled
into opposition to Muhammad Reza Shah's government when Rostam's
father was killed by an army officer. Rostam was initially motivated by a desire
to take revenge for his family, but his feelings later evolved into a more
broadly based ideological commitment. His growing commitment brought
him into contact with Kurds and other minorities fighting for their political
and cultural rights, and ultimately with political exiles and leftists abroad.
His death at the hands of the Islamic Republic's revolutionary guards has

ensured that his memory will be preserved among the Qashqa'i, and his heroism is undoubted. In the end, however, his death is not without its quixotic
aspects. Why is this so?

There is an aura of tragedy about the encounter between the Qashqa'i and
the central government, for each side pursued what it perceived as worthy
goals. Qashqa'i efforts to salvage their way of life collided with the shah's efforts to centralize and control the rural inhabitants of Iran and bring about
what he perceived as the benefits of modernization. (These policies were continued, although in different ways and for some different purposes, by the
Islamic Republic.) For Qashqa'i opponents like Rostam, such plans amounted
to ethnocide. For the shah and his officials, Qashqa'i opposition was perverse,
if not treasonous. The brutality of the shah's agents (and the greed of those
who coveted the Qashqa'i lands) insured the opposition of individuals like
Rostam. In the wider context, it seems unlikely that the Qashqa'i could continue to follow their way of life in an increasingly populous and modernizing
Iranian society. In that sense, one may legitimately wonder about the ultimate
futility of their resistance, even as one honors it.

Because a significant proportion of the 55 percent of Iranians who do not
speak Persian as a first language and who do not identify with Persian culture
are tribal minorities (Baluch, Turkmen, Bakhtiyari, Qashqa'i, Shahsevan,
Lurs, and many Kurds and Arabs), there have been many such clashes since
the 1920s, when Reza Shah began to create what he viewed as a modern
nation-state. Thus the situation of the Qashqa'i has parallels elsewhere in
Iran. More generally, one also thinks of other minorities: the Kurds of Turkey, Iraq, and Iran; the Berbers of Algeria and Morocco; the Druze of Syria,
Lebanon, and Israel; and the bedouin in many states. (See the contributions
by Lila Abu-Lughod, Edmund Burke, and Julie Oehler elsewhere in this volume for more on tribal people.) —Ed.


Golgaz handed her son Rostam a miniature Quran to kiss and then
placed it on a tray and held it high. Tears filling his eyes, Rostam stooped
to pass under the tray and then, without a backward glance, walked away
from his mother's tent. She feared she would never see him again, as she
always feared whenever he left home after another furtive visit. Each
time he departed abruptly, without warning; each time he could never
manage to stay more than a few hours with her. She did not understand
why he seemed so driven to leave his family and tribal territory. She did
not know what kind of life he lived while he was gone, and she worried
about his safety and his encounters with strangers. She had always expected that he would remain with her, marry her brother's daughter, and
present her with grandchildren. Now he was gone again, and she wept.

Rostam was born in 1949 during the arduous spring migration, and
his family and tribal group of Qashqa'i nomadic pastoralists traveled
from winter pastures in the foothills of the Zagros Mountains of south-

ern Iran to summer pastures three hundred miles away to the north, high in the alpine valleys of the Zagros. When Golgaz's labor pains began, her husband, Morad, notified men in his camp that he would not travel the next morning as planned. The men replied that the location provided good grazing for their flocks and said they did not mind postponing the move for a day. In the meantime, they sent their camels and other pack animals, used for transporting all their possessions, into the mountains for browsing. Several women from nearby tents came to assist with the birth and help with domestic tasks. A baby boy was born after several hours of labor. He was Golgaz's eighth surviving child, and delivery had become increasingly easy with each new birth. The women cooked a strengthening mixture of wheat flour, sugar, and ginger in clarified butter for her. Golgaz's sister Guhar told the family's eldest son about his new brother, and he passed the word to Morad. People in camp rejoiced at the arrival of a new "warrior," and men fired rifles into the air in happiness and celebration and in order to frighten evil spirits away from the infant.

When her son was forty days old, Morad gave him the ancient Iranian, pre-Islamic name Rostam. Many Qashqa'i families used ancient Iranian and Arabic/Islamic names for their sons and Turkish names for their daughters. Morad held close to the traditions of his ancestors and chose names of people legendary in tribal history for all his children. He believed that his lineage descended from central Asian Turkish warriors who were part of Chingiz Khan's armed guard.

When Rostam was six years old, his father decided to send him to the tent school newly established in the winter and summer pastures of his tribal group. The school was part of a tribal program created by a Qashqa'i entrepreneur with financial assistance from the United States and Iran's Ministry of Education. With eight children, as many boys as girls, Morad did not need Rostam's labor full time, and he appreciated the benefits of literacy and knowledge. He especially hoped to equip Rostam with the skills necessary for him to interact with the surrounding Persian-dominated society. None of Morad's other children had attended school, but he had taught his sons the rudiments of reading and writing. He had received several months of instruction in reading and writing as a youth. His father had supported the *ilkhani*, the leader of the 400,000-strong Qashqa'i tribal confederacy, and the *ilkhani* had allowed the young Morad to attend school in his camp for a brief period.

Rostam attended school regularly and appeared to flourish there. His teacher was a Qashqa'i man who was comfortable in his surroundings. The government had earlier tried to send young urban Persian men to teach the Turkish-speaking Qashqa'i, but the experiment had failed. In 1960, having completed the five years available, Rostam did not object when his father suggested that he continue his education in a town school. His three brothers performed with skill their tasks in animal husbandry and agriculture, and his absence from home did not much affect the family economically. During autumn, winter, and spring for several years, Rostam lived in Farrashband, the town closest to his tribal group's winter pastures, and attended school. He and several other Qashqa'i adolescents rented a room from a Persian merchant there. After examinations in late spring every year, he rode by horse to summer pastures far to the north in the mountains northeast of the rolling plain of Khusrow Shirin, lived with his family there, and helped with pastoral and agricultural tasks. He assisted his family at the beginning of the autumn migration and then rode by horse alone to Farrashband when classes resumed.

In 1962 Muhammad Reza Shah proclaimed a White Revolution, which included a comprehensive land reform program. To exert state force over the still powerful Qashqa'i tribal elite, government officials announced plans to implement land reform first in Fars province, where the Qashqa'i *ilkhani* and his family had governed vast stretches of land. Morad and his father and grandfather had used pastoral and agricultural land near Farrashband that the Qashqa'i *ilkhani* had controlled, one area now targeted by government officials for confiscation. Morad and other members of his tribal group depended on this land. In charge of some tribal affairs since the shah exiled the Qashqa'i *ilkhani* from Iran, an army officer ordered the headmen of seven Qashqa'i tribal groups to appear at his headquarters in the town of Firuzabad. There he notified of the government's intention to confiscate their land and assign it to Persian-speaking nontribal peasants in the region.

Morad was outraged by the announcement. He had done nothing to warrant being excluded from his ancestral pastures, and the peasants now said to be taking his place had never cultivated crops there. Confronting the army officer, Morad and several kinsmen angrily stated their grievances. The officer beckoned to his armed escort and ordered Morad and his kinsmen to leave; when the unarmed men refused, the officer yelled at his guards to seize them. Years later people were still uncertain about what happened next. But after the skirmish, Morad lay dead, and his nephew Bizhan lay badly wounded. The officer ordered his guards to seize Morad's cousin Jehangir and then telegraphed army headquarters in the city of Shiraz to seek reinforcements because, he claimed, the Qashqa'i had attacked his headquarters. Several Qashqa'i headmen who had witnessed the violent confrontation left town in order to notify Morad's family and group of the catastrophe.

Rumors of some sort of trouble in Firuzabad reached the Qashqa'i boys in school in Farrashband; Rostam hastened home to find out what had happened. As he hurried up the mountain slopes to his group's winter pastures, he could hear wailing in the distance, and he feared for the fate of his family. As he rounded a bend near his father's winter camp-site, he heard his mother's laments and knew instantly that someone close to her had died. He saw her crouched in the dust by the tent, beat-ing her hands against the sides of her head and ripping at the front of her tunic. Her hair, always carefully tended in many neat braids down her back, was disheveled, and she made no effort to cover her head or neck. Repeating a verse of a Qashqa'i dirge, her sister Rokhsar la-mented, "Go tell my sister, 'Rip the front of your tunic, loosen your braids, and scatter your hair on the tombstone.' " Rostam's father's brother Hushang came forward to tell him that his father had been killed, and then the uncle sadly assembled a few men to go to Firuzabad to retrieve the body.

Two days later, near sunset, the men returned to camp with Morad's body draped over the back of a horse. They had hoped to return sooner, but army officers had refused to release the body. Hushang had sought assistance from Hajj Abdul Rasul, a Persian merchant and moneylender in Firuzabad with whom Morad had been acquainted, and the man had pleaded with the authorities to allow the family to bury the body in com-pliance with Islamic tradition.

Men and women of Morad's lineage and subtribe gathered at his tent while Morad was washed and prepared for burial, and then they accom-panied Khalifeh, the one man in their group able to recite the required Quranic passages, to a nearby graveyard. On the seventh day after the death, people convened again at Morad's tent for ritual observances. A sheep had been slaughtered for the commemorative meal, and women not closely related to Morad prepared meat and rice. Rostam and his brothers served as hosts of the gathering and accepted people's condo-lences. At the beginning and ending of the meal, men mournfully re-cited a few Quranic verses, and everyone wept.

Soldiers in Farrashband notified Hushang that Bizhan, wounded in the skirmish, had died in jail. Hushang brought his body back to camp, and the group sadly held another funeral. The two murdered men, con-sidered victims of the shah's regime, had left wives and children behind. Also retained by the army after the skirmish, Jehangir was reportedly moved to prison in Shiraz.

Remaining at home with his mother and siblings, Rostam decided to postpone returning to school in Farrashband. His family needed him. Military authorities periodically summoned Hushang to Farrashband and Firuzabad to interrogate him about the activities of men in his group. One day they announced that they were moving ahead to seize his group's winter pastures, to punish it for the violence, and they or-dered the group to leave immediately for summer pastures. They hoped to forestall any organized protest against the events that had occurred and took advantage of the nomad's mobility and changing seasonal residences. On the forced migration north, the small group entered higher, colder altitudes where no grazing was yet available for their animals. During the trek, Rostam heard that the government had also confiscated pastureland from other Qashqa'i groups whose members had protested against new land policies. Several men told him about skirmishes between Qashqa'i men and the rural police (gendarmes), who had attempted to restrict the nomads' travel between tribal territory and towns. Qashqa'i men were routinely harassed by the army and gendarmes when they traveled outside tribal territory, but these harassments were escalating. Rostam learned of the government's imminent plans to confiscate all guns and rifles held by the Qashqa'i. Coupled with the murder of his father and cousin and the loss of pastureland, the announced confiscation was a turning point for Rostam. Guns were the Qashqa'i people's primary means of defense and offense and were the major symbol of Qashqa'i power and autonomy.

As the nomads neared Shiraz, Rostam heard rumors that two young Qashqa'i men, distant kinsmen of his, had escaped after a confrontation with gendarmes and had sought refuge in the mountains nearby. When a shepherd returned to camp with the news that he had met the two men, who appeared to be without food, Rostam told his sister to bundle the sheets of flat bread she had just baked and to pack dates, onions, tea leaves, sugar, and a small metal teapot. Carrying the supplies and armed with a rifle, Rostam abruptly left camp without a word to anyone. He followed the directions given by the shepherd. After six hours of hard climbing up the mountain slopes and across a small valley to another slope, he reached a rock face shaped like a gazelle's head, and he called out using wild bird songs. Soon an answering call came, and he showed himself. A man some distance away waved his felt hat (identical in its unique shape to Rostam's own and the marker of Qashqa'i identity), and he approached. Two young men near the mouth of a cave exchanged customary greetings with Rostam. The rest of the day he sat in a secluded spot in the sun with Shapur and Kaikavus and talked about the events that had occurred during the past month. The two men had of course known about the murder of Morad and Bizhan. They told Rostam of their own plans to obstruct the movement of army convoys to and from Firuzabad. He said he would join them. First, he noted, he wanted to return home briefly to see his mother and collect ammunition and supplies. The three young men agreed to meet four days later at a secluded location in the mountains northwest of Firuzabad.

When Rostam met up with Shapur and Kaikavus again, they plotted their revenge against the army officer responsible for the two men's deaths. Word that Shapur and Kaikavus had become *yaghi* (rebels, outlaws) had spread among the dispersed Qashqa'i nomads in the vicinity, and several of their cousins joined them. Two young Qashqa'i men who had recently been released from prison also sought them out, and within several months a small band of fluctuating size, but at times as large as fourteen people, had formed. They plotted small-scale, lightning attacks against isolated gendarme posts in order to seize arms, ammunition, and supplies. They held pity for the frightened conscripts who were their own age or younger and who came from impoverished families, and they avoided engaging them in violence. The rebels impeded the movement of military vehicles in and near Qashqa'i territory by setting up road barriers and firing on the stalled vehicles from rocky hideouts in mountain passes. Members of the band took pride in demonstrating the military's weakness and vulnerability and asserting their own and Qashqa'i power. They were quite successful in these aims, and their reputation spread. Young men admired their courage, and older men reminisced about the rebels and outlaws they had known in the past. Adolescent girls sang romantic ballads about the rebels. Families of the rebels provided provisions, and other Qashqa'i nomads were generous in their help. Especially given the proximity of the Persian Gulf and the active smuggling trade there, arms and ammunition were not difficult to acquire. The rebels always wore their two-flap felt hats, a cartridge belt, and often a diaphanous beige cloth cloak called a *choqqa* that they tied with a tasseled cord. Qashqa'i warriors had worn these cloaks during battles in the past.

Rostam stayed with the small group on and off for several years. Members came and went. Periodically, with caution, he visited winter and summer pastures to see his mother and other family members. He arrived at night, slipped off during the day to hide in the nearby mountains, and left in the night, newly provisioned and glad for the familial contact. The government had carried out its threats to confiscate the group's winter pastures, but most of the nomads were fortunate to have found new pastures in nearby mountains, and they cooperated with neighboring Qashqa'i groups in the cultivation of the crops necessary for their own and their animals' sustenance. Occasionally Rostam traveled to the city of Shiraz by taking a circuitous route and blending with other rural people who were on their way to and from market. In Shiraz he met other young men who opposed Muhammad Reza Shah and his regime. Some were university students who told him about political activists elsewhere in Iran and who provided him with some understanding of revolutionary ideologies and struggles in other parts of the world.

By 1965, bolstered by escalating military aid and new technology from the United States, Iran's army and gendarmerie were increasingly effective in their surveillance of and control over Qashqa'i territory. Small Qashqa'i rebel bands similar to that of Shapur and Kaikavus had found it difficult to secure safe mountain retreats, travel freely, and escape from attacks. The government attempted once again to disarm the Qashqa'i, and the young men could no longer carry arms openly during their travels. After the army and gendarmes attacked and killed or captured other Qashqa'i rebels and outlaws, Shapur and Kaikavus decided to disband their own group and find other means of protest. Both men were killed several months later in a skirmish with gendarmes.

Rostam returned home, and this time he decided not to hide. As far as he knew, he had never been identified by state authorities as a member of an outlaw band. When officials had inquired about his whereabouts, for the purpose of conscripting him into the army, his uncle reported that he was a high school student in Shiraz. A year had passed since the last inquiry. Rostam was not comfortable staying at home for long periods, however. His elder brother who had married and fathered children now headed the household, and Golgaz was glad for the company and help of a daughter-in-law and grandchildren. Her second son's bride also proved to be a competent, cooperative worker. The family was still able to hire a shepherd, a young impoverished man, for their sheep and goats, and the brothers cultivated wheat and barley in winter and summer pastures. They sold and traded sheep, goats, wool, goat hair, and dairy products in Firuzabad and Shiraz for cash and needed commodities such as salt, rice, and tea. They were indebted to urban merchants and moneylenders, as were practically all Qashqa'i, and high and rising interest rates troubled them. The family survived economically without Rostam's presence, however, and he did not see a role for himself at home. His mother wanted him to marry and establish a family, but he said he was not ready. Besides, he noted, no girl in his extended family appealed to him. He was entitled to a share of the household's animals but only after his three brothers had set up their own independent households. As youngest son, the "son of the hearth," Rostam was by custom the one eventually responsible for filling his father's place at home and caring for his mother, but he saw with some regret that his elder brothers had already assumed that role.

After several months at home, a restless and bored Rostam returned to Shiraz and sought out the friends he had made there. Although he wanted to continue to act against increasing government restrictions on the Qashqa'i and the loss of their political autonomy, enhanced military surveillance and control made that difficult. The government's treacherous capture and execution in 1966 of the rebel Bahman Qashqa'i, nephew of the Qashqa'i *ilkhani*, was another turning point for Rostam. He considered attending high school in Shiraz but then rejected the idea. He was not qualified or adequately prepared to attend university.

Rostam accompanied his friend Selahaddin, a young Kurdish man from a small village near Sanandaj in northwestern Iran, back home for the New Year's holiday in March. He intended to return to his own family after a week but was drawn to Selahaddin's friends and was excited by their discussions of the problem of Kurds in Iran and neighboring Iraq and Turkey. He decided to remain in Kurdistan for a while. Sympathetic to this sensitive young man who no longer had a father, Selahaddin's father invited him to stay with his family. As Rostam helped out there, he saw that although the family lived in a village, its livelihood was similar to that of his own family in its dependence on both pastoralism and agriculture. During the evenings and on Fridays, he met young Kurds and became aware of the plight of this nation of people oppressed by the states under whose authority and control they fell.

In 1967, disturbed about news of renewed military attacks against Qashqa'i rebels and outlaws near Firuzabad, Rostam decided to travel to Europe to meet with Khusrow Khan, one of the exiled leaders of the Qashqa'i confederacy. Several Kurdish friends wanted to talk with Kurds in exile from Iraq and Turkey, and Europe was the safest, most accessible location for their gathering. Travel by bus from Tabriz to Munich was inexpensive, and the young men hoped to find ways to meet their expenses while visiting Europe. Rostam located Khusrow Khan Qashqa'i, who was widely known to frequent a certain café and a nearby antiquities shop in Munich. Rostam's Kurdish friends traveled on to Paris. Khusrow Khan was distressed as he heard Rostam's firsthand reports about the severe measures the Iranian government was taking against the Qashqa'i. Forced into exile thirteen years previously, Khusrow Khan had received money from the Iranian government that its agents said compensated him for land it had confiscated from his family. He used some of it to support the living expenses of young Qashqa'i men abroad, including Rostam. He hoped to build support for the future, when he would return to Iran and resume tribal leadership.

Rostam remained in Europe for ten years and supported himself by a variety of temporary unskilled jobs and some aid from Khusrow Khan. Periodically he visited other European cities and met members of other national-minority groups in Iran, particularly Kurds and Baluch. He encountered many expatriate Middle Easterners and heard them tell familiar stories. He was struck by the common fate of almost all their groups: military surveillance and control, economic oppression and neglect, and cultural discrimination.

Rostam was initially drawn to leftist groups in Europe that were composed of people from Iran and other Middle Eastern countries, but none of them spoke directly to the concerns he held. He grew to be particularly distrustful of many Iranian leftists of Persian background. Although Persian Iranians seemed sympathetic to the political problems he had faced in Iran, they appeared to him to be more interested in exploiting the Qashqa'i as a strategic and military weapon in their larger struggle. They said they cared about minority rights, but their ideas and programs for a new form of society in Iran did not adequately address minority issues, and they seemed overly concerned about changing the conditions of what they termed the "backward" minorities. They viewed the nomadic pastoralism practiced by Rostam's family and other Qashqa'i as archaic and pointless, they described Qashqa'i economic and political systems as feudal, and they perceived Qashqa'i social systems as patriarchal and oppressive. They said they intended to eradicate these practices and systems and transform these people into a proletariat in a unified Iran. Rostam was offended by their attitudes and knew that these goals were ridiculous and, besides, impossible to achieve.

In 1971 and 1975 Rostam returned briefly for visits with his family. Although he had originally left Iran legally, he had not fulfilled the military service required of Iranian men, and he worried about being apprehended by the authorities. The shah's repressive secret police, SAVAK, was active and powerful, and Rostam feared staying more than a few days with his mother. SAVAK had infiltrated Qashqa'i society; no one knew exactly who all the agents and informers were, although rumors of their identities proliferated. On each visit Rostam entered and exited Iran illegally through Kurdistan, with the help of Kurdish friends. He considered staying in Kurdistan and assisting the struggle for minority rights there, as an affiliate of one of the leftist groups that were active. Most of these groups held non-Kurdish members; as a Qashqa'i, he believed he would fit in. He also considered joining the Marxist-oriented rebellion in Dhofar in the southern Arabian peninsula. Muhammad Reza Shah was providing military aid to the sultan of Oman in his efforts to end the rebellion in Dhofar, and a few Iranians opposed to the imperialist aims of the shah and supportive of the rebellion had gone there to foil the effort.

When Rostam returned to Munich in 1975, uncertain as to his future, he met again with Palestinian men and women who were engaged in their own nationalist struggles against the state of Israel and other enemies. Many of them had received military and other training in camps of the Palestine Liberation Organization in southern Lebanon, and he asked them about the possibility of going there. They provided him with false documents, and in 1977 he passed through Turkey and Syria to Lebanon. Rostam spent a year in a PLO camp there and then returned to Munich.

The rise of protest in Iran against Muhammad Reza Shah in 1978 excited Iranian youth in Europe. Rostam joined their discussions and grew increasingly agitated to return to Iran. He expected Khusrow Khan

Qashqa'i to formulate a plan for the Qashqa'i people in the escalating struggle in Iran and was disappointed to find that he had not yet voiced any specific policy or program. In late 1978 when Khusrow Khan traveled to the United States in order to discuss the situation in Iran with Qashqa'i and other people, Rostam returned to Iran, again through Kurdistan, and went immediately to see his family in winter pastures.

During the past decade, Rostam's brothers, uncles, and other patrilateral kin had purchased small plots of land and built two-room mud-brick houses near their former winter pastures, for they expected that the economic and political conditions for nomadic pastoralism would continue to worsen. Their expectations had not proven false, and they were glad that they had settled before the government had forced it upon them. They named their new village Moradabad, after Rostam's father as well as the reputed founder of their lineage. One of Rostam's brothers and a hired shepherd continued to migrate seasonally between winter and summer pastures with the family's sheep and goats.

Rostam spent many evenings talking with his kinsmen about the years of his absence and his ideas concerning how to improve the status and position of the Qashqa'i in Iran. He spoke of his association with Khusrow Khan, a man they all admired, especially for his military stand against the shah in the 1940s and 1950s, and they eagerly anticipated his expected imminent arrival. Several young men talked about volunteering their services to Khusrow Khan as his armed guards, a role performed by their fathers and grandfathers for previous paramount Qashqa'i leaders. Rostam sought out the Qashqa'i teacher assigned to his group and was surprised to find that although they shared a hatred of the shah, the teacher laughed about the prospects of the paramount Qashqa'i *khans* ever assuming a position of leadership in Iran again. The time for "tribal" leadership was over, he proclaimed. Iran had entered the "modern" era, he declared.

In early January 1979 Naser Khan Qashqa'i, Qashqa'i *ilkhani*, returned to Iran from twenty-five years of exile in the United States, and hundreds of Qashqa'i people came to Tehran to greet him. By then the tide had turned against Muhammad Reza Shah, and on 16 January he fled Iran, never to return. Two days later Naser Khan and a large escort traveled by car to Shiraz in the south. Several thousand Qashqa'i people gathered in secure Qashqa'i territory south of Firuzabad to welcome him. As he joined the gathering, Rostam expected Naser Khan to announce a course of action for the Qashqa'i in these turbulent times, when state institutions were weak or nonexistent, but he did not, partly because of advanced age and his caution in acting after having been in exile for so long. His personal style of leadership, one traditional for Qashqa'i leaders, was to hold council with the tribespeople he respected, allow a consensus to emerge from these often large public gatherings, and then possibly act if it was warranted. When Khusrow Khan arrived in Iran some days later, the situation became tense and complicated, for the two *khans* (who were brothers) held different notions about the roles they should play and the actions they should take in support of or against the new revolutionary Islamic regime. Unlike many of Iran's national minorities, the Qashqa'i were Shii Muslims, but they did not share the fundamentalist interpretations of Islam propagated by the Ayatullah Khomeini and his supporters. The *khans* debated their plans but reached no decisions. Out of loyalty to Khusrow Khan, whom he still regarded as his patron, Rostam remained close and served as a lieutenant. He delivered messages, carried out instructions, and tried to involve other Qashqa'i youth.

Some Qashqa'i men who had associated with Khusrow Khan in Europe had also returned to Iran, and they too were puzzled by the lack of specific programs and policies. Several joined nationwide Persian-dominated leftist groups then active in Iran, but Rostam did not trust many of their members and feared they would exploit him because of his Qashqa'i tribal connections. Although many non-Qashqa'i leftists continued to view him as politically naive, they did expect that he and his "tribe" would be useful in any forthcoming military struggle in Iran. They appreciated the vast numbers of armed and militarily prepared Qashqa'i men and their strategic location near oil fields, a major urban area (Shiraz), and the Persian Gulf.

After national elections in 1980, Khusrow Khan Qashqa'i was elected to the first parliament of the newly proclaimed Islamic Republic of Iran. Muslim clerics and their supporters formally questioned his credentials and then sent revolutionary guards, the new regime's main military arm, to arrest him. Days later, after beatings from revolutionary guards, he was released from prison and sent to his sister's home in Tehran. Instead, he headed to Qashqa'i territory in the south. Revolutionary guards attempted to intercept him and then began to plot attacks against his small group of family and other supporters. Several hundred Qashqa'i men, including Rostam, joined in the defense, and a small insurgency rapidly formed in Qashqa'i territory. Members of three pan-Iranian leftist groups, all non-Qashqa'i men and a few women, attached themselves to the insurgency. Naser Khan, his son Abdullah, Khusrow Khan, and their respective supporters disputed about the presence of the non-Qashqa'i leftists. Unable to agree, the three men set up separate but affiliated camps for a while. Rostam remained in Khusrow Khan's camp and continued to serve as a trusted assistant.

Because of the close proximity of the insurgent camps to Rostam's family near Farrashband, he was often able to visit home. Revolutionary guards, gendarmes, and the army exercised little control over the rugged mountainous area, and Qashqa'i people and others were often able to travel with impunity. Rostam's mother feared for him each time he left home after a brief visit, but his stories about the sometimes pleasant life in the insurgent camp (especially the camaraderie established among the Qashqa'i members) and the infrequency of attacks against it reassured her.

By the spring of 1982 the small group of Qashqa'i rebels was isolated, beleaguered, and demoralized. Revolutionary guards had increased the intensity of their attacks. Concrete expressions of support from within the Qashqa'i confederacy, which had been low-level from the start, were diminishing. Abdullah, son of Naser Khan, died suddenly of suspicious causes, possibly intentional cyanide poisoning, several hours after a battle with revolutionary guards. Dispirited about his son's death and in poor health himself, Naser Khan was encouraged to leave Iran. Even loyal supporters of Khusrow Khan worried about the advisability of continuing to maintain the insurgency. Revolutionary guards intensified their surveillance of roads in the camp's vicinity, and travel was impeded. In July a mediator in Shiraz, supportive of the small Qashqa'i group, arranged for Khusrow Khan and the remaining fighters to receive amnesty if they surrendered to the Shiraz authorities. After much deliberation, Khusrow Khan and some others from the camp secretly entered Shiraz to await the conclusion of the negotiations. A spy from within the insurgency, some Qashqa'i later stated, reported on Khusrow Khan's location, and revolutionary guards seized him. Khusrow Khan was later tried, sentenced to death by an Islamic court, and tortured. Then, according to many reports, he was publicly shot in Firuzabad (some say Shiraz), possibly after having already been killed. Controversy concerning the circumstances of his death continued for years, and soon many legends arose about him. Some members of the insurgency had remained in their mountain stronghold and attempted to find their own way to sanctuary. Most of the key members of the insurgency were later executed or arrested or driven into foreign exile.

Rostam had waited in the mountains until he thought that Khusrow Khan had safely reached Shiraz, and then he traveled alone by foot toward Farrashband. En route, he was ambushed by revolutionary guards sent out from Firuzabad to watch for stragglers from the insurgent camp. They shot Rostam as he struggled to escape and then roughly loaded his body into the back of a Land Rover.

No one in Rostam's family ever discovered where the revolutionary guards took him or where he was buried. Golgaz often visited her husband's grave and pretended that her son was buried next to his father. As she bent her head toward the ground, she murmured that only the earth could hear her and that only the soil of that undug grave could bear and share her endless pain and grief. "O heavenly earth, let my beloveds be held in your caring arms, and let my Rostam sleep in your lap. When they are awakened [on the Day of Judgment], tell them that I was not here to complain but to inform them that new *alamdars* [flag holders in wars] have been born to fight for their tribe."

## A NOTE ON SOURCES

The names of many people in this account, including the name Rostam, are pseudonyms, and I have changed some place-names. This account is augmented by my anthropological, historical, and archival research on the Qashqa'i people of southern Iran. I was in southern Iran in 1963–64 when Qashqa'i rebels were active, and I was acquainted with several of their families. I conducted anthropological field research among the Qashqa'i in 1970–71, 1977, and after the revolution in 1979 and 1991. I also conducted interviews with and collected oral histories from many Qashqa'i individuals (in Iran and in exile abroad), particularly current and former tribal leaders, members of the Qashqa'i insurgency of 1980–82, and men and women who had been fugitives from the Iranian government. A former classmate of mine at Shiraz University in Iran, who became a medical doctor, treated wounded Qashqa'i rebels in the 1960s and later told me about their lives. Two Qashqa'i men, Manucher Dareshuri and Mohammad Shahbazi, offered helpful suggestions for this essay, as did Gene Garthwaite.

## SUGGESTIONS FOR FURTHER READING

My two books on the Qashqa'i will provide readers with the historical and anthropological context of this account: *The Qashqa'i of Iran* (New Haven: Yale University Press, 1986), especially chapters 11 and 12, dealing with Iran under Muhammad Reza Shah Pahlavi and the Ayatullah Khomeini's Islamic Republic; and *Nomad: A Year in the Life of a Qashqa'i Tribesman in Iran* (Berkeley: University of California Press, 1991). In "Tribes and the State in Nineteenth- and Twentieth-Century Iran," in *Tribes and State Formation in the Middle East,* ed. Philip Khoury and Joseph Kostiner (Berkeley: University of California Press, 1990), I discuss the historical importance of tribes and tribal confederacies in Iranian history. Pierre Oberling provides a brief account of Qashqa'i rebel activity in the 1960s in *The Qashqa'i Nomads of Fars* (The Hague: Mouton, 1974), 210–15. In *The Last Migration* (London: Rupert Hart-Davis, 1957), Vincent Cronin offers a fictionalized account of a military confrontation between the Iranian state and the Qashqa'i in the early 1950s. For a novel about a young Kurdish peasant in Turkey who became an outlaw and bandit, I suggest Yashar Kemal's *Memed My Hawk* (New York: Pantheon, 1961). Eric Hobsbawm's *Bandits* (New York: Pantheon, 1981) offers a historical study of the phenomenon of social banditry, while David Hart discusses the applicability of Hobsbawm's notions to the Middle East in *Banditry in Islam* (Cambridgeshire: Middle East and North African Studies Press, 1978).

Farhad Kazemi and Ervand Abrahamian in "The Nonrevolutionary Peasantry of Modern Iran," *Iranian Studies* 11 (1978): 259–304, discuss forms of political protest in rural Iran. Edmund Burke, III, and Ira Lapidus provide an edited collection of studies about social movements in the modern Middle East in *Islam, Politics, and Social Movements* (Berkeley: University of California Press, 1988).

# TWENTY-ONE

# An Iranian Village Boyhood

*Mehdi Abedi and Michael M. J. Fischer*

What a personal odyssey is Mehdi Abedi's! From boyhood in the small village of Dareh, south of the city of Yazd in south-central Iran, to schooling first in Yazd and later in the city of Qum (the seminary city of Iran) on the eve of the Iranian revolution, and finally to Rice University in Texas where he is now an anthropologist, his life has been one of remarkable changes. In this selection, Abedi (with Michael M. J. Fischer) tells of growing up in Dareh in the 1950s and 1960s.

His story is a warmly nostalgic look backward at a world that has now vanished forever as a result of the many changes modern Iran has experienced. Although Dareh is but a small village, one is struck immediately by the enormous vitality of its social and cultural life and by the density of human interactions. We meet a colorful group of characters who appear to have stepped out of the pages of a nineteenth-century novel—the headman, the Hajji, the washer of the dead, the midwife, the barber, and the various individuals who served (with more or less competence) as teacher in the village school.

At the center of everyone's interest was the annual enactment of the passion play at Ashura, the Shiite festival that commemorates the killing of Imam Husayn by the evil Umayyad general Shemr. For the small boy Abedi was then, it must have been a wonderfully exciting time. Selection for the roles in the play became the occasion for intense competition among the villagers. All over Iran, similar passion plays were held on this occasion and were no doubt acted with the same gusto. In the Ashura passion play, the Islamic revolutionaries were to find a rich symbolic vocabulary to denounce the shah (portrayed as the new Yazid) and his allies.

Fischer and Abedi's account also touches upon the latter's life and education in the nearby city of Yazd (where his family resided in the winter months) and the central place that Islamic education played in his life. Through Abedi's experiences we come to understand the cultural roots of the Iranian revolution and how firmly grounded the Shiite tradition is among the Iranian people. At the heart of this tradition is the *Quran*, which was memorized by some urban and rural Iranian boys as well as by some girls. For many Iranians, it is clear, religion offered much that was spiritually nourishing— although it could also be utilized by politically ambitious clerics. Ironically, the shah's educational reforms worked to increase further the influence of the *mullahs* and of the Shiite clergy through the founding of new seminaries and schools and the expansion of the media.

Finally, one must note that Abedi's story is unique in having been written in close collaboration with his coauthor and friend Michael M. J. Fischer. Is this account biography, or autobiography? Or is it a new genre? How do we situate this story alongside the more recognizably biographical contributions to this volume? —ED.

Dareh (Valley) is the name of the little village in which I was born. In the legal documents it is called Dareh-i Miyankuh (the Valley of the Middle Mountains). It is a poor hill village in a narrow valley of the middle ranges of the Shirkuh Mountains, above the basin plain on which sit the larger villages Mehriz and Manshad, to the south of the city of Yazd in central Iran. Not even many Yazdis have heard of it: from Yazd you take the road to Kirman as far as the Abdul Malik Coffee House, then turn right onto a gravel road, past Mehriz, toward the mountains, and when you come to a branch in the road, you can see the bottom of the village. Villagers distinguish three neighborhoods, or *mahalleh:* upper, lower, and middle. We lived in the middle.

The people of the village tell stories about the good past, the days when water was plentiful, much wheat and barley was produced, melons were grown, and everyone was happy. By the time I was old enough to know the village, it was extremely poor, and more than a third of its population had left to work in Yazd or Tehran. Its primary produce was dried mulberries. My memories are of famine conditions of the postwar and post-Mossadeq period, when children were told to fill their bellies by foraging for berries (*angur-i kuhi* and *panirok*). American wheat was sent, but it was often spoiled and uncleaned.

Among the spiritual or religious features of the village were, beginning at the bottom of the village, the *husayniyeh* (arena for the passion plays on Ashura), the graveyard and a hyena's grave for curing sick animals, a mosque and public bathhouse, and, on the hillside behind the bathhouse, a rock formation that was said to be an imprint of the sword of Imam Ali. In our yard in the middle neighborhood there was a holy tree. In the upper village there was a second mosque and an older holy tree. Above the village was a cave where the Imams were said to have left their footprints, and a mountain ridge in the shape of a camel led by a man and pushed by another. All these sites were visual reminders of moral lessons. The camel shape of the mountain went with the legend that during a time of drought and famine two villagers decided to declare war on God, and so they set out with their camels to reach the highest point so they could talk to God. God turned them to stone, and so they remain as a constant warning to people against blasphemy; Big Brother brooks no revolt. Similarly the sword of Ali was a warning against those who express animosity toward the First Imam: the story was that an enemy had tried to ambush Ali, and in his lightning speed to draw his sword, Ali hit the hillside, leaving an imprint. The hyena grave (*qabr kaftar*) at the desert's edge was used for animals as saints' tombs (*imamzadehs*) were for humans: when animals fell sick they were circumambulated seven times around this grave, and sacrifices, offerings, and vows were made.

The bathhouse was used both for cleanliness and ritual purity: menfolk used it before dawn, womenfolk afterwards. Menfolk were less concerned with bathing and more that they be ritually pure before going off to the fields. Womenfolk enjoyed spending time in the bathhouse socializing and picnicking. But the bathhouse was also associated with *jinn*, perhaps through an association with moisture, and so one was never supposed to go there alone. *Jinn* were said to attack neither those who were totally fearless nor those who were extremely timorous, but only the majority in between. They did not attack the timorous lest they have heart attacks and die; all *jinn* in this village were Muslims and did not want to have the blood of anyone charged to them. They feared the totally fearless lest they be seized and have their necks wrung. There was a woman, Zan-i Hajji Daqqaq (Wife of Hajji the Cloth Finisher), who lived between the *husayniyeh* and the mosque, who was possessed by *jinn*, and served as an example to all of what might happen if you failed to exercise caution. She was constantly talking to the *jinn*, screaming at them, cursing them, calling on Hazrat-i Abbas to get them to leave her alone. Her sons had to lock her in when they left for the fields. She must have done something to a *jinn*. She was a living reminder that whenever you pushed a stone down a hillside, as kids loved to do, or whenever you threw out hot water or even whenever you stepped somewhere, you should first call out to warn any invisible *jinn* in the way: *bismillah-i rahman-i rahim* or *parhiz o bismillah-i rahman-i rahim* or just *parhiz* (beware). If you did get tormented by a *jinn*, a *jinn-gir* (*jinn* catcher) would come to divine its name.

The holy tree in our yard had a story that I helped produce. People believed that trees have senses and understanding, especially such that one could talk to them. So if a fruit tree stopped bearing, if one had tried fertilizers and transplanting and nothing else seemed to work, one might try a ritual called *bebur nabur* (cut, don't cut). One placed a saw at the tree's base, and one person pretended to begin cutting it down. A second person would then plead for the tree: "What are you doing, don't you realize this is an apple tree?" First person: "You mean it looks like an apple?" Second person: "No, it gives apples" (thus suggesting to the tree its duties). First person: "Why then does it not give apples? It looks like a simple plane tree to me." Second person: "Please, I beg you, give it one more year, and I guarantee it will bring forth fruit."

We had a tall apple tree in our yard that gave pleasant shade but no fruit. My brother was working in Tehran and had promised to bring us some special black cherry seedlings. My father decided to cut down the apple tree to make room for the new seedlings, but for some reason I jumped at him and began a kind of *bebur nabur* dialogue with him, and Amu Ali, the village *muezzin* (caller to prayer) joined me. My father relented. Sometime later I happened to kill a snake in the mountain, and I buried it at the base of the tree because snakes were thought to be excellent fertilizer, and I would whisper to it: "Please, I want to be proud of you, do your duty and bear fruit." Miraculously, the next year the tree produced an overabundance of apples, but in the following winter, as if exhausted by its efforts, it died, and did not sprout again in the spring.

Near the mosque in the upper neighborhood there was an ancient plane tree that was even more venerable. Someone on an Ashura day had said he had seen it bleeding in sympathy with the martyrdom of Husayn. And so people believed that if they attempted to cut its branches, especially on the festival of Ashura, something terrible would befall them.

Such folklore provides the weft in the rich anecdotal tapestry of the village's sense of its place and its social composition through the lives of its highly individualistic characters. It is a human tapestry viewed with much humor, as well as suspended judgment: only God knows what is possible; and in a materially hard world, folkloric elaboration provides humane comfort and endless material for storytelling sociability. A few characters may serve to illustrate.

At the top of the upper village lived a wealthy Hajji and usurer (*no-zulkhor*), who had connections with both the police and the clergy. (Ayatullah Saduqi of Yazd used to stay at his house.) One day a truck delivered a bag of melons for him. The driver called out to Hajji that he was dropping off the purchase, and left. I and some other boys stole the largest melon on top. When Hajji discovered his loss, he cursed us and our fathers at the top of his lungs. We waited until very late to return home, hoping our parents would be too tired to beat us. They were not. We were beaten soundly enough so that our cries wafted through the village to Hajji. The next day we planned revenge on Hajji. We decided to stone his windows. Hajji's house was the only one to have glass windows. We did not realize that when the lights were on he could not see out, so we waited until he turned out the lights before throwing stones. When the lights came on we stopped. Hajji's house was the highest up the mountain slope, so we simply climbed above it to throw stones. Hajji could not figure out what was going on: somehow he did not think it was us. Instead he yelled at his two wives that one of them had thrown hot water carelessly on the heads of the *jinn*, and he read out the prayer against the *jinn*. Then he called a diviner. We were afraid the diviner would discover us, and I was very close to confessing to my mother, but fortunately I held back, figuring there would be time if he actually knew. The diviner, however, concluded it must indeed by the *jinn*, and that the house was haunted. As a result, Hajji sold his house and moved to town. It was not until years later that I told my father what had happened, and was surprised to learn that none of the boys had told their parents.

Among the other characters of the village there was first Hasan Kadkhoda, the headman, with his pipe and handmade tobacco pouch. He used to be the servant to the previous *kadkhoda*, Hajj Mirza Agha. As was always pointed out, he was a "nobody." Hajj Mirza Agha had fourteen wives and many sons. Being a large landowner, he needed cheap labor. Instead of hiring labor, he married many women, mostly widows, who were happy to be assured daily bread. In contrast, Hasan Kadkhoda had only one wife, and she had only one eye. She was a bitch, and we children were terrified of her loud mouth.

Then there was Rubabeh, the midwife. She was about seventy and lived with an unmarried daughter who had been blinded by smallpox in childhood. Rubabeh was the female healer of the village, curing with herbs. She also baked the most delicious bread. She had a saintly reputation for her piety, her healing, her religious knowledge, and for helping bring so many babies into the world. She herself was also the mother of several men of solid reputation.

There was also Maryam, the female washer of the dead. She was even older than Rubabeh. Most children feared her due to her occupation, but I was used to her since she visited our house frequently. My mother liked her, and my father would tease her by asking her to be his concubine. She was always murmuring prayers, and there were stories about the times God had answered her prayers immediately. Before falling asleep at night, I was told, she repeated the principles of her religion (*usul-i din*) and the names of the Imams so that if she should die in her sleep, they would be able to answer the questions of the angels of death. Whenever there was a drought, people would ask her to pray for rain. I once asked how she did it, and my father suggested that we kids go with her up the mountain to the cave where the Imams had left their footprints. So one day, two of my sisters and I went with her. This pilgrimage was my first "long trip." Since it was the middle of summer, I knew that Maryam could not ask for rain: there are proper times for asking things of God. But at the cave Maryam began to shout and cry. As her voice echoed in the mountains, I experienced a mixture of fear, excitement, joy, and awe. We then entered the cave: there was a puddle of water and some birds flying about. Maryam said the birds were messengers of God. We sat down for a meal, and departed before sunset. My father admired Maryam and would say she was worth more than several men. He would frequently tell the story of the year the month of Muharram fell in the winter, and he tried to cancel the annual passion play, which he supervised, because of the snow. Maryam objected, saying snow was a blessing, and if we abandoned the religious activities of Muharram, next year there would be no snow, and hence also no water in the spring for irrigation. She took a shovel in hand and shamed the menfolk into helping her clear the village square for one of the best Muharram *taziyehs* (mourning rites) ever held.

Ali "Dallak," the barber, shaved the men, pulled bad teeth with his pliers, and ran the village bathhouse. During his military service he had learned to read and write and so was something of a religious authority. He circumcised all my age-mates. I was circumcised when I was two. I remember that he called me: "Amu [reciprocal for paternal uncle-nephew], come here, let me see your little dodo and how it has grown." Then snip with a razor. I was so scared I pissed on him. I was then handed over to a woman. My mother was not there, but my father was. There was no ceremony, and certainly no talk of being a man. Children were not supposed to know about sex. The foreskin is supposed to go to an unmarried woman, who chops it up in a mortar and pestle and eats it, to help her catch a husband.

And of course there was my father, who always bragged about his calligraphy, his ability to understand religious issues, and his ability to cure illnesses with talismans. If a girl could not find a husband, if a woman's husband no longer liked her and wanted another wife, for any ill, my father had the book of talismans and prayers. He was the male healer for the village, combining herbs, powders, liquids, and tablets, as well as talismans and prayers. For curing, in most cases, he did not charge. He had a shop in which he also sharpened knives, sickles, and saws, repaired broken china and stone cooking pots. For this he was paid by the villagers in kind: eggs, yogurt, dried nuts, and other agricultural products. Even peddlers from outside the village often took payment for their wares in kind.

My father was also the supervisor of the passion plays for some forty years, and people would gather at our house from both the upper and lower village on the festival of Ashura. From there a grand procession of floats and *dasteh sineh-zani* (flagellants, mainly boys and young men) would go to the *husayniyeh* down at the bottom of the lower neighborhood.

For two months before Ashura ("the tenth" of the month of Muharram, anniversary of the martyrdom of Imam Husayn on the plains of Karbala) my father would prepare, collecting clothing for costumes, carpets and props for the floats, and reserving particular horses to be ridden. Many items were stored at our house: endowed by the villagers for the passion plays. But no one would refuse a request to lend a fine carpet or *chador* (veil) or animal. The villagers firmly believed that ill would befall anyone who did not participate in the Ashura events. The best horse in the village was reserved for Shemr, the evil general of the Sunni Syrian army, because he had to be able to catch Husayn. The second best horse was reserved for Ali Akbar, the elder son of Husayn, because it took time for Shemr to catch him; and traditionally Ali Akbar would fall from his horse so that he could be caught by the aging Shemr. The laziest horse in the village was used to carry the Fourth Imam, the only male who survived the massacre at Karbala, because he was sick and did not fight. For a month or so my father would supervise rehearsals of the chief actors. Shemr was usually played by the husband of my eldest sister. Shemr had to be tall and have a loud voice with which to frighten people. He was dressed from head to toe in red. Occasionally, when he was available (he lived in the city), my brother-in-law's brother would play Shemr, because he had blue eyes (as Shemr is said to have had). Husayn had to be a man in his forties with a full beard. Imam Sajad, the Fourth Imam, was played by a sick old man, in many villages an opium addict, but in our village there were no opium addicts—almost no one was rich enough to support an opium habit—so the part was played by one addicted to a *qaliun* (hubble-bubble).

There were only so many lead roles. Most men participated as porters for the heavy floats. In other villages the floats might be carried by trucks, but our village was too steep and narrow. The floats illustrated all the major events in the life of Imam Husayn for the ten days preceding his martyrdom and the days immediately following, when the women and children were taken off as prisoners to Damascus. The procession was accompanied by lines of black-shirted men beating their breasts with their hands or chains and chanting rhythmic dirges mourning the fate of Husayn. They all wore Arab *kafiyahs* or headbands (*aqqal*). Only the sick and disabled stood on the sidelines with the women and girls.

Beginning when I was five, I was cast for several years as the barely nubile bride of Qassam (the son of Husayn, the Second Imam). I was given this role partly, no doubt, because I was the son of the producer of the show, and partly as a reward for (or out of my father's pride in) my already being able to recite the Quran. In addition, I was part city boy, cleaner, better dressed, and better behaved than the other village boys—the sort who might be trusted to blow their nose in the fine silk *chador* reserved for the wife of Qassam. The role was intended to make the young girls cry, identifying with the tragic fate of this young widow. I had little white sugar balls (*noql*) to hand out, received as blessed sweets. In second grade, I finally refused to play a woman any longer. What triggered the refusal I no longer exactly remember, but I remember bursting into angry tears at either being pinched, winked at, or obscenely teased as if I were a girl.

Such teasing and humor had a regular place: the man who played Zeinab (sister of Husayn, who led the women and children after the massacre until the sickly Fourth Imam could assume his leadership role) always had a big mustache, and when someone would make a rude comment to him, he would show his mustache from under his *chador*. Typically he had an obscene tongue as well and would respond to such propositioning with retorts like "Yes, I'll sleep with you. Bring your mother too." There was less such humor during our passion plays than the ones I saw in the city, but afterwards there would be a lot of ribald mockery of the *taziyeh*. Shemr and Zeinab would replay their repartee from the passion play in obscene variations such as the following:

> *Shemr.* Agar to Zeinab-i, pas doldolat chist?
> If you are Zeinab, then what's that penis?
>
> *Zeinab.* Khoda danad ke in gusht-i ziadist.
> God knows it is an extra piece of meat.

And indeed some of the acting could stick to the actor. Thus someone named Mahmad who played the role of Shemr might come to be called Mahmad Shemr, even if it caused him to bristle and see red.

Once the procession of floats reached the lower village, it would enter the *husayniyeh* and circumambulate counterclockwise. The men were the actors on the *husayniyeh* floor, while women sat up on the walls (*ghurfeh*, "reviewing stand"). Shemr would gallop into the center, calling for Husayn to show himself and announcing to the audience: "I'm neither Shemr, nor is this the land of Karbala; I'm just playing the role." This formula was partly used to fend off the danger that the onlookers would become so enraged at his killing of their beloved Imam that they would kill him. ("In some villages," goes the archetypical Iranian comment, "people actually killed the person playing Shemr.") Partly the formula was to allow Shemr to shed tears, to empty himself as it were, so that he could then take on the hard-hearted role. Then Husayn would enter, crying to the people: "Is there no one to help me?" Ali Akbar would then gallop in, dressed in a white shroud, stained with blood, and sewn with the arrows that had penetrated his body. He always was played by someone of draft age and was the heartthrob of the girls.

The time frame of the passion play was in fact a mythic, rather than a chronological, one, for, of course, all the events were presented on the floats simultaneously prior to and during the action in the center of the *husayniyeh*. Thus the head of Husayn was already on a pole, and the good Christian who attempted to intercede on Husayn's behalf was seated on a chair, dressed in safari khaki and shorts, pith helmet, with binoculars, watching the events. The climax of the play came first with Shemr killing Ali Akbar: the lad would fall off his horse and roll in the dust as Shemr cut off his head, while Husayn stood by and cried or feigned crying. (Both actual and pretend tears were regarded as having merit.) Finally, Shemr would kill Husayn, and everyone would rush into the middle, beating their heads in grief.

Afterwards people rushed to eat the special wheat stews (*ash-e gandom*) that were cooked in massive cauldrons. These communal meals were supplied either from perpetual endowments, vows made during the year, or by richer villagers. They usually contained the meat of a freshly slaughtered lamb. I remember with amusement scenes of people eating stew communally off big trays, jockeying to make sure they were sitting next to someone relatively clean with whom to share their dipping.

Such communal meals were also important during the holy month of Ramadan (during which Muslims are enjoined to fast from dawn to dusk). In Ramadan one received double merit for good deeds. The rich paid their debts to God by cooking cauldrons of stew to distribute, sharing the meat of a slaughtered lamb, and sending gifts of dry provisions (e.g., rice) to their neighbors. My grandfather served in his day as the village timekeeper: he was one of the first in the village to have a pocket watch, and just before dawn he would sing hymns of praise (*monajot*) to the First Imam to waken people. Traditionally villagers would start their fast with the rooster's crow. The first pocket watches did not change things much, since people only could tell time when the two hands came together at noon and midnight. Thus watches were called *zohr-kuk* and *qurur-kuk* (crow of noon, crow of midnight). Just before dawn my grandfather would sing out the formula *abast o teriak* (only time for a "sip of water and a pull of opium"). It is said that my father's father (he died before I was born) would often substitute the phrase *kaseye tut-i khoshk o kuzeh ab* (only time for a "bowl of dried mulberries"—the main produce of our village—"and a jug of water"). Then he would conclude with *tanbal kahnha ya allah* ("Get up you lazy bums!"). After he died, this role was taken over first by Amu Ali (Uncle Ali), of whom it is said, the first time he saw a radio, he recited the *shahadah*, the credo of Islam, and in mock surprise he exclaimed, "So here is the proof of what the preachers say, that at the end of time people can hear each other no matter what the distance." (Radios were enormously popular, and after the first one came to the village, everyone else immediately had to have one.) Then Akbar-i Ramazan took over the role of calling people to the fast: he eventually became the father-in-law of my father, when my father took a second wife after the death of my mother.

My mother was a city girl, the daughter of Gholam Husayn Vasel, a shopkeeper, Sufi, *zurkhaneh* (traditional gymnasium) master, popular storyteller, wit, and interpreter of Rumi's *Masnavi*. He had married the daughter of a rich merchant, Hajj Muhammad Karim Esfahani, who had come to Yazd from Isfahan. Hajj Muhammad Karim's wife was named Maryam, and her father was Yusuf Aghaii, a Jewish rabbi who had converted to Islam in a striking episode. My mother would often say: "The children of Yusuf Aghaii are scattered throughout the world. But we do not know very many of them." What she meant was that children of converts assimilate among Muslims without leaving much trace, but they carry a certain kind of character legacy.

Several morality plots interlace in her invocations of my great-great-grandfather. First there was the story of Yusuf Aghaii's conversion. As you know, Jews were not allowed into the produce bazaar during the day, but only at the end of the day. Being *najes* (carriers of pollution), they could not touch the produce lest it be declared polluted. To ensure that Muslims got first pick as well as religiously pure food, Jews had to wait until the end of the day to shop. Late one day Yusuf Aghaii went to buy some yogurt. He dipped his finger in it to see if it was still good, and rejected it as sour. The shopkeeper raised a ruckus, crying that Yusuf had defiled the entire container of yogurt. A crowd gathered, and things started to turn ugly. Yusuf, in an effort to escape, said: "I may be as good a Muslim as you." The shopkeeper retorted: "Let us go to the *mujtahid* and see." So the crowd took Yusuf to the *mujtahid*, who publicly forced him to eat some yogurt and meat together, thereby violating Jewish dietary rules. It is said that thereafter the Jews rejected him, but that his father, also a rabbi, asked to be allowed to name Yusuf's first child: it was a girl, and the name chosen was Maryam. Now Yusuf had studied both Hebrew and Arabic in Jerusalem, and so, it is said, when he became Muslim he did not need to study any Islamic jurisprudence: he knew it all and was as learned as any *mujtahid*.

One day when I came home as a child, very upset that I was not a *sayyid* (descendent of the Prophet, entitled to wear a green or black turban), my mother consoled me by saying that we were another kind of *sayyid,* that through Yusuf Aghaii we were descended from Haroun (Aaron), the brother of Moses, and that this could be seen in our entire family's gift of gab and rhetorical flair. Haroun, of course, was known for his silver tongue, and the story is well known that when the baby Moses was brought to the pharaoh, the pharaoh tested him by placing before the child some dates and some red-hot coals. The diviners had suggested that if it were just an ordinary child, it would be attracted to the bright red objects, but if this were the future prophet, it would know better and take a date. The child in fact began to reach for the coal, but the angel Gabriel took its hand and caused Moses to pick up the coal and put it on his tongue. Hence Moses stuttered, and when he went to plead his people's case before the pharaoh, God advised him to take Haroun along. And so the majority of Jews are relatively quiet types, but the descendants of Aaron are loquacious and persuasive. And hence: "The children of Yusuf Aghaii [Jewish converts] are scattered throughout the world, but we do not recognize them as such."

Jews, of course, were ambivalent figures in my mother's discourse. She would use Yusuf Aghaii both as reproof when she scolded me and as explanation when I did something intelligent. In the negative vein, she used to cite the popular *hadith, al bala lil awlia* (the people of catastrophe/sadness are friends of God), identifying Jews as not friends of God: when Jews raised their faces to God, the angels would immediately demand God grant their wishes so that the stench of Jews would disappear. But when the faithful prayed, the angels would tell God to delay granting their wishes so that they might look longer on their faces. Thus it was often repeated that Fatima, the daughter of the Prophet, had to wait eighteen years for her wish to be granted.

My mother's father, Gholam Husayn Vasel, must have been a prosperous young man to have married the only daughter of Hajj Muhammad Karim, but he was a Sufi in the true sense, spending all he had, and not valuing the material world. Originally he was a *mazari* (processor of henna). He owned a factory and helped others to establish similar factories in Yazd and Ardakan. (Yazd is still known as a center of henna processing. The raw material comes from farther east in Kirman province.) He had traveled a great deal and composed an epic poem about his adventures, which ended:

> Abul Qassem sits like a mouse.
> Creditors raise hell.
> One claps his forehead,
> Another beats his breast.
> Most upset of all is the broker.

Indeed Gholam Husayn had to sell the business to pay off his debts. He later bought a small grocery. It caught fire and burned. For the last

fourteen years of his life he was blind, and he died destitute. He seemed
not to mind: the world was but a passage to the real life. But I think it
was after the death of his young wife that he lost interest in the world.
He raised his son and three daughters with difficulty, managing to educate them and marry them off, albeit none lived up to his mark. His
son, Abul Qassem, a tailor, married the daughter of a *mullah* but had no
offspring. His youngest daughter, Khojasteh, married a coppersmith
and had three sons and a daughter, all of whom are educated and relatively prosperous. The eldest daughter, Marziyeh, married a sugar-shop
employee, who suddenly disappeared for seven years, then reappeared
with a good education from India, and became a customs clerk in Ahwaz. They had a daughter (Rakhshandeh) and three sons: Muhammad-
Ali Sirjani became a physician and major in the army and died a suspicious death in the recent revolution; Mahmud became a high school
teacher, and Mehdi died at age eighteen shortly before I was born, contributing to the conundrums of my own naming.

My mother's father's death is among my earliest memories. When I
related this memory to my mother many years later she was quite surprised. His bed was in the middle of the summer room, and everyone sat
around him. The barber came and trimmed his grey beard, but when he
touched the mustache, grandfather stopped him, waving his hand to say,
not this part. Then a few minutes later (my mother corrected me that it
was a few days later), when I was crawling near the courtyard pond with
a little bell around my neck, my mother suddenly came into the courtyard, wailing.

My mother, Farkhondeh, was the middle daughter. Beautiful, with
thick black hair down to her knees, always braided and hanging on
her back, she was witty, a living encyclopedia of poetry, a *hafez* of the
Quran (a *hafez* is one who memorizes the entire Quran), a weaver, and a
professional dress weaver. The neighborhood women loved her and
called our house *bagh-i delgosha* (garden of the open heart), because she
had a way of making even the saddest person laugh and because despite
our poverty she was the most generous of souls. She had her most beautiful moments with God, when she melodiously sang the Quran and
prayers. Despite my love for my father, I must say, she was a world
wasted in his house. Once I asked her why she had married him. She
said it was her fate.

My father, the spoiled only son of a relatively well-to-do farmer, had
been encouraged by his parents to marry a city girl. My father's father
owned a house in Yazd in the same neighborhood as my mother's family.
Periodically he would come from Dareh to collect the rent and to sell
dried mulberries. My mother's family had fallen on hard times and so
was happy to give their daughter to a villager who could at least guarantee steady food. Otherwise a villager could never have dreamed of

marrying a granddaughter of Hajj Muhammad Karim. In the village, my father owned some land and was well connected. His father's sister had married the eldest son of the then *kadkhoda* (headman), Hajj Ismail, who must have owned half the village. His village occupations and religious roles I have already described in the preceding section.

If the date on my birth certificate is to be believed, I was born on the tenth of Shahrivar 1331 Shamsi (31 August 1952). I was the sixth surviving child. My oldest sister, Safa, had already married two years earlier and had a son. She married the eldest son of my father's only sister. My brother Ahmad was the second child, and there were three other sisters: Ezzat, Fatemeh, and Robab. My mother was to have, all told, fourteen pregnancies, of which seven survived. (I have a younger brother.) According to my mother, she was baking bread in the basement kitchen when she felt the labor pains. Everyone had gone to the fields to pick fruit. The old midwife, Rubabeh, was a neighbor and could be called in an emergency, but my mother thought she had time to finish the bread. When she realized there was no time, it was too late, and she could hardly move. She called out a few times, but no one heard. She began reciting prayers, hoping someone would stop by. So I was born. She cut the cord, wrapped me in some clothes, put me under a basket with a stone on top, so no animal could get at me, and went to call Rubabeh. When everyone returned, there was joy that I was a boy, that is, on everyone's part except my elder brother, who felt his special status threatened.

My father named me Mehdi, but since my eighteen-year-old cousin (mother's sister's son), also Mehdi, had just died, my family decided to address me as Gholam Husayn, or Gholi for short, the name of both my grandfathers. The name Mehdi was used only on the birth certificate, and I was seven before I learned my real name. That happened because when I was registered for school in Yazd, my legal name was given, and when the teacher called out "Mehdi Abedi" at first I did not respond, though I had a vague feeling it might be me. I had never liked the name Gholi, which I associated both with the word for ghouls (*ghul*) and the word for a small bell (*ghuri*) that had been tied around my neck as a toddler. So I went home and said I wanted to be called Mehdi. The custom of changing an infant's name, if there was a death or illness in the family, or even to "sell" the child to another set of parents, was a kind of evil-eye avoidance, to confuse the forces of harm so they could not find or identify the child. It is of historical interest that the name Mehdi was not particularly popular earlier in the century but became very popular for children of my age cohort. This was no arbitrary flux of fashion but a kind of campaign launched by Muslim believers to thumb their noses at the Bahais (who claimed that the Mahdi had already come in the person of Bahaullah).

Similarly at the same time it became popular to call the Mahdi or Imam Zaman, Ala Hazrat (His Majesty) to deny the use of that title by the shah. Pro-Khomeini activists, however, soon called for a ban on this practice, as well as on all monarchical titles for the Imams: thus they asked that one no longer refer to the Eighth Imam, Imam Reza, as Sultan or Shah-i Khorasan; nor should one call Ali, Shah-i Vilayat. Instead the Imams ought to be called Abd-i Saleh Khodah (Righteous Servant of God). The struggle between religious sources of legitimacy and royal ones were symbolized in cities like Yazd by the *azan,* the call to prayer, which served as a public timekeeping device, and by the drum and trumpet sounds (*naqqareh khaneh* and *surna*) at dawn and dusk issuing from atop the governor's palace. My mother used to say she could always especially tell from the vigor of the latter how stable the government was: when loud and martial, the governor was in full control; when the sound was more playful, it was a harbinger that the musicians could feel the governor on the defensive and liable to be deposed. When Reza Shah was deposed, she reported, people said the trumpets' sound bursts seemed to be saying *tu kos-i zan-i shah* (up the shah's wife's . . . ).

I did not get to Hafiz with the *mullah* Monavvar. I got through the Quran, at which point I celebrated my first *noql kardan,* a ceremony in which sweets and coins and nuts mixed together would be sprinkled over the young scholar's head, which other children could scramble for; and there would be a gift for the scholar. I remember with some embarrassment that my mother wanted to do the ceremony, but we were so poor that she could only afford the *noql* and not a gift. I knew the situation, and so I also scrambled for the *noql* and coins, probably to the dismay of my mother.

When I was five we spent the winter in the city (Yazd), and I was sent to a pious woman *mullah* to learn the Quran. In the Yazd area, *mullah* is the proper term for one who teaches the rudiments of literacy. (Hence Jews were often addressed with the title *mullah,* because they were almost universally literate.) Her name was Monavvar, and she had about ten students, each at a different level. While teaching, she also made bags for a henna company, and we sometimes helped. She taught me the alphabet and the reading of the first sura of the Quran. I already knew much of the Quran by heart because my mother was a *hafez* and she often recited parts of it. It was a tradition to have a celebration (*noql kardan*) when students finished the first sura; the first, second, and eighth *joz* (thirtieths) of the Quran; and of course when they finished the whole Quran, at which time they were assumed to have acquired literacy in Arabic. In addition to the round sugar balls mixed with nuts and coins that were sprinkled over the scholar's head and the gift for the scholar, the teacher also would be given gifts relative to the family status of the child.

Following memorization of the Quran, students went on to the Persian poet Hafiz as an introduction to Persian literacy. Various things might follow Hafiz: the *Masnavi* of Jalal al-Din Rumi was particularly popular. All of this was just reading, not writing. My older sisters learned the Quran and Hafiz this way. They can no longer really read, but they can open Hafiz and "read" the familiar verses they have half memorized. Such literacy was referred to as *siahi ba sefidi farq gozashtan* (knowing black from white, that is, the print from the page). This is the connection between the Persian term for literacy, *savad*, and the Arabic word for black, *sud*.

Following the celebration, we went back to the village, where I was sent to another *mullah*, an old shroud weaver. Despite the high infant mortality rate, there was barely enough work for her to make a living making shrouds, so she also taught the Quran. Each student had a little carpet or goatskin on which to sit, which we kept at her house. Going to this *mullah* could be terrifying, for she would threaten to send us to the *surakh-i mar-mush khaneh* (the snake-mouse hole, namely, the dark basement, which was particularly scary in a village mud house perpetually falling into ruins), or she might use her knitting needle to draw blood from the back of our hands or she might bastinado the bottoms of our feet if we did not do our lessons properly. I did not like her and soon quit.

I was placed with another *mullah*, a young widow, a weaver with long, dark hair. Her husband had died during a hunting trip from a fall in the mountains. She had a lovely voice and would sing with the rhythm of her loom. She taught us the rules of ritual cleanliness, and the daily prayers. We were mischievous kids, and there were opportunities for mischievousness when we were sent to the river to do the ablutions for prayer. There were trees that provided cover from being watched too closely. Our leader was a girl of about eight or nine. She liked to take her pants off, and we liked to watch. In the villages, children who are around animals learn about sex earlier perhaps than children in the city, even if they do not connect sex with pregnancy. We would play at sex, comparing penis sizes, having erections and fellatio. One day of course someone saw us and raised a fuss. The big girl never came back to learn the Quran.

I had learned just over half the Quran when I quit. My mother decided it was enough for the time being. It was a bad year of drought. Many villagers had left to work as construction workers in the city. There was nothing to eat except bread made of American wheat. For some reason it was uncleaned, and one day a piece of bread baked with this wheat got stuck in my mouth. When my mother pulled it out, it was found to contain a large thorn. She angrily threw away the rest of the bread and declared that she would no longer live this miserable life in the village and subsist on charity. She would go to the city and work as a maid for her mother's brother, and she would take me: I was old enough to earn a little money. My father got very angry. But a few days later we packed for the city and left.

## A NOTE ON SOURCES

This essay is simplified and excerpted from a longer piece recently published as the first chapter of our *Debating Muslims: Cultural Dialogues in Tradition and Post-modernity* (Madison: University of Wisconsin Press, 1990), where we explain the collaborative process of writing:

> We have worked together on a variety of projects since 1970 when Fischer as a young graduate student in Yazd hired Abedi, still in his teens, to translate Islamic texts. We helped each other to learn the other's language and culture. What began as Abedi's effort to convert Fischer and Fischer's use of Abedi's argumentation as an anthropological access into the world of Shi'ism, gradually turned into a deep friendship and genuine set of collaborations. Abedi's autobiography consists of stories Abedi has shared over the years; some he wrote down at Fischer's urging, some were elicited orally in rich memory-laden "bull sessions." We had fun retelling them and shaping a chapter around them, Abedi reminding Fischer about Yazdi places, people, events and practices. Yazd was home to Fischer for some two and a half years (1969–1972), and he helped celebrate the birth of Abedi's first son, Reza, there. In 1975 Fischer spent the academic year in Qum, and Abedi came with his wife and child to live with him for three months, and to work as a research assistant on the project that eventuated in the book *Iran: From Religious Dispute to Revolution*. In 1981 Abedi came with Fischer to Rice University to pursue a Ph.D. degree in anthropology, and as we completed this manuscript, we also celebrated the birth of Abedi's second son, Maysam Morad (p. xxxii).

## SUGGESTIONS FOR FURTHER READING

For accounts and memoirs of Iranian life, see Erika Friedl, *Women of Deh Koh: Lives in an Iranian Village* (Washington, D.C.: Smithsonian Institution Press, 1989); Shusha Guppy, *The Blindfold Horse: Memories of a Persian Childhood* (Boston: Beacon Press, 1988); Michael M. J. Fischer, "Portrait of a Mullah: The Autobiography of Aqa Najafi Quchani," *Persica* 10 (1982): 223–57.

See also the novels by Fereydun Esfandiary, *Day of Sacrifice* (New York: McDowell, Oblonsky, 1959), and Taghi Modarressi, *The Pilgrim's Rules of Etiquette* (New York: Doubleday, 1989).

On Iranian Shiism, see Roy Mottahedeh, *The Mantle of the Prophet: Religion and Politics in Iran* (New York: Pantheon, 1985). See also Michael M. J. Fischer, *Iran: From Religious Dispute to Revolution* (Cambridge, Mass.: Harvard University Press, 1980); and Hamid Algar, *Religion and State in Iran, 1785–1906* (Berkeley: University of California Press, 1969).

# TWENTY-TWO

# Gulab: An Afghan Schoolteacher

*Ashraf Ghani*

As in Morocco, Yemen, and Iran, other Islamic states where pastoralist tribal forces maintained their power into the twentieth century against weak governments, the politics of Afghanistan have been characterized by sharp conflict between the forces of tradition rooted in the countryside and the forces of change based in the cities. In fact, the Afghan experience can be seen as an exaggerated variant of that of the region as a whole. Yet Afghanistan is also different from these other states. It ranks at the bottom of most international development statistics in meeting basic human needs. This disturbing fact can be starkly represented as follows: the total annual consumption of energy in all forms by an Afghan tribesman, it is said, is equivalent to the amount of energy it takes to produce one soft-drink can. Because of the huge gaps between rich and poor, modern and traditional, rural and urban, in Afghanistan, the struggle between groups favoring change and those seeking to maintain the old ways has taken on a particular intensity. It is therefore understandable that a murderous civil war (which still continues at this writing) should have erupted.

The life of Gulab, the Pashtu-speaking schoolteacher from the city of Khost in eastern Afghanistan whose biography is here presented by Ashraf Ghani, can be situated in the midst of and characterized in terms of this struggle. Gulab is the classic man in the middle. In 1978, on the eve of the civil war, he found himself besieged by the demands of conflicting political groups, each of which claimed to have *the solution* to Afghanistan's problems, and each of which sought his support. The choices were mutually contradictory. To select one was to deny a part of himself. Hence Gulab's paralysis. Ghani's portrait of Gulab makes clear what the stakes were for ordinary Afghans and why the situation was so explosive.

Through Gulab we come to understand the importance of the internal social and political divisions of Afghanistan. Some divisions are linguistic, like that between the Persian (Dari)-speakers based in the west of the country and in the cities, and the mostly rural and tribal Pashtu-speakers in the central

and eastern districts. Others pit the rural forces, dominated by the tribal aristocracy, against the government and merchants in the urban centers. Islam
itself is divided between local and Sufi groups, which tended to support the
status quo, and a host of competing and mostly urban groups inspired by radical Islamic doctrines imported from Pakistan, Egypt, and Iran. We learn that
the radical Islamists and their equally radical Marxist opponents were both
predominantly urban; both required a sharp break with established customs.
Until the start of the civil war in 1978, neither had much appeal for the predominantly Pashtun tribal groups.

The biography of Gulab provides a guide to the turbulent world of Afghan
politics in the 1970s. To situate more precisely his life, we might here briefly
summarize the central dynamics of modern Afghan political history. Until the
early 1970s, Afghanistan was a monarchy dominated by urban-based supporters of modernization, grouped around the Pashtun leader Muhammad Daud,
in alliance with elements of the mostly Pashtun tribal aristocracy. Because of
Afghanistan's strategic location between Iran and Pakistan and its common
frontier with the Soviet Union and China, the cold war years were ones of
active competition in Afghanistan between Soviet and American influences,
mitigated by a tacit agreement between the two superpowers not to compel
Afghanistan to choose sides.

The status quo was challenged in 1973, when Daud suppressed the monarchy in a coup d'état in order to introduce a program of drastic reforms. Because of a political miscalculation, his regime failed to develop a solid political
base and was compelled to resort to repressive policies and an alliance with
the United States to stay in power. The competition between Islamist and
Marxist groups for supporters intensified. Eventually, the political contradictions of the government provoked a coup by the army and the intelligentsia, in
which Marxist factions played a leading role. When the new regime adopted
an ill-considered series of radical measures (including a far-reaching land reform program, an end to usury and to the Islamic marriage practices) this
challenged the power of the tribal aristocracy and generated widespread popular opposition. It is at this point, just before the outbreak of the civil war,
that we leave Gulab. —ED.

Just as the thick dark of the night was giving way to the pale light of
early dawn the ringing of the alarm clock shook Gulab out of his sleep.
He hastily got out of his cot and, after making his ablutions, rushed to
the local mosque. With a sigh of relief, he noted that other people were
still arriving. He was keenly aware that some people were keeping a
close record of his attendance, as well as of his other activities. As he me-
chanically performed the rituals, his mind wandered over the conflicting
demands that were ripping his life apart.

Like everybody else in the mosque of Khost in southeastern Afghanistan, Gulab had been born in the vicinity of the town. He was thirty or

thirty-one years old. As dates of birth were not recorded, he did not know his exact age, but he knew the tribal lore well. He remembered the times spent with his father, memorizing the names of his seven paternal ancestors, as required by custom. His father had made sure that Gulab and his three brothers knew the names of the various lineages and clans that jointly made up the Pashtun ethnic group. They were also told about the groups that were allied together and those that carried on feuds.

When Gulab was a boy, his father owned four acres of irrigated land and about forty watered by rainfall in a village fifteen miles east of Khost. He was also involved in the illegal trade between Khost and towns across the border in Pakistan. The biggest item of trade at the time was wood. Some of the now barren mountains were forested then, and others had a much thicker layer of green. But people had to make a living, and nobody was concerned about the changing nature of the scenery or the erosion that deforestation would precipitate.

In those years, Khost was not a particularly healthy place. It was infested with malaria, and the people preferred their cooler villages on the upper hills to the damp and flat valley in which the town was located. Few people wanted to settle in Khost for long. Yet a government garrison had been stationed in the town since the mid-nineteenth century, and the governor of Paktia province spent the winters in the town.

But it had not been Gulab's lot to avoid Khost. He remembered his first trip there well. One day when he was about six years old, he and his brother Sur Gul, who was a year younger, were told to put on their fine clothes and were taken to the town. In those days there were no trucks or buses linking the villages to the town, and the boys were put on a donkey while the older men walked. One of Gulab's two sisters was married to a man whose village was about two miles from Khost, and the brothers were at first told that they would be staying there for some time. In fact, they were to attend the school in Khost for the next six years.

Gulab's father was illiterate. He had not allowed his eldest son to go to school and, as it later turned out, was not going to permit the youngest one to enroll either, but his dealings with the governmental machinery had convinced him that it might be useful to send his two middle sons to school. So in 1956 Gulab and Sur Gul found themselves in school.

The two boys were terrified by the discipline. Whenever they felt the need, teachers and headmasters used the stripped branch of an almond tree on the students. Most of the students were much older than the two brothers; some had spent two or three years in the same grade without learning to read or write. As the central government held the headmaster accountable for the number of enrollments per year—public schooling was in theory compulsory—those students unwilling to attend the classes were dragged there by the school's orderlies. A generous bribe to the headmaster was the only way their parents had to release them from their misery. After their pleas to return to the carefree life of the village were rejected, Gulab and Sur Gul accepted the inevitable and passed their exams regularly. Despite their acclimation, they cherished their three-month summer vacations, which they spent in their home village, sharing the schemes of their age-mates.

Graduation from the elementary school brought about a longer period of exile for the two brothers. Through some connections in Kabul, a member of their lineage learned that the government had established two special high schools for students of the border areas. Unlike other schools in the capital, in the special schools the language of instruction was Pashtu. In addition to room and board, students were granted a monthly stipend. The relative persuaded Gulab's father to enroll Gulab in one of the high schools and to send Sur Gul to a military school, also located in Kabul.

This time, the trip was longer and more strenuous. After tearful partings from their mothers, who entrusted each with a bundle containing clothes, some home-baked cookies, and a cone of refined cane sugar, a band of thirty boys from villages surrounding Khost headed toward Gardez, the provincial capital. Steered by five elders from different clans, the group took three days to walk the one hundred or so miles separating the two towns. They spent the nights in mosques or guest houses of the various clans along the way. It rained on the last day of their trip, and when they reached Gardez not only were they soaked but the sugar in their sacks had melted, permeating all their clothes with a special smell. The owners of teahouses, which also served as guest houses, refused to receive them at first until one of the elders accompanying them found a local friend who intervened on their behalf.

Gardez was much larger than Khost; its size and the number of soldiers pacing its streets awed the boys. They listened with fear as some shopkeepers described the methods of torture that the governor administered to those who dared defy his orders. However, the sight of the trucks on which they were to be taken to Kabul overjoyed them. The trucks were loaded with wood on which they had to sit, but this was the first time most of them were to ride in a vehicle, and they were thrilled at the prospect and pleased to not be walking. They sang Pashtu martial and love poetry and were amazed at the speed of their journey. The trucks were making about ten to fifteen miles an hour!

Covered with dust from the dirt road, they reached Kabul after about ten hours' travel. Henceforth, Gulab's and Sur Gul's lives were to be intertwined with the rapid tempo of political change in the capital. Nobody had any inkling of what the future held in store, of course, and when he was taken to his room in the school and shown his bed, all that a tired Gulab desired was blissful sleep. The night was quiet, but with dawn the new adjustments began.

Life in school resembled that in a military barracks, and there were elaborate rules for what could and what could not be done. The rest of the city remained a great mystery to Gulab and his fellow students. On holidays and Fridays they walked around the town and even at times managed to see a movie, but they never made any real contact with the local people. Gulab slowly mastered the Persian language, but the opportunity to use it was basically confined to the classroom and his weekly rounds in the markets of Kabul. Gulab spent six years in the school, yet not once did he have a meal in a house. The only home he visited was that of the principal, but not for social purposes. The principal was building two new houses for himself, and to avoid hiring labor, he assigned teams of students to work on the site.

In these years, Gulab's perception of Afghanistan underwent radical changes. Textbooks told him of an indestructible country that had managed to resist all attempts at annexation and conquest for some three thousand years. While he readily imbibed this part of the nationalist credo, he was more ambivalent about the portrayal of rural revolts. The textbooks painted an image of a progressive central government whose designs were destroyed by the bigotry of the rural people. Not far from his school was a monument called the Minaret of Knowledge and Ignorance, which celebrated the victory of the reforming government over the rebels of Khost in 1924. But Gulab had heard a different story about Khost. The elders of the village had told him that they had been resisting a despotic government's interference in their customs and its demands for revenue. At home Gulab himself had repeatedly sung some of the antigovernment poetry of the period. To say the least, he was confused by the discordance of the two versions.

During their three-month summer vacations, Gulab and his brother went back to their village near Khost. Transportation now reached the town, and the boys rode on the back of trucks. They were becoming adolescents, and there was talk of looking for suitable matches for them. As the last year of high school approached, the boys' family arranged their engagements to two girls from nearby villages. Since they had never seen the girls before, they spent long hours wondering what they looked like. Custom allowed the future mothers-in-law to arrange for the couples to meet without the knowledge of their husbands, who played the role of stern patriarchs. Gulab and Sur Gul were finally permitted to see their future wives in the presence of their mothers, but nobody quite knew what to say, and they just stole glances at each other. By that time, vacation was over, and the boys had to return to school.

Life in school was suddenly transformed. A spate of high school student unrest and widespread political agitation at Kabul University had erupted following General Muhammad Daud's ouster as prime minister, a post he had held for about a decade. The movement had taken five years to reach Gulab's school, which was finally in the throes of overdue change.

Food in the school had always been bad. It was common knowledge among the students that part of the funds assigned to their upkeep was diverted to pay for the principal's new houses. Nobody had dared to complain, taking for granted that all government bureaucrats were corrupt. On hearing that the Ministry of Education had considered similar complaints from the students of Kabul University, some of Gulab's classmates decided to follow their example. They even convinced a number of students, including Gulab, to accompany them to the university to talk to the college students.

This was Gulab's first visit to the university. He was amazed to see so many extremely well-dressed girls and boys and, at first, took them to be part of the staff, only to learn they were all students. A number had their own cars, and others used chauffeur-driven governmental cars. When he expressed his surprise at this wealth, a friend commented that these students came from a class other than that to which people like Gulab and himself belonged. Seeing the expression of bewilderment on Gulab's face, the friend explained that the word "class" expressed the difference in wealth and social standing of different segments of society.

Gulab knew that in his village there were people called *mala,* which meant "filled with food," and those called *wigi,* which meant "hungry." He knew that the size of landholdings in Khost was unequal. But a considerable part of the land of one person, if not all of it, would not be enough to pay for one of the cars the students were driving. A thought suddenly flashed through his mind: if the sons displayed so much wealth, how wealthy must the fathers be!

The sight of the university made such an impression on Gulab that he could not absorb the advice he and the other students were given on how to voice their discontent. The idea of bringing their complaints to the Ministry of Education, however, was circulated among his fellow students, and although most were frightened, they all agreed that the situation was intolerable. A few days later, some students challenged the authority of the principal by refusing to eat their supper. Infuriated, the principal reacted by trying to beat one of them. Others came to his rescue, and a melee broke out between students and orderlies. Some teachers intervened, and soon a representative of the Ministry of Education arrived at the scene of the fight. After inquiries that took almost a month, the school got a new principal, the food improved, and there was no more talk of working on housing sites in the evening.

Soon it was time to prepare for the entrance exam to the university. Only by accident did the students, who were familiar only with writing essay examinations by rote, learn that it was to be of the multiple-choice type. A friend from the university volunteered to explain what this meant and even gave them a trial exam. When the examiners came from the university, they took only a couple of minutes to explain the procedure before administering the exam.

After some six months of anxious waiting, Gulab learned that he had been admitted to the School of Natural Sciences. He was granted a place in the dormitory, where he was to share a room with five other people, none of whom was from the vicinity of Khost. Two were Pashtu-speakers, but the other three spoke hardly a word of it. Also, all professors lectured in Persian. Gulab made a strong effort to understand what was said in class, but he was acutely aware that the students from Kabul made fun of his accent. Not wishing to risk ridicule, he grew reticent in class and would not take part in discussions.

Life in the dormitory was different. Gulab thought it funny that he was becoming closer to his Persian-speaking roommates than to the Pashtu-speaking ones. These last two came from major landowning families, and everybody was soon aware that they had used forged documents on their family income in order to qualify for the subsidies provided by the university. They carried sufficient cash to go regularly to restaurants and movies. When in a good mood, they even spoke of their exploits with women and told Gulab that they made regular visits to prostitutes. Gulab, who had never been told that one could have access to a woman outside the bonds of marriage, now realized there were many things he did not know and braced himself for future surprises.

Gulab's three Persian-speaking roommates came from a background similar to his own. One from the valley of Darwaz, in the province of Badakhshan, told Gulab that his village was right on the bank of the Oxus River, which bordered the Soviet Union. Gulab was amazed to learn that there was a large town on the Soviet side of the border and that it had an airport where some fifteen to twenty planes landed every day. Gulab had been to the airport of Kabul only once, but the description of the Soviet airport convinced him that it was much larger than the Kabul airport. And, he marveled, the airport of the Soviet capital must be even larger than that of a provincial town.

He also learned that people in Badakhshan spoke several languages and that Persian was not, in fact, his friend's mother tongue. It was the same with another of his roommates, who came from a small village in the province of Balkh, in northern Afghanistan, and whose mother tongue was Uzbek. Only the third roommate, who came from Hazarajat in central Afghanistan, was a native Persian-speaker, but even his accent was not like that of Kabul. Although the boys at first hesitated to trust each other, they gradually found that they had a lot in common. Other differences, however, gradually came to the fore.

All were aware that there were students who were members of various political parties, and Gulab had even heard some of them deliver speeches on oppression and class struggle in a corner of the campus where a forum was regularly held. Toward the end of the first semester, one of these boys, who lived in the next room, approached Gulab and asked whether he would be interested in reading some of their literature. Gulab said he would not mind, and the student gave him three novels written in Pashtu by Noor Muhammad Taraki, who was to become president of Afghanistan some ten years later, after the coup of April 1978.

These books centered on a description of life in rural Afghanistan and of migrant Afghan labor in British colonial India. Religious dignitaries were condemned as parasites, and the consumption orientation of the rural and urban upper classes was deplored. But the books also had a positive message. In each one, the chief character was made to declare that if the working people united, they could put an end to this condition of inequality and abolish the stratification of society.

Gulab was favorably impressed and asked his contact for more material. Meanwhile he discussed the books with his three roommates. To Gulab's surprise, one of the boys told him that although the author claimed to be a socialist, he was in fact a Pashtun chauvinist and that most of his followers were Pashtuns. The second said that he could not possibly agree with an atheistic author, and that Islam, although abused like any other religion, was capable of being generated from within. True equality, he said, had only existed during the reign of the first four caliphs. The third one disagreed with all of them, declaring that the Soviet Union, which had inspired the author in advocating a method of peaceful struggle, was no longer revolutionary. He maintained that the only revolutionary country in the world was the People's Republic of China, that the only true harbinger of the future was the Maoist group in Afghanistan. Taken aback, Gulab did not know how to respond. When his three friends realized that he had not, in fact, joined the party of Taraki, they each urged upon him their own literature and implored him to meet with their comrades, who would explain their course of conduct to him in detail. Although Gulab agreed to take a look at their material, he had to prepare for his examinations and did not get around to reading it until the next year. But the discussion in the room continued, and while Gulab listened, each of the three boys stuck to his position and attacked that of the others.

One day just before the beginning of the summer vacation, Gulab's brother Sur Gul, who was attending the military academy and whom

Gulab now saw only occasionally, came to his room in great excitement. He had been granted a scholarship to pursue his studies in the Soviet Union and would be leaving in six months. Training was provided by the USSR, the only country offering military aid to Afghanistan. The brothers rushed to the bus station—by now buses were running to Khost—and told a relative who was a bus driver to inform the family of Sur Gul's good fortune. A week later Gulab and Sur Gul left for home.

The family had changed during their absence. Gulab's father and elder brother were now involved in smuggling Pakistani cloth to different provinces in Afghanistan and in taking wood from Paktia province into Pakistan. The father was also negotiating to become the agent of a company that imported spare truck parts to be smuggled into Pakistan. The family, with a group of friends, had bought some camels for transporting the goods across the border. They had also invested in a minitruck, and Gulab's youngest brother, who had not been sent to school, was transporting people and goods between Khost and the surrounding villages. The family members were wearing better clothes and eating more meat and rice than during Gulab's childhood.

Upon the boy's arrival, the topic of conversation became Sur Gul's impending departure and the responsibilities of the family. Although everybody had heard that the Soviet Union was an atheistic country, the father and elder brother were not particularly worried by this and were happy that Sur Gul had been granted the scholarship. An officer who was related to a business associate had told Gulab's father that recipients of these scholarships advanced very rapidly in their careers and were bound to be entrusted with important governmental posts. Obviously, all the family would gain from his influence.

The discussion turned to the marriage of the two boys. As Gulab was older, he was expected to marry first. The plans had been that Gulab's marriage would take place in a year and Sur Gul's in three years. But Sur Gul's imminent departure changed the whole picture. The family could not meet the expense of two marriages on such short notice and yet did not know how to avoid hurting Gulab's feelings and violating the custom. Sensing the dilemma, Gulab came forward and said there was no need for him to marry at the moment, that he would go and explain the problem to his future in-laws. The father and the elder brother agreed and advised Gulab that when he paid his visit, he should take a sheep and some special presents. Without the consent of Sur Gul, it was decided that his wedding would take place in a month.

On the eve of the occasion, Gulab's father, his four sons, and some of the elders of the village drove to the bride's village and gave her father the last installment of the bride-price. Half of the money had already been given at the time of the engagement. The total sum amounted to fifty thousand *afghanis*—the price of one acre of irrigated land—and the family spent another ten thousand on the marriage ceremony itself. The teenage bride was brought to Sur Gul's village, and during his five years in the Soviet Union she stayed with his family.

Meanwhile, Gulab gained the confidence of his future mother-in-law, and several times she allowed him to visit his fiancée alone. Gulab found her quite pleasant and was fairly happy with what fate had brought him. He was so busy during all these months that he completely forgot about the literature that his roommates had given him. He saw the books again as he was preparing his bag just before leaving for Kabul.

The political climate of Kabul was as intense as ever, and Gulab soon found himself in the midst of conflicting demands. There were frequent demonstrations, speeches every day in the special corner of the campus, and intense discussions in the dormitory on the merits and shortcomings of various parties. Professors took sides more or less openly and actively tried to build a loyal following among the students. There were allegations that grades reflected the political beliefs of the students more than their competence. There were also rumors that some of the professors took bribes and that most of the rich students were passing without studying. There was even talk that some members of the faculty took advantage of female students. Everyone was full of accusations, and Gulab did not know whom to believe.

As he slowly read over the material that he was given, one question bothered him more and more. What did all this have to do with Afghanistan? He read the Chinese attacks on the Soviet Union and those of the latter on the former. He read fragments of a piece on how out of ten hours of work the workers were given wages for only five, but there were very few industrial workers in the country. Even the literature of the Muslim group dealt with Syria and Egypt. Gulab spent most of the year considering the merits of the pieces he was reading and preparing for his exam.

From time to time, his father and two brothers from the village would visit him on their way to other provinces in Afghanistan. Gulab's father even spoke of buying some land in northern Afghanistan. Gulab's involvement in the family economy was minimal; he was never asked his opinion and kept his thoughts to himself. But even in his own mind he did not know how to react to the relative expansion of his family's resources.

When Gulab returned for his vacation, plans for his wedding were under way, and he was soon married. By the time he left, his wife was expecting a baby. Gulab, of course, had no income of his own, and all the expenses of his wedding and the maintenance of his wife were paid by the family. He took advantage of every major holiday to visit home, but as the trip took two days each way, he could not make it as often as he wished.

By Gulab's third year of studies, things at the university were in turmoil. Demands for the establishment of a student council led to a full-scale student strike, and the government stopped supplying food to the dorms and asked the students to leave. Although the university was officially closed for some time, committees of students and faculty met regularly and became even firmer in their demands. Students raised funds from inside the country, and even Afghan students from abroad sent money to provide food for the university. It was during this strike that Gulab became known as a sympathizer of Taraki, although he had not officially joined his party. One day he was taken to Taraki's house, which was located only a couple of miles from the campus. Taraki was a plump man with a clean-shaven head. In his humble manner, he told the group that their demands were legitimate and that history would prove them right.

Gulab was becoming fairly active in the strike when he received a message that his father was seriously ill. He reached home just in time to witness his father's last words, a request that his sons remain united. With the death of his father, the authority in the house passed over to the elder brother. Since harvesttime was approaching and the family had been deprived of an active member, the elder brother asked Gulab to oversee the management of the house. Gulab stayed the summer until the university reopened. During this time his wife gave birth to a son.

Back for his final year at the university, he continued his political activity, which now included trying to recruit others to his beliefs. He was told by members of Taraki's party to make use of his knowledge of local conditions to attract the sympathies of students from the region of Khost. Although some joined, others were quitting. The membership of the various groups was not stable, and there was much crossing over. Gulab himself did not feel particularly bound and still did not join Taraki's party officially. There were more strikes, more protests. All of the city was gripped by the debates in parliament on the question of languages. A proposal for turning Pashtu into an official language was being considered, but for months the quorum was not met. There was also pending a treaty with Iran on the division of the waters of the Helmand River, which had become an issue throughout the country; this was portrayed as an act of national treason by all the opposition parties. Just as Gulab was preparing for his final examinations in the university came the coup of 1973.

General Muhammad Daud, cousin and brother-in-law of the king and prime minister from 1953 to 1962, overthrew the monarchy and declared the republic. A large number of the posts in the cabinet were given to junior officers, who according to rumors were sympathetic to the parties on the left. Yet open political life in the country came to an end, continuing only underground.

Gulab received his B.A. in chemistry and was assigned to teach high school in the valley of Aryoub in Paktia province. Aryoub was not very far from Khost, but as it was not on the road between Kabul and Khost, Gulab had never been there. As he rode on the back of a truck toward Aryoub, he was amazed by the beauty of the forest that unfolded in front of his eyes. Unlike the semibarren valleys that surrounded Khost, the mountains were all densely covered with trees. To his dismay, he learned that even from here the wood was increasingly taken to Pakistan. The only government-owned forest was located near the border, and only there did some reforestation take place.

Gulab did not expect the school where he was to teach to be built like the one in Kabul, but he was not prepared for what he saw. The high school, which served about six hundred students, was an old mud house, and most of the classes were held in the open air. Whenever it rained, classes had to be canceled. Next to the school was an unfinished two-story concrete structure; Gulab was told that this was to be the new school, but that contractors and government officials had stolen from the allotted budget and it remained uncompleted. The minister of public works of the new regime had come to the valley, but despite the petition he was presented with by the teachers, the only outcome of his visit was a report in the national newspapers stating that he had been satisfied with the 95-percent completion of the work.

Although all of Gulab's teaching of chemistry was confined to illustrations on the blackboard, he found the students attentive. Only he and the principal, who had a B.A. in literature, were graduates of the university. The other ten teachers had anywhere from six years of schooling to specialized training in teachers' institutes. Despite the seeming geographical isolation of the place, currents of ideas from the rest of the country were very much present. Students quickly started asking Gulab about the political movements in Kabul, and he found out that the teachers had very definite commitments.

Whereas students and teachers were divided along lines similar to those found in Kabul, there were also movements among the peasantry aimed at the revitalization of Islam. A number of theology students, trained in schools in Pakistan, were coming back and trying to teach the peasants what "true" Islam was all about. Gulab also heard of the emergence in a neighboring valley of a soldier as a holy figure; in six months the man had a major following. When the more orthodox *mullahs* challenged him to a debate, his lack of knowledge of Islamic sources was exposed, and he was forced to leave.

While in Aryoub, Gulab sent the major part of his salary home. His wife and child were not with him, and he found his assignment cumbersome. Two years went by. Finally, through some friends and relatives, he secured a contact in the Ministry of Education and managed to be transferred to Khost. The town had changed considerably. There was a German-operated hospital, as well as a center for reforestation. Shops built of concrete were replacing the old mud structures, and buses and taxis left almost every hour for Kabul. Half of the road to Kabul had been paved; this section could be traversed in about two hours, while the unpaved portion required from four to five hours. Students and teachers were politically active, and the deputy governor, who had had no formal education himself, kept a wary eye on their activities.

Gulab's elder brother had visited Mecca and was now known as Haji. He had expanded his operations and had even bought a house in Khost, where all the male members of the family stayed when they had to remain in town. The youngest brother had also married. Sur Gul was back in Afghanistan and had a post in the armored division in Kabul, but he did not have a house of his own in the city, and his wife had to stay with the rest of the family in the village. Every other week he went to see her and his daughter. (Gulab too had a daughter now.) Although Sur Gul did not share his thoughts with the other members of the family, he confided to Gulab that he had secretly joined Taraki's party and that conditions in the country were coming to a head-on collision. Dissatisfaction with Daud was growing because officers in the regime were being fired, and the regime was drawing closer to Iran.

When one day in April 1978 Gulab heard on the radio that as a result of their demonstrations in Kabul Taraki and some other members of the party were arrested, his thoughts went to the safety of his brother. Two days later, however, Daud was killed while resisting a coup, and Taraki became president, prime minister, and chairman of the revolutionary council. Two of Gulab's professors were appointed to the cabinet, as well as some friends of Sur Gul from the armored division. Gulab soon learned that Sur Gul, having played an important role in the coup, had been appointed garrison commander, fulfilling the duties of a general. Because Sur Gul was now too busy to leave Kabul, he asked that his wife and daughter be sent to join him. He had been given an apartment and could provide for them. When Gulab took Sur Gul's family to Kabul, he was asked to join Taraki's party and was told that if he wished, his transfer to another ministry in Kabul could be easily arranged. He answered that he would join the party but preferred to stay in Khost for a while.

Most of the people in the country were stunned by the takeover by Taraki's party and could not really believe it. Many were happy that the old regime had come to an end, and people in Khost were pleased that

Taraki was giving his official speeches in Pashtu. Neither the king nor Daud had ever done so, although ethnically they were Pashtuns. But after some months, disturbing news started to emanate from Kabul. There were rumors of mass arrests and torture of people whom Gulab had gotten to know in his years at the university. There were also rumors that Russians were in charge and that in response to local armed resistance the government had dropped bombs on villages in the province of Jalalabad. Parties of people arrived from Kabul and crossed the border to Pakistan. Soon, a number of them were crossing back into the Khost region, openly declaring that they were going to fight the government. Religious dignitaries asserted that religion was in danger, and landlords and moneylenders said that the state was going to confiscate all the belongings of the wealthy. Everybody was taking sides, and people seemed hesitant to speak in front of Gulab.

Government officials said that they were not afraid of any party and that whoever opposed them was reactionary and would be punished. They soon showed that they were not talking lightly. One day, people who came from the Aryoub Valley brought the news that planes had bombed the neighboring valley. One after the other, reports of bombing came from every corner of the country, including almost every valley of Paktia province. Business came to a standstill, and few dared go to Kabul.

In the midst of all this uncertainty, Sur Gul sent his family back to the village. He wrote that he could not live with an ignorant rural wife and was going to marry a member of the party from Kabul. This news made Haji and Gulab's youngest brother so furious that they disowned Sur Gul. Haji also announced that he was going to join the opposition and cross the border; the youngest brother said he was going with him.

Gulab, by this time, was under considerable pressure and did not know what to make of the situation. On the one hand he was witnessing considerable suffering; on the other, every day the radio was proclaiming the glories of the revolution and its achievements for the toiling people. But then came another piece of news. Taraki had been removed from office and replaced by his deputy, Hafizullah Amin. Some weeks later, Taraki's death was announced. Then came news of a huge attack by some four hundred tanks on the town of Gardez, a display of muscle by the central government intended to intimidate the rebels. Khost, by that time, was more or less isolated, and few dared move out of it. Gulab was still teaching in the high school, but the number of students was decreasing. Whereas previously nobody had ever asked him whether he prayed, now he had to attend the local mosque and pray with the congregation. The people who showed concern were not strangers; they were his in-laws and kinsmen, who told him openly that unless he sided with them, they could not guarantee his safety.

Thus, all his life unrolled in front of his eyes in the early chill of a December morning in the mosque of Khost. Gulab realized that he had to make a decision soon. He could join his brother in the capital by becoming a member of the bureaucracy and embracing the ideology of the emerging regime, but he would have to sacrifice his ties to the community where he was born. He could ally himself with his other two brothers in rebelling against the central government; in so doing, he would affirm traditional family ties at the risk of becoming an émigré, severed from his homeland. Neither route could promise safety and security, for the future was too uncertain.

Just as the prayer ended, a soldier came running in, shouting that the Russians had taken over the capital and that President Amin had been shot. There was sudden silence, then a great flurry of noise and activity. Gulab knew that there was no more opportunity for postponement. All his life he had been hesitant about making clear-cut decisions; now he could no longer delay. Either choice was going to be painful.

The sounds in the mosque slowly emerged, and there was a cry of *Allah u-Akbar*—"God is great." Yet as he looked out of the window, Gulab could see the red flag of the regime unfurling in the wind on top of the government building.

Gulab is one of some thirty thousand teachers in Afghanistan. In a country where the majority of the people are illiterate, teachers have a very important role to play in implementing the social policies of the new regime. Most of the membership of the leftist parties also comes from the ranks of the teachers. All were confronted with more or less the same choice.

## A NOTE ON SOURCES

This essay is based upon fieldwork conducted in Kabul and the provinces of Afghanistan, including the town of Khost, during the period 1973 to 1977.

## SUGGESTIONS FOR FURTHER READING

Unfortunately, most of the works on the Afghan civil war in English are generally poorly informed and highly ideological. Readers interested in learning more about contemporary Afghanistan should begin with Louis Dupree, *Afghanistan* (Princeton: Princeton University Press, 1980).

On the civil war, Olivier Roy, *Islam and Resistance in Afghanistan* (Cambridge: Cambridge University Press, 1986), is recommended. See also M. Nazif Shrani and R. Canfield, eds., *Revolutions and Rebellions in Afghanistan* (Berkeley: Institute for International Studies, 1984); and Hafeez Malik, ed., *Soviet-American Relations with Pakistan, India and Afghanistan* (New York: St. Martin's Press, 1987), especially the present author's "The Afghan State and Its Adaptation to the Environment of Central and Southwest Asia," pp. 310–33. Also my "Persian Literature of Afghanistan, 1911–1978," in *Persian Literature*, ed. Ehsan Yarshater (Albany: State University of New York Press, 1988); the evolution of urban elite Farsi culture is discussed on pp. 428–53.

# TWENTY-THREE

# Sumaya: A Lebanese Housemaid

*Leila Fawaz*

Wars and civil strife have played an enormous role in the lives of Middle Eastern men and women in the twentieth century, as we have seen in the preceding biographies in part 3. Nowhere is this truer than in Lebanon, where a bitter civil war has raged since 1975. Even at this writing (1991), despite the reestablishment of the authority of the state (under Syrian auspices), it is by no means clear that Lebanon's sufferings are over.

The story of Sumaya's life helps us to understand some of the forces that have shaped Lebanon in the postwar era. One is the collapse of the Lebanese peasantry. Between the 1950s and 1980s, Lebanon was transformed from a country with 40 percent of the population engaged in agriculture to one with fewer than 10 percent. The declining fortunes of Sumaya's family in the village of Dakkoun are typical of many Lebanese peasant families. The crash of the Intra Bank in 1966, in which Sumaya (along with many others) lost most of her savings, was a major event that helped expose some of the simmering tensions between the Lebanese establishment and the Palestinian bourgeoisie. The religiously mixed neighborhoods of West Beirut, such as the one in which Sumaya lived, fostered the development of strong ties that transcended ethnicity. Her friendship with the family of the Shiite Muslim janitor who lived in her building may have afforded her a measure of safety when the neighborhood was overrun after 1979 by Shiite migrants displaced by Israeli scorched-earth tactics in southern Lebanon.

Sumaya's life also helps us to understand the civil war differently. For example, we learn that, despite widespread belief to the contrary, mass communal violence was uncommon. While there were massacres, they were caused by the activities of organized political groups and militias and were not the spontaneous unleashings of sectarian rage. As sociologist Selim Nasr has argued, the militias killed people; neighbors did not slaughter neighbors. On the contrary, groups sought shelter from the fighting among other groups. Civil society persisted throughout.*

*Selim Nasr, "The Militia Phenomenon," *Middle East Report*, no. 162 (1990): 7.

In addition to illuminating the resilience of the Lebanese in the face of the unspeakable catastrophe that has descended upon their society, Leila Fawaz's biography of Sumaya, a retainer in her parent's house, brings us into contact with the class system of old Lebanon, in which patron-client networks worked to bridge the gaps between rich and poor, rural and urban, and provide avenues of advancement for many less fortunate people. It was socially acceptable for young Maronite women of poor peasant background to work for a time as live-in maids or kitchen helpers in bourgeois homes in Beirut. Most such young women later married and started families of their own. Certainly such employment was preferable to working in a factory or as a domestic employee working by the hour.

Sumaya was the third of her extended family to find employment with the Tarazis, a Greek Orthodox family in West Beirut. Through a cousin, her father arranged for her to become a maid in the Tarazi household; two distant cousins had preceded her there. Eventually she became accepted as a member of her employer's family. Close personal relationships between employers and domestic servants, now rare in the United States (where the cash nexus has dissolved the sentimental fictions that used to mitigate to an extent the harshness of the class system), were common in Lebanon.

Sumaya's fierce devotion to her adoptive family (that of her employer) and to her neighborhood and network of friends makes her case singular. At first she was a reclusive and irritable presence in the Tarazi household, going about her chores with diligence, but refraining from forming close attachments with family members. As a result of a botched thyroid operation in her childhood, her health was a constant preoccupation for her and probably contributed to her isolation. Eventually her condition was diagnosed, and medication was prescribed that gave her a measure of physical well-being.

When Beirut descended into chaos following the outbreak of the civil war in 1975–76, Sumaya began to come into her own. As the fighting spread to her West Beirut neighborhood, her Greek Orthodox employers sought refuge in East Beirut or elsewhere. Sumaya alone remained, sustained by her indomitable sense of purpose as the guardian of the family home and by her strong attachment to the neighborhood. Her survival attests not only to her own remarkable personal qualities but also to the strength of the patron-client system in Lebanon, of which loyalty was a prime value. In view of the ways in which class tensions helped to destroy the old Lebanon, there is much irony here. —ED.

Sumaya, now a woman in her forties, lives in an empty, half-destroyed apartment in war-torn Beirut, still serving the family she has always worked for, though they themselves have long since left Lebanon. She came to them as a teenage girl in 1960, when it was no longer easy for affluent families in the Lebanese capital to find maids from among the peasants of Mount Lebanon. Placing one's daughters in service in the capital—the financial and commercial center of the Middle East—was more honorable and better paid than sending them to work in a factory or in a public institution such as a hospital or government building or, worse, to do housecleaning by day for various households or businesses, a job for poor Kurdish and Metwali (Shii) women that no respectable mountain Druze or Christian would contemplate.

The affluent families who sought them often took girls younger than their own children. Lebanese maids were regarded as preferable to maids from Egypt and Ethiopia, whom everyone regarded as dishonest and lice-ridden, or to maids from the Philippines or Sri Lanka, who spoke only English and had to be hired through placement offices. The cost of the contract and travel made it difficult for an employer to get rid of a maid if she turned out to be unsatisfactory.

For the Lebanese maids and their families, the small-scale social structure of Lebanon was their best protection against abuses. No social security or welfare system protected domestic help; what did protect them was familiarity with one another's families and backgrounds, and sometimes even personal acquaintance. People tended to hire members of families who came from their own native region or from their own religious or ethnic group. Paternalism and personal ties were common among people who did business together, and these connections extended to the hired help.

Many of these Lebanese girls stayed with the same family for decades. Even though some of the family might not even know a maid's full name, it was not uncommon for its members to take care of a maid when she was sick or grew old. It was not uncommon either to let her have her way in daily matters, such as what to cook for lunch—the big meal of the day—or what television program to watch, as if she were part of the family.

The shortage of Lebanese maids added to their security in the 1960s and 1970s. The few who were available could easily find generous pay and good working conditions. Being in demand gave them some of the protections and some social benefits other societies guarantee through social welfare. They had bargaining power in their dealings with their employers. Ladies avoided boasting about how good their maids were for fear they would be stolen away by higher bidders.

Sumaya exploited her bargaining power to the full to build herself a secure and pleasant nest with her family. She had been sent to work in Beirut to support herself and help support her family. Her father, a small, fragile, and self-effacing man, was burdened by the responsibilities of raising four children. One of them was retarded and kept in Dayr al-Salib, a Maronite monastery northeast of Beirut. Sumaya almost never mentioned him. Her father had been married twice. His first marriage had produced Sumaya and another girl. When his wife died, he re-married and acquired sons, one of whom was the retarded boy. Sumaya was very young when her mother died, and she was raised by her step-mother. She was very mistrustful of people.

Sumaya's world was dominated by men. She almost never referred to her stepmother or her mother, but she talked readily about her father and brothers. She invariably saw to the requirements of her male em-ployers before she concerned herself with orders of any woman, al-though she herself was a paragon of female initiative, courage, and hard work. Men mattered; they made the important decisions.

Sumaya came from the Maronite village of Dakkoun, in a southern, religiously mixed district of Mount Lebanon. It is a village of a few thou-sand inhabitants, now occupied by Druze. It is in a part of the Mountain where destitution was comparatively rare, but people were poor. The subsistence of many families, including Sumaya's, was marginal. Little ever happened there, and when anything did, it was a great event. The recent arrival of electricity had been one of these great events. Enter-tainment was provided by weddings and funerals. The outside world, particularly the political world, touched the village only rarely. Elections and civil wars were noted; otherwise the villagers took no part in the struggles of the capital and other cities on the coast.

The family livelihood depended on a small plot of land on which Sumaya's father grew fruits, vegetables, and the olive trees that provided the family with oil and soap. Like the other peasants, Sumaya's father tried insofar as was possible to be self-sufficient, but the plot could not produce enough to cover all the family's needs. Hence his decision to put his eldest daughter in service in Beirut.

Sumaya's father heard of a Beiruti family looking for a maid through the village network. He got his daughter the job through a distant cousin in the village—almost everyone was related by blood ties or mar-riage. The cousin's son Sami was already employed as a cook in the household where Sumaya was to go. Later, yet another relative of Sumaya, a younger and prettier female cousin by the name of Nawal, joined her and Sami in that same house.

The decision to send Sumaya into service had been prompted by other considerations as well. Sumaya's marriage prospects were poor. She was plain, short, and very thin, the last no virtue among a peasant population, however chic it may have become among the Westernized city people. Her most serious drawback, however, was the sickness she suffered that sent constant spasms through her arms and legs. The vil-lagers thought she was epileptic and that no one would ever marry her. To help cure her, friends and relatives in the village had lit candles, burned incense, blown leaves, and prayed, but all to no avail. Poor, ill, deprived of motherly affection, and a source of some embarrassment to her family, Sumaya had indeed no reason to expect much from life. No wonder her severe face almost never broke into a smile.

When Sumaya started working, her only assets were her youth and the ability to dust and mop the floors. From the start, she struck her employers as clean, well groomed, and well organized, meticulous, and methodical—so much so that as time passed she became very strict about routine and grumbled when it was disturbed. That rigidity had its usefulness, however, because it helped her to maintain a semblance of normality when chaos descended after the outbreak of war in 1975.

Sumaya was also intelligent and quick, though she used her intelligence mainly to come up with sarcastic rejoinders or to bicker with the lady of the house. It also fed her bitterness. She was well aware of the social restrictions her health had brought upon her; at times, she seemed to resent the fact that her father had placed her in service in Beirut, although she looked forward to his relatively rare visits. She was sensitive also to the chasm that separated her from the Beiruti milieu in which she worked. She resented the children of the household in which she labored for all the privileges they had and took for granted.

Her intelligence also helped her improve her lot. She learned quickly and was soon doing all sorts of chores, including cooking. She would have liked to go to school, and she spent hours learning the alphabet and numbers from the children. She questioned them endlessly and with such determination that she eventually was able to write a little, take down telephone numbers, calculate bills, and read a bit. She also developed an interest in current events, especially after war broke out in Lebanon, and followed the news closely on the radio and television. She made acute comments about factional politics and the war that showed solid common sense.

Her poor health continued, however, and her evil temper kept her from getting along with the noisy and demanding children or with the other servants. But servants came and went—to different jobs or to get married and have children, as every successful village girl was expected to do. Sami and Nawal moved on: Sami to become a chef in the grand house of a magnate of the district he came from, and Nawal to marry. Sumaya, however, stayed until whatever dreams of marriage and family she may have had faded away. Her attacks grew worse. She suffered from severe cramps and convulsions; her fingers were freezing as she did the daily chores.

One day, while making *kibbi* (a national dish made of ground meat, cracked wheat, onions, and pine nuts) her hands became paralyzed, and she could not move them at all. At the charity ward of the American University of Beirut hospital, she was examined by a resident, who found out that as a child she had had her thyroid removed because of a large goiter. The surgeon in the squalid hospital had also removed her four parathyroid glands. She was neither abnormal nor diseased, but simply the victim of a mistake. She had endured village sympathy and mockery and missed marriage because of someone else's error. The diagnosis of Sumaya's condition changed her life. Treated with massive doses of calcium powder (pills were too expensive, and she had difficulty swallowing them), her health improved as Lebanon's political health grew worse. She gained weight and felt better; she began to smile, to be friendly and self-assured.

When life began to smile on her, she began to take steps to ensure her old age. For her labor, she received the usual wages. Even though her pay was steadily increased, almost from the very beginning inflation ate away at her income, as it did that of hundreds of thousands of other low-paid people. She started at a modest sixty Lebanese pounds a month (the dollar was then worth about three Lebanese pounds). Although she sent some money to her family, she was also able to save. However, with the bad luck that in the early years seemed to dog her footsteps, she put her money in the Palestinian-owned Intra Bank. At the time it seemed a good move. The Intra Bank had started as a small money-changing bureau but had grown to become Lebanon's leading bank. It had branches in every major Arab city and in the principal capitals of Western Europe and North and South America. Its success, however, aroused the envy of established Lebanese political and financial circles. When a run on the bank in 1966 forced its management to appeal to Lebanon's central bank for help, the latter refused, despite its enormous assets. Sumaya was among the thousands of small investors who suffered from the bank's collapse.

Like others who had been hit by the collapse of the Intra Bank, it took her a while to renew her faith in banking. But after one of her employers' neighbors helped her recover some of her losses at the Intra Bank, her savings grew. The safest investments in Lebanon were thought to be jewelry and land. Although other maids invested in jewelry and, however poor, could be seen with gold teeth in their mouths and with gold bracelets on their arms, Sumaya chose land. In 1973, she began sending money to her family to construct a small apartment for retirement next to their small house. They built it a room at a time as she saved her money. A bedroom and a bathroom were completed.

Sumaya now felt lucky. Now she was doing better than the relatives who once appeared so successful. Sami the cook had committed suicide. No one knows why; perhaps he was having trouble providing for his large family. Hoping for a son, he had fathered eight daughters—a terrible burden on him, as well as a terrible disappointment. Sons are the providers for their parents in old age. Sami grew more and more depressed until one day he shot himself. Nawal was widowed with a child two years after her marriage. Since husbands provide both support and standing in society, this was very hard on her. Sumaya, who had never had all these things to lose, enjoyed her life in Beirut.

Sumaya first began to show affection to pets, then children, and eventually adults. For a long time she had shown none to anyone. Then, a dog named Oscar broke the ice. The son of the household brought Oscar home in 1978. She fought his arrival bitterly and complained of the additional work. When he arrived, she refused to prepare his food, forbade him access to any part of the apartment she could stop him from going into, and generally made everyone wish the dog had never appeared. Then slowly but surely Oscar won her heart, and she became more attached to him than to anyone or anything anyone could remember. Within six months, Oscar was her favorite companion. They became inseparable. She played with him, walked him, and took care of him. Every day she took him all around the quarter and across al-Sanayeh, one of the very few public parks left in Beirut. Everyone in the neighborhood became used to the familiar sight of Sumaya, pocketbook and house keys in hand, strolling happily with Oscar on a leash.

So attached to Oscar did she become that she refused to leave him when in 1982 the Israeli siege of West Beirut forced many of its inhabitants to flee. Not Sumaya. Since there was no way to get the dog to East Beirut or into the two-room cottage where eight members of the family had sought refuge, she stayed in West Beirut. Eventually the bombing and shelling drove even her out of the quarter, but by then she could take Oscar along. She went to Faraya, a ski resort in Mount Lebanon where members of the family owned a chalet. There, Oscar enjoyed the countryside and ran around with Sumaya until it was possible to return to Beirut.

In the meantime the children who had long since grown up and gotten married began to bring back their own babies. Sumaya learned to love the next generation as much as she loved Oscar. She retained some of her acid tongue when dealing with their parents, but she could not resist the appeal of the young ones. Through them, she came as close to experiencing family love as she had ever done. She also began to make friends. She became particularly attached to a dressmaker in the neighborhood by the name of Geneviève and to the building's janitor Hasan. Geneviève was a Maronite, like herself, but Hasan was a Shii from the south of Lebanon. He had worked in the building for years. He had seven children and was proud that his eldest worked in a bank. He felt very protective of tiny Sumaya and took care of her as if she were his sister.

Sumaya became something of a snob; at least, she insisted that her friends be "respectable." After the war broke out, a tough ruffian and militia gang leader by the name of Abu Muhammad came to live in one of the two basement apartments of the building. He was eager to be accepted by the neighborhood and tried to be friendly. But Sumaya disapproved of him, kept him at a distance with her severity, and never allowed any friendship to develop between his family and herself. In contrast, she befriended the occupant of the other basement apartment, a widow by the name of Thérèse who had learned the skills of a manicurist to support her family after her husband died under mysterious circumstances; he was a low-ranking policeman who, it was rumored, took to dealing with arms when the war broke out. His service as a policeman, however, and the fact the family had lived in the building for years apparently made his widow acceptable.

Sumaya took particular pride in one of her respectable friendships. Across from the apartment where she worked lived a well-off family with a schizophrenic daughter named Hoda, who was kept at home and regarded as an embarrassment by the family. No one in the neighborhood talked to her, and children were afraid of her odd looks and ways. When she was feeling well, however, she craved company and spent hours on the balcony overlooking the other apartments. Sumaya herself, in between chores and especially after the noon meal, used to sit on a rear balcony attached to the kitchen, facing the balcony where Hoda spent her time. Sumaya and Hoda somehow started talking, their voices carrying over the open space separating the two buildings. Then Sumaya took to visiting Hoda to take lessons from her on how to count and read. Sumaya was proud of having for a friend the daughter of someone of the social standing of her employers. Unlike most people in the neighborhood who shunned Hoda and called her crazy, she felt compassion toward her. One day, however, she became frightened when Hoda got out of control and talked and behaved in a very odd way. Shortly after, Hoda was committed to a mental hospital by her family. She is still there, and Sumaya has not seen her since. Geneviève and Hasan are still in West Beirut, and Sumaya sees them daily.

The war in Lebanon coincided with a rewarding time in Sumaya's life. The worse Lebanon became, the better she felt. For the first time in her life she had friends and good health. She had nothing to lose before the war started. She is as close to happiness as she has ever been. Her inner strength has also helped her cope with thirteen years of relentless war. A small, determined, courageous woman, she alone guards the apartment whose owners have departed for safe havens in Europe and the United States. Daily she copes with power outages, water shortages, telephone breakdowns, shelling and bombing, news of kidnappings, and death. Most of the apartments in the neighborhood are now deserted or occupied like hers by the servants of owners. They stay to keep refugees from squatting in the apartments, which can happen the instant they are vacated.

The family apartment is now half-destroyed; the best furniture is stored away. It looks desolate. It has also been hit many times in the battles and skirmishes between rival neighborhood militias. On several occasions, its windows have been shattered, replaced, and shattered again. On one occasion, a bomb exploded in one of the basement apartments directly under Sumaya's, shaking the building and starting a fire that raised and cracked its marble floors. Everywhere there are signs of desolation and damage, but Sumaya continues to clean and care for it as if it were in its best and most elegant days.

Sumaya also helps take care of the building. Before the war, it too was very elegant; its black iron gates always stood open. Now they are always locked to keep out the marauders who roam the streets. Still, Sumaya and her neighbors continue to wash its marble steps and its hallways and keep its elevator clean. Even before the war, the responsibility for public spaces was mainly in the hands of the owners; the municipality did little. Now it has almost ceased to function altogether. Sumaya keeps the stairs and walkways clean to fight the ravages of war in her own way.

As Sumaya learned to cope with daily life under the changing fortunes of the family and the war, she grew from housecleaner to housekeeper. At the death of the head of the house in 1976, she took charge and, subtly but surely, transformed her relations with his widow from those of a subaltern to those of a companion. By then, the two daughters of the family had gotten married and had moved away. The son then left at home was in turn married in 1979. The following year, he and his bride moved in with his mother when it had become too dangerous to live apart and too difficult to keep in touch. Through it all, Sumaya continued to take charge of most daily matters and sought the family's advice less and less often, until she dispensed with it almost entirely.

Sumaya's strength of character became apparent whenever there was shelling and bombing. Like everyone else, she was no doubt afraid, but she rarely showed it and never lost her self-possession. On one occasion in 1984, when the Shii militia reestablished their control over West Beirut after days of terrible fighting, Sumaya, her employer, the employer's son, wife, and two-year-old daughter spent the night in a minuscule ironing room considered best protected from shelling. Sumaya remained the calmest of them all. In the morning, Sumaya was the first to emerge. She went to the kitchen and cooked macaroni and meat so that the baby would have a proper meal.

She began to show affection for the family more and more often. She discovered how attached she had been to the two older children who had gone abroad. One daughter, who always sought her advice on what to wear and what to do, returned for a visit to Lebanon. When she left again, Sumaya was in tears. It was the first time anyone remembered her crying.

She has adamantly rejected offers that would move her to Christian East Beirut or to Rabiya, a suburb east of town where Sumaya's employer, after she was widowed, was considering moving into a grand villa, now rented to the British ambassador to Lebanon, which belonged to one of her daughters and her son-in-law who resided abroad. The villa was relatively safe and spectacularly beautiful, with the best that money can buy in Lebanon and abroad. They also promised not to add to Sumaya's burdens, for the villa was in the care of two servants. But again Sumaya refused, and so the widow rejected the villa and went abroad. Other offers were as firmly rejected. She prefers to stay in the only neighborhood and apartment where she has roots. She is not likely to change her mind. Although she is a Maronite woman living in a Muslim militia-dominated area, she is so at home there that the militia who surround the apartment call out their greetings to her when she goes for groceries or to clean the balconies.

As Sumaya was left alone in the apartment, the process by which she had slowly acquired responsibility for it was completed. When in 1987 a member of the family visited Beirut, she was left with the distinct impression that she was Sumaya's guest. By then, Sumaya had moved the television from the kitchen to the sitting room. At the same time, she never ventures into family bedrooms and fiercely protects them from intruders. She continues to sleep in an attic, and she takes no advantage of the many spacious rooms left empty.

The war has not left her untouched either. The small apartment for her retirement is outside her reach, for her Maronite native village has been taken over by Druze. Her savings are melting as the Lebanese pound loses more and more of its value. Her three thousand a month should be a great improvement over the sixty Lebanese pounds she started with. But the pound has lost its value relative to the dollar (the dollar is now worth some four hundred Lebanese pounds). The rate of inflation is very high and continues to escalate unchecked, putting beyond Sumaya's means the simplest luxuries and even elementary necessities.

The war has made refugees of her own family, and she is out of touch with them for long stretches of time. When war broke out in the Mountain in 1983, Maronite Lebanese Forces warned the villagers in Dakkoun that they were about to fight the Druze and told them to go seek refuge for the night in Damoor, a Christian town on the coast between Sidon and Beirut. The villagers had no choice but to depart, but they were never able to return. The Lebanese Forces lost, and the Druze took the village and gave out its houses to their own refugees. Sumaya's family left without belongings, but her stepmother at least had the presence of mind to take their identity cards and what little cash they had.

For some time, Sumaya was without news of them and had no idea what had happened or whether they were dead or alive. She learned later that they had at first found refuge in a Maronite convent near Sidon; then, a few months later, they had taken a boat from Sidon to Jouniye, another port in the Christian-dominated area north of Beirut. From there, they reached Ashrafiya, the Christian quarter in East Beirut and settled in with their son Ilyas.

Ilyas, Sumaya's half-brother, was in no condition to take care of them. Devoid of both schooling and skills, he had always had trouble keeping a job. Sometimes he lived in the village, sometimes in West Beirut. During the war, he moved to East Beirut. He got odd jobs, usually as a waiter or kitchen help. In one of these jobs he lost half a finger in a blender and was never compensated for it. In East Beirut, he also found jobs from time to time. He now lives in Sin al-Fil, a suburb in East Beirut. He rents a room in an apartment that once belonged to a Druze family but has now passed into the hands of Phalangists. His parents share his room. Sumaya gives them money and occasionally makes the dangerous crossing between East and West Beirut to visit them.

Sumaya's sister has fared a little better. Before the war she married a school-bus driver and lived with him in Ashrafiya. When the war made it unsafe for parents to send their children to school in buses, her husband lost his job. He emigrated to Australia, and that is where they now live. Sumaya's family responsibilities have increased, as she is the only one of the family who has a steady income and lives nearby. But none of them will accept her sister's offer to come to Australia.

Sumaya also keeps in touch with her other relatives. One of her cousins works as a taxi driver, shuttling between the village and Beirut. He carries several taxi fares at once. One day one of his fares began to tell the other passengers about his troubles. He had lost everything. He did not know how he was going to take care of four children orphaned by the war and left in his charge. Sumaya's cousin offered to take care of one of them; he was married but childless. The man agreed, and Sumaya and her family, poor as they are, were pleased to acquire yet another relative.

Sumaya's struggle with ill health helped her to develop the moral qualities needed to survive the hardships of urban warfare. She exemplifies the courage and resilience of the neglected silent majority who remain in Lebanon against all odds.

## A NOTE ON SOURCES

Information on Sumaya's life has been gathered from interviews with her and with Claire Tarazi, Randa and Nakhle Tarazi, and Hoda and Eli Saddi.

## SUGGESTIONS FOR FURTHER READING

The best introduction in English to modern Lebanese history is Kamal S. Salibi, *The Modern History of Lebanon* (New York, 1975). It should be supplemented with works by Toufic Touma, Dominique Chevallies, Samir Khalaf, Boutros Labaki, John Spagnolo, and Leila Fawaz (for complete references, see the bibliography following the chapter by Akram Khater and Antoine Khater).

The war in Lebanon has been extensively examined. The most useful works include Kamal S. Salibi, *Crossroads to Civil War: Lebanon, 1958–1976* (Delmar, N.Y.: Caravan Books, 1976); Walid Khalidi, *Conflict and Violence in Lebanon: Confrontation in the Middle East* (Cambridge, Mass., 1979); Richard Augustus Norton, *Amal and the Shi'a: Struggle for the Soul of Lebanon* (Austin, 1987); Roger Owen, ed., *Essays on the Crisis in Lebanon* (London, 1976); Fouad Ajami, *The Vanished Imam: Musa al-Sadr and the Shia of Lebanon* (Ithaca N.Y., 1986); and Nadim Shehadi and Dana Haffar Mills, eds., *Lebanon: A History of Conflict and Consensus* (Oxford: I. B. Tauris, 1988).

A number of memoirs and novels convey the atmosphere of the Lebanese civil war. See especially the novel by Hana al-Shaykh, *The Story of Zahra* (London, 1986). Also Elias Khoury, *Little Mountain* (Minneapolis: University of Minnesota Press, 1989); and G. Khoury, *Mémoires de l'aube* (Paris, 1987).

# TWENTY-FOUR

# Abu Jamal:
# A Palestinian Urban Villager

*Joost Hiltermann*

Abu Jamal has seen a lot: the end of the British mandate over Palestine and
the incorporation of the West Bank into Jordan in 1948, the defeat of Jordan
and the Israeli occupation of the West Bank and Gaza after the 1967 June
war, the "iron fist" policies of the Israeli military government in the early
1980s, the outbreak of the *intifada* (the Palestinian uprising that began in December 1987 and continues to the present). Abu Jamal has managed to survive by taking whatever jobs fate chanced to blow across his path. Thus far he
has been (among his other occupations) a shepherd, a Red Cross relief
worker, a soldier in the Jordanian army, a laborer, a waiter, the manager of a
small café, a construction worker, and a welfare recipient. With this
background, Abu Jamal escapes sociological classification. He is illiterate and a
widower (his wife died in 1986). Due to an accident on a construction site in
West Jerusalem, he has been unable to work since 1973. Most of his large extended family are landless peasants; many work in the fruit and vegetable
trade in Ramallah. Abu Jamal lives in a house rented from an absentee owner
in the West Bank town of Ramallah, supported by his sons and a meager Israeli welfare allowance.

The Israeli occupation has affected Abu Jamal and his family in countless
ways, drastically constraining his movements, his possibilities for work, his access to services. Life has become increasingly hard. None of his four working-
age sons have been able to acquire a regular trade, though they have learned
to read and write. All have spent periods in Israeli jails for resistance activity,
and the fines imposed by the authorities have been a heavy drain on the family treasury. The two oldest daughters are married and live at Se'ir near Hebron. Two young sons and three daughters live at home.

The outbreak of the *intifada* in December 1987 was followed by sharply
worse living conditions for Palestinians. The strikes and increased militancy of
the Palestinians were a response to the brutal "iron fist" policies of the military authorities in the preceding years (under the terms of which beatings,
jailings, and shootings of Palestinians escalated). They also represented the

emergence of a Palestinian leadership within the Occupied Territories capable of undertaking an unprecedented mobilization—in coordination with PLO officials based in Tunis. Because of repeated strikes and Israeli-imposed curfews, living conditions worsened. One means of coping was the development of the informal sector of the economy (in which Abu Jamal was a participant): itinerant peddlers, backyard gardens, chicken farms, etc.

Joost Hiltermann first wrote this sketch in 1987 and revised it in 1989. By this latter date, the *intifada* had been going for two years. His essay reflects the Palestinian sense of optimism about its effects on Israeli society then current and the hope that some solution to their desperate situation might yet emerge. By mid-1991 these hopes had largely faded.

In some respects the life of Abu Jamal recalls that of the Tunisian villager Muhammad Ameur, whose biography can be found in part 2. Neither man fits the portrait of a classic *fallah*, or peasant. Both are fond of the male sociability afforded by the café, and despite a lifetime of work at a variety of jobs both found themselves late in life marooned pretty much where they started, if not economically behind. But Ameur lives in independent Tunisia, while Abu Jamal lives under Israeli occupation in the West Bank. The contrast is a revealing one. —ED.

The sun was setting over Ramallah as I bent my head and, after a short knock, stepped into the dimly lit house in the Haret al-Jiryis in the old city. Abu Jamal sat glowering in a corner of the small, damp room, his hands raised over the coals that lay smoldering in the *kanoun*, drawing intently on his cigarette of homegrown tobacco—what is known in the villages as *hisha*.

Abu Jamal had no reason to be cheerful: his son Nasr had decided to divorce his wife of six months, Nuha, who returned to her father's house in Se'ir. She was what is commonly referred to as *hardana*, disgruntled and unwilling to go back to her husband until he came to fetch her. Now Abu Jamal was faced with the prospect of rocking the family boat—Nuha's father being his cousin, after all—in addition to having to pay the deferred amount of the bride-price (*al-mahr al-muakhar*) for the divorce, if in fact it was to take place. Given his precarious standard of living, it was probably the second punishment he feared most.

Abu Jamal does not fit in any neat sociological category. Historical processes have thrown him and his family among the in-betweens of human society, who constitute, however, a major component of Palestinian society. Raised in a family of peasant origins, he is definitely not a peasant: he lives in the city, feeding off the crumbs it provides him and his offspring. He is definitely not a worker in the proletarian sense, as he has moved around in the lower reaches of all possible economic sectors:

agriculture, industry, services. If ever he had a career, it is fair to say that his was a career in honing his survival skills, at scraping through by the skin of his teeth. He and his wife raised eleven children, who will support him until his death.

Abu Jamal was born the oldest son of Abd-al-Fatah Ghanam al-Furukh, in Se'ir, a village northeast of Hebron, in the year 1936. Abd-al-Fatah moved with his small family up to Ramallah the same month that Abu Jamal was born. A landless shepherd, he was unable to sustain himself, his wife, and child in the native village, and the city beckoned with the prospect of work in the booming stonecutting industry and with the support of those relatives who had preceded him in his journey northward.

Unable to find housing near the Manara, the square that is the hub of the twin towns of Ramallah and al-Bira, Abd-al-Fatah moved around from place to place, finally settling in the old city of Ramallah in a house owned by the Shunara family. Aziz Shunara, like many Ramallah Christians, had made the big move to America, leaving his property for rent at a rate that, due to rent-control regulations, is low today compared with new housing: one hundred Jordanian dinars per year (or about twenty-five dollars per month). By the early 1980s, the al-Furukh clan (*hamula*) had become firmly ensconced in the original town of Ramallah, its twenty families (*dawr*) making up perhaps one-fourth of its population. They share this small area of one square kilometer surrounding the fifteenth-century mosque with other Se'ir families (the Shalaldas, the Umturs, the Jaradats) and a number of families from Dhahriya, south of Hebron. Now relatively few of the original Christian families remain in these old parts.

Immigration from the economically depressed Mount Hebron (Jabal al-Khalil) region northward, which started in the late nineteenth and continued throughout the twentieth century, permanently altered the character of Ramallah's old city. The Hebronites are referred to as Qaysis, as opposed to the Yamanis; both are putative lineages whose members make up the population of the modern Middle East. The differences between the two groups, if they exist at all, are political, not ideological, and families are known to have switched allegiances in the past. Both lineages are represented in Ramallah and the villages in the subdistrict; clashes between them over territorial claims and rights of passage characterize local history. When the first Hebronites came to Ramallah in search of work, being Qaysis, they became retainers for the local landed Qaysi families, working as sharecroppers in the olive and fig cultures and taking the side of the Qaysi families in the latter's conflicts with the Yamanis. They later moved into the building trade and the service sector; in the 1940s, for example, most porters in Ramallah were Qaysis from Hebron.

Being an underclass, the Qaysis from Mount Hebron, who are Muslims, have suffered their share of discrimination at the hands of the established Ramallah families, Qaysi or Yamani. In fact, most Christian Ramallah families refer to themselves as Qais, which, though the same word, is pronounced quite differently from the "Qaysi" with which they designate the Hebronites; in Ramallah, the word Qaysi has now become synonymous with riffraff. The Hebronites, however, continue to refer to themselves as Qaysis with a fair measure of pride. When I asked him about it over a dish of rice and *liya* (the fatty deposits stored by goats near their buttocks, a village delicacy) Abu Jamal declared in his strong southern peasant accent: *Ana min al-Geisiya*—"I am a Qaysi!"

As a boy in the 1940s, Abu Jamal contributed to the income of the growing family by shepherding, running errands, and carrying goods for people. He attended the school run by the Roman Catholic church in Ramallah, but quit after three years. As a result, he never learned to read or write. He has two vivid recollections of World War II. He remembers the blackouts in 1945, when residents were ordered by the British occupying forces to cover their windows with blankets or paint them blue; and he recalls the British soldiers celebrating in the streets of Ramallah after the final victory of the Allied forces. Memories of the war of 1948, and what Palestinians refer to as the Disaster (*al-Nakba*) that followed it, lie closer to the surface. "We were not scared," Abu Jamal recalls now, "because the war stayed far from Ramallah. We trusted that the Arab nations would expel the Jews, sooner or later. Our people used to carry out acts of sabotage and raid Israeli farms and camps. In Ramallah we did not notice much of this." With the defeat of the Arab armies, an uneasy peace came to the area, and with it thousands of refugees expelled from their native lands. Abu Jamal worked the next two years for the Red Cross, distributing relief packages to the newly dispossessed.

At age fifteen, Abu Jamal journeyed to Aqaba to haul goods in the Hashimite Kingdom's southern port: wheat, phosphates, whatever arrived in or departed from this busy port city, Jordan's gateway to the Fertile Crescent. He would return home every forty days or so and stay with his family for a week until new ships arrived and the demand for labor peaked. In 1952 he voluntarily joined the Jordanian army. He remembers training, guard duty, patrols, and occasional skirmishes with the Israelis entrenched across the Green Line, only meters away.

Four years into his army service, at age twenty, Abu Jamal wedded the daughter of his aunt and uncle in Se'ir, as is the custom in Palestinian villages. Um Jamal was barely thirteen when she was sent to Ramallah into marriage. Close kinship ties dictated a minimal bride-price—itself one more reason, aside from the traditionally strong identification with the clan, for a young man of humble means to marry within the immediate family. The oldest son, Jamal, was born two years later. Twelve children followed, two of whom died at an early age. Um Jamal was strong of character, and her stewardship over the family through times both rough and very rough was natural and unchallenged. She was the one who encouraged the children to study, and she would even help them with their homework, though she herself could neither read nor write. Her influence extended beyond the immediate family; others in the neighborhood, as well as more removed members of the clan, treated her with a great deal of respect. When she succumbed to illness and died in 1986, she was deeply mourned and missed by all who knew her. Her youngest child, Ahmad, was only five years old at the time.

At the birth of his first son in 1958, Abu Jamal left the army and set off on a career as roving laborer in Ramallah, performing irregular tasks such as loading and unloading trucks and moving from coffee shop to coffee shop as a waiter. By 1965 he had saved up enough cash to open his own café near the Manara, where he developed his considerable skills as a comic orator and working-class socialite, the antihero who plays the clown at village gatherings and is the butt of many an affectionate joke. Still today he is fondly referred to as Abu Shaham—the Fat One—by his friends and relatives.

The Israeli occupation came brusquely on the unsuspecting Palestinian population of the West Bank and Gaza in 1967, as Abu Jamal recalls:

> Airplanes came flying over. But it was more of a game than a real war. The Arab leaders were lying to us. People were scared. They had Deir Yassin [a Palestinian village near Jerusalem whose 261 inhabitants were massacred by elements of the Irgun, Stern gang, and Palmach on 8 April 1948] in mind. Some were so scared, they fled across the bridge [into Jordan]. I was scared, but I could not leave; I did not want to leave. When the situation got dangerous, we used to go down into the cellar underneath the house. When the Israelis came, we moved to Ein Kinia [a village west of Ramallah] to hide. There was water there for the kids, and shade. Jordanian soldiers were taking off their uniforms and putting on civilian clothes. After one day we returned to Ramallah. The Israelis said that everybody should go to their houses and raise a white flag on the roof. So we put up a white flag and kept it for about a week, like everyone else. We were under curfew, and soldiers searched all the houses.

Normal life remained paralyzed that June, and food was scarce. "There was no flour in the shops," Abu Jamal relates. "So we went down to the UNRWA offices, which were closed, and broke them open to take the flour that was inside. Soldiers were looking on and asked what we were doing. 'We are hungry,' we said. 'We want to eat.' They said they wouldn't stop us."

Abu Jamal's career as a coffee-shop operator did not survive the war. Although he reopened the café later in 1967, he grew increasingly apprehensive about his position in such a public area as a coffee shop, given the proliferation of collaborators, the scourge of the Israeli occupation, and the influence they had on the atmosphere among his customers. He shut down the shop shortly thereafter and sold the business finally in 1971. For two years he worked in the building trade for Israeli contractors ("with the Jews") in West Jerusalem, until he dropped a stone on his foot. After a three-month stint in the hospital, he retired from the labor force. Since then, he and his family have scraped by on the meager welfare check he managed to draw from the Social Affairs Department of the Israeli Civil Administration in the West Bank and on the occasional income from his chicken trade, usually illicit. Toward the late 1970s, the burden of providing the family's subsistence was gradually transferred onto the backs of his sons as they reached their teens.

Today Abu Jamal lives in the house of the absentee Aziz Shunara, which consists of two small buildings, each containing two rooms, located on the square that abuts the Ramallah mosque. Abu Jamal's cousin (who is Um Jamal's brother) and his cousin's wife (who is Abu Jamal's sister) live twenty meters across the way; other relatives are just around the corner. Relations with the remaining Christians are cordial, and confessional differences, which do exist and sometimes are even articulated, play a minor role in the life of the neighborhood.

The bonds with the village remain strong, both because of its significance as the family's birthplace—as Abu Jamal explains—and because of continuing close family ties. Relatives travel back and forth almost daily, if not for family visits, then at least for the frequent major family occasions like births, weddings and funerals, or religious feasts like the Id al-Fitr and the Id al-Adha. Intermarriage ensures that these bonds will not soon diminish. Those members of the clan in Ramallah who still own land in Se'ir return seasonally to the village, where many have retained an abode or where their children have chosen to settle. Most of the landless Ramallah contingent work in the fruit and vegetable trade around the *suq* in the old city or are employed irregularly either in Ramallah or inside Israel, usually in construction.

Some of the al-Furukhs have come into money through the years and have moved into new housing elsewhere in Ramallah or in al-Bira. Some of the young men even ventured across the ocean in search of greater opportunity, often finding life in the United States harsh but profitable. Many of these married a second wife in the States to obtain the much-coveted green card, and some of them never returned to their first wife and the children they sired in Ramallah. Abu Jamal's younger brother Musa managed to make it to the United States in 1978, married, stayed, earned some money, and then was shot to death under yet unsolved circumstances in Boston in 1983. His wife in Ramallah, a mother of six, was forced to look for work in order to survive, since Musa's American wife received most of the small estate. She now cleans houses and offices at five dinars (approximately fifteen dollars) per day and must otherwise rely on the irregular labor of her oldest son, a boy of sixteen.

In spite of or perhaps because of tight kinship bonds, fights among close relatives are frequent and reverberate throughout the extended family. Marriages are a major source of friction, and because of the custom of marrying both a son and daughter off to a daughter and son of a brother or first cousin, the whole clan may get embroiled in minor disputes. At one point in the summer of 1988, relations soured between Abu Jamal and his cousin (his sister's husband) Abu Anwar across the square following a disagreement about the (negligible) inheritance of the husband of Abu Anwar's sister in Se'ir who passed away in July 1988. Abu Saket's death triggered a fight between Um Saket and her oldest son Saket—as well as Abu Anwar's family in Ramallah on the one hand— and Saket's wife, Jamila, who is Abu Jamal's daughter—and therefore with Abu Jamal's family in Ramallah on the other. False rumors fed the squabble. Abu Jamal, for example, claimed that Abu Anwar had poached some of Abu Jamal's chickens from the boxes in front of his house, a charge vehemently denied by Abu Anwar, who subsequently launched a smear campaign against his cousin in the neighborhood. Rejected by her husband Saket, Jamila became *hardana* and returned to Ramallah; Nasr's wife, Nuha, who is a daughter of Abu and Um Saket, was sent packing to Se'ir in exchange. After a couple of weeks, the contestants grudgingly assented to make peace.

Life under military occupation has taken its toll on the family of Abu Jamal. His sons are involved in various trades, but usually for short stretches and at low wages. Although they can read and write, they have not learned any particular trade or skill. Jamal, the oldest son, was managing a coffee shop in an office building at the Manara until he was arrested for membership in a group that was planning armed attacks against the occupation in the summer of 1985. He was sentenced to two-and-a-half years in prison. Nasr, the second son, has intermittently worked at the local Tako tissue paper factory at 60 dinars (180 dollars) a month, including overtime. He spent ten months in jail in 1985–86 on the accusation of being a member of a group that threw a Molotov cocktail at a car driven by agents of the Shin Bet, the Israeli internal intelligence service. Two other sons, both in their late teens, work odd jobs. Khalid took over Jamal's place in the coffee shop when the latter was in prison, and Umar has also worked at the tissue paper factory, at a mere 45 dinars a month, since he is not married. Umar spent three months in prison in 1986 on the charge of throwing stones; as part of Umar's sentence, Abu Jamal had to pay a fine of 140 dinars (about 420 dollars).

That same year Abu Jamal himself was caught transporting chickens from a hatchery in Bet Shemesh inside the Green Line to Ramallah in the West Bank without a license (i.e., without paying taxes), and was ordered to pay a fine of 140 dinars to the authorities. In addition, his chickens and the boxes containing them—at a total value of 450 dinars—were confiscated. It is sometimes difficult to believe how families like Abu Jamal's are able to save up money for the only major expense of their lifetime, the weddings of their sons. According to his own calculations, Abu Jamal shelled out between 4,000 and 5,000 dinars, part of which he borrowed from friends and relatives, for the wedding in July 1986 of his son Nasr—the one who later made several attempts at divorcing his wife, which itself would have cost the family 1,000 dinars, along with the predictable upset in familial ties.

The biggest jolt to the family was the death of Um Jamal in August 1986. Mourning the absence of her two imprisoned sons and virtually pining away because of the uncertainty surrounding the fate of a brother who apparently "disappeared" in Syria, she was not able to muster the necessary physical resources to withstand a bout of hepatitis, nor could her family muster the necessary financial resources to put her up in a hospital to protect her from the constant demands at home. At age forty-two, Um Jamal had come to wield considerable power in the family, virtually running it single-handedly, as Abu Jamal was either away looking for chickens to transport or socializing in the coffeehouse near the *suq*. The gap had to be filled by the second generation: Abu Jamal's younger daughters (the older ones having married and moved back to Se'ir), like Ferial, who had to quit school with her mother's death, and Jamal's wife, Anam, who at age twenty-four had five children of her own to take care of.

Abu Jamal's immediate family circle was thus further reduced. His own father, Abd-al-Fatah, died in 1970. But his mother, Luliya—the Hajja (honorific title given to a woman who has made the pilgrimage to the Muslim holy places at Mecca and Medina)—is still around, a spunky old woman in her seventies and a real tease, who will alight anywhere on the ground in the small neighborhood but who will never ever sit down on a chair. One of Abu Jamal's brothers and two of his sisters died at a very young age; another sister did not survive an illness at age eighteen (an "act of God"—*min Allah*). Now two sisters remain: Um Anwar, who lives across the square with her family, and Um Abbas, who lives with her children in Se'ir while her husband travels back and forth between the village and Ramallah, where he sometimes works selling watermelons and other goods in the market. A picture of Abu Jamal's father, Abd-al-Fatah, a beautiful black-and-white reproduction of the man in his later years, still adorns the wall of Abu Jamal's house.

Traditional village mores remain the organizing force of the Ramallah community, an *idée fixe* indelibly impressed in the consciousness of these semiurbanized villagers. It is as if the social structure of Se'ir has simply been lifted out of the original village to be reproduced intact in the city, minus the social relations generated by immediate access to land and the fruits it engenders. The weight of Ramallah's economic life gravitated long ago toward the dividing line with al-Bira, leaving the old city a peninsula bordering on the main part of town, a virtually self-subsistent (but barely so) economic and social entity with links, not primarily to the Ramallah and al-Bira commercial hub, but to the native village, and through the village to the money that is repatriated by its offspring in the Gulf states and in the United States. The longevity of the community is in doubt, however, as more and more of its members seek their fortunes elsewhere. The older generation is fading, and the Ramallah municipality, faithful to the plans first developed by the late mayor Karim Khalaf, has begun to earmark some of the aging houses for demolition.

In the mid-1980s, women activists linked to the recently founded women's committees tried to interest the women in the neighborhood in their social and cultural activities. So far they have had little success. One reason is the traditional prohibition on village women from moving outside their houses and outside the immediate family circle. Another reason lies in the political affiliation of the committees, which tend to identify with the more progressive blocks in the Palestinian national movement. Abu Jamal's family, like most of the families in Ramallah's old city, displays an unwavering identification with the mainstream grouping in the national movement, and their allegiance to Abu Ammar (Yasir Arafat) as a leader is absolute and unquestioned. In fact, the political action of the residents of the old quarter extends as far as the edge of their communal territory and is usually a direct response to overt repression.

Before the uprising (*intifada*) that began in December 1987, these people were at the heart of the demonstrations against the Israeli occupation—for example, in December 1986 (following the killing of two students in Birzeit) and in February 1987 (during Amal's siege of the Palestinian camps in Lebanon). Their activity consisted of throwing stones at soldiers and burning tires in the general area of the *suq* and the mosque. Although the demonstrations involved mostly children and teenagers under eighteen (especially girls), the older generation gave their full moral support. One turbulent day in late 1986 I ran into Abu Jamal near the *suq* carrying bags of vegetables and groceries; he had taken it upon himself, in the absence of Um Jamal, to do the shopping for the family. Yet—with a whiff of tear gas still in the air from that morning's encounter with the army—this was positively the only day since the death of Um Jamal in August that I saw Abu Jamal with a spark in his eyes and a big grin on his face, as he, like everyone else, was momentarily bathing in a rediscovered sense of self.

The *intifada* tapped long-dormant energies in the neighborhood, while providing new outlets for pent-up frustration and resentment against the occupation. Altercations between children and soldiers, previously the exception, became part of daily life in 1988, and the Haret al-Jiryis was affected as much as any area in Ramallah or elsewhere. In contrast to earlier times, few displayed fear of facing the army, and families have been immeasurably proud of those among their children and siblings who were touched directly by the army's "iron fist." On 8 February 1988, for example, soldiers came to the Haret al-Jiryis to suppress demonstrations that were taking place throughout the town. They ordered residents to remove the barricades of stones, old metal, and other scrap materials that local youths had erected in the narrow alleyways. People refused, which led to an argument. In the melee, someone threw a rock at the soldiers, who responded by spraying rubber bullets at the group of people that had amassed on the square near the mosque, and beat men, women, and children at random, following them even into their homes. Abu Jamal's youngest son, Ahmad, was hit in the buttocks by a rubber bullet. Abu Jamal's daughter-in-law Anam was beaten and could still not move her badly swollen arm after a week. Anam's four-year-old daughter, Amal, was hurt, too. Both had been inside their home at the time of the incident, attacked by soldiers who forced their way into all the houses in the neighborhood.

Many youngsters have been arrested during the uprising, but usually on flimsy charges or on no charges at all, and they would often be released after a few days of punitive detention in prison camps, where they were forced to run the gauntlet of soldiers' rifle butts and verbal and physical abuse. In mid-December 1987, two weeks into the uprising, soldiers came to the house of Abu Jamal and arrested Nasr and Umar, as well as their cousin Khadir from across the square, and took them to the prison camp in Dhahriya, which was opened specifically to accommodate those arrested during the uprising. There they spent twelve days, along with hundreds of other boys averaging age sixteen, packed together in tiny rooms, deprived of washing facilities, and forced to use an overflowing trash can as a toilet, with few blankets and little food. They were released without being interrogated or charged. The family heaved a sigh of relief; they had been saved the extended anguish and steep lawyers' costs that usually accompany the arrest of one of their children. Two weeks later, the soldiers came and arrested another of Abu Jamal's sons, Khalid, who did a similar ten-day stint in Dhahriya and was then released, also without charges. He shrugged as he recalled his experience later; shared collectively by so many of his peers, it had become part of an unremarkable routine.

Not so for deaths. Abu Jamal's family so far has been spared the loss of one of its relatives, but the neighborhood has felt the army's fire. On 20 February 1988, a soldier of the Druze Border Guards fired three bullets at point-blank range at Abdallah Ataya, a young man from the village of Kufr Naima who was fleeing through the *hara,* killing him instantly. In tune with the spirit of the uprising, the whole neighborhood pitched in and erected a marble monument on the spot where he fell, committing the event to the collective memory. Months later, Um Anwar would recount what happened, describing in detail how the young man's brain had lain splattered across the alley that runs next to her house.

As the violence continued, flaring up and receding throughout the year, people tried to make do despite the turmoil, adjusting their lifestyles to the new realities of the uprising. For some, the hardships suffered by others brought unexpected benefits, though no one gained economically from the uprising in absolute terms compared with the previous period. The commercial strike, for example, that was set by the Unified National Leadership of the Uprising to start every day at noon proved a boon to those whose contribution to economic life had always been marginal. In an effort to reduce their losses, shopkeepers in the major towns converted their merchandise to wholesale after twelve, charging street vendors and peddlers with the task of selling their wares from street carts or neighborhood stalls. This informal economy proliferated, defying official strike hours and thriving throughout the afternoon and into the early evening.

Seizing the opportunity, Abu Jamal opened a candy and lemonade store in the doorway of his two-room house, competing with his sister's family across the square for the patronage of the children in the neighborhood, whose regular supply from the corner grocery had been cut off. Even though half his merchandise was consumed by his own children, his income was supplemented by the wages brought home by his sons Khalid and Umar. (The latter found work in an Israeli bakery in Holon across the Green Line.) Nasr, meanwhile, still married to the recalcitrant Nuha, traipsed mopishly around the neighborhood unemployed, incurring the scorn of family members, who were unanimous in designating him as incorrigibly lazy. At the same time, Abu Jamal continued his chicken trade, but the increased police checkpoints on West Bank roads raised the risk of his illicit Bet Shemesh runs, and the income from his feathered contraband was thus reduced to a trickle. By the summer of 1988, he was quietly expressing the intent of doing the rounds of local charities, because although he was loath to admit it, he could no longer make ends meet.

Once the euphoria and pain of the first violent months had worn off, the uprising gradually evolved from a much-discussed exception to the regular way of life, and families like Abu Jamal's made the transition almost unnoticed. One day, eight months into the uprising, in the late afternoon, Abu Jamal was sitting on a stone in front of the house of his sister, Um Anwar, clutching a cup of tea. As usual, the discussion among the various members of the family centered on the latest events in the neighborhood: demonstrations; clashes; army patrols late into the night; soldiers perched in a newly established watch post on the roof of a nearby building, throwing stones at those in the *hara* who dared to leave the sanctity of their homes after nightfall.

Suddenly kids, the oldest perhaps seven, came running out of the little alley, past the monument to Abdallah Ataya, crying *Jaysh! Jaysh!* (The army! The army!) The whole *hara* leaped to their feet, seeking to verify the news. "Where are they?" "In the *suq!*" "How many?" "Just one!" "Only one? It can't be!" "Only one," an older boy who turned the corner confirmed. "It is a trap (*kamin*)!" Scores of children, boys and girls, rushed, stones in hands, past the mosque to the road that issues into the *suq*, then halting, waiting for the *jaysh* to appear, ready to defend the neighborhood, ready too, given the army's inclination to open fire without warning, to give their lives.

After a few minutes, things returned to normal as the *jaysh* failed to make an appearance, except for the fading whine of a jeep engine in the distance toward the Manara. Abu Jamal sat down again in the falling twilight, sighing, lamenting, "Oh, oh, oh, the world is a mess. They are making a mess of everything." "But," his nephew, sitting next to him, retorted, "the uprising is doing a lot of damage to Israel!"

Presently Abu Jamal looked up from the small cup in his hand, a broad grin smoothing out the furrows that mark his face. He beamed as he repeated after the boy, forgetting for a moment his own economic predicament and his intention to turn mendicant, "Yes, it is doing them harm. It is doing them a lot of harm!" And he adjusted his blue hand-knit cap with a slow motion of his hand, rolled himself a cigarette of *hisha,* and calmly drank his tea.

## A NOTE ON SOURCES

This essay is based upon conversation with Abu Jamal and his family over a period of more than four years (1985–89), when I got to know them and they me on an intimate basis. I lived a mere five-minute walk from their neighborhood for three years before moving to Jerusalem, and after that I visited them intermittently until my departure in December 1989. The present essay is a revised and expanded version of my article "Seasoned Migrants to the North," which appeared in *MERIP Reports*, May–June 1987.

## SUGGESTIONS FOR FURTHER READING

Palestinian society under Israeli occupation has been the subject of a number of important recent studies. See in particular Said Abu Rish, *Children of Bethany: The Story of a Palestinian Family* (Bloomington: Indiana University Press, 1989); Naseer Aruri, *Occupation: Israel over Palestine*, 2d ed. (Belmont, Mass.: Association of Arab-American University Graduates, Inc., 1989); Ibrahim Wade Ata, *The West Bank Palestinian Family* (London: Routledge and Kegan Paul, 1986); Paul Cossali and Clive Robson, *Stateless in Gaza* (London: Zed Books, 1986); and Rita Giacaman, *Life and Health in Three Palestinian Villages* (London: Ithaca Press, 1988). My own book *Behind the Intifada: Labor and Women's Movements in the Occupied Territories* (Princeton: Princeton University Press, 1991) examines the role of Palestinian labor unions and women's organizations in the politics of the West Bank and Gaza.

The human rights of Palestinians under occupation are examined in al-Haq, *Punishing a Nation: Human Rights Violations During the Palestinian Uprising, December 1987–1988* (Ramallah: Al-Haq, 1988). The journal of Raja Shehadeh, a Palestinian human rights activist lawyer and cofounder of al-Haq/Law in the Service of Man, although set in the period before the uprising, conveys the realities of life under the occupation. His *Samed: A Journal of Life in the West Bank* (New York: Adama Books, 1984), also published as *The Third Way: A Journal of Life in the West Bank* (London: Quartet Books, 1982) is of particular interest.

A number of American and Israeli authors have discussed the impact of the occupation on the Palestinians and on Israeli society. See especially David Grossman, *The Yellow Wind* (New York: Farrar, Straus & Giroux, 1988). Also Amos Oz, *In the Land of Israel* (New York: Harper & Row, 1987); David Shipler, *Arab and Jew: Wounded Spirits in the Promised Land* (New York: New York Times Books, 1987); Thomas Friedman, *From Beirut to Jerusalem* (New York: Farrar, Straus and Giroux, 1989); David MacDowall, *Palestine and Israel: The Uprising and Beyond* (London: I. B. Tauris, 1989).

The PLO, United States policy, and the international context of the occupation are discussed in Noam Chomsky, *The Fateful Triangle: The United States, Israel and the Palestinians* (Boston: South End Press, 1983). On the dynamics of war and peace, see David Hirst, *The Gun and the Olive Branch* (London: Faber and Faber, 1977).

There are a number of books on the *intifada*. See especially Roger Heacock and Jamal Nassar, eds., *Intifada: Palestine at the Crossroads* (New York: Praeger, 1990); Michael Hudson, ed., *The Palestinians: New Directions* (Washington, D.C.: Center for Contemporary Arab Studies, 1990); Zachary Lockman and Joel Beinin, eds., *Intifada: The Palestinian Uprising against Israeli Occupation* (Boston: South End Press, 1989). For an Israeli view, Ze'ev Schiff and Ehud Ya'ari, *Intifada: The Palestinian Uprising—Israel's Third Front* (New York: Simon and Schuster, 1990).

# TWENTY-FIVE

# Haddou: A Moroccan Migrant Worker

*David McMurray*

David McMurray's portrait of Haddou, a Moroccan migrant, presents us
with yet another facet of the new Middle East: Arab labor migration to Western Europe. The presence of ever greater numbers of Arab workers in the
European economy is a sign of the internationalization of labor (as is the
presence of Mexicans and Hispanics in the United States) and the globalization of the world economy. The sources of this migration are complex; its
consequences for the future of relations between Europe and the Middle East
are considerable.

As in the United States, where World War II hastened the dissolution of
the black peasantry in the South and led to the massive civil rights movement
of the 1960s, the end of the war brought momentous changes for North Africa. One result, to be schematic, was the independence movement of the
1950s and 1960s. A second was a large-scale peasant migration to the cities
not just of North Africa but increasingly of Western Europe as well.

As part of the latter trend Haddou, a Moroccan Berber from the region
around Nador, left his home in northern Morocco in the 1960s and voluntarily expatriated himself to seek work. By this time migrants from North Africa
had already established a beachhead for themselves in Western Europe, where
they did jobs that no Europeans would do anymore. Initially, migration was a
seasonable phenomenon. But by the late 1970s and 1980s it had led to the
emergence of large permanent communities of migrants—with an increasingly problematic insertion into European society. The rhythms of Haddou's
life largely follow this script, though not without complications.

On one level, Haddou's biography can be read as a story of economic success. We can trace his ascent from his early low-paying jobs as a young man in
northern Morocco (the same region of origin as Muhammad El Merid, whom
we met in part 2) to positions of growing income and security in France and
Germany. By careful planning and much hard work, he had achieved his original goal: to construct an imposing home in which he could live in his old age,
surrounded by his married sons and their families. In his dreams, then, he

resembles Assaf Khater, whom we encountered in part 1 (as well as many a successful Sicilian and Polish immigrant to the New World who elected to return to his village of origin to vaunt his new-gained wealth).

Yet this reading contrasts with Haddou's own sense of his life. Despite a measure of worldly success he has not, for all of that, achieved happiness. His years of hard work and voluntary deprivation have gone for naught, and he finds himself in his fifties alienated from his family, his authority not respected. As far as his children (whom he sees only one month out of a year) are concerned, his primary role is to bankroll their desires for the latest consumer items. Even his eldest son, Driss, who now also works in Europe, is a disappointment to him. Instead of sending monthly remittances to the family, as the Moroccan family-centered ethos requires, Driss spends his income on himself and his Dutch girlfriend. (Haddou's feeling of betrayal and his sense of the breakdown of family values give him a lot in common with the Tunisian Muhammad Ameur and the Palestinian Abu Jamal, whose lives are also presented in this volume.)

By the mid-1980s, when this essay was written, Haddou was no longer content with an annual migration to his village of origin. The years of deprivation and loneliness had taken their toll, his estrangement from his children had chilled his welcome. He had begun to establish himself and his wife, Thraithmas, in Düsseldorf. While it is unclear what he eventually decided, one possibility was that he would gradually sever his ties with Morocco and make his home in Germany. If so, he would join the increasing numbers of Turks, West Africans, Yugoslavs, and other recent migrants who have put down roots in the new multiethnic Europe. —ED.

Haddou sat on the bed, thumbing through his passport. It was full of entry and exit stamps from his many trips between his family in Morocco and his job in Düsseldorf, Germany. As the pages flipped he stopped again to look at the visa he had received from the German government just that afternoon. He had to smile, for this newest visa guaranteed him a court hearing before any deportation measures could be taken against him. It made him feel relaxed. He did not need to fear every time the boss yelled at him or every time the border guards interrogated him. He had had very few close calls over the years, but you could never be too careful. He thought of that time when while riding his bicycle to work the cops stopped him, claiming he had run a red light. They said to him, "Hey, where do you think you are, Turkey? Here in Germany we obey the law. Do that again and you'll be riding that bike back in Istanbul!" Haddou was upset that they assumed he was a Turk. It further irritated him that they assumed he disobeyed the law when in fact he bent over backwards to keep his nose clean. With the new visa he would not have to jump every time a police car passed him.

He looked up at the railway calendar on the opposite wall next to his television set. He could not make out the date exactly, for now, at fifty, his eyes were going bad. He put it up mainly for decoration anyway. The calendars were free, given out at the train yard where he worked. He often thought of getting glasses but did not, because he suspected that the railway company might consider him unfit to continue working. His job consisted essentially of copying down the numbers of each boxcar on each train as it came into Düsseldorf. So if he was having trouble seeing and they found out about it, well . . .

Haddou's thoughts always drifted back to Morocco whenever he found himself alone in his railroad company apartment. Thinking about the visa this time set him to remembering what his life had been like before he started migrating to Europe.

As far back as Haddou could remember he had worked. Everyone did. Everyone except his oldest brother, that is. Haddou's father determined that his four younger sons would work and pool their wages so that the eldest would be able to attend school in Fez. Even Haddou's father pitched in. He supplemented the produce from their small farm with wages earned in Algeria. Every year in early May Haddou's father left for Oran province in Algeria to work the harvest on the farms of the French *colons* (settlers). He would then hurry back to harvest his own barley crop the month after.

Haddou's first job was as a ticket taker on the local bus route between Kariat Arkman, a small town near his *char*, or lineage settlement, and Villa Nador, the Spanish provincial capital of the whole region. He got the job during the great drought of 1944–45, when he was only seven years old. Prior to that he had worked on the family farm, watching the goats or helping with the planting and harvesting. The drought proved to be so bad, however, that his father was forced to sell the goats—and that was after the goats had eaten what little of the barley actually sprouted that year.

The whole of northern Morocco was under Spanish protectorate control from 1912 until 1956, the year of Moroccan independence. Villa Nador sprang up in the late 1920s as the easternmost Spanish administrative center. Nador paled, however, in comparison with Melilla, a purely Spanish city less than fifteen miles from Nador on a peninsula jutting out into the Mediterranean. Melilla had been a Spanish garrison and trading center on the coast since the end of the fifteenth century. It exerted a stronger influence than Nador over the surrounding countryside by providing menial jobs for the local Moroccans and by consuming much of the surplus produced on farms in the area. Eventually Haddou found a job running produce into the Spanish city. Every morning throughout the early 1950s he loaded up a donkey cart with eggs or vegetables or fruit—depending on the season—and delivered them to the Melilla market.

When in his late teens, Haddou finally landed a good paying job working in Kariat Arkman in an automobile upholstery shop. Since the business was owned by a Spaniard and all of the customers were Spaniards, when the Spanish population in the region began to decline after independence, so, unfortunately, did the business. Before it closed, however, Haddou managed to save enough money to get married. That same year he and a friend from the shop decided to emigrate to Europe to look for work.

Haddou got up from his bed to make himself a cup of tea. He had a one-burner hot plate and three little teacups. While he was measuring out the tea leaves into the pot, he thought back to his first job in Europe and the very beginnings of his "dream house" idea, as he called it.

Haddou had started as an unskilled construction worker on a job in the outskirts of Paris. He lived in a shack on the site to save money. Many other North Africans lived there also. They guarded the site during the night in exchange for their room. That is how Haddou met the big bosses. Every Saturday evening after work had finished, the architect, contractor, and their cronies returned to the job site. Haddou would open the gate to let them in, after which they would enter his guard hut and pull out the cards and liquor and proceed to play poker until early in the morning. Haddou's job was to wash their cars and then wait outside and stand guard in case of trouble. Since he was a Muslim, they reasoned, he did not want to go out on the town or to play or drink with them. He could thus be trusted to stay nearby, sober and alert. He could also be trusted to guard their liquor stash during the week. They did not have to worry about his taking a nip behind their backs. They did not see the need to pay him extra for his special duties either.

One Saturday night as Haddou sat in the dark, the cars all clean and shiny, the architect came out to stretch. Haddou seized this opportunity to request once more that the architect sketch out a floor plan for Haddou's dream house. He did not know what he wanted exactly from the architect, he just knew that the man was very well educated and very talented and that whatever he designed Haddou would be proud to build. This time the architect obliged Haddou. He quickly sketched on a scrap of paper the rough design and dimensions of a floor plan.

Haddou carried that scrap with him for years, unfolding it every time he thought of his future dream house. He slowly managed to save enough from his wages to put a down payment on a small plot of land on the edge of the city of Nador. That was in the late 1960s. By 1975 he had saved enough to start construction of the house. His land no longer stood on the edge of the city. Nador had grown so much in the interim through migrants relocating their families in the city that Haddou was now starting out to build his house on one of the nicest streets in Nador.

Haddou took his architect's design to a local draftsman to be filled in. He then hired a construction foreman to round up a crew and get started. They came from the region of Ouarzazate in southern Morocco, just like most of the other construction workers in Nador. Haddou liked them because they worked hard for little money and without complaint. They had migrated in search of work just like himself.

The house rose slowly over the next decade. Each year Haddou saved enough to pay for a few months of work. The first year they laid the foundation. The second year they raised the support pillars and laid the first floor. The third year, as soon as the ground-level garage was enclosed, Haddou moved his young family in. He wanted them to start attending the city schools as soon as possible—even if that meant setting up house in the garage. He did this because his vision of the family's future included good schools and then good jobs for all of his boys. He had grown up in the countryside without benefit of education and did not want that to happen to his children.

The dream house actually contained four apartments of five rooms each, two apartments to a floor, each the mirror image of the other. When they grew up, Haddou figured, each of his boys and their respective families would get an apartment. As the house was being built, he occasionally reflected on how similar it looked to all of the other buildings in the neighborhood. This was odd because the French architect had never been to Nador and thus did not know what the houses looked like there. What Haddou found out later was that the majority of draftsmen in Nador were unlicensed and more or less trained by each other. Therefore the same three or four blueprints were reproduced with slight variation by most of them. Haddou's architect's design had been quietly but efficiently reworked by the local draftsman to conform to Nador standards.

All of this reminiscing was making Haddou homesick again. He finished his tea, put the passport back in his pocket, and reached for his coat. By the time he stepped outside his apartment in the company's housing complex it was almost dark. He walked to the phone booth on the corner, entered, closed the door, and dialed the number he had dialed countless times before. Hassan, his second son, heard the ring and picked up the phone at the other end in Nador, Morocco. "Is your mother there?"

Haddou always asked first about his wife, Thraithmas. He was crazy about her, as devoted to her now as he had been at the time of their marriage. In 1958 she had begged him not to go to work in Europe. He assured her that he would return regularly. Unfortunately, he had had to wait a long time before his first vacation. His eldest son, Driss, was already over two years old by the time Haddou initially saw him. Even now, after thirty years of marriage, Haddou and Thraithmas has spent less than three years total in each other's company.

In the beginning of his sojourn in Europe Haddou kept in touch with his family in Morocco by means of professional runners whose job it was to transfer money and messages back to Morocco. As the migrant communities grew in Europe, runners were replaced by migrants, and Haddou came to depend on fellow workers from his tribal region to help keep up contact with his family. The migrants took turns relaying greetings and gifts back and forth for each other's respective families. Those who could write sometimes used the mail, but many complained that their letters never arrived or had been opened before arrival. Moreover, the petty bureaucrats in the post office in Nador often forced the migrants' families to buy "lottery tickets" or pay some other form of bribe before receiving their letters from overseas. The postal workers, who made very little money working for the state, were jealous of the uneducated migrants and their relatively large European salaries. They thus seized the opportunity provided by their positions to profit from the migrants.

The migrants' other option was to arrange to make a long-distance telephone call from one public telephone to another. This often proved difficult, however, for international connections took a long time in the early days, reception was bad, and the whole province had to use the same little office in Nador, which created long lines.

The first big change in means of communication came with the spread of the tape recorder, particularly the cassette recorder. The actual voices of the migrants could now be relayed to the families instead of just their secondhand salutations. A minute or minute-and-a-half conversation cost as little as the stamps on the package.

By the mid-1980s, the private telephone had become the communication medium of choice. The wait for phone installation sometimes lasted three or four years, but the freedom it provided from theft, censorship, waiting in line, and general worry was worth it. Most importantly—from Haddou's point of view—the telephone reinstated the migrant as master of the house, whether he was there or not. Migrants in Haddou's position, that is, those who moved their families into the city from the country while they continued working in Europe, customarily demanded that their wives remain in the house during the migrants' absence. Worrying about the well-being and fidelity of the women back home occupied a good share of the migrants' time. Haddou was no different. Once they installed the phone in his house in Nador, however, Haddou could call any time of the day or night to find out if his wife was there. During any given week he called at least three times, always at a different hour and on a different day so as not to establish a pattern. That way no one in the house could plan their activities around his phone calls. He also kept the phone dial in Nador locked so no one could call out but could only receive calls. He could thus monitor and manage the activities of his whole family thousands of miles away. In effect, Haddou transformed the telephone into a technology trap.

Haddou also controlled the household by controlling its purse strings. He sent a monthly stipend through the Moroccan Banque populaire. The bank had established branches throughout Europe and gave the migrants a fair exchange rate to make it easier for them to send money home. The bank had to do something, because most migrants did not trust the banking system. Migrants traditionally brought the biggest share of their earnings home with them at vacation time. Money changers in the Nador market or in the nearby Spanish port town of Melilla then bought the migrants' European currency and sold them Moroccan dirhams. Haddou and the others who worked abroad did this because they feared that the government might some day confiscate their earnings if they deposited them all in Morocco. Besides, the migrants did not want Moroccan officials to know how much they earned so that they could avoid paying Moroccan taxes. They still brought the lion's share of their earnings home this way. Now, however, Haddou also transferred about fifteen hundred dirhams (approximately two hundred dollars) a month to his account in Nador. His son, Hassan, would write a check on the account for the family. Haddou would then telephone instructions as to how the money was to be spent.

Yet try as he might to enforce his will upon them, Haddou's family found ways to subvert his authority during his absence. Even his loving wife, Thraithmas, dipped into the family's monthly stipend. For example, every week or two Thraithmas's mother came to visit. She would stay for a few days and then return home with a little money and some tea, sugar, or meat given to her by her daughter. The mother gladly accepted the food paid for by her daughter because she was dependent on a pitifully small pension from the Spanish government given in recognition of her husband's death during the Spanish civil war. Over seventy years old and beginning to stiffen up, she was also glad of the chance to forgo the hour's walk needed to reach the weekly market nearest her country home.

Hassan, who was in charge of the accounts, skimmed the most. He exaggerated the extent of his school and clothing expenses regularly. Occasionally he pocketed money earmarked for bills and then spent the money in cafés and on other forms of entertainment enjoyed by the richer boys on the block. Even little Murad, Haddou's youngest son, pocketed the change from the daily shopping trips it was his duty to perform. The whole family habitually ran up credit at various stores, which Haddou then had to pay off during his vacation.

These problems with the children began early and at the top for Haddou. Driss, the eldest, disappointed him first by not passing his *baccalauréat* (high school graduation exam) and then by becoming a migrant. Haddou had always intended that he alone would migrate so that none of the others would have to leave home. Unfortunately, when Driss was visiting his maternal uncle, a migrant in Lille, the Socialist government of France declared an amnesty for all foreigners working without papers. Driss's uncle quickly talked his boss into hiring Driss so that he could apply for papers and a visa. The plan worked, and Driss got a job in a warehouse in northern France. But that was only half of the problem, according to Haddou. What was worse, Driss begged off contributing to the household budget from his own salary by claiming that the European cost of living ate up all of his savings. Yet Haddou knew only too well that Driss's major expense happened to be his weekly trips and gifts to a certain Dutch girlfriend Driss had met while she was on vacation in France.

The family's insubordination troubled Haddou constantly. He felt he had worked all of his life just to provide for them and yet they were not appreciative. All they ever asked for was more money; all they ever complained about was their "small" family stipend. He had poured his savings into a piece of property and then built a four-apartment building on it, all for them. He had never asked for anything more than to be allowed to retire back in Nador on a comfortable German pension, to live surrounded by his children and their families, all under one roof in a building of his own creation. Was that too much to ask? Now, however, his eldest son wanted to quit his job in France and move in with his girlfriend in Holland. Since his second son had failed the *baccalauréat*, he would not be able to go to university or find a decent job in Morocco. Maybe the two youngest sons would mature and prosper, though they seemed no more likely to fulfill their father's dream than the older brothers.

The frustrations of being an absent head of household preoccupied Haddou as he walked back from the phone booth to his apartment. Haddou partly blamed himself for the family's failure. He had not been there to raise the children properly and knew he could not make up in one month for eleven months of absence. He also suspected that his children did not entirely respect him, for he, like many other migrants, had never lived in the city and thus had few of the social graces typical of the nonmigrant fathers of his children's friends. What was worse, Haddou had none of the contacts needed to ease his children's access into good schools and jobs. Years of giving and receiving favors and of sitting in cafés with men of influence were needed to develop a network of acquaintances. Haddou had spent his adult life out of the country, which meant that his circle of acquaintances was strictly limited to men he had known before he migrated. He was thus in the unenviable position of having an income and house commensurate with a high status but none of the personal prestige needed to get others to do his bidding. The children, he sensed, resented him for this.

On the other hand, Haddou knew how to work for something he wanted, and the children did not. They expected it all to be laid out before them. They disdained manual labor and assumed, instead, that only white-collar jobs were respectable. Take last winter when the sewer pipe backed up. Haddou jumped right in and dug up the pipe while the boys disappeared. They were embarrassed to have the neighbors see their father digging in the dirt. Yet what did they think their father did all year to earn money that kept them from having to work? He deserved their respect if only for that.

At least Haddou's daughters were loyal. Fatima, the older one, had last year married without complaint a successful migrant working in Holland. The man had approached Haddou requesting that Fatima live abroad as his second wife while his first stayed in Nador with their children. People in the neighborhood were aghast that Haddou consented to give his daughter away as a second wife. They said that showed what a country bumpkin he was. A good city family would never stoop so low. But Haddou defended his actions by claiming that the man was from his tribal region, earned an excellent income, owned a nice house in Nador, and was a migrant—in short, he was just like Haddou himself and therefore a good match for his daughter.

Haddou's other daughter, Malika, never gave him cause for concern. Her high school grades were impressive; she did particularly well in French. Yet she also helped her mother with the cooking and cleaning in the house and even found time to take sewing classes from a seamstress a few blocks away. In Haddou's eyes, Malika was the model daughter. He daydreamed on occasion of keeping her unmarried and at home so that she could tend to his needs in his old age. He justified this by saying it would be a pity to separate Malika from her mother, because they were so close. Unlike the others, Malika never asked him to raise the monthly stipend.

Haddou could not help smiling as he closed the door to his apartment and took off his coat. It was Malika, after all, who had said he looked like Charles Bronson and that he should stop working and start making movies. Bronson's mustache was smaller and his eyes not as round as Haddou's, but otherwise he had to agree with her: the resemblance was striking. Maybe he would buy a VCR this time to take back with him on his upcoming vacation to Nador. That way the whole family could watch Bronson movies together.

Haddou chose to take his vacation and return to Nador during the month of December. The winters were cold in Germany, and he no longer wanted to compete for space with the hundreds of thousands of Moroccan migrants who returned in July and August. He disliked the crowded Spanish highways and the crush at the boat docks and the Moroccan border caused by the summertime returnees. It had grown so bad in recent years that some migrants now wasted a week of their vacation time just getting home. Once back in Nador, the streets became jammed with the migrants' Mercedes. Every summer weekend, one procession after another of honking cars followed by fireworks displays created a ruckus, all due to the dozens of weddings taking place simultaneously. This was caused by the migrants' families back home, who found brides for the unmarried male migrants and arranged for their weddings to coincide with their vacations. The locals, too, preferred to marry in the summer, hence the noise and confusion of that season.

The changed nature of the wedding celebration also added to the mayhem. Prior to the influx of peasants and migrants into Nador (in 1960 Nador's population was seventeen thousand; in 1985 it was eighty-five thousand) weddings took place within the confines of the village and kin group. However, the tremendous growth of the city, the creation of neighborhoods full of strangers, and the dramatic rise in family income following labor migration to Europe led to the development of open, lavish matrimonial displays. The families of newlyweds used fireworks, Mercedes-Benz corteges, and professional, electronic orchestras to compete with each other and to make a big splash in front of the neighbors and relatives.

Haddou personally disliked the lavish displays because the only marriage he had been responsible for, that of his elder daughter, Fatima, was a secret affair carried out quietly behind closed doors and windows, due to the shame attached to his daughter's becoming a second wife. He justified his displeasure at large public weddings in more sweeping and general terms though by citing the wastefulness of such extravagance. Why should he, a hardworking father with dependents, squander his savings on celebrations meant to impress strangers? On the other hand, he did not mind competing with his neighbors when it came to building a big house or decorating its facade. That kind of social competition required no face-to-face interaction or mastery of urban etiquette.

Making sure his children were reasonably well dressed and had imported electronic toys to play with on the street was another form of social display of which Haddou approved, for as a migrant he was in a position to purchase cheaply such foreign articles. Haddou, like all the other Moroccan migrants, always brought home presents for the whole family. In his family the boys normally received shirts and pants, while Thraithmas and Malika got scarves and dresses. The boys proudly wore their German clothes—when they fit—but the women tended to leave theirs in the closet, since the clothes Haddou picked out were often too ugly or too risqué (sleeveless, for example) to be worn in Nador.

Haddou also brought back items from Germany for the house. Like many Moroccans, Haddou considered foreign-made goods to be superior to domestic products. In fact, so strong was the allure of commodities from industrial Europe that Haddou carried back items as small as faucets and door handles made in Germany, not to mention tea glasses, pots and pans, and tablecloths. Driss, the son with the self-professed high living costs, tended to buy cheap presents for the family from Spain, Taiwan, or Hong Kong when he returned, and then to claim that they were really made in Germany or France.

One year Haddou brought back a Mercedes-Benz for a colonel in the Moroccan air force. He met Haddou on the train to Rabat. They started talking, and the man ended up contracting with Haddou to purchase a car in Germany and then drive it back to Rabat for him. The colonel, in turn, saw to it that Haddou met no resistance from Moroccan officials. Thus protected, Haddou seized the opportunity to load the car down with items for his own household, including a television, a sewing machine, folding chairs, and bundles of towels. No one asked him for bribes on that trip.

Haddou set about brewing another pot of tea. He realized as he thought about his own vacation that he had to make a decision soon on whether to bring Thraithmas to Düsseldorf that year. Since the mid-1980s, when Murad became ten and could be left in the care of his brothers and sisters, Haddou had begun to bring Thraithmas to Germany to stay with him for a month each year. When it was time for his mother to go, Hassan would wake up while it was still dark, go down to the taxicab stand, and bring a car right up to the front door. Thraithmas would heavily veil herself and then quickly step out of the house and into the car. She and Hassan would then take the taxi to the Oujda International Airport long before anyone in the neighborhood awoke. Once in Düsseldorf, Thraithmas would change out of her Moroccan dress and into Western clothing. Haddou insisted on that. He remembered too well when she first arrived in Germany wearing her *jallaba*. All eyes were upon her, staring at her as if she were a freak. When she wore her Western clothes, no one paid attention. Luckily for Haddou, unlike her mother, Thraithmas had never tattooed her face with the markings of her natal region, so nothing about her attracted the Germans' curiosity.

Haddou deeply appreciated her visits. She brought with her delicacies from Morocco: almonds, prepared barley dishes, pickled lemons, olive oil, fresh mint. She also made his favorite food, *limsimen*, a fried bread of many layers made by folding the dough again and again. More than anything else, Thraithmas's visits broke the monotony of Haddou's existence in Düsseldorf. Without her, his routine consisted of waking early, making tea on the small hot plate, riding his bicycle down to the rail yard, and then working as long as they needed him. He would ride home after finishing, change his clothes, and go out to buy a little food for supper. He then watched television for awhile or flipped through a magazine before going to bed. The weekends were mainly reserved for washing clothes and straightening up his room.

The only excitement of the week occurred on Saturday afternoons, at which time Haddou liked to walk down to a certain tearoom in a nicer neighborhood where German women gathered. There he would sit for a few hours, listening to their conversations. Sometimes when the place was full, women even sat at his table. They would start to ask him about his homeland or about his religion. Haddou enjoyed these little exchanges very much because they were practically his only informal contacts with the locals. During the rest of the week he talked to Germans only as a worker talks to a boss or as a customer talks to a storekeeper. The women at the tearoom were the only Germans who showed Haddou any consideration.

With Thraithmas around, Haddou had no need for the Germans. What is more, when he woke up in the morning she had his tea ready. When he got home at night she was cooking his supper. During the day while Haddou was working, Thraithmas would often go across the hall and sit in the apartment of the railway widow who lived there. They watched television together and communicated through gestures. That was enough. They just enjoyed each other's presence. When Haddou returned at night or on weekends, he and Thraithmas sometimes went shopping in one of the big discount department stores. She doubly enjoyed these outings because she, like other relatively wealthy migrants' wives, was not allowed to go out shopping in Nador. By going out with Haddou in Düsseldorf she could also buy more tasteful clothes for the family back home—at least clothes that fit. She also enjoyed buying inexpensive perfumes, soaps, and candies to place around the house in Nador on special occasions and to give to guests when they visited.

Perhaps more than anything, Haddou appreciated Thraithmas's visits because they provided him with a sense of stability and worth. Her calm and respectful manner toward him, her familiar way of speaking, her correct behavior, all reminded him that he belonged, as a proud believer and father of a family, to an Islamic community with a set of values and way of living totally distinct from his present European surroundings. He had not always felt this way. During those early years in Paris no one had been overly concerned with strictly maintaining the religious practices and precepts of their Islamic homeland. They were too busy working. Besides, there was only one mosque in all of Paris.

Sometime during the 1970s a mosque opened in Haddou's quarter of Düsseldorf. It began as a room where Muslims could gather and pray. An Egyptian led the prayers. Haddou visited the mosque once or twice, but he did not know the other men. They seemed too serious anyway and were too interested in trying to run his life. One day while Haddou was in the train yard recording the boxcar numbers of the most recent train to arrive, a Turkish worker from the mosque approached him and asked him to join an Islamic group then forming. They wanted to petition the boss for the right to stop work during prayer times. Some companies in France had even set aside rooms to be used as mosques—right inside the factories. Maybe the Germans could be persuaded to do the same thing.

Haddou refused to have anything to do with the man or his group and their objectives. He said he was in Europe to earn money, not to pray. God had given him two hands and a strong back to use to provide for himself and his family. Who was going to put food on the table back in Nador if he decided to spend all day at the mosque? In any case, he did not need a bunch of bearded migrants telling him what was and was not Islamic.

And look at the way the religiously militant migrants were greeted back home! The cops at the Moroccan customs bureau treated them like criminals. They knew who the troublemakers were because the government spied on the migrants in Europe. The consulates and the Moroccan migrants' associations were full of spies who kept track of everyone. When the migrants got to the Moroccan border, the customs agents went through all their possessions, looking for religious tracts. They even began confiscating the migrants' audio and video cassettes. Supposedly the militants smuggled the sermons of subversive preachers into the country on these tapes.

Locals in Nador also complained of the way the bearded migrants came home and preached to them about the "true" Islam. The locals viewed them as hicks from the countryside who had spent most of their adult lives in Christian Europe. Now they were coming back every vacation to Islamic Morocco and had the gall to preach to the people who had never abandoned their country and its religion.

Haddou had to admit, however, that it was the risk of being fired from his job and then deported from Germany that weighed most heavily on him and kept him from getting involved with the group. The Germans used any excuse to get rid of foreigners. Even with his new visa he did not entirely trust them, so he was going to continue to make sure he never arrived late for work or left early. If they wanted him to work night shifts outside in the train yard in the middle of winter, he would still be there. He would even continue to have his paycheck deposited directly into his account so that the bank could automatically pay his rent and utilities bills. That way he would never miss a payment and give the Germans a reason for firing him.

Haddou had to admit that he respected the Germans as well as feared them. They worked hard, built good products, and kept their streets and parks clean—more than he could say for the Moroccans. The Germans were also honest with you. If you asked them a question, they would tell you the answer. If a Moroccan knew, he would never tell; if he did not know, he would make something up. On the other hand, unlike the Moroccans, the Germans were morally bankrupt. The family meant nothing to them. Old people were all sent off to live alone in homes for the aged. Daughters and wives went about scantily clad, even drinking and talking to strangers if they so desired. The men were too weak to keep their families in line. What was worse, they were all racists, young and old. It was best to steer clear of them, for nothing good ever came from mixing. The Germans knew nothing of the proper Islamic way of life. Haddou knew this through one of his friends who had married a German woman. At first the man had been enthralled with his new wife and her Christian way of life. He danced and drank and even began to eat pork. Soon, however, their marriage deteriorated, and he rediscovered his Islamic heritage. Nonetheless, she refused to maintain an Islamic household. The couple ended up with two kitchens in the house: one for her pork and alcohol dishes and the other for him, free of impurities. The man now spent most of his free time at the mosque in the company of other strict believers.

"Why don't you just go home?" Haddou thought to himself on many occasions. This is what the racists wanted, too. Haddou's answer was always the same: "To do what?" Most Moroccan men's answer to this would be to set up a shop and sell something. But Haddou felt himself to be unsuited to the life of a small merchant. They were not involved in productive activity anyway, just buying and selling what others had made. In any case, he needed contacts to make a good profit. Otherwise no one would buy from him, and the Moroccan bureaucracy would slowly bleed him to death without a patron to protect him. Even if he wanted to make some kind of productive investment, the banks were not safe, laws were not enforced, and, besides, in what kind of manufacturing could he invest in Morocco that could possibly compete with foreign manufactures? The government favored imported goods by keeping import tariffs low. What was worse, the Moroccan consumer was convinced that quality came only from abroad. The only domestic products worth buying consisted mainly of foods and traditional clothing. If he chose to produce them, who would buy his modern shoes, for example, when they could purchase imported Italian shoes? Or who would buy his Moroccan-made shampoo when they could buy it from France or Spain? Even dinner plates imported from Taiwan were preferable to those produced locally. The Moroccan government made matters worse by throwing their support behind commercial activities producing for export. In the region of Nador that meant growing citrus fruit for Europe. But citrus grew locally only on irrigated land, and most of the good, irrigated land had been bought up long ago by wealthy men with contacts. They had been told of the planned irrigation system before everyone else and had bought the land at a cheaper price in order to take advantage of the development. Today that land was too expensive to buy. Equally vexing was the fact that many of the prices for crops grown on unirrigated land were controlled by middlemen and the government in such a restrictive manner that they barely repaid the farmers' investments—and then only during good years. No subsidies existed to carry the farmers during the bad years, which in recent times had far outnumbered the good.

Given these conditions back home, Haddou never could understand why so many Europeans expected the migrants just to pick up and leave. They acted as if the migrants had come uninvited. On the contrary, he and the millions of other migrants from around the world were in Europe because the European governments, factories, and shop owners originally asked them to come work. The first time Haddou went back on vacation during the early 1960s, his boss gave him hundreds of work contracts to hand out to people in the Moroccan countryside who might want to join him in Europe, so eager was the boss to expand his migrant labor force. No, migrants did not originally knock down the door; it was opened for them. Unlike the better organized and more demanding European workers, migrants could be made to work harder and longer or to do dirtier and more dangerous jobs, thus providing greater profits for their European employers. As Haddou saw it, the real dilemma was that Moroccans were dependent on Europe no matter what they did. They could stay home and—if they were lucky enough to find a job at all—produce goods for export to Europe, work on assembling and distributing products legally imported from Europe, illegally smuggle products in from Europe, or, like himself, they could just pick up and go to work right in Europe. Directly, or indirectly, in Morocco or abroad, they were all working for the Europeans.

Being a migrant in the modern world is serious business. Moroccans like Haddou know this well, for he and close to a million of his compatriots have left their families and homeland in Morocco in order to earn a wage a thousand miles away in the countries of Europe. They have had to learn how to navigate through the Moroccan bureaucracy, which selectively issues or withholds necessary papers and passports, as well as how to master the complex European system of visa and residency requirements, which determines how long—or even whether—they can stay. Along the way they have been victimized by an array of corrupt Moroccan and European officials.

The migrants' vulnerability increased during the 1970s and 1980s. On the Moroccan side, their allegiance to the state has come under suspicion, particularly with the growing influence of Islamic revivalists in the migrant community. On the European side, the growing power of right-wing groups places a further burden on the migrants, who now find themselves threatened physically by racist thugs and legally hemmed in by restrictive legislation.

Yet it would be a mistake to see Haddou and migrants like him as merely pawns, pushed about by political and economic forces out of their control, for in spite of official harassment, forbiddingly long distances, and minimal time spent with their families, migrants continue to invest their own sacrifices with meaning by committing themselves to the betterment of the lives of their dependents. As the career of Haddou reveals, however, the male migrant's vision of what constitutes a good life, a good family, or even a good father is often at odds with the perceptions of others close to him. It may be difficult to agree with the way Haddou managed his familial affairs and relations, but it is not difficult to respect his ability to sustain, in the face of what amounted to almost lifelong hardship and privation, his commitment to what he valued most: the construction and maintenance of an economically stable and emotionally nurturing household.

### A NOTE ON SOURCES

My wife, Joan Gross, and I spent most of 1986 and 1987 living in Nador studying the impact of migration on the region, which is how we came to know Haddou and his family, whose stories, of course, provided the sources for this article. For obvious reasons, we have not given his real name. Fulbright, Social Science Research Council, and American Institute of Maghrib Studies dissertation grants made our stay possible.

## SUGGESTIONS FOR FURTHER READING

The study of international migration is an industry in itself so I will mention only a few of the more theoretical works on this general topic. Michael Piore's *Birds of Passage: Migrant Labor and Industrial Societies* (Cambridge: Cambridge University Press, 1979) still stands as one of the best mainstream neoclassical studies of the field. Alejandro Portes and John Walton's *Labor, Class and the International System* (New York: Academic Press, 1981) is a good Marxist study. Stephen Castles, Heather Booth, and Tina Wallace have written a more militantly committed, though no less theoretical, work entitled *Here for Good: Western Europe's New Ethnic Minorities* (London: Pluto Press, 1984).

On the Moroccan context, most important for this article is David Seddon, *Moroccan Peasants: A Century of Change in the Eastern Rif, 1870–1970* (Folkestone: Dawson, 1981), which is one of the best sources of information in English on the history and development of the region of Nador, as well as on the early years of migration from that region.

Most Moroccan researchers write on the subject of migration either in Arabic or French, the two national languages of Morocco. One important work in French is Tahar Ben Jelloun's account of the sexual frustrations of migrants. See his *La plus haute des solitudes* (Paris: Seuil, 1979).

Several Moroccan novels concerning various migration experiences have been translated into English. Some of the most interesting come from the collaboration of Paul Bowles and Mohammed Mrabet, notably their *Love with a Few Hairs* (London: Arena/Anchor Books, 1986 [1967]), which chronicles the life of a migrant to Tangier from the eastern Rif. Bowles has also translated Mohamed Choukri's *For Bread Alone* (London: Grafton Books, 1987), the autobiography of another Rifi from Nador province who was forced to migrate to Tangier. See also Driss Chraibi, *The Simple Past* (Washington D.C.: Three Continents Press, 1989).

Finally, Ali Ghanem's *A Wife For My Son*, trans. G. Koziolas (London: Zed Press, 1984) describes in depth the familial stresses and strains accompanying an emigrant's attempt to work in Europe while maintaining a family in Algeria. It has recently been made into a film.

# GLOSSARY OF SELECTED TERMS

| | |
|---|---|
| *alim (pl. ulama):* | Learned man, especially in law and other religious studies |
| *amir (pl. ashraf; fem. sharifa):* | Title held by a politico-military commander or his companions |
| *ayan:* | Notables |
| *ayatullah:* | Highest rank in Shii hierarchy of scholars qualified to pronounce independent judgment in religious matters |
| *baraka:* | Blessing; holiness; spiritual power inherent in a saint |
| *bey:* | Turkish title |
| *bibi:* | Daughter of an Iranian tribal leader, or *khan* |
| *dhikr:* | Sufi ritual |
| *fakir:* | Sufi |
| *fatwa:* | Formal legal opinion issued by a *mufti* |
| *fiqh:* | Jurisprudence; the discipline of elucidating the Sharia |
| *habous:* | See *waqf* |
| *hadith:* | Reported words and deeds of the Prophet Muhammad based on the authority of a chain of reliable transmitters |
| *hajj:* | Annual pilgrimage to Mecca |
| *ilbeg:* | Leader of an Iranian tribal confederacy |
| *ilkhan:* | Leader of an Iranian tribal confederacy |
| *ilm:* | Religious knowledge |
| *imam:* | Leader of prayer; in Shiite usage, the leader of the Muslim community |

| | |
|---|---|
| *intifada:* | Palestinian uprising against Israeli occupation in West Bank and Gaza that began in December 1987 |
| *jihad:* | War in accord with the Sharia against unbelievers; in Sufi usage, the moral struggle of the individual |
| *kadkhoda:* | Iranian village headman |
| *karamat:* | Miracles |
| *khalifa:* | Successor; local official; a Sufi master |
| *khan:* | Caravansary; building given to diverse commercial and industrial purposes; Iranian tribal governor under *ilkhan* or *ilbeg* |
| *kulughli:* | Descendent of Ottoman military officer and local woman (Maghrib); a family caste |
| *madrasa:* | College of law and other religious studies |
| *Mahdi:* | Person who will appear at the end of days to establish Islam over all unrighteous forces |
| *makhzan:* | The Moroccan government |
| *mellah:* | Jewish quarter or ghetto (Morocco) |
| *millet:* | In Ottoman Empire, non-Muslim communities benefiting from special administrative status |
| *muezzin:* | Individual who performs the call to prayer |
| *mufti:* | Muslim jurisconsult |
| *mujahid (pl. mujahidin):* | Warrior for the faith (in *jihad*) |
| *mujtahid:* | Scholar with authority to interpret Islamic law, especially in Shiite Islam |
| *mullah:* | Local Shiite teacher |
| *muqaddam:* | Head of a local Sufi *tariqa* |
| *murabit (pl. murabitin):* | Sufi teacher; head of a saintly lineage |
| *pasha:* | Ottoman governmental official |
| *qabaday:* | Urban gang leader |
| *qabila:* | Tribe |
| *qadi:* | Judge according to Sharia law |
| *qaid:* | Local governor (Maghrib) |
| *saddiqim:* | Locally venerated Jewish saints (Morocco) |
| *sayyid:* | Descendent of Husayn, son of Fatima, the daughter of the Prophet |
| *shabab:* | Young men; retainers of a shaykh (Lebanon) |
| *shahid:* | Martyr |
| *Sharia:* | Islamic law; more generally, Muslim belief and practice |

| | |
|---|---|
| *sharif (pl. ashraf):* | One who traces his descent to the Prophet |
| *shaykh:* | Elder; head of a Sufi order (Maghrib); landlord (Lebanon); head of an artisan guild |
| *Shia:* | Muslims who hold to the right of Ali and his descendents to lead the Islamic community |
| *sinf (pl. asnaf):* | Artisan guild |
| *Sufi:* | Follower of a mystic path, or *tariqa* |
| *sultan:* | Title of a ruler, head of state |
| *Sunni:* | Most Muslims, who accept the authority of the first generations of Muslims and the validity of the historic succession of caliphs, unlike the Shia and Kharijis |
| *tariqa (pl. turuq):* | Sufi way or brotherhood |
| *ulama:* | Scholars learned in the Sharia; see *alim* |
| *waqf:* | Pious foundation or endowment of properties to provide income for religious purposes |
| *zawiya:* | Sufi *tariqa;* Sufi center for teaching and other activities |

# CONTRIBUTORS

*Mehdi Abedi* is research associate and lecturer in anthropology at Rice University.

*Lila Abu-Lughod* is associate professor of anthropology at New York University.

*Eqbal Ahmad* is professor of social sciences at Hampshire College.

*Lisa Anderson* is associate professor of political science at Columbia University.

*Fakhreddin Azimi* is assistant professor of history at the University of Connecticut (Storrs).

*Lois Beck* is professor of anthropology at Washington University in St. Louis.

*Kenneth Brown* is reader in sociology at the University of Manchester.

*Edmund Burke, III,* is professor of history at the University of California, Santa Cruz.

*Julia Clancy-Smith* is assistant professor of history at the University of Virginia, Charlottesville.

*Leila Fawaz* is professor of history at Tufts University.

*Michael M. J. Fischer* is professor of anthropology at Rice University.

*Ashraf Ghani* is professor of anthropology at John Hopkins University.

*Joost Hiltermann* is a writer who lives in Washington, D.C.

399

*Nels Johnson* is senior lecturer in anthropology and politics at Richmond College (London).

*Akram F. Khater* is a Ph.D. candidate in history at the University of California, Berkeley, and Mendenhall Fellow in History at Smith College.

*Antoine F. Khater* is professor of physics at the Université de Maine, Le Mans (France).

*Philip S. Khoury* is associate dean of humanities and social science and professor of history at the Massachusetts Institute of Technology.

*David McMurray* is assistant professor of anthropology at Oregon State University.

*Julie Oehler* is a writer who lives in Salinas, California.

*Stuart Schaar* is associate professor of history at Brooklyn College, City University of New York.

*Abdullah Schleifer* is professor at the Adham School for Television Journalism at the American University in Cairo.

*Daniel Schroeter* is assistant professor of history at the University of Florida, Gainesville.

*David Seddon* is reader in the School of Development Studies at the University of East Anglia.

*Ehud R. Toledano* is professor of history at Tel Aviv University.

*Sherry Vatter* is a Ph.D. candidate in history at the University of California, Los Angeles.

*David N. Yaghoubian* is a graduate student in history at the University of California, Berkeley.

*Sami Zubaida* is reader in politics and sociology at Birkbeck College, the University of London.

Compositor: BookMasters, Inc.
Text: 10/12 Baskerville
Display: Baskerville
Printer and Binder: Sheridan